ONE MORE RIDE ON THE MERRY-GO-ROUND

Tiziano Terzani (1938–2004) was an Italian journalist and writer, best known for his extensive knowledge of twentieth-century Asia, where he lived for thirty years. He was the Asian correspondent for the German weekly *Der Spiegel*, while also collaborating with the daily newspapers *Corriere della Sera* and *La Repubblica*.

Born in Florence, Italy, in 1972, as the foreign correspondent for *Der Spiegel*, he opened new bureaus for them in Singapore, Hong Kong, Beijing, Tokyo and Bangkok. After witnessing key historical events like the defeat of the Americans in the Vietnam War, the transformation of Mao's China and the collapse of the Soviet empire, Terzani decided to make India his home in 1994, spending his final years in a small retreat in the Himalayan ranges above Almora.

When he died in July 2004, *Times* London described him as a 'legend in his own time'. Terzani's passionate curiosity about the fate of man in the modern world became increasingly more important to him than the journalistic concerns of economics and politics. *A Fortune-Teller Told Me* (1995), which describes his travels by train, ship and elephant following a warning from a fortune-teller in Hong Kong to avoid airplanes, became an inspiration to millions of readers, helping them change perspective on their own lives. *The End Is My Beginning*, a discussion with his son about the great journey of life, was made into a feature film in Italian and German.

One More Ride on the Merry-Go-Round, first published in Italy a few months before his final journey, tackles the age-old question of how to live and die, and became an instant best-seller for its down-to-earth approach to exploring the spiritual dimension in an ever more materialistic world. An international literary prize is awarded every year in Tiziano Terzani's name.

Felix Bolling is a translator and traveller. He never stays still at one place for long.

Also by Tiziano Terzani

Pelle di leopardo (Leopard Skin: Vietnamese Diary of a War Correspondent), 1973

Giai Phong! (*Giai Phong! The Fall and Liberation of Saigon*), 1976

La porta proibita (*Behind the Forbidden Door: Travels in Unknown China*), 1984

Buonanotte, Signor Lenin (*Goodnight Mister Lenin*), 1992

Un indovino mi disse (*A Fortune-Teller Told Me*), 1995

In Asia (*Asia*), 1998

Lettere contro la guerra (*Letters Against the War*), 2002

Un altro giro di giostra (*One More Ride on the Merry-Go-Round*), 2004

La fine è il mio inizio (*The End Is My Beginning*), 2006

Fantasmi (*Ghosts: Dispatches from Cambodia*), 2008

Un mondo che non esiste piu' (*A World That Is No More: The Photographs of Tiziano Terzani*), 2010

Un'idea di destino (*An Idea of Destiny: Diaries of an Extraordinary Life*), 2014

Praise for *One More Ride on the Merry-Go-Round*

'He decided to use whatever time was left to him to map and make his last journey – to death. He spent much of his last few years living very simply, without running water or electric light in a hut in the Himalayas. There, he said, he learnt how to die.' – *The Times*

'Terzani had a new country to explore, the grimmest and strangest yet most compelling of them all ... with the same patience, clear sight and sensible judgement with which he had reported from Cambodia or Nepal, and in the same bell-like Italian prose, he wrote from the land of cancer. *One More Ride on the Merry-Go-Round* went to the top of the bestseller lists in Italy and has remained in the list ever since.' – *The Independent*

'For twenty-five years Tiziano Terzani has lived in Asia, reporting on the wars and revolutions. He has become a star in a profession.' – *The Guardian*

'Italian journalist and writer who won international fame. His writings, imbued with personal charm, made him a folk hero in his native Italy.' – *The New York Times*

'For almost thirty years, he was perhaps his country's most celebrated foreign correspondent.' – *The Daily Telegraph*

Praise for *A Fortune-Teller Told Me*

'A glorious journey through Asia and through Tiziano's own consciousness, examining slower, gentler and more traditional Asian philosophies and ways of life.' – *The Times*

'The correspondent's gaze, till this point always focused steadily on the societies which he was striving to fathom, now began to turn on himself. His life, his destiny became the new terrain for exploration. He went native in his own skin. The enchanting book that resulted was a huge success in Italy and elsewhere.' – *The Independent*

Praise for *Letters Against the War*

'A fierce indictment of all wars. Terzani, the veteran war correspondent, became a hero to a new Italian generation of pacifists and anti-globalists.' – *The Independent*

ONE MORE RIDE ON THE MERRY-GO-ROUND

TIZIANO TERZANI

Translated by
FELIX BOLLING

First published in India in 2016 by Harper Element
An imprint of HarperCollins *Publishers*

HarperCollins Publishers India, Cyber City, Building 10-A, Gurugram,
Haryana-122002, India
www.harpercollins.co.in

P-ISBN: 978-93-5029-715-5
E-ISBN: 978-93-5029-716-2

2 4 6 8 10 9 7 5 3 1

Typeset in 10.5/15.5 Palatino by
R. Ajith Kumar

Printed and bound at
MicroPrints India, New Delhi

This product is made of FSC®-certified and other controlled material.

HarperCollins Publishers, Macken House, 39/40 Mayor Street
Upper, Dublin 1, D01 C9W8, Ireland

CONTENTS

ONE

DEPARTURE

A JOURNEY WITHOUT SHORTCUTS

We know it happens to a lot of people, but we never think it may happen to me. This had always been my attitude too. So when it did happen, I was as unprepared as anyone, and at first it felt like it was occurring to somebody else. 'Mr Terzani, you have cancer,' said the doctor, but it seemed as if he wasn't actually talking to me. So much so – and I realized this at once, to my own surprise – that I didn't get emotional, I didn't despair. It was as if this whole matter, in the end, was no business of mine.

Perhaps this initial indifference was just an instinctive defence mechanism, a way to stay in control, to keep some distance. It helped me, in any case. Looking in through a set of eyes outside of your self is always useful. It's an exercise that can be learnt.

I spent another night at the hospital, alone, mulling things over. I thought of all those people who'd been there before me and, in these very same rooms, received the same kind of news, and I found their company somehow comforting. I was in Bologna, and I'd arrived there via the usual rigmarole of little steps, each insignificant on its own, but when taken all together, decisive. First, a persistent diarrhoea in Calcutta, then a series of tests at the Institute for Tropical Diseases in Paris, more tests to discover the cause of an inexplicable anaemia, until a shrewd Italian doctor, refusing to be satisfied with the obvious explanations, set about with a strange instrument – a nasty, penetrating rubber snake with a luminous eye – to peer into the innermost recesses of my body. And there he immediately recognized that which, by years of experience, he knew so well.

I was grateful to him for having been competent and clear. Now I would be able to calmly take stock, figure out my priorities, and make the necessary decisions. I was about to celebrate my fifty-ninth birthday and it was natural to turn around and look back at my life with satisfaction as one might from a mountaintop after a climb just completed. What had my life been like up until then? Wonderful! One adventure after another, a true love, no regrets and nothing of great importance still left to be done. If as a boy setting out on this journey I had aimed, as many have, 'to plant a tree, to bring a child into the world, and write a line of poetry' I'd more or less arrived. Almost without realizing it, without too much effort and having had a lot of fun along the way.

That night in the hospital, in the silence broken only by the swishing of cars going by on the wet asphalt outside, and the nuns walking down the linoleum corridors, an image came to mind which has stayed with me ever since. I felt as if my whole life I had been on a merry-go-round, and right from the start I'd ridden the white horse. I'd gone up and down and round and round to my heart's content, without anyone – I realized for the first time – coming to ask if I had a ticket. And in fact, I hadn't. All my life I'd bummed a ride! Well, now the ticket collector was coming through and I'd have to pay my dues. But with a bit of luck, I might just get ... one more ride on the merry-go-round.

The following day began like any other. Nothing around me had changed; nothing outside me reflected the great storm of thoughts that raged through my mind. I even remembered to pick up the linen I had left to wash at the launderette in Porretta Terme a few days earlier. There I changed trains to get to my house in the Apennines mountains at Orsigna. My wife Angela was waiting for me at home, and as soon as I arrived, I suggested we go for a walk in the woods together. After almost forty years of sharing our lives, it was easy to talk and be silent with each other. I promised her I would do my best to make it through, and this was, I think, the only time a tear came to my eye.

I had to quickly decide what to do. My first instinct was that of a wounded animal: to hide somewhere. I suddenly felt very weak, and what little strength I had, I needed to concentrate as best I could. I chose to not say anything to anyone, except my children and those friends who wouldn't understand my disappearance. I wanted to focus and not be distracted by anything or anyone.

Above all I had to decide where to go for treatment, and what kind I wanted to have. Chemotherapy, radiotherapy and surgery, with their apparently devastating consequences, are no longer the only alternatives. Everything these days is open to question; anything official is viewed with suspicion, and all forms of authority have lost the prestige they once had. Everyone feels entitled to judge. As a result, it has become increasingly fashionable to speak ill of classical medicine, and to speak highly of alternative approaches.

Their names at least sound more appealing: ayurveda, pranic healing, acupuncture, yoga, homeopathy, Chinese herbal remedies, reiki and even – why not? – faith healers, Filipino or otherwise. There is always some second-hand story, a person you hear a tale about, but which seems to exist just to get you to believe it, to pin your hopes on any one of the growing number of 'cures' now available. I didn't take any of them seriously, not even for a minute.

Many of these practices originated in Asia, where I had lived for thirty years, and some even have their roots in India, where I now had a home! I myself had no difficulty in turning to these practices in the past. I once took my eleven-year-old son Folco to an acupuncturist in China, who cured him of asthma. Just a year before having to decide what to do with myself, I took my friend Leopold, from France, to the Medical-Astrological Institute (an odd combination, I know!) in Dharamshala to see the Dalai Lama's personal doctor. This doctor felt his seventeen pulses, and prescribed some little black pills for his hepatitis which looked rather like sheep's droppings, but were apparently very effective. What is more, I was the one who had said and written that Western man, in taking the highway of modern science, had been too quick to abandon the paths of ancient wisdom. In seeking to conquer Asia with his blueprint of modernity, he risked causing a wealth of knowledge linked to local traditions to be lost there too.

It was not that I had changed my mind, but when it came to the issue of my own survival, I didn't have a moment's hesitation. I had to turn to what I knew best: to science and Western reason. There wasn't much time, and all the so-called alternative medicines work in the long term – if/when they do actually work, that is. But it was not just this. It was more the fact that deep down, I didn't trust them, and having faith in the treatment and the person administering it is an important and vital part of the healing process.

It helps to be lucky in life, and here too, I have generally had more than my fair share. Fortune did not fail me on this occasion either – or at least that was how I viewed it, which ultimately is the same thing. Among my old journalist colleagues from Asia, there was one, a *New York Times* correspondent and two-time winner of the Pulitzer Prize, I was linked to by a special bond of friendship as a result of our having had several experiences in common. We had both been arrested and expelled from China, and after much more 'important' postings and against all received career wisdom, we both chose India as the country we wanted to cover. Now we were linked by another coincidence. He too had had the same type of illness a couple of years ago – and survived. I went to see him in Delhi, to ask for his advice.

The doctors who had fixed him up, or the 'fixers' as he called them, were in his view the best in the market. I took his word for it. A couple of phone calls, a fax, and within a few days I was in New York, eighteenth on the waiting list for a new type of experimental treatment, at what is probably the cutting edge of modern Western medical science: the Memorial Sloan Kettering Cancer Center, or MSKCC, as they suggest you write on your cheques, in order to maintain a semblance of discretion with your bank regarding your stay at their institution.

After *A Fortune-Teller Told Me* was released, when people asked me what I wanted to write next, I would reply that books are like children. You have to at least be pregnant with them before you can think about having them.[1] However, I used to say that, after so many years in the Far East, if I got the chance I would have

[1] One of the fortune-tellers, Rajamanickam of Singapore, had indeed predicted I would go through a 'difficult patch' in life between the ages of fifty-nine and sixty-one, and that I might even have an operation. He, however, was the only one. The others saw nothing of the kind in my future, and generally all of them said I would live a long life.

liked to go on a journey of rediscovery to the Far West – the Rocky Mountains and the Pacific Coast in the United States. So with the excuse that I had gone to America to, as it were, get 'pregnant', I managed to get them to forget about me.

In the small ads of *The New York Times*, I spotted a one-bedroom flat for rent overlooking Central Park. I went to see it, and took it immediately. Those few square metres of grey carpet were instantly cheered up by a couple of Indonesian throws and a small bronze Chinese Buddha, which I put on the ledge in front of my large, low window. This room was to become my lair for the next few months.

No one but Angela and the people at the MSKCC knew where I was. The phone never rang; no one came to the door. The only means of communication I left open with the world was email, and the odd electronic message in a bottle washed up on my computer's cybernetic shore, which could have been anywhere. These days I find this to be the best, most discreet, and least invasive form of communication.

Everything was perfect. It was just what I had been dreaming of for ages: endless days of freedom, no commitments or responsibilities, and the incredible luxury of being able to just let my mind wander, without interruptions, and without the idea – once an obsession – that there was something else I ought to be doing. After all the noise there had been in my life, at long last I was able to just enjoy all the silence. For years I had been caught up with wars, revolutions, floods, earthquakes – all the great changes that had taken place in Asia. I had been an impassioned observer of lives in danger, lives destroyed and, more often than not, wasted. Now I was merely observing the life that concerned me most of all: my own.

And there was much to observe. After more tests, and the usual round of 'There's a mark here we're not sure about', 'We need to do more tests', 'Come back next week', and 'I'm sorry, I've got some bad news', it turned out that there wasn't just one tumour. There were three, each with its own properties, and each likely to respond to different forms of treatment. It was then that I ended up going through chemotherapy, surgery and radiotherapy, without doubting their effectiveness for a minute, and each time adding my own form of psychological certainty that this was the right thing to be done, and the best option available.

Never before had I felt so made of matter. Never before had I looked at my body so closely. More importantly, I learnt to control and master it, rather than let it dominate me with its demands and pains, its palpitations and retching.

I realized the extent to which, over the years, my biological rhythms and mental states had been conditioned by deadlines, all accompanied by anxiety as a result of having worked for a weekly news magazine. There was immense joy on Saturday and Sunday, when the whole world could crumble but the magazine was printed, and not a word could be added; indifference on Monday, while the new issue was planned; tension on Tuesday and Wednesday, when I had to come up with a new subject and start making notes; discipline and focus on Thursday as the day copy was due for submission; and cautious relief on Friday, in case of further developments. It would merely start all over again the following week and the week after that. From some war front, a capital city where a coup had taken place, while travelling through a country to feel its soul, or following up a story in a bid to reconstruct events. Now every day of the week was the same, with no highs and no lows. It was simply marvellously flat. And no one wanted a thing from me.

Every season bears its fruits; my career as a journalist certainly had. Now, however, I was increasingly finding myself in situations resembling those I had already been in, facing problems I was already familiar with. The worst thing was, I was writing with echoes in my mind of the words and the stories I had written twenty years ago. What is more, even the facts themselves, which I had earlier chased after with the determination of a bloodhound, no longer held the same attraction for me. As the years passed, I had begun to realize that facts are never the whole truth. Behind them there lies something else – another level of reality perhaps – which I was just not grasping, and which I knew in any case had nothing to do with journalism – at least not as it was currently practised. Cancer had provided me with a great opportunity: not to have to repeat myself.

This was not all. Slowly I realized that cancer had also become a shield I could hide behind, a form of defence against what previously had attacked me, a bulwark against the banalities of life, against social engagements and mindless conversation. By getting cancer, I had earned the right to not feel obligated to anyone, to not feel guilty either. At last I was free, utterly free. It may sound odd, and at times it seemed odd to me too, but I was happy.

'Does one really have to get cancer before one can enjoy life?' an old English friend wrote to me. He had heard of my disappearance and asked for news via email. I replied that the news was one of my 'scoops', and yes, from my point of view it was, if not perhaps the happiest time in my life, certainly the most absorbing. Travelling had always been a way of life for me, and I approached my illness as another kind of journey: one that was unplanned and unexpected. I had no maps and was completely unprepared, but it was the most demanding and eventful of any I had ever been on. Everything that took place on this journey involved me directly. I wrote back to my friend asking him to rejoice that he didn't have cancer, but if he felt like attempting an interesting exercise, he could pretend he did, and reflect on how different life is and how different the people and things around us can appear when seen in another – and possibly more accurate – light.

In ancient China, people would keep their own coffins in their homes to remind themselves they were mortal. Some would even climb into them when they had important decisions to make, as if to gain a better perspective on the transient nature of life. Why not, just for a moment, pretend that you're ill and your days are numbered, which they are, in any case? Only then will you begin to realize the value of those days.

In India there is a well-known story about this. A man is chased by a tiger, and falls over the edge of a precipice. As he plunges into the void, the poor man manages to grab hold of a shrub, but soon even that starts to give way. There is no escape; above, the jaws of the tiger await him, below lies the yawning chasm. But then, right within reach, in the rocks of the cliff face, he catches sight of a beautiful, juicy red strawberry. He picks it, and … never in his whole life did a strawberry taste as good as the last one he would ever eat!

The weeks and months of solitary peace I enjoyed in New York were as sweet as could be. But this didn't mean I was ready to let go quite yet. On the contrary, I was trying everything I knew to get help. But how? If I as a person had been responsible for getting my body into this difficult situation, what could I do to help myself get out of it? The doctors I put these questions to between one round of tests and another had no answers. Some understood it was important for me to look for these answers, but no one helped me find them.

In one sense my doctors were like journalists too. They also took into account only what appeared to them to be 'facts', and not the elusive 'other' that might be hiding behind them. I was just a body as far as they were concerned: a body that was sick, and needed to be cured. It was useless for me to say I was a mind too, possibly a spirit, and certainly an accumulation of stories, experiences, feelings, thoughts and emotions, all of which must have had some bearing on my illness! No one wanted to hear such things, not even insofar as my treatment was concerned. What they were after was cancer *itself*, described in such detail in medical textbooks, with its occurrence and survival rates – the kind of cancer that anyone might have had. But not *my* cancer!

The scientific, rational approach I had chosen towards my illness meant I was being treated like a broken-down car, to be used either for scrap or mended, not as a person who consciously, wilfully intends to be put back together and get back on the road.

Indeed, the worthy doctor-fixers asked remarkably little about me as a person, provided my body showed up for the appointments they had arranged for it to be subjected to various treatments.

Do we even know what it is that makes one of our body cells go mad, abandon its vital functions, and transform itself into something so life-threatening?

I went to ask the head of research at the MSKCC, a young man who, I had read, not only had the answer to this question, but was on the verge of making a major breakthrough: discovering the key to the code which makes a healthy cell become unhealthy and vice versa, just as quickly as a light switch is turned on or off.

'We're on the right track,' he said. 'But this is harder than putting a man on the moon.'

The little I managed to understand was fascinating. By pure coincidence, this young man had specialized in precisely my type of illness. But the more I listened to him, the more I realized that his work as an explorer of the mysterious world of life was taking him in another direction from the me-as-a-whole-person mentality, and an even longer way from the me-as-a-body approach.

By digging and going from one detail to another on a smaller and smaller scale, he had managed to get inside one of the millions of codes contained in the DNA of one of the human body's billion-plus cells. But where was *I* in all this? Might I not have had some part to play in flicking my switch the wrong way?

'No. None whatsoever. It was all contained in your code already, and soon we'll be able to reprogramme the part of you that's gone wrong,' he said.

This was comforting, but I was still left with the impression that he and his colleagues were kidding themselves. Once they had found the key to this door, they would realize there was another door behind it, then another and yet another – each of them with a key of their own. What these scientists were really looking for was the key to all keys, the combination of all combinations – the code of God. How did they think they were going to find that?

I never lost faith in the doctors I had entrusted myself to. Quite the opposite. But the more I got to know them, I realized they were trapped in a highly mechanical view of the problem and its solution. Some of them understood my misgivings, and were entertained by my observations, one of which, for example, was to suggest that we thought more carefully about the words we use – might that not help? Every form of language used in connection with this illness involves war, and I too had adopted such language to begin with. Cancer is an 'enemy' which needs to be fought, therapy is a 'weapon', every stage of the treatment is a 'battle'. The 'evil' is seen as something alien which comes inside us in order to wreak havoc, so it must be destroyed, removed or expelled. After just a few weeks of living with cancer I already disliked this way of thinking, and was no longer happy with it.

I had spent some time with this internal visitor of mine, and it was almost as though he had become part of me, like my hands and feet, or even my head, now quite bald as a result of the chemotherapy. Rather than attacking this cancer in any of its incarnations, I felt more like talking to it and making friends with it, if for no other reason than that I now knew it would be there for the rest of my days, in one form or another, dormant or otherwise.

'When you wake up each morning, smile, and say hello to your heart, your stomach, your lungs and your liver; after all, much depends on them,' I had once heard the famous Vietnamese Buddhist monk Thich Nhat Hanh say when he came to Delhi to speak on meditation. At that stage, I didn't realize how useful his advice would be. I began to smile and say hello to my inner guest each day.

The more time I spent with science and reason, the more curious I grew about the magic and madness of the alternatives I had rejected to begin with. Not because I thought I had taken the wrong path – it's the first recommendation I would make to anyone. But though this was no doubt the best option available, I still felt this route had its limits, and that if I were to try others as well, I would come across something different, something complementary perhaps, rather than something alternative.

So when the doctor-fixers in New York told me they had completed their repairs, and that they didn't want to see me again for another three months – three months! It sounded like forever – this was the direction I ran in.

After all the blows inflicted on my body, I decided to give it some respite, purify it from all the poisons I had dosed it with by way of treatment. Above all, I had to get my mind, now used to solitude, back in tune with the rest of the world. The obvious way for me to do this was by travelling, so I set off with the idea of seeing all the other types of medicines, therapies and miracles that could be of use.

The first thing I did was go back to India, where life is always more authentic, where humanity is still most varied, where the hours seem longer, where the old continues to exist alongside the new, and where living and dying seem to be more ancient experiences than anywhere else.

I had been away from Delhi for almost a year, and an old jeweller in Sundar Nagar, who was threading a garland of the sweetest-smelling jasmine flowers to put around an image of Krishna, asked me what had happened when I entered his shop.

'I've been going around hospitals – I've got cancer,' I told him quite naturally, as I wouldn't have told anyone else.

'It must have been the most divine period in your life,' he replied, just as naturally. Indeed it had been. But how did he know?

'Don't you know the story of the Muslim who was thrown out of a mosque and who fell down the stairs?'

'No, I don't.'

'With every stair he hit he felt pain, he suffered, so his thoughts turned to God. When he finally reached the bottom, he was sad that there were no steps left. I imagine something similar must have happened to you.'

Was there a better way of buying a simple money clip to replace the one I had lost in New York? Was there a better form of moral support for the journey I had embarked on, in search of something even I wasn't sure of? Apart from my three-monthly check-ups in New York, I travelled non-stop, going from one place to another, each time following up leads, satisfying a point of curiosity, or checking out a story I had heard about.

Thus it was that I spent a week in an old, basic ayurvedic centre at the southernmost tip of India, run by a young doctor who knew all the sacred writings on his traditional medicine by heart, having learnt them from his grandfather, who in turn had learnt them from his father, and so on. The place itself was beautiful, set amid rice fields near an ancient ruined temple which, legend has it, Rama founded while on his way to Lanka.

Also in India, I did a course and earned a diploma in reiki, while in Thailand I fasted for seven days at a centre specializing in the now highly fashionable treatment of colonic irrigation.

In the northern Philippines I was 'operated' on by the most famous Filipino healer, and the next day I was the first to experience his Pyramid of Asia on the eve of its inauguration, which he had built to become his world healing centre. I spent days going around with a 'doctor-magician' who prepared some special, foul-smelling green potions for me out of bundles of herbs and firewood in a village in central India. I also stayed in the most famous traditional hospital in Kerala where, like the other patients, I was kept awake all night by an elephant trumpeting in the courtyard outside, along with the odd sounds of an orchestra, which had arrived with a troupe of actors to celebrate the festival of the divine protector of ayurveda.

I followed a young Italian surgeon-turned-homeopath all the way to Boston, where he was giving a course on marine remedies. From his old refurbished farmhouse in the nondescript plains of Emilia-Romagna, this man sought to gain scientific credibility for his practice, which he himself recognized had an element of magic to it. I can testify to the positive effect it had on me!

I travelled to Hong Kong to meet an old Chinese billionaire

and philanthropist, who wanted to leave a treatment for cancer as his gift to mankind before he died. He had invested part of his fortune into the research and production of a mushroom extract, which Chinese tradition has always seen as miraculous.

At Chiang Mai in northern Thailand, I met up with my old friend, Dan Reid, an expert in Taoism and *chi gung*. Every morning under his guidance, I performed ancient Chinese exercises in an attempt to harness the 'cosmic energies' he had just finished writing a book about.

I attended a cancer sufferers' support group in California, in an isolated, windy complex of old buildings high up on a cliff top, with a view of the ocean that filled the mind with immensity. There were nine of us, and I have emotional, but also amusing memories of them all. Immediately after that I tagged along with a master of yoga and a musician, both of whom were Indian, and who taught me to take up various yogic positions and 'open the channels' so the music could filter through to my body's fibres and cells, and stimulate new vitality. It was the kind of music that spoke straight to the heart. It certainly did me a power of good, whether or not it got as far down as my cells!

Also in India, I tried to see Sai Baba, a holy man to whom thousands of miracles are attributed. However, on the day I arrived at his ashram he was elsewhere, so I took this as a sign that we didn't need to meet.

En route I also visited some of the holy places of Buddhism and spent a number of days at Varanasi. But as is always the case, when you look for one thing you find another, and gradually my vast collection of doctors, specialists and healers grew.

Occasionally, I even tried some of the 'medicines' that were offered to me, and everywhere I went I collected stories of people who had been 'miraculously' healed, of treatments ascribed to some potion or the other. I heard an equal number of stories involving people who had refused the normal therapies they had been offered by Western classical medicine and turned to alternative treatment instead, only to end up dying as a result.

If I had thought I needed to make a clean break with the past and begin a new life in order to help cure me of my illness which was due, probably, to the life I had been living, surely I was now on the right track. I was spending time with different people, facing different problems, and thinking different thoughts. I myself had changed, and not just physically. At this point, the only thing left to do was take one more step and cross another wholly Indian line.

I decided to spend three months in an ashram, studying Sanskrit and meditating on the one great question man has always asked, and one which lies at the heart of the Vedanta, the last part of the Vedas and the philosophical essence of the most ancient holy Indian scriptures, namely: 'Who am I?' And seeing as the answer to this question was not 'journalist for whatever newspaper', 'author of such-and-such a book', or 'sufferer from this or that illness', I tried to stop being what I had always been, to stop calling myself by my own name, to have no past and become 'Anam', meaning no name. In my view, this was the most appropriate name for a person who had spent his whole life trying to make a name for himself!

Slowly, laughing at myself all the while and smiling at what had become of me, I had gone from me as a-body-suffering-from-cancer and being treated at one of the best medical institutions in the world, to me as a-body-suffering-from-cancer-plus-all-the-other-stuff-that-goes-along-with-it being treated in the most spartan of ashrams. It involved studying classical Hindu texts, chanting Vedic hymns, and sitting on the floor eating out of a steel bowl with my fingers, instead of one of the diets I had so carefully chosen in New York. But I ate whatever happened to be on the menu at the time – always a matter of chance, but usually boiled chickpeas!

'So, have you spoken to God?' an old friend of mine asked me when I went to see him as I passed through Paris.

'I'd have to meet him first in order to speak to him,' I replied, to avoid answering. He probably thought I'd gone off the rails while in India. But I hadn't converted to Hinduism or Buddhism, I'm not a follower of any guru, nor have I gone back to my own religion. Though I have rediscovered the pleasure of sitting in silence in a beautiful church steeped in ancient faith, one such as San Miniato al Monte in Florence.

I'm just a seeker without too many preconceptions, without fear of the new or ridiculous. Did I discover a cure for cancer in the course of my searches? No. But at least I'm now sure that no such cure exists because there are no shortcuts: not to health, happiness or wisdom. None of these things is instantaneous. Everyone has to find their own way and make their own path in life.

After so much travelling, did I come back to my starting point of believing only in science and reason? Did I come back to believing that the Western way of dealing with problems was really the best? Not at all. Now I believe, more than ever, that nothing should be ruled out a priori, and that it is always possible to find someone or something of value in even the unlikeliest of places and circumstances. Miracles? Of course they happen. But I'm now sure that everyone must be the author of their own. Above all, I'm convinced that our knowledge of the world and ourselves really is very limited, and that behind the appearances and facts, there is a truth which eludes us, because it eludes the network of our senses, the basis of our science and so-called reason.

There is no doubt the West has made huge progress in understanding the human body. I do admit though, I've always been somewhat bemused by the fact that Western science is based on anatomy – a science which involves dissecting corpses – and I do wonder how one can hope to understand the mystery of life by studying the dead. But the West has made no progress in terms of understanding what is invisible, immeasurable and imponderable, inside or outside our bodies, that which sustains and links us to the other forms of life, and makes us part of nature. Indeed, we may have even gone backwards in this respect. Psychoanalysis and psychology barely scratch the surface of the invisible world, as though embarrassed by this great mystery which no science can ever hope to resolve, precisely because it is a science.

This is why medical research has no choice but to become more and more specialized, to go from the small to the smaller. But should not another form of research, not necessarily scientific, proceed in the opposite direction – from the small to the large?

Perhaps subconsciously, I wanted to see my problem as more than just a cell that had gone mad – I was looking for another answer than just a switch in a code of my DNA that had broken – that I ended up in a small stone house with mud walls in the Himalayas. Here, with my heart lighter than ever, free of all desire and ambition, and the most immense sense of peace, I watched the first sunrise of the new millennium as though it were the dawn of creation itself. Some of the highest peaks on earth emerged from the cosmic darkness tinged with a pinkish glow, and seemed to restore hope in the eternity of life and death. Never before had the gods felt so close.

I was the guest of a most learned Indian man, over eighty years in age, who had done nothing all his life save reflect on the meaning of life. He had met all the great masters of his age and now lived there alone, convinced that the one true master is the one we all have inside ourselves. At night, when the silence became so dense it echoed, he got up, lit a candle, and sat in front of it for several hours. Why?

'To try to be myself,' he replied. 'To hear the melody.'

Occasionally, this old man would climb the wooden stairs to my house, after his afternoon walk in the woods on the footsteps of a leopard which one night had eaten his guard dog. I would heat some water from a nearby spring on a gas stove, and make us two cups of the China tea I take with me everywhere.

'All forces – visible and invisible, tangible and intangible, male and female, negative and positive – all of them have arranged for us to be sitting here in front of the fire drinking tea!' he would say, with a peal of laughter that was pure joy to listen to. He would quote Plotinus or Boethius, sometimes the Upanishads, a verse from the Bhagavadgita, William Blake or a Sufi mystic, and set off on one of his highly idiosyncratic theories of art or music, or a confession of his own version of 'original sin' – that of always having set greater store by 'being' rather than by 'doing'.

'And the melody?' I asked him one day.

'It's not easy. You have to prepare yourself, then sometimes you can hear it: it's the melody of the life inside, one which sustains all lives, where everything has its place and everything fits – good and evil, health and disease – the inner life, where there's no birth or death.'

The days passed as I watched the ever present mountains alone, motionless, a symbol of the utmost stability, yet – like everything else in this world – continuously changing and impermanent. In the process, with the presence of this lovely man I had met by chance, I felt the long, tortuous journey I had commenced at the hospital at Bologna had reached its end.

I decided to tell the story of my journey, mostly because I know how encouraging it is to hear the experience of someone who is already some way along the path you yourself have to take. I also did this because after a while my journey ceased to be in search of a cure for cancer, and became one for the 'disease' which sooner or later we all have to come to terms with: our own mortality.

Is this really a disease? Something to fear, an ill to be avoided?

'Imagine how crowded the world would be if everyone was immortal and we all had to hang around forever. If alongside us there were also those who had gone through the ages, they too immortal!' my old companion said one day during a walk in the woods. 'We have to realize that life and death are merely two aspects of the same thing.'

Achieving this is perhaps the real goal of the journey we all embark on the day that we are born, a journey which I too profess not to know much about, apart from its direction – I now know it goes from the outside to the inside, and from the small to the large and then the larger.

The pages that follow present the story.

TWO

NEW YORK

THE MAN IN THE MIRROR

It was like being in an aquarium, and I was the fish; eyes agape, breathing through an open mouth. I was sheltered from the elements, stuffed full of antibiotics, vaccinated from the merest rumour of a cold – something which in my case might prove dangerous, the doctors said – there I sat, alone in the silence of my tank, motionless for hours at a time, staring out at the frantic world that began just beyond the glass wall: New York.

My apartment was on the fifth floor; low enough to have a good view of the street and its unending pageant, but sufficiently high to discern, through the big north-facing window, the swath of trees that marked Central Park and behind it the Manhattan skyline.

That strange world on the other side of the glass, with its flat, muffled sounds appeared to me as bizarre and remote as it would have appeared to a fish. My head felt empty, capable of only the haziest of thoughts, my bones ached, and my limbs had lost all their strength. The scurrying legs of all the people as they bumped into, or bustled past each other, issuing perfunctory greetings to acquaintances before scuttling away again, appeared to me so out of step with my rhythm that I would sometimes laugh out loud. Nor did the natural cadence of the sun, reassuringly punctual in its rising and setting, match my body's rhythm. I would often fall asleep during the day and remain awake all night amid the sounds of police cars, fire trucks and ambulance sirens whose maddening wails added yet another layer of anguish to the darkness.

For months my window was my only companion; from it I saw marathon runners surge past, and snow blanket the city. I watched squirrels chase each other across the bare winter trees before vanishing beneath their spring foliage. From it I followed the adventures of a number of amiable tramps who, surrounded by their bundled belongings and mounds of plastic bags, took the time to enjoy a spot of sun.

From the window I imagined the destinies of several small-town girls I saw stepping off the arriving Greyhounds, a few clothes and countless plans stowed away in enormous black shoulder-slung holdalls. I observed the odd relationships that seemed to exist between dogs and their owners as well as those, often odder still, between the owners themselves. It is amazing how much one can learn from simply standing at a window, how far the imagination can travel beginning from the smallest detail or gesture.

It is also amazing that even a place as anonymous and plain as that apartment could become a 'home'. Often, returning from a stroll with the feel of cold sweat on my back, I would find myself counting the steps that remained, already savouring the moment when I would open the iron door of 5/C and breathe in the by now familiar rented-room smell which I tried, vainly, to smother with sandalwood incense.

On moving into the apartment I had draped bright Indonesian

batiks over all the mirrors that an interior decorator had installed to give the apartment illusion of size. The only mirror I left uncovered was the one above the bathroom sink. Whenever I stepped in, I was met by this swollen, yellow, glabrous guy who scowled intently at me as if expecting to be recognized, even though I'd never in my life seen him before. Yet he was always there, waiting in that mirror. Sometimes the scowl would contort into a knowing smirk which was even more repugnant, but this didn't discourage him and in his way he kept on trying to talk to me. He said that we'd known each other for almost sixty years, that he was, in point of fact, me. I gradually became accustomed to this new bloated, pallid and hairless version of myself.

Aging gracefully is an art the Chinese have spent centuries trying to perfect. Having lived among them for years, I believed I had learnt some of its rudiments and tucked the knowledge safely away for when my time came. I liked the idea of growing white-haired and wizened, perhaps even cultivating a set of handsome bushy eyebrows. I hadn't reckoned on the effects of chemotherapy. But neither had chemotherapy reckoned on me! Not wanting to find clumps of hair in my comb, two days into my first cycle of treatment I went over to Angelo's, the corner barbershop and said I wanted a radical makeover. I told him to shave off all my hair, which hung down to my shoulders.

'I'm just about to close. Why don't you sleep on it? Come back tomorrow,' Angelo said. 'I don't want you dousing my place in gasoline!'

The following day Angelo did what I requested, but stopped short of my moustache. That, he said, I would have to remove myself. I'd had it since 1968 when Richard Nixon won the US presidential elections and I, then a student at Columbia, lost a bet. For nearly thirty years the moustache had been a part of how I saw myself, and I was surprised that it took less than a minute to learn to live without it.

An old school chum, Alberto Baroni, now a famous gerontologist in Florence, once told me, 'The old people who suffer the most are those who have set great store by their image during their lives. They're the ones who find it hardest to recover when that image is suddenly disfigured by a heart attack or stroke or some other illness.' I was determined to get through this ordeal, and had no compunction about burying the old me along with his moustache and flowing locks.

The last day of his existence was a strange one indeed. Still wearing my old face so the bank clerks would recognize me, I went to the Banca Commerciale Italiana on Wall Street to withdraw some money to keep in the apartment. I decided to make the journey home on foot, a considerable hike. The sun was out, there was a slight breeze in the air and I, still the old me, clad in white, bursting with energy, with my long hair and moustache walked back along Fifth Avenue across Manhattan, watching myself in shop windows as I went past. In a few hours, I thought, he'll be gone. It was almost amusing, this idea of becoming someone else. During my life, I'd met a number of people who were able to juggle two, sometimes three, parallel existences. As much as I would have liked to join their club I was never able to.

'Hey Tiziano, what are you doing in New York?' Outside the Disney superstore, who should appear but an old journalist colleague from *Libération* and his wife, arms open wide in greeting.

'What a surprise seeing you here. All in white as always. We recognized you a mile off. Why don't we meet for dinner tonight?' I'd last seen him in Ulan Bator, when he'd told me he was working on a historical novel set in Mongolia.

'So, have you finished it yet?' I asked.

'Are you kidding? I've written more than a thousand pages and still the monster keeps growing. It's worse than cancer! It grows and grows but I'm sticking with it.'

I had to laugh at this, but neither he nor his wife understood the reason for my mirth. Had I suggested the image to him? I mumbled my excuses and made a quick getaway.

Before my appointment with Angelo, I needed to consider my wardrobe. Or rather, I had to decide how I was going to dress this new me. One thing I was certain of: if I was to cope with the disease there could be no regrets, no nostalgia for the past, and above all no illusions of going back to being who I was before, should I make it through. So I may as well have done away with that extrovert, the sociable guy who wanted to be liked, with his white duds and slightly arrogant mien; after all, he was the one whose cells had gone haywire. Why? Maybe because of who he was. So all the more reason to change him. I had to detach myself from his lifestyle, his habits, his favourite colours. Not that I fully believed what my head was thinking, but I let it think on, all the time taking notes from the sidelines.

In New York, on one of the streets I took, trying to constantly vary my route to and from the hospital, I chanced upon a store called Duffy's Cheap Clothes for Millionaires where everything seemed tailor-made to my requirements. Though I've never actually been a millionaire, I always felt like one. Plus I've always bought my clothes on the cheap. Finding designer clothes in upmarket boutiques isn't exactly a treasure hunt. At Duffy's, among the remaindered stock of last year's trends, there was plenty to discover. In a few minutes, for very little money, I managed to gather all I needed for my new wardrobe: two tracksuits in blue and black; tennis shoes, sports socks, gloves and two woollen caps, one blue and the other violet, to cover what would very soon be my cue ball of a head.

The idea behind chemotherapy is simple: cancer cells have a certain malign aspect, that of replicating and reproducing themselves. Chemotherapy is a mix – a 'cocktail' – of powerful chemical agents which, once introduced into the blood stream, roam around the body on a search-and-destroy mission to eliminate the rogue cells. The problem is that it isn't only cancer cells which go forth and multiply. Hair cells, along with those of the palate, the tongue and other mucous surfaces like the intestines share similar characteristics, which, though healthy, are attacked along with the diseased cells. 'So you could say it's a bit like napalming a jungle, laying to waste thousands of trees, in order to kill a monkey perched on a palm tree,' I suggested to the nurse, as she studiously mixed the first batch of the cocktail that would shortly be introduced into my bloodstream.

As I said this, I was thinking of the Viet Cong and how the American military, during the Vietnam War, defoliated entire regions of forest, destroying vast stretches of vegetation simply to deprive the resistance fighters of a place to hide or food to eat. The logic was the same, and now I would have to bow to that very logic if I wanted to come out alive. From the first fiery-red drops that slithered one after another from their transparent sac down a plastic tube and entered my veins, it seemed to be working.

The effect was immediate and overwhelming. A strong taste of iron filled my mouth and I felt my head flare up as though it was hit by napalm, the flames quickly spreading through my body down to my fingertips. Plumped in a comfy armchair that seemed to have been requisitioned from a spaceship, I had the luxury of flowers, modest but real, on the window sill and was listening to the lovely young nurse telling me her dream of living in a beach house in California. I felt at ease, in good hands; I liked the gaudy hue, almost phosphorescent, of the liquid entering my body. It seemed to confirm its efficacy, and I was disappointed when the nurse attached a new bag to the drip. It was the final ingredient to her cocktail, a colourless, water-like liquid that I couldn't imagine having any effect whatsoever. I suggested she dye the anaemic solution a nice emerald green or purple and fortify its chemical muscle with psychological persuasiveness. 'Neat idea!' the nurse laughed.

She was an astute observer. Watching her patients, she could see each had their own way of dealing with chemotherapy; there were those who used meditation, those who brought their Walkman Stereos to listen to music as the dyes did their work. Some became nervous, suffering through the treatment as if under torture, maybe because, psychologically, they refused to see it as a possible cure and couldn't accept its debilitating consequences.

'You seem to be enjoying this,' the nurse said to me.

What choice had I but to grin and bear it? It seemed like the natural thing to do.

For me, chemo was the first phase of a 'strategy', after weeks of tests, checks, visits to specialists, trudging from one floor to another of the vast edifice of MSKCC, I decided it was my best chance for survival. Well, that's how the sternly laconic doctor in charge of my case presented it to me. In her fifties, she was a skinny woman of rod-like bearing, whose terse pronouncements occasionally softened into a delicate smile. From our very first encounter I felt she was someone I could trust. I was happy to hand myself over to her care. Following the chemo – the cocktail best suited to my condition, she said, had been perfected by a team of Milan doctors in whom she had the greatest confidence – there would be an operation. Once the wounds from the surgery healed,

I would start radiotherapy, a process still at the experimental stage, developed by an Israeli doctor heading the hospital's radiology department.

A small, sturdy individual with a Freudian tuft on his chin, whose curiosity went beyond the confines of medical science, he seemed to radiate healing power even without his machines. At least that is the impression I first had on meeting him when I impulsively decided to volunteer for his 'experiments'. I was the eighteenth patient to do so.

'And the other seventeen?' I asked him.

'All survived.'

'For how long?'

'Two years ... but it's only been that long since we first started this treatment.' Since then I always referred to him as the Radiator.

The surgeon turned up in khakis and a denim shirt. Short and fat with blonde hair, his beer gut bespoke Teutonic origins. And Herr was his surname, which means 'My Lord'. What struck me was the unflinching blue of his eyes, his tiny hands and sharp, cuneiform fingers. Had I been Louis XVI facing the guillotine, I would have preferred the job be done by someone as precise as this man obviously was. He seemed absolutely sure of himself after having made a primary incision that ran from above the navel to the back. What he did not tell me was that during the operation he would also have to remove a rib.

'What are my chances?' I asked him.

'Excellent, if you survive the other cancer.'

Well, it was better than none at all, especially since this was the word of 'The Lord', as I had mentally rechristened him.

Prior to each of these phases, I was examined by the speleologist, a young endoscopist whose microscopic video camera could go wherever tissue needed to be scrutinized. He went caving into my body about ten times in all and nobody, I believe, can claim to know the inner me better than he.

All told, the labours of these various 'fixers' were to take six or seven months. I tried to bargain with the doctor responsible for coordinating 'repairs', wanting to quicken the work, postpone some steps, cut short others. 'Couldn't the operation wait another year?' I pleaded.

Looking me in the eye, she answered, 'Mr Terzani, you wait – you die.' If that was the case, I had no choice. So the bargaining stopped.

This was why I liked chemo. I clung to it as a rope someone had thrown to save me from both the tiger above waiting to pounce and from the abyss below. I intended to go through with it conscious of every drop entering my bloodstream, monitoring the slightest effects it had, taking part in its workings, mustering all my attention. For me, chemotherapy was the beginning of what could have been one more strip of life, one more ride on the merry-go-round. I liked that in hospital jargon the day of the first injection was referred to as 'Day One' and starting from then a schedule would be laid out for the various tests and treatments I would have to undergo. For me too, it was 'day one' … the beginning of a new era, my second life.

After a couple of hours I was allowed to get up, but I felt completely exhausted. My bones ached as though I'd been beaten with billy clubs. I couldn't say they did not warn me. I gathered what strength I had left to make the walk home across Central Park. A half-hour stroll this time took twice as long. I felt like I was gliding, high on drugs, but it was nice to know I could still make it on my own. The doctor had advised me not to interrupt my daily exercise routine, if possible. Among many other things, I had to drink as much water as I could, up to three or four litres a day, to eliminate the cells killed by chemotherapy. I followed her instructions to the letter.

There was something deeply consoling about believing in doctors and their advice. It helped immensely. I imagine praying would have had a similar effect, but I had no idea how to pray. It even seemed a bit ridiculous to bother God, or whoever was up there, to concern himself with something as insignificant as my illness.

Between one cocktail and another, there was a two-week hiatus during which I had strict appointments to keep along with a string of other medicines. I was also to inject myself with steroids, inserting a small syringe into the folds of flab that covered my stomach. Steroids would help the white corpuscles reproduce, though they were a further blow to my bones, especially the sternum and pelvic bone. The two-week interval was to work off the effects of the bombardment and to restore my body to some kind of normality, readying it for another attack.

Body. Strange how we hardly notice its existence when we are healthy, taking its functions for granted. However, it suddenly becomes the all-consuming centre of our attention if we fall ill. Simple acts such as breathing, urinating or defecating become essential matters that determine our happiness or suffering, causing anguish or relief. Following the instructions I'd been given, I monitored all of my body's vital functions, trying to correct irregularities where I could. But by doing so, I became even more aware of how much I depended on this body, how much its mood determined my own, and how great an effort I had to make to not become its slave.

I've always felt that anyone with a strong enough will can be 'free' even in prison. A recent and fine example of such strength of will is Palden Gyatso, a Tibetan monk who managed to survive thirty-three years of torture and solitary confinement in Chinese prisons while remaining free in spirit. But how free is a person if the prison in question is their own body? And in any case, what is this blessed 'freedom' that people are always going on about these days? Asia has an answer, in the form of an old story.

A man presents himself before his king, famed for his great wisdom, and asks him, 'Sire, tell me, does freedom exist in life?'

'Most certainly,' replies the king. 'How many legs do you have?'

The man looks down, somewhat surprised by the question, and answers, 'Two, My Lord.'

'And are you able to stand on one alone?'

'Naturally, sire.'

'Let's see you then. Upon which leg do you wish to stand?'

The man ponders for a moment, then lifts up his left leg, shifting all his weight to his right.

'Excellent,' says the king. 'Now lift up the other leg.'

'But sire, that's impossible.'

'You see? There is your freedom. You are free, but only to make the first decision, that is all.'

And what choice did I have? To what extent was I my body? What relationship did we share? And were we really 'the two of us'? Or was my mind, the part which I so strongly identified with – simply one of the body's many functions and thus completely bound to it?

With death ever present as a possibility amidst a welter of pain, anxiety and feelings of melancholy, I questioned myself this way, even if I had no answers.

I thought of my body as a costume I had borrowed at birth, that sooner or later I should be able to, and must be able to, return without the fear of remaining unclothed. Yet, would that really work? There was one thing I was certain of: my mind was aware of my body, but was it aware of me? Well, if it wasn't, it would bloody well have to be. It had to recognize that I was there too and that it couldn't just do as it pleased.

The most immediate effects of chemo were on the stomach. Lacking self-control, it tried to spit out what it considered poison. To prevent this, the hospital gave me a small bottle of some very expensive pills to consume if necessary. I managed to not take a single one. The moment I felt my stomach launch one of its revolts, I sat cross-legged on the floor before a little bronze Buddha I had placed on the window sill. Closing my eyes, I focused my mind on my stomach, imagining I was stroking it, soothing it with soft words. At least that was the impression I gave myself. Maybe I was just lucky. I didn't want to delude myself into thinking that what John Coleman had taught me in a meditation course in Thailand could adequately substitute for my doctors and their pills, no more than it could replace that malignant yet benign fluorescent-red liquid. But it helped.

Despite my aspirations to be something other than a body, something less subject to mutation or decomposition, a body I was and a body I would remain. It would be wise then, to pay attention to the things that kept my body functioning, on which everything else now seemed to depend.

'What we are is 97 per cent what we eat,' the young MSKCC dietician told me. I had been referred to her for advice on the best diet for dealing with chemotherapy. 'The industrialization of food has created major imbalances in our bodies and is a serious health risk. So what you should try to do is to eat as naturally as possible.'

To help my body, she asked me to drink lots of herbal infusions. I was to avoid cow's milk – which was too fatty – and stick to soy milk. I could indulge in low-fat yoghurt and eat plenty of fruit. If I insisted on remaining vegetarian, as I had become almost by osmosis since living in India, I would have to eat tree loads of nuts, pine kernels, almonds and also a variety of seeds – pumpkin and sunflower seeds were particularly recommended provided they weren't too salty.

'Make sure the dishes you eat are colourful; red, yellow, green and black vegetables should all be mixed together. Eat a lot of broccoli, leeks and as much garlic as you like. Two or three times a day make yourself an "everything" shake: carrots, apples, spinach, and lots of berries, especially blueberries. And when you have an orange or grapefruit, make sure to eat the white too. Anything containing fibre is good in your case and will help regulate your intestines,' she said.

And I, as if still in my old journalist skin, took notes.

During my life I'd never paid much attention to what I ate, whether a dish was salty or not, boiled or fried, and in no time I became extremely aware of everything that I ate. I became an assiduous frequenter of organic food shops and an attentive reader of packaging. I learnt to look for lists of ingredients that producers were required to declare by law. Steering clear of anything containing preservatives, artificial flavouring or colouring, I became obsessed with the dangers of eating polluted, unnatural food. I disposed all the Teflon pots and pans I found in the apartment and re-bought them all in cast iron. I cooked every meal in the simplest and most natural way.

What disgusted me most were foods made with genetically modified ingredients. Those malefic food giants who tampered with nature for the sake of enormous profits did not ask themselves what the result would be, both for the human body and the environment, of their playing God. Their products sit on the supermarket shelves, are consumed, and no one knows the diabolical consequences of doing so.

If our body is primarily made up of what we eat, perhaps the cancer too, undeniably a part of my body, was caused by what I had eaten. The reasoning struck me as flawless and with mounting horror I now recalled all those wonderful Chinese dishes from dirt-caked kitchens, soups from the streets of Indo-China, hundreds of things that whether from hunger, boredom or conviviality, we stuffed into our gullets. In India there are castes of people – such as the more orthodox Brahmins – who eat only what they have cooked in receptacles they wash themselves; some consider the choice of a cook a spiritual rather than a practical matter. These Brahmins believe that the person who prepares food unconsciously imbues it with their influence. Should a cook have a lowly soul, the dish will be sprinkled with a negative charge that will inexorably pass on to the one who eats it. Scientifically speaking, this is absurd, for no science can verify the existence of such a negative charge, nor can it measure the intensity. But people will go on believing in it. Absence of proof is not proof of absence.

The doctors were amused by my reflections between one test and another. But not one paused to believe there could be an element of truth in this way of viewing the world, something that eluded the grasp of science.

For years scientific research claimed that vitamins were of vital importance for the treatment of illnesses. Now, however, several studies have revealed that they were of little or no use. For nearly twenty years we were convinced that salt was dangerous for those who suffered from heart disease. We now know that this is not the whole truth. Doctors always informed us that a high-fibre diet was effective in preventing colonic cancer. Now it seems this is not the case.

Articles would regularly appear in the US press, citing studies carried out by universities which demonstrated that certain vegetables were more useful than others in fighting cancer. Some of the suggested vegetables were onions, Brussels sprouts, carrots, tomatoes and even broccoli, but they had to be no more than three days old. It was the same for fruits – prunes and blueberries were essential – and spices, especially turmeric and cumin. These momentous discoveries have become objects of ridicule over time. *The New York Times* once stated: 'People suffering from stress are much more vulnerable to colds than non-stress sufferers.'

Why shouldn't we think that at the root of mad cow disease lies the fact that for years we have forced upon the planet's most vegetarian animal a daily diet of crushed bones and meat of other animals? Though scientifically this argument may seem specious, to me it sounds right; ruminating on the recycled corpses of other murdered creatures has driven cows mad. It is that simple. Wouldn't we humans risk a similar fate if we woke up one day to discover our morning coffee had been ground from the toasted bones of our relatives? Or that the juicy steak on our plate was the thigh of our neighbour's murdered son?

Can science explain why dogs become so attached to people? Or why salmon, after being at sea for years, are able to locate the estuary they were born in and swim up it to deposit their spawn before dying? And how, in an experiment conducted at the time of the cold war, did mother rabbits caged up in a Soviet ship's hold know their little ones were being killed at irregular intervals on an underwater submarine?

The person most amused by my freestyle lucubration was my doctor-fixer, though she was careful not to become enmeshed in their logic. Nor would I have wished her to. I certainly didn't want her to admit her science was equally relative and that its history was a stream of truths that turned out to be errors in the light of later truths. My mind simply got its fun by quibbling. Inside, however, I desperately wanted to trust the science on which I had staked everything.

'Say, Mr Terzani,' my doctor asked me one day, 'I've heard you've given all your doctors nicknames. What's mine?' Fortunately I didn't need to dissemble. Playing on her surname which was Portlock with 'portare' meaning 'to bring', I substituted a single vowel and decided to call her 'Bringluck'.

I was extremely careful of what I put into my body, food being my primary concern, but equally important was air. We can survive for several days without eating, and it can be a salutary exercise for it to do so now and then. But without air it won't last more than a couple of minutes. I couldn't choose the quality of the air, but I could at least learn how to breathe better.

There was an advertisement in the personals that gave me the idea: a Chinese 'master' was holding weekend courses in qigong (literally, the work of the air). Participants of all ages and physical conditions were welcome. I wrote to them, paid the enrolment fee, and at 9 a.m. on a Saturday morning I found myself in a huge room in the fashionable Bowery district, an ex-industrial makeover with a wooden floor to gentrify its iron columns. Part of a general movement that has seen old textile works and elegant nineteenth-century warehouse buildings transformed into art galleries. Master Hu's seminar provided an excellent example of this new type of consumer experience. In place of rows of immigrant girls bent over sewing machines – the sweatshop labour that made the US garment industry a fortune – were approximately fifty young to middle-aged women and two of us men. We listened intently to Master Hu as he explained to us in broken English, interspersed with the elucidations of his assistant-cum-spin-doctor, 'one of China's oldest secrets'. I immediately understood from his accent that the spin-doctor was Italian. The Korean girl at the front desk must have been his partner.

Like the pranayama practised in India, qigong is the art of controlling one's breathing, directing its vital force from the lungs to various other parts of the body. Having lived among the Chinese for many years, I had often witnessed crowds of people, especially the elderly, practising such slow, highly focused movements at dawn in public parks and I had become aware of their therapeutic value. In Beijing, after an operation for cancer, my wife Angela's friend was sent by her work unit on a course of qigong, which she claimed was of great benefit.

When I was arrested and expelled from China, I had just begun to take lessons in this ancient mind–body gymnastics. I wish I had finished the course, instead here I was in New York, listening to Master Hu's banalities. 'The qigongI teach you, if practised correctly, will change your character, make you more likeable, and for women, make it easier to find a husband.' Poor Master Hu had only just arrived in the States and hadn't yet realized that such politically incorrect reasoning here had gone the way of the dinosaurs.

I spent the day learning a number of exercises: the first taught me that one breathes by expanding one's chest, the others taught me to breathe not simply by opening the ribcage but also the stomach and lower abdomen. One exercise in particular involved standing with both knees slightly bent and feet apart in line with the shoulders, imagining we had a ball of energy in our hands held immobile at the height of the navel. After ten minutes of this, we had to imagine the ball revolving, first in one direction, and then the other. 'Now try separating your hands,' said Master Hu. 'You will see how difficult it is. For some impossible, I think.' Several particularly zealous students found their hands locked in an unbreakable 'magnetic field', but I wasn't one of them.

A final exercise consisted of closing one's eyes and, keeping the knees slightly bent, feet firmly planted in the ground but imagining the head rising to dizzying heights. This one I liked because it was close to my ideal of fulfilment: to be rooted in things, but still free to dream.

After the first day's lesson, I introduced myself to the Master and asked him to tell me his story. I soon found myself in a vegetarian restaurant, with his circle of adepts, along with the Italian spin-doctor and the Korean receptionist. On our way there, the spin-doctor told me how he had come to the US after completing his military service to look for work as a goldsmith. Having no luck, he quickly discovered that 'being a healer is more interesting'. It was certainly more lucrative. He had attended an array of martial arts courses from kung fu to judo, akido to t'ai-chi-ch'uan before meeting Master Hu, and the two of them decided to partner-up, each making use of the other's talents. The Korean had tagged along after she lost her job at a pharmaceutical company, hoping to become a healer herself.

Spin spoke in glowing terms of the Master's 'miracles'. He told me how he could move things from a distance, make sheets of paper and other objects fly simply by the force of the energy he emitted. 'I've just learnt to cure a migraine but he, he can do anything,' Spin concluded. One of the Master's specialities was curing cancer. Spin swore he'd witnessed certain tumours literally shrink by 50 per cent after only one session of exposure to Master Hu's 'energy'. According to him, the Master could have cured Pope John Paul II's Parkinsonism. But how could he have informed the Vatican? Master Hu was equally confident of being able to help Giovannino Agnelli, the nephew of one of the richest industrialist families in Italy, who was at MSKCC during those weeks, but the Master didn't know how to contact him. I was careful to not mention that I was a patient there too. It had been terribly odd to find myself in Agnelli's company, following a meeting-cum-interview in India and after a series of unlikely coincidences with similar malady and in the hands of the same team of fixers.

All Master and his entourage needed to do was perform a 'miracle' on somebody famous enough to get Hu's name known. This is how the world worked, after all. The only thing that counted was the market; profit was its sole morality and everyone had to hack their way through the jungle as best they could. All I could say was I didn't like it.

Master Hu's story however struck me at once as charming and at the same time pathetic. Born in Gansu province, one of the poorest and remotest in China, he grew up in the village his family had lived in for centuries, thanks to the 'secret' they had been blessed with: the ability to cure burns. The secret was actually quite simple. They would put melon rind in terracotta containers which would then be buried three metres underground and left for several months. The liquid produced from the rind had miraculous properties. One simply had to rub it on the burn to make it heal.

I imagined the main street of a typical Chinese village, the low slate-roofed houses with their floors of beaten earth, peasants going about their business and burn victims arriving from all over to be cured. Now what do we have? Globalization, the free market, a whirlwind spin of ideas and desires that have led to the young Hu to become 'Master' Hu, broker for the world's most sought-after commodity: hope. The hope of a cure for cancer, for which there exists no guaranteed treatment yet.

'You see that woman at the other end of the room? The one you were next to.' Spin asked. 'She doesn't want anyone to know, but I can tell you, she has breast cancer. She decided she isn't going to let them operate, or do chemotherapy, she is going to leave it to Master Hu.' Sure, I had noticed her. Pale, looking afraid, she had sat by herself during the lunch break, propped up against a wall, extracting a Tupperware jar from her bag which contained a greenish swill, the fruit no doubt of some other piece of ancient Chinese or modern macrobiotic wisdom. She sat there sipping it in joyless silence. What a world!

Back home, Spin would perhaps have become an honest goldsmith, young Hu could have carried on the family tradition, the Korean girl might have found happiness somewhere. Instead, here they were, shipwrecked on a foreign shore, momentarily united in their common effort to survive, selling to this poor lonely woman the illusion that their quackery could do more for her than chemo or whatever else Western medicine, with all its limits, had to offer.

The second day was dedicated to repeating the first day's exercises and observing Master Hu perform some of the 'miracles' Spin had foretold me about. The Master had one of his students sit on a chair and measured her blood pressure. Then he stood behind her and went through his exercise routine, transferring his energy to her. He measured her pressure again to check how much it had gone down.

And yet I couldn't help staring at the thin, pallid-faced woman in the corner, not far from where I was standing. She followed the Master's every gesture in an almost trance-like state. It was her life after all, and she had the right to choose how to live it or end it. But was she really free to choose? Without this option, this 'alternative', she would probably have already had the operation, gone through chemo, and would have been out jogging in a park somewhere.

Was it qigong's fault? Obviously not. Qigong itself was a wise thing; there was something eminently healthy, ancient and true in the idea of having the power to shape one's own breath, or at least soothe a person with one's own energy. What was unbearable, at least for me, was how out of place this all was, transplanted from one world to another, removed from its natural context and made over into a supermarket commodity with its attendant bumf listing the litany of illnesses, acute and chronic, that Master Hu claimed he could cure with qigong.

In the Temple of Heaven Park, in Beijing, those gestures, performed at sunrise by old Chinese in their cloth slippers to the sound of nightingales in brightly painted cages suspended from the branches of a weeping willow made perfect sense; in a New York loft, none at all. Even Master Hu himself seemed ill at ease in his role.

All ancient civilizations have studied the art of breathing and remarked on the connection between breathing and the mind, and perhaps the soul too. In India, for example, some believed that through breathing one could attain an awareness of the force that supported the universe itself. A yogi, noticing how certain slow-breathing animals like elephants and snakes lived much longer than species such as dogs and monkeys whose breathing was more rapid, spent years devising special exercises to slow the rhythm of their breathing, thus increasing their lifespan, so it was said, to 150, or even 200, years.

Another Indian belief is that the time we are allotted by fate cannot be measured in years, days and hours – after all, these are our inventions – but only in breaths. And since we normally take around 21,000 breaths a day, 630,000 a month and over seven-

and-a-half million a year, slowing down this rhythm is a way of buying time. All it requires is exercise.

But if such practices are to have any value, they have to be difficult, esoteric, beyond the reach of ordinary mortals. They must be mastered through tremendous sacrifice and dedication. If made available to all, they lose their meaning and their potential efficacy. To retain its power, a mystery has to remain a mystery.

But qigong was very popular. On the way out I listened to a gaggle of girls enthuse about it: 'I've tried Yoga and reiki,' said one, 'but this is the first time I think I really, you know, feel something.' Spin and his Korean girlfriend were at the front desk selling T-shirts embossed with the yin–yang symbol, videotapes of past lessons and bottles of the Master's smelling salts to ease the effects of cold and stress. There were also piles of leaflets and flyers announcing the imminent opening of a new studio in Soho at only $150 a session.

I was glad to have over sixty streets to walk on the way home and the prospect of returning the following day to my doctors, who had no illusions about curing anything, though they had promised to try.

The reason I had to undergo chemotherapy was that my original condition, where my cells reproduced slowly and non-aggressively, had suddenly undergone a 'mutation'. The new version was extremely rapid and ferocious and chemo was supposed to stall this mutation. But in the meantime the treatment was causing a mutation in myself.

After several weeks of treatment my body had become unrecognizable. Every day I would notice a new change, changes which were hard to spot at first, but soon became more prominent. I felt like a mutant. My senses numb; everything felt dull to the touch. Taste and smell too were badly affected. My fingers felt like shards of glass. My fingernails, lacking the strength to nick an orange peel, soon turned brown, sepia-tinted like those of a nineteenth century photograph. My teeth had become yellow and my gums were so acutely sensitive that even the softest bristled toothbrush felt like a cheese-grater. I had cramps in my feet, often to the point of total numbness. One of them began to bend oddly, the nails of the big toes turned black and fell off. My face and belly were constantly swollen.

My head was the hardest thing to bear: I felt my thoughts would no longer gel. I've never considered myself particularly intelligent and have always admired people who could perform four or five mental somersaults around a single idea. I, on the other hand, could manage two at most, but now my head was incapable of elementary exercises, such as remembering to remove the keys from the door, or to turn off the gas under an empty pot, or even to drink the camomile tea I prepared every evening before going to bed which I would then awake to find cold in its cup.

At times, I felt I was living in a trance: objects I thought I had a firm grip on would suddenly slip out of my hand. The distance between the sofa and the kitchen was about three paces but those were the number of minutes it took me to get there. My whole body had slowed down, it had lost its sense of balance. I frequently had the sensation of floating on water. Though I lived in a space not more than forty square metres, I was constantly misplacing my pen or glasses.

I kept a pair for reading while lying on the sofa and was terrified of losing them. Of all the objects I had accumulated in my life – carpets, furniture, statues, Chinese calligraphy, paintings – the thing I cared most about now were my glasses. Strangely, my thoughts often returned to a spindle-shanked old hermit, a disciple of the Dalai Lama, whom my son Folco and I had once visited in the mountains of north India. He passed his days in tranquil solitude, reading the holy scriptures under the roof of his tiny stone shack, recumbent in the wooden box that served as a bed and in future would be his coffin. What if he had lost his glasses? Perhaps a young monk might have made the journey down to Dharamshala to fetch him another pair, but the old hermit would have to wait weeks, months even for the joy of reading his smoke- and time-yellowed books.

My glasses seemed like a fabulous treasure. I read a great deal, though without digesting or retaining anything, simply enjoying the moment of reading. I read collections of poetry and, just as at eighteen when I read *The Magic Mountain* during a spell in the hospital, I now devoured stories of illness: William Styron's depression, Norman Cousins's spondylitis for which he had his own personal therapy based on a combination of hearty belly laughs and massive doses of vitamin C.

Then there was the sun. All my life I'd loved basking in the sun, on mountain tops, by the seaside, on the banks of the Mekong. Now I found myself automatically walking on the shaded side of the street, avoiding sunlight like the plague. My fixer, Doctor Bringluck, explained how chemotherapy would cause irreversible damage to the pigmentation of my skin. She had been adamant: 'You will never be able to sunbathe again, ever.' I had smiled and she, thinking I meant 'We'll see,' added in her seemingly sadistic, but in fact deeply considerate way, 'Mr Terzani, you stay out in the sun, your brain will fry.'

The strangest thing, however, was that even my personality seemed to have undergone a mutation. I had become indecisive, I felt fragile and vulnerable. Those fluids had the power to alter my state of mind. Unlike Angela, I'd always loved horror movies, with their creaking doors and knife-wielding psychos. Chemo changed all that and now such films terrified me. I couldn't sit through one for more than two minutes.

I felt my mind becoming dull, but it was accompanied by a great calm, and this provided tremendous relief. When I started therapy, I had been psychologically unstable: a vaguely negative thought that popped into my head soon whipped up into a maelstrom. Every voice sounded like a scream. Going up a staircase was like climbing a mountain. Even the simplest conversations bothered me, not on account of what was said, but because my head felt like a barrel half-filled with a liquid element that, once disturbed, would go on sloshing indefinitely.

Meditation taught me that to silence the mind, one should not try to resist thoughts, but bring them to conscious awareness and accept their presence. They were more likely to disappear this way. I thought I would be able to do so with regard to my initial state of mind, and also because of a loss of physical strength I was able to find an oddly precarious, but extremely pleasant sense of equilibrium. My dreams too became light, serene and free from anguish, like the dreamer himself.

Sometimes, waking up in the morning, I would feel a shadow of depression lying in wait, but it soon wafted off, not like the awful black hole I would earlier feel myself tumbling into every day. What I felt now was more like a sense of distance, one that made the world irrelevant or no longer interesting enough to live in. The cancer wasn't such a tragedy, after all. One day, while watching a film on TV, I was struck by a phrase that I ordinarily wouldn't have noticed, but it brought a smile to my lips. 'I know I'm going to die, but I don't know when. That's what's killing me.' It was a variation on Woody Allen's famous gag: 'I'm not afraid of dying, I just don't want to be around when it happens.'

Another curious aspect of my new condition was the change in my relationship with time. In my dual fascination with the solid wealth of the past and the future with its fog of uncertainties, I had always regarded the present as a matter that could be enjoyed only once it had congealed into the former tense. But that was no longer the case. I found I could enjoy those moments for hours, days on end, with no need to plan or expect anything.

And so I spent my days reading, gazing out of the window, sleeping when I was tired, enjoying my scaled-down existence as though none of what happened beyond these walls had either flavour or smell, or was of the slightest import. I browsed through *The New York Times* every morning with the same detachment as would an ant or a bee. The world it spoke of seemed to me impossibly remote.

Every country I lived in, I would adopt a different mode of reading the newspaper. In China, I always began with the editorials because there, I soon learnt, was where the real news was to be found. In Japan, where I'd started playing the stock market, my main interest was the financial section. But in New York, what attracted me were those pages that seemed to have disappeared from European newspapers: the local obituaries, the pages where communities kept their records of the great, the good and the not-so-good. Reading them, I realized how little difference there was between my fifty-nine years and the ages of those who had died 'after a long illness', 'of a heart attack' or 'after finally losing his battle with cancer'. Sometimes there was no difference at all.

I found it odd, this journalistic insistence in attributing a specific cause to every death. Nowhere was it written that a person had simply died of being born. Even on days when I was extremely tired – the tenth day after each session of chemo was the worst – I did all I could to stick to my self-imposed routine, a sign I hadn't given up the fight yet. There are those people who stop brushing their teeth or neglect to comb their hair if they fall ill, as though none of it is worth the effort, that their bodies, the root of all their suffering, no longer deserve their love or respect, only their abhorrence and contempt. I wasn't going to be one of them. So I went for walks in Central Park, I meditated under a tree for half an hour, a bit of gym, breakfast, and a stomach injection. Then a lengthy hike, as much as fifty blocks.

Even if it was sometimes hard to recognize, it was the only body I had and the least I could do was try to keep it in some kind of shape.

Some days I was so exhausted when I got back to my apartment that I lacked the strength to even turn on the computer to send Angela my daily email. It was one of the few remaining ties I had with the world and the only one that was of any real importance to me. I had wisely decided to spend this period alone, with no company to enjoy but also no one to worry about, making it easier to focus my attention and energy on my own situation.

Like a tempest-tossed old frigate might jettison ballast – kegs of gunpowder, barrels of rum, everything that once seemed indispensable – to keep from going under, I had decided to reduce human contact, those I had kept out of habit or simple courtesy, to the minimum.

My world had become one of silences, empty hours and pointless meanderings. There was a wavering peace I had managed to preserve by sealing myself off completely from the winds that blustered beyond the handsome windows of my apartment. I would spend hours observing the changing complexion of a skyscraper on the East Side: black at dawn, like a monolith outlined against the clear orange sky, shading to grey in the full light of mid-morning, a splendidly lit taper after dusk when the lights on the upper floors came on and the whole building became a torch, casting a glow over my sleepless nights. Days would pass without a single word being spoken or heard, days when I could hardly bring myself to mumble a customary 'good morning' or 'good evening' to the Dominican caretaker when I would go for my daily walk or to get something from the store.

My head gradually became emptier, my heart less embattled. Time went by faster than it ever had before. As far as my apparent uselessness went, I felt no anguish, no sense of responsibility. I had nothing to do, dream of, hope for. I loved not having to talk. For once, I could put away the role I had played all my life, no longer having to recite that same old script! All those friends I had plied with impressions and anecdotes on returning from some trip, consumed like so many bottles of wine. I was sick of the journalist I had been, with the endless need to be received by ministers and presidents for interviews, or to cajole ambassadors into giving visas to enter their prickly countries. I felt like the profession had deformed me; always having to get a foot in the door, ingratiate myself, be remembered, accepted, gather enough information, anecdotes or quotations with which to cram an article. It was over, finally. That Tiziano Terzani no longer existed, torched out of existence by the fiery-red liquid of chemo.

I began *A Fortune-Teller Told Me* with the words: 'Life is full of opportunities. The problem is to recognize them when they present themselves, and that isn't always easy.' In 1993, I recognized one such opportunity in a prophecy that I would die in an air crash if I flew that year – so I didn't fly. It seemed my cancer was presenting me with another. I'd often joked about how I dreamt of closing up shop on my journalism career, pulling down the shutters and affixing the note: 'Out for lunch'. Well, I had finally succeeded. I was now definitively 'Out for lunch'. It was as though cancer was the excuse I'd been looking for all along.

Physically, I was beginning to resemble Marlon Brando's Kurtz in *Apocalypse Now* and, in his words, I was like 'A snail slithering along the edge of a straight razor'. Though I was, objectively speaking, an abomination, I convinced myself I didn't look too bad, that I was in good shape. When I walked into the hospital it was with my head held high and a smile on my face. To anyone who inquired how I was feeling, I replied, 'Wonderful,' and the amused smiles of the staff, relieved of having to pity me with the usual consoling platitudes, served to bolster my sense of well-being. After all, the alternative I had was to play or not play the victim. Instinctively, I chose the latter.

I thought I should at least make good use of my experience, so I attached to the table where I wrote my diary, the verses written by a Korean Zen monk of the nineteenth century.

Do not ask for perfect health
That would be greed
Make suffering your medicine
And do not expect a road free of obstacles
Without their flame your light would expire
Make use of the tempest to free yourself.

I began to think of my illness as an obstacle, one that would teach me how to leap. The question was whether I would have the strength to jump across to reach the other side. Perhaps the illness harboured a secret message, perhaps it was here to teach me something. I went so far as to imagine I had unconsciously wished the cancer on myself. For years I had been trying to escape from routine, slow things down, discover another way of looking at the world. Now it all seemed to add up. Even physically, I had become another person.

Donning my tracksuit, sneakers, woollen hat and gloves, I wandered around the city; I was amused by the thought of all the colleagues I might encounter. They would never have recognized me in this garb. I could easily have stopped at some corner, extended my hand, mouthing one of the city's familiar refrains: 'Hey brother, spare some change'; 'Can you help me out, man? I'm a Vietnam vet.' Had I done so, the editor-in-chief of *Der Spiegel* in New York would no doubt have distractedly dug into his pockets for a nickel without realizing who I was.

But which I would that be? Certainly not the one an old friend of mine – one of the few who knew the reason for my being in New York – had known and seen regularly for thirty years. He was staying at Essex House, a hotel just down the street from my apartment. 'We can meet halfway,' I told him on the phone. 'Just keep walking towards Columbus Circus.'

From a distance I could see him making his way towards me, but without seeing me, he just brushed past looking straight ahead, seeking my face in the oncoming crowd.

THE TWIN LIGHTS OF THE CITY

In India they say dawn is the most splendid hour. The night's shadow still hovers in the air and the day has not yet fully risen. Light and dark cannot be distinguished and for a moment, if one is attentive, they can dimly intuit that things in life, which appear to be sharply contrasted, light and dark, true and false, are in reality merely opposite sides of the same coin. Distinct but not twain, like man and woman, creatures of wonderful diversity who in love come together to become one. This is the hour when the rishis, the ones who 'see', meditate in solitude in the Himalayas, charging the air with positive energy, allowing novices to look within themselves in their search for the answers to all their questions.

In New York too dawn was the best time of the day, the hour when the air did seem charged with something resembling goodness, even hope. The impression was due to the sun's first reassuring rays dissolving what, in my infirmity, I could only describe as the terrors of night. But it was also on account of the city itself which, at that hour, was at its most poetic; it was steeped in a crowdless hush. Bits of waste paper flitted like gulls along the deserted avenues while tramps lay curled asleep in their blankets near to the subway air vents, and the odd taxi prowled the streets in search of a client. Strange columns of white steam issued intermittently from mysterious holes in the asphalt, like the breath of dragons still slumbering below in Manhattan's warm viscera. In the twofold light of that hour the city appeared to be immersed in its own form of meditation.

I loved New York. When I had the strength I loved to roam the city on foot, sometimes for hours on end. At times it was impossible not to sense the weight of labour, pain and suffering each of its skyscrapers embodied. Staring up at the United Nations building, I would think of how many words, how many lies, how much blood, sweat and tears had been spent in the vain attempt to control a humanity that refused to be controlled. I would stroll past famous hotels like The Plaza and The Waldorf Astoria that continued to play host to half the world's dictators, heads of state, government officials, spies and respected murderers, thinking of the decisions made and the conspiracies hatched in those sumptuous rooms that had changed the destinies of several countries, overturning regimes, eliminating opponents, making dissidents vanish into thin air.

Here it was, all the modern world's reasoned insanity, packed into these few marvellously exuberant miles of concrete and steel between the Hudson and the East River whose rippling water reflected a clear blue sky. Here was the stone heart of the rampant, dispiriting materialism that was slowly changing the face of humanity; capital of the new imperial tyranny that threatened to engulf us all, the empire whose subjects we were becoming and against which I had always felt the instinctive urge to rebel: globalization.

Yet, it was in this ideological epicentre of everything I hated, that I had come for help, to seek salvation. This wasn't the first time either. At the age of thirty I had arrived in New York weighed down with the frustration of working for five years in a company, to try to start my life over. Now here I was again, this time hoping to extend my deadline. On that first occasion I had sensed a deep contradiction between my gratitude to America for what it offered – two years of paid freedom to study Chinese at Columbia University as preparation for a career in journalism in Asia – and the contempt, resentment, even hatred I sometimes felt for what the country represented.

In 1967, when an enthusiastic Angela and I arrived in New York Harbor off the *Leonardo Da Vinci*, which we had boarded in Genoa the week before, the US was engaged in a dirty, unjust war through which it hoped to impose its will on impoverished South-East Asian people whose only weapon was their stubborn resolve not to give in: Vietnam. Now, using more sophisticated, less visible and therefore resistible forms of aggression, the US was trying to force upon the entire world not only its commodities but also its values, truths, definitions of good and evil, progress and terrorism.

At times, watching the elegantly dressed executives step in and out of the well-appointed office buildings on Fifth Avenue or Wall Street, I began to suspect that these were the men to be wary of and protect ourselves against. In their smart leather cases, camouflaged as 'development projects', were plans for pointless dams, toxic factories, dangerous nuclear power stations and venomous new TV channels that once installed in a country could cause more damage and casualties than an aerial bombardment. Weren't they then the real 'terrorists'?

As people began to pour on to the streets, the charm New York held for me vanished, replaced by what seemed a monstrous jumble of desperate lives, each chasing some dream of joyless riches or tawdry happiness.

By 8 a.m., not far from where I lived, Fifth Avenue was already swarming with people. A strong whiff of perfume assaulted my nostrils with every woman who brushed past me to duck into one of the office buildings, paper bag breakfast in hand. What a way to start the day. I thought of the inhabitants of Florence who, on entering the Bar Petrarça in Porta Romana don't just order coffee but caffè latte or caffè macchiato or a creamy cappuccino without froth. In New York, coffee for most people is a dose of acidic mouthwash in a paper cup that is imbibed through a plastic lid shaped like a baby's dummy, so that one can drink it on the move while it's still hot. The early-morning crowd generally consisted of, good-looking, lean but hard youngsters. They were a new race, cultivated in fitness centres and vitamin shops. Some of the older men I imagined I had seen before in Vietnam. Then officers in the marines, they would have swapped their tunics and regalia for a businessman's uniform, worn it with the same stiff-backed self-righteousness, still 'officers' of the same empire with the task of gathering the rest of the world to the bosom of their global village.

At the time that I was living in New York, the city had not yet suffered the terrible wounds of the 9/11 attacks and the sleekly implacable Twin Towers still dominated downtown

Manhattan. But even then America was hardly at peace, either with itself or with the rest of the world. For more than half a century the Americans, though not once having to defend their home front, have never ceased to find themselves at war: first it was with Communism, Mao, guerrillas in Asia, South American revolutionaries; then it was Saddam Hussein and now Osama Bin Laden and Islamic fundamentalism. They were never at peace, always going all out with guns blazing. For all their wealth and power they were nonetheless deeply uneasy and continually dissatisfied.

I recall reading a study carried out by the London School of Economics (LSE) on world happiness in *The New York Times* one day. The results were surprising: Bangladesh, one of the poorest countries in the world, turned out to be the happiest. India came in fifth, while the United States was in the forty-sixth place!

Sometimes I had the impression that people who really appreciated the beauty of New York were only a handful. Apart from myself, who had nothing to do but walk the length and breadth of the city, everyone else I saw seemed locked in a struggle to survive, to escape being crushed, forever at war: whichever war that may be.

One war I was unaccustomed to, having lived for more than twenty-five years in Asia, was the battle of the sexes, fought in a single direction: women against men. Seated at the foot of a large tree in Central Park, I would watch as they ran past: healthy, tough, self-confident, though somewhat robotic. They jogged around the park in provocatively clinging leisurewear, drenched in sweat, ponytails bobbing behind them. Later they would change into their office uniforms – black two-piece suits and court shoes, carrying black computer bags, hair loose and still wet from the shower, beautiful and cold, with an arrogance, a contempt that was also physical. Everything my generation might have considered 'feminine' had disappeared, purposely erased by a perverse new desire to remove all differences, make everything equal, transform women into ersatz men.

Folco, who grew up in Asia, told me of an incident. Shortly after beginning his studies at the New York University (NYU) Film School, he had tried to open a lecture hall door for a female classmate and had been stopped cold by her response: 'Hey, what's the deal buddy? You think I can't open the fucking door by myself?' I thought this might have been an exceptional case, but here it appeared to be the rule. And the more muscle and arrogance women acquired, the more timorous and indecisive men became. If men were still needed for the purpose of conception, they would simply be summoned when the time came and promptly sent packing after use. And the result? A tremendous unhappiness. It seemed to me, especially if what I saw from my vantage point under the shade of the tree was to be the play's second act: countless women alone in their forties and fifties, smoking cigarettes, walking their dogs who appeared to have been named after former male companions: 'Bill, come here!', 'No, Bill, you mustn't cross the road by yourself,' 'Come on, Bill, home now.' Weren't these the same women who a few years ago had padded around the park in search for the perfect body? These women had spent their youth on warrior dreams of freedom, but instead had won for themselves a realm of solitude, facial tics, wizened skin and, so it appeared to me as I watched them, withering melancholy.

My thoughts would often return to the women of India who have remained so feminine to this day, so differently sure of themselves, more womanly at forty or fifty than in their twenties. By no means athletic, just naturally beautiful. And then, Indian women of that age, like their Western counterparts were never alone. They were always part of a family or group, never left abandoned or uncared for.

From my window I would often witness a 'house move' as some girl from another part of the country arrived in New York with her life in a holdall. I imagined her reading small ads in the paper in search of a room to rent, a gym and most importantly, a job. I imagined her on her lunch break going into a salad bar, standing at the counter, picking at her organic greens with a plastic fork. And for the evening's entertainment a course in Kundalini yoga that promised to reawaken the sexual energy she might need for that once divine act which had now been reduced to a sports performance ... with points.

In the end, this girl too, like a moth attracted to the dazzling lights of New York, would finish up in the human bonfire that made the city glow. In ten, maybe twenty years, she might become one of those desperate women I saw in MSKCC waiting for test results or an operation, silent and afraid, and without a friend or relative in sight.

Perhaps by living alone, you lose the measure of things. But the silence improves your hearing. During my walks I would catch stray rags of speech, remarks that would echo in my ears for hours afterwards. All anyone ever seemed to talk about was money or their personal problems. Most conversations were like arguments, the words constantly straining with pent-up aggression.

'He's disgusting, totally disgusting. He's like a baby,' said one woman, perhaps referring to her husband. I had no idea babies were revolting. Once I came home with the word 'ferocious' bouncing around in my head. I had heard it used in three separate conversations that day. The most amusing incident happened one morning when I overheard someone at Central Park chatting with a person hidden behind a hedge say in conclusion, '… and remember, don't forget to take care of the baby.' The 'baby' they were referring to was a toy dog, tugging at its lead.

One's first impression of America is that there's something extremely alluring and warmly effusive about its people. When the immigration officer who checked my passport and entry card at the airport inquired about my purpose of visiting the US, I replied, 'To cure my cancer.' He looked at me sympathetically and with a warm smile said, 'Good luck,' as he stamped my passport.

One soon realizes, however, that this directness, this off-hand, almost familiar way of dealing with people, is simply a technique. It is a social trick every American learns and that is taken for granted. The truth is that every rapport is lined with suspicion, the whole of life is a matter of protecting oneself. In the big stores these days, everything including handkerchiefs now carry an electronic device which, if not deactivated at the till, triggers an alarm. Bookshops, record stores and clothes boutiques are under the constant surveillance of plain-clothes security who prowl the shelves adjusting their earpieces like presidential bodyguards. Every transaction is subject to meticulous control, it being naturally suspected that you are an impostor wielding a stolen credit card. I would immediately leave certain shops when asked to hand over the modest Indian cloth bag I'd evidently brought to hide stolen merchandise.

A society whose members are so deeply distrustful of each other and in which there is no shared set of values, must continually resort to legal channels to regulate even the smallest transaction. That is the American way. It's this unremitting threat, together with lawyers who administrate it, which has become the bugbear of every social bond, whether it is friendship, love, working partnerships or simple trust.

A new highly American way of making some extra money is to denounce a company for racial discrimination, a boss for sexual harassment, a lover for rape or a doctor for malpractice. Before every single medical check at MSKCC, I had to sign a waiver unburdening the institution of all responsibility in case something went wrong. Before an endoscopy, for instance, I was made to sit through a video which, among other things, detailed the percentage risk of not waking up from the anaesthetic. 'You understand everything, right? Now if you would please just sign here,' said the nurse, who was perfectly aware of the absurdity. Digging into her own Italian origins, she sang 'Volare' to put me at ease as the first drops of that magical concoction drew me into sleep, happy to be in a clean bed among all this highly trained medical expertise, a product of the society I internally railed against and in which I had now placed my hopes for survival.

Naturally, I wasn't the only one who had come to America to seek my salvation. Everywhere I looked were fellow-travellers on the hope trail. The caretakers of my apartment building were all immigrants: the oldest had come from Santo Domingo; the youngest from Kosovo; the corner news stand was run by a Pakistani, the greengrocers by a Korean; the boy who sold flowers on the freezing sidewalk was from Ecuador; the taxis I took to the hospital when I was late for my appointments, nearly all driven by newly arrived immigrants, as could be seen from the nameplate every taxi driver was required by law to display. Many were Haitians, happy to be recognized as such and addressed in French. Others were from Bangladesh, occasionally there were Africans – who did not take kindly to being confused as African Americans. For me the most fascinating were the Russian Jews for whom I had developed something of an affection during my travels in Central Asia at a time when the Soviet Empire was crumbling and each of its republics gained their independence. Second-class citizens had only one aspiration before and after the transition: to emigrate to Israel or the US.

'When did you leave Russia?' I asked one.

'Not Russia, the former Soviet Union. I am from Moldavia. We are Europeans.'

'And how do you find it here? Do you like living in America?'

He looked at me in the rear-view mirror to ensure he was not about to cause mortal offence and then continued, 'America? America is a Gulag, a work camp, but with better food. If I say this to Americans, some get offended, but what can I do? They are Americans and now I too am an American.'

He had already tried to emigrate in 1979, but managed to do so only in 1991. He was now living in Brooklyn's Brighton Beach. Once a black neighbourhood where even McDonalds had been forced to close, it was now booming with an almost entirely Russian-Jewish population and their shops, restaurants and synagogues.

In the former Soviet Union as he called it, he'd been a businessman. 'I was buying furniture for 20,000 roubles that I would resell for 50,000. For a pair of shoes at eighty roubles I would make 120. And all this without having to pay sales or income tax. That was good about the former Soviet Union. No taxes. It was risky, I mean I could have gone to prison any time, but I managed to stay out of trouble. Here they tell me I'm free, but nobody is free in America, not even the president. Over there I was free. Here they say I'm economically free but it's not true. They say this taxi is mine, but it actually belongs to the banks. We're all slaves of the managers who in turn are slaves of someone else.

'In the former Soviet Union if a woman has a child she stays home for months. Here only two weeks after my wife has our baby, her boss is calling her, telling her she has to get back to work. Two weeks! Don't get me wrong, I'm grateful to the United States for giving me citizenship. I managed to avoid the civil war back home in 1994. I managed not to kill anybody or be killed but what I have here is not life. Yesterday I left home at 6 a.m. and got back at 9.30 p.m. only to leave again this morning at six. It would be better to sleep in the car.

'And it's not just me: here they all live life like this, even the rich guys where you live or on Park Avenue. You know how I know? Because I take them to their offices. They wave down a taxi and when they get in, they can't even close the door because they have a paper cup full of coffee in one hand and a bagel in the other. When they tell me where to drop them, I don't understand nothing because their mouth is full, you know?

'And when they get out, it's the same. With both hands occupied they can't get the door shut. In the former Soviet Union we had time to spend with our families, take long walks, talk with our friends. Here I get vacation for ten days in a year if I'm lucky. But even then, I can't relax because I know while I'm gone the mailbox is filling up with bills to pay.'

Since the Soviet Union's collapse in 1991, more than half a million, mostly well-educated Jews have arrived in the US, many settling in New York. This is the secret to America's continuing vitality and to New York's in particular: there's always a new wave of immigrants ready to sacrifice everything in the hope they can make it here. During the 1930s and '40s, it was the Jews from Germany and Europe, later the Chinese, Koreans and Vietnamese. Now the Chinese are again knocking on the doors along with the Indians, with even more Jews this time from the former Soviet republics.

For a country this huge, whose few original inhabitants

were methodically exterminated and dispossessed of their land, immigration was a congenital necessity and a multi-ethnic society became the obvious consequence. It is odd how these facts, in part the result of actual genocide, are now presented as a model, almost a virtue, and how on the basis of its experience the US now fosters the myth of a globalized, multiracial, multicultural society of the future: a potpourri that by continually renewing itself guarantees vitality and development.

The truth is that there is no global solution for the people of the earth. The best solutions are inevitably those which take local conditions into account. What works in the US does not necessarily work elsewhere, just as what is hazardous to one place may not be to another.

This is true even of medicine. If a New Yorker were to eat like an inhabitant of Ladakh they would soon die of a heart attack from consuming all the butter, together with the almost total lack of fruits and vegetables typical of north India. Yet in Ladakh, heart disease is almost unknown because the people live in the open air and eat organic produce. They don't require fitness centres to stay in shape but get plenty of exercise simply by walking great distances. They don't know the meaning of the word 'stress' and live their lives in utmost serenity. They also have their own way of fighting diseases. To a woman suffering from hepatitis, the amchi, the local shaman-cum-doctor, prescribed a cure of 'intense and vigorous sexual intercourse'. The results greatly surprised anthropologist Helena Norberg Hodge who recounted the episode in her wonderful book, *Ancient Futures*, writing: 'After only a few days, the woman's condition had noticeably improved.'

Never had I felt as European as I did in the US. Though I had come here to resolve my health problems, I soon began to feel that the solutions this country proposed were not always right for other people and their difficulties. Immigration was a classic example. Though this is undoubtedly going to be a crucial problem for the West's own future, Europe with its particular history and set of social conditions which are completely different from those of the US, would be making a grave error in adopting American remedies.

I was thinking of what Luciano, an old friend whose Florentine roots were centuries old, said to me one day: 'It's alright to let in a few Moroccans, Tunisians, Senegalese and Albanians, but you have to draw the line somewhere. I mean, where is it going to end? Say, one day there's a referendum to decide whether or not to knock down the Duomo, the main renaissance cathedral in the centre of Florence, to make way for a new car park, that lot would vote for the car park, I'm sure.' Racism is in the end a question of numbers, and his was a typical reaction.

Despite all its rhetoric about global society, the problems in the US are far from being resolved. Consider the situation of the African Americans. When I first arrived here more than thirty years ago, they finally seemed to have emancipated themselves and found a way into mainstream society. Now they were being pushed further and further into their ghettos. For them, every new wave of immigration was a step backward.

New immigrants arrive bursting with hope, willing to sacrifice everything. America gives them the impression that they will make it, if not the first generation, then the second, maybe even the third. But for the Blacks who have waited generations, that change will not come about; for them it's a different story. They seem spent, their hopes exhausted. Unlike the Chinese, Russian or Indian immigrants who scale the socio-economic cliff face knowing they can rely on the safety net of a solid traditional family, African Americans lack even that support. For them, family is a thing of the past. 75 per cent of Black infants are now born out of wedlock.

A quick look around is enough to see that despite its pretensions of democracy, American society is still deeply divided and unequal. Occasionally, I saw things that reminded me of Johannesburg under apartheid where I had lived for some time in the early 1960s. During the day the city was all in white; white the crowds on the street, white the people in shops and offices. It was not until the evening, when everything had closed and the bustle of city life shuffled off stage, did a stream of Blacks emerge from the innards who swept, cleaned and kept things running. Who, after completing their work, would climb aboard the 'Coloured Only' buses which would ferry them back to the townships. Something similar was happening in New York too. Certain neighbourhoods or tracts of the subway seemed reserved exclusively for a racial minority, while walking past the basements of stores and restaurants you would only ever see Blacks or Hispanics taking out the garbage. Even the human landscape of my beloved Central Park, the wonderfully well-kept lawns of which were now the responsibility of a private company run by a group of well-to-do ladies, changed colour according to the time of day. Almost completely white in the morning, it was full of joggers, cyclists, dog owners, birdwatchers and morning strollers. It would then gradually darken in hue after 9 a.m. as Black nannies appeared pushing their white charges whose parents were cloistered in their office blocks by now.

One of the USA's greatest talents is that they produce highly positive images of themselves that they go on to believe in and persuade others to do so too. The movie industry has played a crucial role in this. For Americans and a large section of the world's population, American history is not book history but that which unravels on a screen where the Americans are always the 'cavalry' arriving in the nick of time to save the day from the 'red-skinned savages', or the Nazis, the communists, the guerrilla fighters, terrorists or aliens.

While not shirking from the task of confronting American society's ills, Hollywood has its own special way of presenting and resolving them, complete with the obligatory happy ending that both ideology and commerce demands. Democracy, justice, equality and values that are blatantly denied in reality find themselves constantly reaffirmed in the realm of representation. Fiction takes the place of news, and propaganda steps comfortably into truth's shoes.

In the US, the advertising and public relations industries have evolved into highly sophisticated machines of psychological manipulation and there is nothing, be it God, war or an electrical appliance that isn't first slickly wrapped in some bamboozling verbal formula or glossy packaging before being launched into the market. The truth is therefore constantly screened, facts often sidelined or forgotten. So every appalling act of injustice, exploitation or violence routinely ends up coated with a reassuring patina of 'all's well that ends well'. Say, a poor Haitian immigrant were to be seized one evening by officers of the New York Police Department (NYPD) and subjected to beatings, torture and abuse, some big-shot Los Angeles (LA) lawyer would come running to his defence, 'so that his suffering should not be in vain', 'so that the likes of this will never happen again'. He probably did this for the million-dollar damages the city of New York would have to pay the poor victim ... and his attorney.

To arriving foreigners, every country has its own particular quality, one that is immediately revealed in some person, thing or incident they happen to encounter. In India, for me the characteristic trait was absurdity. I recall being struck by a story I read in the papers while eating breakfast my first morning in

Delhi where I had come to set up base. The article concerned a man who had achieved a measure of fame in his youth by getting his name into *The Guinness Book of Records* – an important honour everywhere in the world – for having eaten more nails, stones and broken glass than anyone else on earth. Now almost completely forgotten, he was dying of starvation in a village in the state of Bihar and had requested a government subsidy.

Back in America, what struck me on this occasion were accounts of violence: a fourteen-year-old living in the cosy loop of home, school and PlayStation had befriended a forty-year-old man while surfing the Internet. Several chats later the man invited the boy to join him for a walk on which he subjected him to rape, and then at the hands of his buddies, gang rape. The boy confided in his parents who sent him to see a psychotherapist. A few years later, alone in the house one day, he happened to answer the door to an eleven-year-old boy who was going around asking for donations for his school fair. He grabbed the kid, raped him, strangled him and bundled his body into a suitcase which he dumped that night in a nearby forest.

In Kentucky another fourteen-year-old boy had arrived at school one day, pale and armed with two assault rifles, he went on a shooting spree, killing three girls, in imitation of another teenager in Mississippi.

'What's happening to America?' was the cry in all the major newspapers. TV commentators screwed their faces into masks of contrition. And yet one only had to zap through the channels to grasp the obvious; without fail you'd chance upon a scene in which someone was being beaten, slammed against a wall, killed, burnt, strangled or sexually assaulted.

And yet this is all part of progress, the price we have to pay to continue on the road forward. But where does that lead? Sometimes it felt as though I were living on the brink of a cataclysm, that this increasingly strange society, composed of people more 'mutant' than myself, was gradually going insane. I even read that to kill the bacteria present in meat Americans eat, it is exposed to radiation. Didn't this make it even more carcinogenic? This question was never posed.

In another article, it appeared that a town in the state of New York had installed surveillance cameras in a nursery schools so that mothers could check on their kids from their office computer screens and thus, their minds set at rest, get on with their work. Is this considered progress?

At the end of his life Freud too had begun to ask whether humanity's much vaunted conquests could really be considered signs of progress. In one of his last essays, *Civilization and Its Discontents,* after beginning with an ode to technological progress, progress which permitted him the joy of hearing his son's voice thousands of miles away, Freud reflects that had there been no railway to take his son so far away from him, he would never have needed a telephone to hear his voice.

Walking to the hospital, as I watched columns of smoke billowing from a power station's giant cooling towers, I thought of this country's immense human furnace whose fires of progress, modernity and cancer generation upon generation of immigrants continued to stoke. If the Americans had become the world's foremost cancer experts it was on account of their industries, food, fertilizers, weapons and their way of life which caused more cancer than any other nation. It made sense: the more cancer victims, the more doctors and therefore, more expertise.

There were days when, no matter where I went, all anyone seemed to talk about was cancer. A leaflet in the morning paper warned me that one of the most common chemical agents used in dry cleaning had been classified as carcinogenic and only a new type of laundry could guarantee its clients' safety. I came upon a demonstration one day while I was out for a stroll in Central Park; thousands of women were marching in support of breast cancer research. One day I arrived at the hospital to learn that a well-known colleague, an American journalist one year younger than me and himself a client of the institution, had just passed away. His wife left me a message saying she wanted to meet, believing she had discovered a link between a number of correspondents, all of whom suffered from some form of cancer. Having covered the war in Vietnam, she said, it was likely that we had all been exposed to Agent Orange, the defoliant deployed by the US army which had led to all kinds of infant deformities which thirty years on continued to afflict newborns in Indo-China.[2]

I didn't believe this was my case, but there is certainly known to be a terrible connection between weapons and cancer, just as the disease can be linked to electronics, food and chemical products. The food industry has forced upon the human body a diet that is unnatural, whose consequences are impossible to predict. But who has an interest in opening this particular can of worms? Medical research, like any other branch of research, is almost entirely financed and controlled by huge industrial corporations who are in no way burning with the desire to know the real causes of cancer. On the contrary, they believe, 'Finding a cure for cancer is easier

---

[2] An estimated 100 million litres of Agent Orange had been sprayed on the forests and rice paddies of Vietnam and Laos by the American military, the first time in human history a chemical weapon for mass destruction had been used in a war. The US had also been the first power to use nuclear weapons on Japan in 1945 and prior to this had been pioneers in biological warfare, distributing blankets infected with the smallpox virus to Native Americans during the nineteenth century.

than establishing its causes.' It is also much more profitable: cures mean medicines which in turn mean big bucks. What's more, the quest for a cure is projected towards the future and fuelled by those two great economic catalysts, hope and optimism.

And so we go on living in conditions that undoubtedly provoke cancer, but no one seems to do anything to change it. Meanwhile, the hope is that someone, somewhere, will come up with a cure and naturally the news on that front is all 'good' news. The headlines routinely announce 'an important breakthrough', 'a major step forward'. As a young researcher at MSKCC put it, we always seem to be 'on the verge' of a major discovery, just a short step away from the solution. Flipping through these articles I would fall into the same trap on occasion. One study demonstrated that a diet of uncooked food reduced the possibility of cancer by over 80 per cent. Too bad the study referred solely to cats! A pharmaceutical company announced they had perfected a new drug for reducing tumours. The numbers were staggering, but I would have had to become a lab rat to benefit from the treatment, it was well known by now that treatments which worked on this particular guinea pig did not necessarily have the same effect on human beings.

The truth is that thirty years on from its launch, the 'war on cancer' declared by President Nixon – perhaps to take minds off the other war being fought in Vietnam – is far from over. And though progress has been made concerning certain types of cancer, the total number of people who die from this disease each year in the US has not diminished.

However, even this 'truth' did not fully convince me. I wasn't interested in the percentages of incidents, recoveries or relapses. There was something doubtful about this whole business of statistics. As Charles de Gaulle once said, 'If you eat two chickens and I don't eat any, statistically speaking we have each eaten one chicken.' I preferred to see myself as a special, highly subjective case, rather than a theoretical probability.

During these solitary months I spent in New York, Angela came to visit me on two occasions and, like all great joys, her visits were also cause of great worry. Despite all that we had in common, we now belonged to two different worlds. I to the world of the sick with its logic, priorities, pains, rhythms and, above all, its extremely peculiar sense of time, while she belonged to the healthy with their plans, desires, deadlines and future certainties.

It was one thing to exchange daily emails on a computer and quite another to find ourselves facing each other across a space of a few square metres. Her imminent arrival anguished me terribly. We had banned telephone calls which we considered too aggressive and which gave a false illusion of proximity. Emails were ideal. Angela's, recounting her days in Florence, were like the log of a vanished ship that had been swallowed up centuries ago by the high seas. They spoke of things and people that were to me like shadows, the silhouettes of barely remembered ghosts. Yet they were my saving anchor, and here was yet another thing science could not explain: the mere thought of a person whose existence justifies one's own was itself a life-prolonging medicine.

Angela was greatly understanding of my need to be alone, to put between us a distance that we knew was only physical. I had found a precarious equilibrium and was afraid that the slightest breeze could topple me over. Knowing she was there for me was a benediction. Among the memoirs of illness I had read in that period, there was one that struck me in particular: Paul Zweig's autobiography, published shortly after his death. All of a sudden, he had fallen ill. One day after weeks of checks and worry, his doctor announced the diagnosis: cancer. He went home and told his wife, and she presented him with divorce papers to sign in reply. And what of love, commitment and loyalty? Here was another 'modern' tale, another American tale.

The distance that emerges between the healthy and the sick is one that puts human relationships to the test. Illnesses cause a rupture with the prevailing order of things, but also create one of their own. If a sick man steps across the border into another country, the logic of the healthy of that place becomes something irrelevant, absurd, even offensive. I realized this one day when, waiting my turn for a medical exam, I saw in our dishevelled, sallow-complexioned, track-suited, woollen-capped, tagged and braceleted midst, a handsome, well-dressed man who was tanned, healthy and sported a pair of designer sunglasses. Here to collect someone no doubt, his presence was a thorn in our eyes, an unjust affront to our dignity. 'Get out, get out of here!' were the words that echoed in my head.

One of the nicest things about being ill is the retreat of desire, that unconscious awareness that it's really not worth buying another pair of shoes or going to a carpet sale. The healthy cannot understand the sick and this is how it should be. Whatever the attitude to their illness, there is in sick people a kind of torpor, woven from weakness but also from serenity which the healthy, with all their sympathy, cannot fully understand. On the contrary, they take it as a sign of resignation and believe they have to help the sick struggle against it. And yet illness has its own logic, a logic whose function is perhaps to psychologically help the sufferer face the prospect of the end.

Angela came from her country to enter my world, a world in which nothing was familiar or recognizable, beginning with myself. She had last seen me in my usual white garb, flowing locks and moustache but now instead, waiting for her at the airport was a hairless man dressed in black wearing a skullcap on a bald and purple head. This was a man from a wholly different tribe.

An instant brotherhood springs up among the sick. The ego that elsewhere had to constantly affirm or defend itself, sank into a state of placid tranquillity inside a hospital. Having crossed its threshold and immersed oneself in the regulated warmth that kept the chilly world of the healthy at arm's length, there was no longer any need for that ego to exist. I remember Folco once saying, 'Whenever I feel I'm lacking something, I think about India. There, everybody lacks something or the other. Food, a hand, a nose. Whatever it is I lack seems nothing in comparison.' I felt something similar every time I entered MSKCC. Every one of the hospital's floors was dedicated to some form of cancer. The one that moved me most was the children's ward. I'd been lucky. Unlike them I'd already had a life. But perhaps this wasn't the whole truth. Perhaps what I saw was the fruit of other lives, the effect of karma piled up over several existences. Faced with these gaunt, emaciated bodies, sometimes transparent to the point of being no longer human, it was Hinduism, of all religions, that seemed to offer the most comforting explanation for such monstrous injustice.

In the waiting rooms of the various wards I observed the other patients, trying to imagine the stories that had brought them here. At once I recognized the first-timers, the ones still attached to the outside world, those who behaved as though their presence here was some kind of mistake, just as I recognized from their fearful expressions those who had just begun chemo and those who were already accustomed to its mutations; some who'd given up hope and some who were clearly going to pull through.

But what was that common factor we all had which brought us from different paths on to the same one?

One day I found myself sitting next to a man who appeared to be in his early fifties. Tall, spindly and sallow-faced, his body was completely hairless. I realized from the way he was staring at me that he wanted to talk. Finally, pointing at my watch, he said in a broken and heavily Russian-accented English, 'That is made in Russia. You are a refugee too?'

I replied, 'In a manner of speaking … and yes this watch was made in the Soviet Union, in 1991. It was one of the last things they did as a gift to the Buriati who were celebrating the 250th anniversary of their conversion to Buddhism that year. I bought it from a Mongol for $5 at the Chinese border.' I slipped the watch off my wrist to show him the Cyrillic inscription.

The watch was a simple wind-up model that needed to be set every morning or every night. The most striking aspect about it was the fact that you'd never see it in an advertisement. In the middle of its white, square dial was an image of a meditating Buddha wrapped in an orange cassock. Even the Dalai Lama, during our meeting in Dharamshala, had been unable to take his eyes off it. Knowing his favourite pastime was mending watches, I had said to him, 'Your Holiness, this watch works perfectly,' a remark that triggered one of his marvellously inimitable laughs.

My neighbour's wife, one of the healthy people there and an extremely forward woman, quickly cut into on our conversation which, seeing she was more fluent in English, she clearly wanted to steer in her direction.

'Are you Jewish?' I asked them both.

'I am,' she said proudly. 'But he isn't. He's Russian, but they said the Russians couldn't stay in Uzbekistan any more. Thanks to my being Jewish, we both managed to come here as refugees.'

The man's mild eyes had an expression that was sweet, yet pained and embarrassed, and he left it to his wife who was speaking loud enough for all to hear, to recount their story. Back in Uzbekistan he had been an engineer, supervising gold mines, but in New York the only job he'd been able to find was as a nightwatchman at a warehouse.

'Nothing, nothing,' he said.

'But that's how it must be,' she admonished him. 'When you come here as a refugee, you can't expect anything, you have to start from the bottom. As a driver, a caretaker, a nightwatchman, whatever.'

He just smiled and repeated, 'Nothing, nothing ... a nightwatchman.' He'd fallen ill after only eight months on the job and was suffering from lung cancer.

'It was the stress,' his wife said.

'Nothing, nothing, stress,' he echoed.

Stress! Naturally. The stress of having a wife like his, of being Russian in a country where he didn't know the language or customs, where everything he'd struggled to learn during his life was now worthless. 'Stress, stress,' he repeated, as though trying to make us laugh. They had already removed one of his lungs, but the disease had spread to the other. The couple were convinced I was a refugee like them, though they never asked me where I'd escaped from or for what reason. 'Here in America, we are all like this, all refugees,' they said.

In a sense she was right. There were many immigrants among us waiting: Chinese, Vietnamese, more Russians from the former Soviet republics. Perhaps cancer really did have something to do with stress, the stress of being uprooted. This was undoubtedly the case for the Russian sitting next to me. He felt lonely, America had little to offer him and the only words that issued from his lips while his wife was telling other stories were, 'Nothing. Nightwatchman. Stress.'

Leaving the hospital, I too felt terrified by the emptiness that surrounded me. Climbing into a taxi, I heard the meter click into operation, and with it the odious voice of a famous actress: 'Wow! Cats have nine lives ... but you, sad to say, have only one ...' I didn't need her to remind me.

'... So be good and buckle up!'

Sound advice, undoubtedly, but I'd never felt less inclined to heed it as I did then.

New York may well have been 'nothing', but it had everything. If you were attentive, a day wouldn't go by without something interesting happening in the city. Quite by chance I'd read that Robert Thurman, professor of Asian religions at Columbia University, an expert on India and father to the famous Hollywood actress, Uma, named after Shiva's betrothed, was giving a lecture in one of The Bowery's 'alternative' centres.

The hall was packed with a mostly female audience. These women with their antennae, ready to pick up the tempting signal of the new with its accompanying risks, but more able than men to separate the genuinely authentic from the bogus, are always the first to know when something is, in human terms, just not working. The topic of the conference was supposed to be Tibetan Buddhism, but Thurman spoke mainly about America.

'At the present time the West appears to be the best starting point from which to attain illumination. In no other part of the world has humanity been closer to Nirvana than in America. Here, one can fully understand the meaning of the void and of nothingness because here we already live in nothingness. We are nothing, our human relations are nothing and we regard others as nothing. "How you doing Jim?", "What's up John?" Certainly, we may be warm in our greetings, but in reality we care nothing for others and treat them as though we are meeting them once in our lives and will never see them again. If only we knew that we have always been together and are destined to be so for all eternity!'

I liked the man's irony.

'Does anyone in this room know anything about Buddhism?' he asked the audience. Many raised their hands.

'Which of you have had an out-of-body experience, been transported elsewhere, forgetting everything and having the shock of returning to your body?'

A good-looking young man accompanying an older woman with copper-coloured hair – the woman was obviously his lover – got to his feet and proceeded to recount an amazing tale which moved the woman to embrace him even more tightly when he sat down again. He was one of the lucky few who had gone on an astral voyage.

'No, no,' said Thurman. 'The experience of which I speak is by no means exceptional. It happens to us all, every night, when we fall asleep.'

He went on to suggest that death too was perhaps such an experience and not the end of consciousness as the West had taught us to believe. It was simply a form of falling asleep. 'Yama, the bull-headed demon, comes to bludgeon us and take the body away. But we are not the body, no matter how fiercely we identify with it, how much time we spend keeping it in shape, buffing, polishing and repairing it. We spend a fortune on the body, even if we know that one day it is going to rot and decompose into nature ...' The audience hung on to his every word.

'... But we are Americans,' he went on. 'And the pursuit of happiness is not simply one of our constitutional rights, it is our most important national pastime. And that's okay because happiness can also be an occasion for reflection. Somebody who wins a million dollars in the lottery realizes he's suddenly lost all his friends. Why?'

The gist of all this is that life is an opportunity to know oneself; the society we live in is moronic because its pure materialist core is a denial of everything we are: the remains of countless lives.

'Look at my jaw, for instance. It is the result of a number of previous lives, lives composed of tolerance, compassion and self-control that have gradually transformed my original jaw. Once upon a time this jaw came equipped with huge fangs which I used to defend myself and attack others, now those fangs are no more ...' There were smiles in the audience and I had the impression that a seed of novelty had been successfully planted.

I came out of Thurman's talk feeling strangely buoyant. Only a couple of days ago, a friend had written to me saying he was contemplating suicide. His professional and personal lives were both in tatters. Later I realized I had finally found the words to reply to him: the weights and measures, the values on which we imagine our lives depend are nothing more than conventions. They form the way in which we regulate our lives, but in doing so add unnecessary weight to our existence. However, they are not the determining factor. Success and failure are highly relative terms by which to judge an event or time of life that is itself transient and impermanent. What appears to us as unbearable today will in ten years seem irrelevant. Why not look at today's horrors with the hindsight we will have then? I felt relieved, although I was hardly in a position to give myself the same advice.

Thurman's talk had been a breath of fresh air, air whose intelligent provocations blew against the prevailing winds. This was New York. Within this society, every taut and twitching nerve end strained towards happiness, the kind Thurman had ridiculed for its spurious absolutism, however much we wished otherwise.

Within this society there also existed a fringe group who refused to accept the vapid materialism of daily life, who aspired to do other things and who, however absurdly, sought another way, people who in one way or another resisted.

It didn't take me a long time to discover one of the main centres of this 'resistance' movement. It was the smell that brought me there. One morning, while walking along Spring Street an iron gate swung open. As a girl stepped out on to the sidewalk, a familiar whiff of incense assaulted my nostrils. My curiosity had been awakened and before the gate could swing shut, I had slipped inside. I stumbled upon the New York Open Center, an adult education college, a social club and an alternative supermarket. On the notice boards were detailed descriptions of the various courses the Center offered, from herbal medicine to dietetics, reflexology to yoga. There was also the usual array of alternative medicine's treatments and therapies. The bookshop from which the incense smell had wafted, together with a constant background of 'meditation music', was well stocked in New Age literature, CDs, cassettes and other 'alternative' materials. Going in and out of the classrooms were the usual raggle-taggle band of 'others', mainly well-souled females. The atmosphere was pleasantly laid-back.

I approached the information desk but before I could open my mouth the girl behind the desk looked at me and with a wide smile and said, 'Wow!'

'What is it?' I asked, failing to understand the reason for her amazement.

'You look, wow, amazing, you know?'

'You think so?'

'Yeah, you know, you've got like this aura all around your body. You must be really happy!'

A lean grey-haired guy beside her, who had been following

our exchange, intervened at this moment: 'Yeah, yeah. It's true. You have a wonderful smile. A real aura.'

No doubt this was a sales tactic they laid on anyone who signed up. But at that moment I was convinced I really did have an aura and in the end I enrolled in a course on Tarot reading. I regularly attended these sessions twice a week for two months. The teacher was Italian American and the other 'students' were mainly women, but there was one bizarre fellow who arrived in the uniform of a bank manager or lawyer which he removed to reveal a white sweatsuit underneath. Before each lesson, he would shuffle into a corner and strip off his trousers, shirt and tie to reveal his true inner self that lay under the mask he wore for survival. Amid that strange, in some ways clandestine, tribe of seekers of otherness weren't only those looking for a new port to drop anchor, but some whose affiliations one would never have suspected.

Before being operated on, I had to first meet the hospital's chief anaesthetist. During this visit and his litany of questions regarding prior operations and possible allergies, I noticed he was glancing insistently at my watch.

'Are you a Buddhist?' he asked me.

'No, are you?'

'No,' he replied, pausing a moment to prepare his revelation. 'I'm a Sufi. A Kashmiri Sufi.'

Good God, Kashmir! I had spent weeks there covering the bloody tug of war between India and Pakistan over what was one of the most beautiful lands on earth and I had stood on the smoking ruins of one of its finest mosques. A structure carved entirely out of wood, it had once been a place of worship for the Sufis, the Muslim mystics under the sway of Hinduism and Buddhism, though during my stay in Kashmir I had never encountered a single one. Although a few certainly still lived there, they were probably too scared to come out in the open, forever persecuted by orthodox Muslims who regarded them as heretics. But here in New York, my anaesthetist was a Sufi, and happy to be one, a regular doctor standing in his white lab coat. I had to imagine him dressed in a long woollen tunic – the Arabic word *suf* means 'wool' – his hands raised, spinning on his axis in one of those dervish dances whose vertiginous pull would whip him into a state of ecstasy enabling him to touch the divine. I sympathized with him: alone in a society with which he felt no connection, a society where he clung to his search for something higher, an end that wasn't merely survival, finding his particular answer in the Sufis' way of 'being in but not of the world'.

Jalal Al-Din Rumi, one the greatest Sufi poets born in 1207 in the region known today as Afghanistan wrote, 'There are thousands of ways one can kneel and kiss the earth. Beyond ideas, beyond what is right or wrong, is a place. Let us meet there.'

My anaesthetist at MSKCC had found that ideal site in Kashmir, a place unreachable now, no more than an exotic name on a map. From there, in the form of a dance, had come to him the hope of something more, something without which life would be unliveable. Every weekend he met fellow Sufis in a New York loft or a country house where they read poetry and spun for hours to the rhythm of a music whose straining crescendos accompanied their 'ascent' in a mystic rite which was the symbol of life itself. Just as neutrons and electrons spin around the nucleus of an atom or the stars and planets spin around the cosmos, we spin on the earth, rising from it and returning to it as dust. The dance, he told me, had drilled a hole in him, a void in which he felt truly free. It was one that removed him from his daily existence and brought him closer to the divine.

This was something I too was missing and until then I had never really needed. Walking on the streets of New York, I realized I'd never heard or seen a single procession or festival, not a single god shouldered by the faithful, nor an allusion to anything deeper.

Everywhere I'd lived in Asia, except communist China, reference to the divine was constant; not just in ceremonies and rites but in the language and in people's everyday gestures. A Japanese fishmonger would open his shop every morning after sprinkling a handful of salt over the pavement outside; in Singapore, Thailand and Malaysia, incense smoulders in temples to propitiate some deity; in India, the way people greet each other, joining hands at chest height and slightly bowing the forehead while pronouncing the word 'Namaste', means 'I salute the divinity I acknowledge in you.'

I often found myself thinking of India and of our apartment there under whose windows trains of camels or elephants carrying their daily ration of grass in their trunks would pass. We would be woken up in the middle of the night by the resounding clang of bells from a Sikh or Muslim procession. Sometimes I would spot an Indian face in the New York crowds in whom I recognized a distant relation, so much more familiar was he to me than the Americans.

One day during a downpour when I was late for an appointment with my fixers, I waved down a cab whose driver was a Sikh with a bushy black beard and wearing a sky-blue turban.

'Can you take me to the Memorial Sloan Kettering, Sardar*ji*?'

Addressing him as 'Sardar' with the respectful suffix 'ji' was enough to create a bond between us. He told me he was from a small village near Amritsar, the site of the famous Golden Temple, the Sikhs' equivalent to the Vatican. Living in New York, he made approximately $3,000 a month, half of which he managed to send home. Forty-seven years old, he had 'another thirteen to live'.

'Thirteen?' I asked. 'How do you know that?'

'My God told me, twenty years ago when I was still back home in India,' he replied. 'And I am content. A man who has lived sixty years shouldn't be sad to die. Naturally, no one wants to die, but there are so many of us on earth that we must make room for others ... and the age of sixty seems the right time to bow out.'

'Listen Sardar*ji*,' I said. 'I'm fifty-nine. I have cancer, which is why you're taking me to a hospital. Do you really think I have to die at sixty?'

'Oh no, sir. You look like you are in good health. But what does your God say?'

'I don't know, I don't really have one. Though a number of fortune-tellers told me I would live to a ripe old age.'

'Naturally. A man like you in tip-top condition ...'

Pulling up in front of the hospital, he turned to me, joined his palms and bowing both to me and to the God he saw in me, said, 'Namaste. Good luck.'

'Namaste, Sardar*ji*.'

I was then back in the white world of the hospital for my date with that fiery-red liquid.

I made the return journey to my apartment on foot. Back in my burrow, feeling exhausted, I sat by the window. In the limpid rain-washed air, the view was splendid. The skyscrapers on one side were painted gold by the dying sun's rays, while those on the other side stood coldly metallic in the shade. The streets below were full of people of all races wearing the strangest clothes imaginable. Suddenly, above my building, two giant military helicopters appeared out of nowhere, hovering at roof level. Was it an attack? An invasion? Martians? Even if it was, no one would have been surprised. The Americans live in a world of science fiction where anything is possible. Even if it was announced that the president had been kidnapped, it would be nothing out of the ordinary, as people have already seen such incidences in movies.

The helicopters continued to circle. The humanity I lived among was already that of the 'Day After', and I, in the surreal suspension of this wilderness of solitude and having neither desires nor plans, felt like a telephone conversation on hold with Muzak in the background.

I sometimes truly felt like an alien in America. On some occasions I could no longer stomach the banality of its endless chatter, the robotic courtesy of its people and the electronically processed telephone voices. I had zero tolerance for the kilograms of advertising I had to jettison from the Sunday edition of *The New York Times* and for the standard invitation of waiters in every cafe and restaurant in the land to 'enjoy' whatever this mysterious entity we were supposed to be enjoying. What added to the city's daily cacophony at Christmas was the endless loop of '*Jingle bells*' on the streets, in shops and lifts; there was no escaping it.

Once, after a long walk, I stepped into a bookshop but found I couldn't stay for more than two minutes. Even there, '*Jingle bells*' was playing loudly through the store. I rushed outside in the cold and on the sidewalk saw a shivering man selling hotdogs, a plastic sheet barely covering his mobile stall.

'Where's the nearest subway station?' I asked him.

'At the end of this block, on your left.'

From his accent, I realized he was one of my beloved Russian Jews, the people with whom years before, while writing *Goodnight Mister Lenin*, I had passed many a pleasant hour conversing, laughing and sipping tea in Central Asia.

'*Spassiba,*' I answered, which meant 'thank you'.

He looked at me as though I was an apparition. With a warmth I hadn't felt all day, he said in a hesitant voice, '*Pozhaluysta.*' This meant 'you're welcome'.

And once again, cheered by this small sign of mutual recognition, we turned with a smile to resume our different, but equally strange lives in this refugee camp, this human furnace, this safe harbour, the gourmet gulag which for both of us was New York City.

PIECES OF THE SELF

Among the various exercises, many at least 2,000 years old, that aspiring young Tibetan monks are put through at the Institute of Buddhist Dialectics is one we should all practise every now and then: establishing the location of the thing we are all so attached to – the 'self'.

'Could it be in our names?' suggested the old lama to his students who sat in two rows, cross-legged behind their little tables. 'No,' he continued, 'because the name can change without the self doing so.' And yet there are so many who identify with their names, and even more with the titles that precede them. It is clear, however, that the self cannot reside in a name.

'In our bodies?' the lama pondered. Evidently, the self has much to do with the body, to the point that without it there is no self. 'But where in our bodies?' The lama then went on and proceeded to mimic the ways certain cultures indicate a different part of their body when pronouncing the letter 'I'. The Chinese say 'I' by placing the index finger of their right hand on the tip of their nose. But can a self live in the nose? Or in the heart upon which Americans place their hand? Or in one's head, the chosen site of those who regard the intellect as the most important of the faculties?

The students listened as he spoke, a few interrupting with their own comments, and the discussion carried on. Then the old lama suddenly produced a rose from inside the drawer of the table behind which he sat and held it up for everyone to see, focusing the class's attention on that single point.

'We all agree that this is a flower, yes?' he said, and with these words ripped off a petal and held it up. 'And is this a flower? No, it's a petal. And this?' he asked rhetorically, once again pointing to the rose. 'This is a flower.' He tore off another petal, then another and another, each time asking, 'And what about this?'

At the end of the demonstration, a small pile of petals lay on the table. The lama held aloft the rose's bare stem to show to the class, once again asking 'And is this a flower? No, not any more. The same can be said for a hand,' he continued, holding up his left hand. 'If I remove one of my fingers and then another and another still, none of those fingers will be my hand and my hand will no longer be a hand either. So the same applies to our bodies as a whole. It is composed of numerous pieces none of which, however, really make us who we are.'

The morning of my operation when a dear old lady, one of the many hospital volunteers, arrived very early and asked me to join her in prayer that the surgeon's hand be swift and true in removing what it had to remove, my mind recalled my visit to the exiled Dalai Lama in Dharamshala. Where was I really? And the surgeon whom I'd baptized 'the Lord', how many pieces could he remove from my body before I vanished altogether?

My mind had little time for its gymnastics, however, being rudely interrupted by a nurse asking whether I intended to authorize my wife to pull the plug in the event of an irreversible coma. 'You understand, this is the law of the state of New York ...' Though I was more gently interrupted by the Kashmiri Sufi doctor whose first injection of anaesthetic made me slide into a profound calm before I lost consciousness completely.

I was told later that the operation lasted six hours. Where my self had been during that time, I had no idea. Had it left my body or was it still suspended there as though in sleep? When I awoke parts of me were missing, but it seemed that for the most part, amid a tangle of incoming and outgoing tubes, I was still there – and so was my self.

This problem of the self had begun in Bologna, where I had the first inkling that medicines and doctors, which I had managed to avoid for several years, had radically changed from the way I remembered them. I was no longer a person to them as much as I was the disease itself. In New York this was even more evident.

There I would be wheeled from one floor to the next, still under the effects of the anaesthetic, which actually made me keenly aware of what was going on during the day, though I would remember nothing afterwards. Clutching a sheaf of forms along with a plastic card containing all my data to present at each port of call – my life credit card, I called it – which lead to even more forms, more pints of various coloured liquids to swallow, tubes, wires, injections that set my mouth on fire and hour-long waits. I was hooked up to various machines, monitors, sonar devices or placed on a narrow bed and pushed back and forth inside a huge brightly lit cylinder which sounded like the howl of a storm, with the instruction to hold my breath for as long as possible. All just to discover what had gone wrong inside of me. At each station a different part of my body – liver, kidneys, stomach, lungs and heart – would be examined. The relevant specialist would never so much as visit or touch me, however, concentrated exclusively on the bits they had to deal with, but on a computer image of them and even more on the spreadsheets of data the printer spat out at the end of the examination.

Looking at the screen, I would see my own liver reduced to a trembling red and green splotch, detached from me, a foreign body adrift outside the gut it had inhabited for sixty years. But as for myself, my whole self or simply as the sum of all these bits, was nowhere to be found. It wasn't even consulted.

During one of these exams, one of the doctors discovered a third cancer and it is to her shrewdness that I owe this extra time. I would have liked to be able to thank her but I never actually met her. All I knew was that she had red hair. I looked for her among the white-coats in the hospital cafeteria but in vain. To make her discovery she never needed to touch me, speak to me, or ask how I was feeling. It had been sufficient for her to peer into her monitor, analyse the intensity of a patch which had swiftly changed colour, and note an inexplicable but statistically proven correlation between my principal disease and this newcomer.

Had we met she might have told me what an increasing number of medical professions maintain nowadays is that the patient's own impressions are irrelevant, the images, numbers and read-outs produced by their battery of machines are infinitely more reliable. Modern medical research is entirely geared towards such objective data, and has no time for the patient's subjectivity. Mine was a case in point since the cancer the red-haired doctor had discovered caused me no pain and produced no symptoms. By the time I became aware of its presence, it would probably have been too late anyway. The machine had known how I was feeling much sooner and much better than I did.

There was undoubtedly something highly positive and efficient in this way of proceeding by being completely detached from the patient and their reactions. Yet the fact that I was treated as a collection of bits, and never as a whole person, left me oddly dissatisfied. I wondered whether the science to which I had entrusted my life might be blind in the same way as the five blind men in an old Indian story I'd once heard. These men were all asked to describe an elephant and the first man, approaching the animal, touched its legs. 'The elephant,' he said, 'is like a temple and these are its columns.' The second put his hand on the trunk and said that the elephant was like a snake. The third touched its belly and claimed the elephant was like a mountain. The fourth found the elephant's ear and said the animal was like a fan. The last man fumbled and took hold of the tail. He said the elephant was like a whip!

While each of these definitions contained an element of truth, we never see the elephant as it really is. So what of my brilliant doctors? Weren't they too in some ways like these blind men? Of course they were. Because they were scientists and science has its limits. A 'scientific' description of an elephant – whether made by a physicist, a chemist, a biologist or a zoologist – would in essence be as partial as those of the men in the story.

This is a problem with science: while it may be accurate, precise, free of dogma and ready to change its theory by replacing it with another, because of its very nature, science's understanding of reality remains irredeemably limited.

To see reality exclusively through the lens of science is to be like the drunkard in Mullah Nasiruddin's tales, the mythic protagonist of countless ironic fables from the Middle East which are now an intrinsic part of Asian folklore. After a night of drinking with his friends, he arrives home and realizes he has lost his keys. He immediately starts searching for them under the light of the road's only street lamp. 'Why are you looking there?' asks a passer-by. 'Because,' the drunkard replies, 'it's the only place I can see anything.'

Scientists act similarly. The world their instruments describe isn't really the world, but an extremely partial representation, an abstraction that doesn't exist any more than numbers do. Though they may be useful to science, numbers are nowhere to be found in nature.

The world we live in is made of mountains, the oceans, green lawns, shrieking birds, barking dogs and numberless people. What does the scientist do with all this? He weighs, measures, discovers laws, analyses the world's phenomena in all their various aspects and tries to explain each which in the end explains nothing. He looks at only the simplest and most obvious things, those which can be perceived by the senses, ignoring all that concerns emotion and feelings, the things that imperceptibly alter the fabric of our lives such as love, or that like greed change the whole world.

And what of the economists, the other kind of scientists, who analyse global demand for a certain product, make predictions based on the health of the stock exchange, or calculate the rate of interest that banks can offer their investors. What can they tell us about things like greed which is devouring the world in the name of so-called 'progress?' Words like 'greed' and 'selfishness' cannot be found in economics textbooks, while economists themselves blithely go on perfecting their science as though it has nothing to with the fate of humanity.

Before starting chemo I'd gone to Chicago to see an old friend from university, now director of the Nuclear Medicine Research Laboratory at Northwestern University, who perfectly embodied the frustrations of a scientist. Pointing at his own forehead, he said, 'I know how every cell in here functions, but I don't know how the brain works.' He had devoted thirty years of his life, first as a physiologist, then as a molecular biologist and then to studying that part of the anatomy; yet he had lost his way. 'Medicine isn't maths, it is biology,' he told me.

Often my dealings with my MSKCC doctors, all of them top specialists, resulted in my thoughts returning to my childhood and our family doctor, Dr Macchioni, who would come to visit me at home when I was ill.

In preparation for his arrival, my mother would fill a basin with water and lay it on a chair. Along with that there would be a fresh piece of soap in a small saucer and, draped over the chair's back, a clean, perfumed towel. Always elegantly dressed, he would arrive sporting a pair of round gold-framed spectacles. Laying his leather bag on the side of the bed, he would ask for our news as he gently probed my chest and back with his stethoscope, peered into the orbs of my eyes and told me to stick my tongue out, after which he would check my pulse, and finally, after washing his hands and scrupulously drying each finger, pronounce his verdict. To my childish eyes, there was something magical in the calm, assured way he had of speaking. His presence was itself a medicine. He had been there at my birth, and had seen two of my aunts die tragically young of consumption and my grandmother of old age. As my mother accompanied him to the door and watched him descend the staircase, repeating the words, 'Thank you, doctor, thank you,' I was already feeling better.

In the numerous dealings I've had with doctors since then, I'm glad to say that most of them were like him. At the age of eighteen I landed in hospital with an infected lung and after several months of ineffective treatments, it appeared that the only solution was to remove the offending organ. Luckily I was snatched from the jaws of the operating theatre by an elderly consultant from Florence. Thanks to his years of expertise and to a new drug that had just appeared on the market, my lung was saved and with it my plans for the future.

Years later, another doctor, this time from Switzerland, was able to spare Angela the nasty consequences of a therapy that had seemed the only possible course of treatment at the time. Angela was thirty-three at the time and had just been operated on for breast cancer after undergoing cobalt-based radiotherapy, which at that time was still a fairly crude affair. And this was in Singapore, of all places! She would have to take a course of diabolical pills for the rest of her life which would provide the vital substances formerly produced by the parts of her body the surgeon would remove. Every doctor we consulted reckoned this supplement to be indispensable, all the while knowing its side effects. One in particular told me Angela would develop extraneous facial hair and would almost certainly end up with a moustache! Instinctively repelled by the idea of her being enslaved to any drug, we decided to look for an alternative. This search finally led to a Swiss clinic where, after several days of tests, the octogenarian endocrinologist asked Angela a rather odd question: 'Are you happy in your life? Do you feel loved?'

I don't know what she said because he had asked me to wait outside. When he called me back into the room, he said that in his view Angela had no need of any medicine and that the two of us and our still-young children could, without cause for alarm, go back to living our lives. The man was obviously a genius! He was someone who didn't reduce everything to chemistry, someone who acknowledged the important and vital role the mind and psyche played in the affairs of the body. From a purely scientific point of view we had no choice but to resort to a chemical substitute, but this doctor believed that returning to normal life, one that was filled with love and serenity would do the same job as the medicine, but without any side effects. Thirty years have passed since then and at the moment I'm still the only one in my family to have had a moustache.

Sadly, doctors whose knowledge of life is equal to their knowledge of medicine and who, despite their scientific training, still consider medicine an art form, no longer exist, especially in the West. Doctors stepping out of our modern universities think only in terms of illnesses, never in terms of those who are ill. Simply put, the patient is a 'bearer of a disease'. Doctors no longer visit patients at their homes where they can see how they live and trace the fabric of their affective relationships. They no longer have the time, the curiosity or the inclination.

Patients both in Europe and North America are beginning to feel a widening gap of incomprehension between themselves and these new doctor-functionaries who scrutinize every part of their body as though it has nothing to do with its owner.

As a consequence, more people are turning to forms of 'alternative' medicine. In a country like the US where the tendency towards specialization is at its most extreme, the annual number of visits made to alternative practitioners already exceeds that made to traditional doctors.

Alternative medicine promises patients a more personalized approach, giving them the impression of being treated as a whole being. For example, the root of a headache may be sought in the soles of the feet, restoring to the doctor–patient rapport that element of mystery and magic, which in itself seems to be of therapeutic value.

'Tell me, madam, when you go to the toilet do your faeces float or sink?', 'Between a piece of chocolate and a lemon, which would you prefer to eat?', 'Imagine you were in a forest and you found yourself face-to-face with a ferocious beast, would you make a run for it or would you scramble up the nearest tree?' Angela, somewhat amused by these questions, tried her best to respond.

We had been living in India for two years. She had injured her toe and the various creams, antibiotics and pills she had been prescribed by the Western-trained, embassy-recommended doctor had been useless. On the contrary, the wound seemed to be worsening. Then an Indian friend suggested we consult an Ayurvedic doctor. I telephoned the president of their association who graciously agreed to receive us in his home in the heart of Delhi. The place was modest and the atmosphere relaxed. The doctor seemed extremely interested in Angela's dreams and asked her about her life, what she had wanted to be when she was a child. He got her to draw a house and a boat and then felt the pulse of both her wrists. He hardly glanced at her foot. At the end of the hour-long consultation he handed us a prescription. He sent us to an old ayurvedic pharmacy in Connaught Place where we watched the chemist prepare several white paper wraps, similar to ones we had encountered in China, which contained powders to dissolve in water.

Angela took the powders at the prescribed intervals, but her toe did not improve. Her experience with Ayurveda had been disheartening and she had to live with her nasty injury for several more weeks. But one evening an old colleague from *Newsweek* came to our house for dinner with a bizarre woman in tow. Around forty years old, she was tall and slender, her beauty offset by a slightly prickly demeanour as though hardened by a life of woes that had also worn down most of her teeth. Originally from Australia, she told us how ten years ago she had been working as a journalist in Hong Kong where she met and married an Indonesian man, even converting to Islam to follow him to his native village in Borneo. She had learnt Indonesian and adapted to the village's strange way of life.

The stories that Nur – her newly given Arabic name that meant 'light' – recounted were like tales from another world. Shortly after arriving in her husband's village, the only white woman to have ever set foot there, she was at the market when the owner of a vegetable stall suddenly turned to her and said, 'I will come to visit you tonight. If you see a silver beetle, don't kill it. It will be me.' That night Nur saw an insect come in through the window and watched it make its way through the house before flying off again, but adjudged it to be mere coincidence. When she returned to the market a week later, the man was able to give her a precise description of the house's various rooms, warning her, 'Beware, there are evil spirits in your house.' He was right. Soon, Nur's marriage began to fall apart and the Bomoh – the local witch doctor – and her adopted family ganged up on her and did their best to make her leave the village. Under the spell of the Bomoh's black magic, Nur's hens stopped producing eggs, the flowers in her garden wilted the moment they came into bloom, certain household objects mysteriously vanished while a series of ominously rusty nails were found in her drawers.

Nur refused to give in and, secretly aided by the greengrocer beetle, began to study white magic and learnt to counter the Bomoh's spells. She remained in the village well after her husband had left and thanks to the powers she had acquired, became a healer there. After recently moving to Jakarta she quickly become renowned for her ability to cure several illnesses. Maybe this included Angela's injured toe too. And so, Nur began coming to our house every day, making Angela lie down on the living-room sofa and drawing the curtains. She would put on some Indonesian music and burn incense and begin stroking Angela's foot, telling her about her life in Borneo and asking about her own. Within a week the wound had completely healed.

How nice it would have been if Nur could heal me, if I could be recumbent in the penumbral cosiness of a scented room, listening as a steady trickle of gamelan music seeped between her tales and my own. But my problem wasn't an injured toe, nor did I have the time to experiment.

'Just try it,' you hear people say. 'Alternative medicine has no side effects. The worst that can happen to you is nothing.' But that too can be a death trap. Many people, hoping to avoid mutilating surgery, the devastations of chemo and the dangers of radiotherapy, have made the mistake of opting for apparently less troublesome, more promising solutions. I remember the fifty-year-old mother of a friend who had consulted a healer to cure her breast cancer. He made her drink gallons of herbal infusions and used a pendulum to evaluate her progress. Several months later, when the woman decided to go back to the surgeon who had advised her to have one breast removed to ensure a good chance of survival, it was already too late. Having wasted precious time, she died.

In recent years, this has become a particularly serious problem. Certain practices that were limited to a small sector of the population were now exposed to every city and neighbourhood in Europe. New Age culture and all things Oriental were spreading like wildfire. In Florence a tradesman whom we'd asked to reupholster a sofa began telling me about the chakra and energy flows that a faith healer had convinced him could cure his colonic cancer with no need for surgery. Even in Orsigna, a sheep farmer friend had told me how he would drive hundreds of miles every week to see a Tibetan sorceress. Fortunately, in his case it was merely for a pain in his leg that gave him a slight limp.

The real problem is that there are no longer any filters or controls. Current laws are inadequate to sort out the chaotic, indiscriminate deluge of information spewed out on the Internet. This has given birth to a realm of half-knowledge and half-truth, the most pernicious and dangerous form of ignorance.

There was a time when doctors, lawyers, architects and engineers would have to produce a degree certificate, signed by their university rector, as proof of their expertise. Today, such certificates are no longer a guarantee of anything. The tale of a successful act of healing or the mere sound of an exotic word suffices. Judges and professional associations no longer have the power to protect citizens who in any case, 'liberated' from the shackles of such tutelage, are not interested in their protection. In this matter, as in every other aspect of 'modern life', it is the market which decides. Anyone selling will find a clientele, and if they finish up the victims, that's their business, or rather, their fault!

One of the most appealing aspects of alternative therapies is the patient's own participation in the healing process, the idea that a lot depends on them and their will. This also means that should the treatment fail, the doctor cannot be held responsible: it's the patient's fault for not working hard enough, for not giving their all. Charlatans thus have the perfect justification for their own ineffectiveness. Frequently, however, the proselytes of alternative medicine – with the term 'medicine' being in most cases no more than an empty boast – are acting in good faith. This was certainly the case of Dan Reed, a fellow Sinologist from my university days in the States and now an expert in Taoism, Buddhism, qigong and Oriental medicine which he himself practised and on which he had written numerous books. I wrote him an email from New York while undergoing chemo, telling him what I was doing there and asking him for suggestions on what I could do to regain my balance and bolster my immune system. If I were lucky, I'd receive some nuggets of wisdom too I knew were buried in his chosen field. A disastrous move, as it turned out. Within a few hours his reply flamed across my computer screen. He told me I was mad to put my life in the hands of these 'white-coated assassins' who aimed to rid me of my cancer by poisoning it but would poison me in the process. Certainly it was a matter of life and death, but there was also the question of the quality of my afterlife to consider! Chemotherapy was the last thing I needed. He believed I should stop treatment immediately before it completely destroyed my organism. The damage, especially to the liver and blood, would be irreversible. How could I have done all this without consulting him first? How could I, after living in Asia for all these years, hand myself over to 'bullshit Western medicine'? So Dan suggested I call a San Francisco number he gave me *immediately* and fix a telephone appointment with a fortune-teller he knew, a true psychic and a great healer who could see everything. 'After thirty years of pilgrimages in Asia, ranging from India to Tibet in search of spiritual gurus and great healers,' Dan wrote, 'I've never met anyone who came close to this woman's powers and vision. You'll realize yourself ... and if you want to know more about what your buddies at MSKCC do to their patients, just read.' There followed a short bibliography I was already partly familiar with, together with the addresses of several websites where I could find damning accounts of the hospital and its methods.

Dan's email didn't bother me in any way. I was perfectly aware of the theories about MSKCC conspiring with the big pharmaceutical giants to rubbish any alternative forms of treatment that might affect the latter's profits. Yet this couldn't alter my conviction that it was my best bet.

Had I contacted the woman in San Francisco, no doubt the

experience would have been an interesting one. She would have 'seen' my entire self and the multicoloured aura that surrounded my body. I would be taught the art of 'positive thinking' and made to participate in my treatment. All the things that were anathema to MSKCC.

Had my illness been scarlet fever or hay fever, I would have called her, if for no other reason but her name, Holly Clarity, which could not have been more perfect for a fortune-teller.

Though I was sure I had made the right decision, I was equally aware that the medicine I had chosen – precisely because it was science and not magic, rooted in physics rather than metaphysics and founded on reason and experiment rather than intuition – could reach no deeper than appearances and what could be perceived by the senses. And for this reason it left me with a sense of emptiness, a void in understanding. I was convinced that perhaps there existed something that continually slipped through science's net – which after all had been designed for fishing in the sea of reality – something important, perhaps the most important thing of all.

The fact that this something couldn't be captured only proved that the existing equipment was unsuitable for the job. Science attempted to understand and explain the world by breaking it into pieces which it weighed, measured, observed and, where possible, reproduced.

I knew full well there was no scientific explanation for a loose slate on a roof landing on someone who happened to be passing by, or why a bullet would miss me and hit someone standing a few feet away. Yet, how could they deny that there might be some kind of cause-and-effect relationship between my life, the things I had seen and done, my frustrations and depressions and my rioting cells?

If it were true that a person's face was the mirror to their life, a reflection of their joys and disappointments, why shouldn't their life not leave its traces at the deepest level of material being – the cells? What I wanted to prove, to myself at least, was that the cancer was 'my' cancer. Not that I wished to blame myself for it, but because I believed that if I was partly the cause of it, I could surely have a part in controlling it too. Maybe this was merely a question of mental attitude but to me it seemed important.

The great nineteenth-century Indian mystic Ramakrishna, whose tales and parables are still recounted today, once said that there were two ways to salvation: the way of the cat which, from the moment it is born, is picked up by the scruff of its neck and carried around by its mother without it having to do anything, and the way of the monkey which must quickly learn to cling to its mother's fur with all its strength. But it was always this figure of the 'mother', of destiny, which saved us. I was determined to give mine a hand.

'I'm afraid you're expecting too much if you think you're the cause,' Lucio Luzzatto, whom I had gone to ask how cancer was born, told me. A tiny, sixty-year-old man from Genoa, he had spent many years in Africa before becoming MSKCC's head of genetics research.

Like great intellectuals who have no need to impress anyone with complicated jargon to explain a simple concept, Luzzatto was able to simplify what to me seemed a matter of dizzying complexity. If I understood correctly, this is how it worked: cancer is a disease of genetic origin that affects soma cells. The genes are the base of our DNA, an identity code unique to each of us. Every DNA is composed of around 100,000 genes, which determine who we are and what we will become. Contained in them is the colour of our hair when we are young and when we grow old, the length of our nose and the length of our life. In some way, genes are our 'destiny'. They reproduce by replicating themselves. And this is where the problems start and where cancerous cells can be produced since it is impossible for genes to reproduce themselves indefinitely in exactly the same way. There is a small chance of an error occurring – as little as one in a million – which is entirely natural. The error might in itself be a small one, but because it can be inherited, it constitutes a mutation and will be reproduced in the next copy and again in the next and so on. Among these mutations are many which are of no consequence, while others may prevent cells from functioning and thus reproducing themselves. Some mutations, however, provoke a variation in the cell structure and these are the ones to look out for.

Luzzatto was keen to stress that mutation is a chance error, nothing bad in itself and in fact entirely natural. 'Without mutations, there would be no evolution,' he told me. A mutation on its own cannot produce a cancer. It is only when a mutation is followed by another and another that a problem becomes serious. 'In your case, for example, it has taken at least five successive mutations, all of which, you have to remember, are chance occurrences!' Luzzatto did seemed convinced, however, that medical science would shortly find a way to prevent such mutations.

'You understand,' he concluded, 'that there's no way you can personally have had any influence on these mutations. But if you want to feel responsible for something, take care of your immune system. That's personal. Even identical twins have completely different immune systems. That, you can more or less make how you want it, it's *yours*. In that sense you have a lot to do with how it'll respond to the cancer and, therefore, with what's going to happen to you in general.'

At last, I no longer need to resign myself to watching the illness do what it was going to do to my body. There was something I could do, a part I had to play, a certain responsibility. My future depended, in part, on myself. I would have been happy to spend hours studying with a mentor like Luzzatto. Here was a scientist that made me cast aside all my regrets about the shamans. As I was leaving his office, I turned to him with one last question that had been buzzing around my head for days: 'What exactly is a disease?'

He looked at me, conscious of the weight of a culture that for centuries had performed mental somersaults around such enigmas, and with a disarming smile, replied, 'That's a fascinating question, but it's easier for me to talk about cancer. On that subject, at least, I have a couple of clear ideas.'

My conversation with Luzzatto got me thinking. While writing *A Fortune-teller Told Me*, I had tried, with a large dose of scepticism I'll admit, to understand whether a person's destiny was written in the lines on their palm, and if there might be people who could decipher it. In the end, though, there was little cause for scepticism. If, as Luzzatto maintained, our destiny was indelibly written in the genes which experts like himself were now in a position to read, why shouldn't it also be etched in the palm of a hand? The only difference was that reading genes was a more modern pursuit, one not enveloped in mystery. Yet its scientific character made it infinitely more disturbing. An individual's future could now be read in their genes and which opened up untold opportunities for its manipulation. Soon, when the map of the human genome was complete, scientists, or rather the few companies who had monopolized this area of research and its related patents, would have exclusive rights to the genetic design of our species. They would also be the sole proprietors of the various tools for cloning.

One group of firms would specialize in producing embryos to satisfy demand for the latest consumer gimmick: babies to order – male, blonde hair, blue eyes, built to last – while others would help employers select from among various candidates those whose genetic readings indicated they had the least chance of developing prostate or breast cancer later in life.

The consequences, both foreseeable and unimaginable, seem alarming. It is as though man has finally reached a stage when he could conceivably play God and stage his own miniature version of the creation. But will God permit him to do so?

I don't remember which language Luzzatto and I spoke, but it was probably English. Though he had graduated in Italy, he was no longer a typical Italian doctor, the kind who didn't bother to button up their white coats once they attained a good position – a symbolic gesture like what animal bones and skulls draped around the neck are to a shaman – and indeed deliberately leaving them flying open as they strut through the hospital wards, their court of acolytes in close pursuit, with an attitude to patients that can best be described as patrician disdain.

Barons, they are sometimes called, though no doubt they would prefer to be called almighty fathers.

American doctors were exactly the opposite. They, at most, considered themselves skilled mechanics. During mealtimes, in MSKCC's enormous ground-floor cafeteria everyone, no matter what their rank, took a tray and joined the queue. It was often impossible to tell whether someone was a doctor, a nurse or a lab technician.

Living in the world of the sick, I soon realized that one of the reasons people abandon scientific medicine for alternative therapies is because of the doctors' attitude towards them, their frequent failure to take the patient's feelings into account or their tendency, whether because of work pressure or legal indemnity, to simply be cruel. The story of Ludovico is particularly significant to me in this sense. A number of its implications continue to perplex me.

Ludovico was not the usual acquaintance who calls one day to get himself invited to lunch or for suggestions on where to go or what to buy in India. He had read one of my books and was in Delhi for a few days, so he asked the Italian embassy for my number ... and I was lucky, for just as I was about to slip into my usual, 'I'm sorry, I'm just about to leave. Maybe we can meet next time' routine, it occurred to me to ask him something.

'Sorry, but what is it you do exactly?'

'Me? Oh, I'm a professional patient.'

An unusual answer, as was Ludovico himself, and the sequence of events that followed, events which, in hindsight, make me wonder whether there might be things in our lives that truly defy comprehension, that are beyond reason's reach.

At the time he called me, Ludovico was forty-six; after trying his hand at several occupations he had become a professional patient. When diagnosed with cancer, he had undergone chemotherapy and the experience had been traumatic to say the least. During the treatment he felt he had been reduced to a serial number and his doctors did not help him find something to alleviate the cocktail's effects. When, at the end of the last cycle, he approached the head doctor to ask whether he was cured, the doctor, tried to sidestep the question, then brutally replied, 'Get it through your head once and for all. There is no cure for cancer.'

Ludovico refused to accept such a verdict. From that moment he had been in search of someone or who wouldn't be so quick to crush his hopes. A Canadian friend suggested he try the Kaisse formula. It is a herbal remedy used by a tribe of native Americans to treat several diseases including cancer. Ludovico became a regular consumer, then a dedicated proselyte. Gradually, an escalating flood of people – sceptics or disillusioned casualties of orthodox medicine – began to turn to him for advice on how to get hold of this 'miraculous' potion. He told me he was in India to study the local medicine and to meet any Ayurvedic doctors he could invite to Italy. For two hours, Angela and I listened to his tale. I liked Ludovico's warmth, though at that time I had no personal interest in his story, neither as a patient nor as a professional of alternative medicine. I had never felt better. After he'd gone, purely out of curiosity, I checked the Internet for information on this potion that I had never heard of. There turned out to be hundreds of links, some of which I looked at, and that was it. Several months after our meeting, I was diagnosed with cancer myself. And what's more, it was the same type as Ludovico's. What a strange coincidence it was!

Our lives became intertwined from then on. His experience and presence helped me enormously. While I was still in New York Ludovico, in spite of his miraculous potion, suffered a relapse. After months of uncertainty and not knowing whether to go on believing in what he had convinced so many others to believe or admit failure and return to the traditional medicine he had rejected, Ludovico chose to go back to chemotherapy and a bone marrow transplant. In the meantime he had learnt not to ask if he was cured. But he continued to take the potion.

I, on the other hand, couldn't help but wonder what had brought about our strange meeting in Delhi. I had difficulty thinking it was purely chance.

One day I woke up to a parcel at the door of my apartment in New York. Inside, wrapped in yellow tissue paper was a kata – a long, thin white silk scarf – that, once touched and thus blessed by a revered lama, is worn by Tibetans as a form of protection or kept in the house, hung from a tanka – a sacred painting – or else draped around a statue of Buddha. This one had come from the Dalai Lama himself.

A friend and colleague from *Der Spiegel* had flown from Hamburg to Dharamshala to interview him and at the end of their meeting, mentioned my name, saying I couldn't be there because I was at MSKCC. Hearing this the Dalai Lama, holding the kata in both hands, ceremoniously touched it to his forehead and, after a few seconds of concentration, gave it to my friend, asking if he would send it to me along with the following piece of advice: 'In case my blessings prove insufficient, tell him he must take all the medicines they give him.'

The last time I'd seen the Dalai Lama, the 'Ocean of Wisdom', he had been suffering from a terrible cold, his voice affected by an insistent hoarseness. This greatly worried my host, his brother. 'Your holiness, are you taking Tibetan or Western medicine?' I asked him. 'Both,' he replied with one of his highly contagious laughs, remembering instantly that he had been late to take his medication, speedily chasing down a quintessentially Western antibiotic with the hot Tibetan infusion an assistant had placed on the little table next to where we sat in his Dharamshala studio.

I wrapped the kata around a little statuette of Buddha that sat on my aquarium window sill, looking out over Central Park. Every day, when I took my medicines I would think of the Dalai Lama's welcome blessing that perhaps charged that strip of white silk.

In 1993, I went into retreat for ten days in northern Thailand to study vipassana meditation. The course was held by an amiable fellow named John Coleman, a former CIA agent who had converted to Buddhism. At that time, 'meditation' was still a relatively unusual expression, and though I lived in Asia I had only heard it used in connection with people who had too much time on their hands, probably for vacationing hippies.

Things have changed since, especially in the West. 'Meditation' has become a part of everyday parlance and many practise, or claim to, practise it.

Thanks to the monstrous, dispiriting process of trivialization that transforms the smallest secret into a product to sell, meditation has now arrived on the supermarket shelves. Advertisements for meditation courses appear alongside those seeking a home for a dog or a pair of Siamese kittens. In bookshops, books on meditation are placed alongside those on yoga, reiki, occultism, Tarot, Tibetan Buddhism, qigong, Taoism, the I Ching, Native American medicine and astral travel. In addition to its traditional departments of history, literature, science, biography and so on, Barnes & Noble now has entire sections devoted to self-help, new age, astrology and health. Those allergic to the printed word can now learn to meditate using audio books. But the fact that these things are now available to everyone means they have inevitably lost their intrinsic value, which, especially in the case of certain spiritual practices, was often linked to the difficulty of their discovery, the 'secret' meaning of their teachings.

A disciple would once have to serve his master for years; fetch him his water, cut his firewood and sweep his hut until the moment he was taught something that let him in on even a small part of the 'secret'. It was not in any way like the instant, boil-in-the-bag wisdom of today which contains nothing extraordinary or precious.

I believe even the language we use today has been infected by a strength-sapping virus. Certain words through their use, reuse, and often misuse, have lost much of their original meaning. We often resort to cliché or banal formulaic expressions. Love, for instance, may be a powerful word, but it would be impossible to love someone or something with the same intensity and passion every day. We can't 'love' a pair of jeans in the same way that we love a person. This is why people who really do meditate never speak about it.

After Coleman's course, I tried to incorporate meditation into my daily routine, though not always with success. If you neglect its spiritual dimension, meditation soon loses its hold and cannot be treated as a daily chore. For me Coleman's course had been a bit like learning to ride a bike. I worked out how the mind could be used to control the body and this seemed to me an art to stow away for safe keeping, an art that would be of great help when in need. As indeed it was.

When I was in Bologna during my initial tests, some of which were extremely painful, I had recourse to what I had learnt from Coleman's lessons: concentrate on the breathing, attune the mind to the source of the pain, imagining it be a knot that needed untying. I had to try and ascertain its colour and shape – whether it is round or square – its dimensions, take note of each blow it dealt me. All this in order to distract the body-self from its suffering and to remind myself that everything was impermanent, everything would pass, even the pain.

We have a mind that we do not use, intelligence that we let go to waste. Or rather, that we use to produce an artificial variety. Though it is one of the most sophisticated instruments we have at our disposal, we treat the mind as though it were of no account. Indeed, we have adopted a more 'modern' attitude and use chemistry to do what we could with our minds. It is regarded as the solution to all our problems. Depressed? Tired? Sterile? Underweight? Overweight? No need to worry, there is a pill for every problem. Why bother finding out why your child is hyperactive when Prozac can easily sort out his restlessness? These days even tens of thousands of children in the US depend on a daily dose of medications in order to function 'normally'.

The same goes for pain whose defeat is considered one of modern man's greatest triumphs. And yet, even this victory is not necessarily a good thing. Firstly, pain has a primordial natural function, that of sounding the alarm. It is pain's job to tell us when things aren't well, and in certain situations it may be more dangerous if we don't feel pain. One of the terrible effects of leprosy is that it destroys the capillary nerves. Not feeling any pain, the sufferer doesn't realize when their fingers or toes hit something and break, or worse, as used to happen in colonies in poor regions, when they were eaten by rats as they slept.

Secondly, by nipping their sufferings in the bud and depriving themselves of the awareness of pain, modern man is unable to appreciate the beauty and relief of its absence. In all the world's great religions, pain is regarded as something quite natural, a normal part of life. Haven't we perhaps missed or forgotten the point of pain? Yet even if this is the case, nobody wants to know, conditioned as they are to think good must triumph over evil, and that existence is not a harmony of contraries.

A vision like this has no place for either death or pain. We deny the existence of death by not thinking about it, ushering it from the sphere of our daily life to where, physically too, it is least visible. Pain we have actually defeated, coming up with a remedy for every one of its manifestations. We have even eliminated from human experience its oldest and most natural form, that of giving birth, on which the pride of motherhood has always been based and with it the uniqueness of the mother–child rapport whose very foundation is perhaps suffering.

But that's Western civilization in which, ever more accustomed to solving problems by external means, we gradually lose those most natural to us. Just as our dependence on the artificial memory of computers causes our own to wither, ingestion of sundry medicines reduces the body's capacity to produce its own.

But can the mind really control pain? Living in India, you hear countless tales or legends saying it can. The logic is this: all our sensations are linked to our consciousness; when we say we see or hear something, it is not with our eyes or ears, but with our consciousness. It recognizes the fact that eyes see and ears hear. In order to not feel pain, one must use the mind to unplug consciousness from sensation. This is exactly what happens when we fall asleep: consciousness makes itself scarce and we feel no pain. The problem is how to attain this state when we are awake.

Yoga affords us this power while alluding to something more fascinating: the ability to transfer pain to an external object. A famous story, almost a thousand years old, recounts such a feat. The protagonist, was Milarepa, a Tibetan who actually existed and became known as one of the greatest yogi of all time. Even now you see him depicted on tankas, a hand cupped behind his right ear as he listens to the world's sufferings.

Born in Tibet in the mid-eleventh century to a family of rich wool merchants who fall into penury following his father's death, Milarepa, in order to avenge his mother whose inheritance has been cruelly usurped by relatives, studies black magic which he employs to provoke their death or ruin. He repents his actions later in life and becomes the disciple of a great master, Marpa the Translator, and for years lives an ascetic existence in the forest, surviving on nettles boiled in a terracotta pot. With time, Milarepa becomes renowned for his wisdom, wisdom more precious for the fact that it comes not from sacred texts, but from his own experience.

One day, a conceited bookish monk, jealous of Milarepa and his fame, decides to kill him. Entrusting the mission to one of his concubines, he instructs her to offer Milarepa a glass of poisoned lassi. The moment he sees the concubine, Milarepa instantly knows what is afoot – the ability to read minds was amongst the many powers he had gained through the study of yoga. But being already quite old and realizing that sooner or later he must die, he takes the lassi from her and downs it in a single gulp.

On hearing this, the monk immediately feels remorse and runs to the old yogi, begging him to lay all his sufferings on himself so that he might expiate his guilt. 'Should I do so,' replies Milarepa, seemingly in perfect control of the pain, 'you would not be able to bear it for even a minute.' But the monk insists, and so, to show him how impossible it would be for him to stand the pain, Milarepa transfers a small portion of it to the door of the room which immediately starts to creak and buckle until the wood snaps under the strain. Witnessing this, the monk throws himself at the old man's feet and begs for his forgiveness, becoming his ardent disciple, in the moment before the yogi gives up his mortal body.

After an operation, one of the first reassuring signs that we are still alive is pain. In my case the pain came in the form of a terrible stomach ache. I felt like I was being pierced by a thousand spears, but which I was quickly able to bring under control. Through meditation? Not at all. It was simply by pressing a button on a remote control I had been given that injected a miraculous discharge directly into my veins making the pain go away. For a while I was calm, until the pain came back and I would have to press the button again. Meanwhile, another electronic device kept count of the injections, shutting off the supply if there were too many. Even though I wasn't aware of this, I pressed the button regardless. The mere act of doing so gave me a feeling of well-being. It was what doctors call the placebo effect: the surprising healing properties of something that in reality has no effect whatsoever, such as drinking a glass of water rather than simply swallowing a pill.

This device in my room was maintained by two young doctors from the Pain Control Unit who visited me daily. I have no idea what the discharges contained, but whatever it was, it helped. Perhaps it was a substance similar to that which the body produces on its own when in need. The moment it experiences a tremendous or potentially fatal pain, it releases a home-made anaesthetic that enables it to resist, which explains why, for example, a soldier whose arm has been blown off can go on running for several minutes as though nothing has happened.

Perhaps this too explains the wonderful story of Sarmad, the seventeenth-century mystic whose tale is still recounted by tour guides at his tomb near Jama Masjid, the great mosque facing Delhi's Red Fort. Upon his arrival in India, Sarmad, who might have been a Jew or a Christian from Armenia, had converted to Islam and had become famous for his wisdom and verses, which he wrote in Persian. And because, 'drunk on God's love', he would dance completely nude in public, 'liberated from all weight, including that of clothes'. A Sufi like my anaesthetist, he was accused of heresy by the court's highly orthodox mullahs. Emperor Aurangzeb ordered that he be beheaded.

'Oh, my great friend,' said Sarmad, addressing his words to God as the chief executioner approached, a scimitar glinting in his hand. 'Today you have come disguised as an executioner, but nonetheless I recognize you. Welcome!' Smiling, he offered his neck to the blade.

There is a similar story of Al-Hallaj, another mystic, this time from the nineteenth century. He was accused of saying that God and truth were the same thing and that man himself was an intrinsic part of that truth. Brought before the sultan, he was told to recant. Al-Hallaj refused and on the sultan's orders one of his hands was cut off. Al-Hallaj nonetheless continued to repeat his thesis and so a leg was removed. But he would not desist in saying, 'I am the Truth,' at which point the sultan gave orders to cut his head off. And still the lips of the severed head continued to form the words: 'Ana 'l-Haqq, I am the Truth,' as it rolled on the floor.

Stuck in bed, with nothing to do but pass the time, I remembered those stories and found them to be of valuable assistance in my attempts to resist pressing the button. To keep the pain at bay, I tried to meditate, I tried to distract my mind, coaxing it towards pleasant thoughts. I told myself the pain was the counterweight to this oft-repeated pleasure. It was only fair that it had finally levelled the score.

I asked myself why following the most unbearable suffering, our constitution ensures the experience is wiped from our minds. We know we have felt it and yet we can no longer recall its intensity or precise nature. I wondered why the word 'pain' refers not merely to physical suffering but to other kinds of affliction. I thought about psychoanalysis, the laborious control unit watching over our other great pain … how fortunate I was to have that button to press. And when I could stand no more, to be able to press it.

At least once a week, on my way home from the hospital, I would stop at the corner of Sixty-seventh and Madison, and take a creaky old lift up to the twelfth floor where there was a small sunlit apartment whose door was always open. For several decades that apartment had been home to a friend of mine, a writer I'd always admired. He was a multicultured man of many worlds; one who should be preserved in a glass case if only to offer future generations a lesson on how, at one time, it was possible to live. But time was fast running out for Niccolò Tucci. Now in his nineties, he had been bedridden for months, but lay there without a murmur of complaint, elegant as always with his immaculately groomed grey beard and long hair which gave him the air of a nineteenth-century Romantic rebel.

Half-Russian and half-Florentine, Nica had come to New York at the end of the 1930s. Here he'd become involved with a group of fellow Italians in the struggle against fascism and where he remained after the war. Writer, pamphleteer and literary Don Quixote of numerous causes, he was always ready with a smart quip or unorthodox slant for problems, both old and new, of the human condition. We'd known each other for over thirty years.

Of the many things for which I was indebted to Nica, one of them was learning to read Dante with a Tuscan accent, free of rhetoric in the manner of a fantastic tale one might recount in a Florence tavern. I also owed to him the rather amusing idea that one should tip a hotel porter on arrival rather than when departing, as well as a joke Gaetano Salvemini had told him and with which I used to console myself every time I tried to learn a new language, a task that became more and more arduous with the years. After recently arriving in the States, Salvemini was struggling to learn English. 'How's it going?' someone asked him. 'Well,' he said. 'At least I'm beginning to understand the things that *I* say.'

To Nica, I also owed the following words of encouragement: 'When are you going to quit with this Jour…nalism and do a bit of Etern…alism?'

Knowing full well that nothing was eternal, he wanted to persuade me to give up my day-to-day, week-to-week existence and had encouraged me to pen down some of my experiences in a more permanent book form. He himself had written several excellent books, some in Italian, others in English, but as he himself put it, 'Crossing the Atlantic, you always end up on the wrong shore.' His faded literary career was testament to this. Even now that he was dying, he was on the wrong shore. The apartment was everything a man of his mould could wish for: its two small well-lit rooms contained a nice desk, a well-stocked library, an old Bakelite telephone and an armchair. On one wall there was an enlarged print of an old black-and-white photo of his parents taken on a beach at Forte dei Marmi, there were a couple of colour snap shots of Tuscany sellotaped next to it and there was also a cutting of an article he had written for *The New Yorker* to mark Gaetano Salvemini's death. He knew he was never again going to leave those four walls on foot.

'You know,' he said to me during one of my visits, 'If I was dead today, I'd be happy.'

'But how could you be happy if you were dead?' I asked him.

'I don't know, because I don't know what death is.'

'But are you afraid of it?' I slowly asked.

He opened his impish eyes wide which glinted beneath his sturdy, still black eyebrows. 'Mamma mia, yes!'

'Come on, Nica. If billions of people before us have managed it, I'm sure we will too.'

'Yes, but if I could at least die somewhere else... Florence, for instance, would be more...' he drifted off, probably in search of the right word.

'More civilized, you mean?' I suggested, picking an adjective at random.

'Yes, more civilized, but also ...' He meandered on as though to himself, talking about a special kind of bread he had eaten on Good Friday during his childhood in Florence.

'These days, you can find it on any day of the week,' I said.

'Isn't it absurd? I think they even use a spray to recreate the smell. You know, in Florence now, there is a chain of bakers that have this smell. When you go in you would think there was an oven right behind the till, but it's all fake. The bread is made in some factory and the smell comes from an aerosol can.' I told him about a French 'aroma engineer' I had met in Calcutta the year before who was trying to sell the Indian car industry a very typical scent; a heady mixture of plastic, rubber and machismo.

But Nica wasn't listening, he was only interested in Florence. For some reason I found myself describing a walk we might have taken together, starting from Ponte Vecchio, then up L'Erta Canina and along Via San Leonardo, stopping in front of the house where the painter Ottone Rosai had once lived and then finishing up on Viale dei Colli. I spoke throughout, telling him where to turn and describing the scene in front of us as he lay there smiling with his eyes tightly shut. What once started on a whim, this game became our ritual.

'Where are we going today?' he would ask as soon as I stepped through his door. And soon, we would be off on another stroll around Florence. Once it was from Piazza Torquato Tasso to Torre di Bellosguardo where we paused to enjoy one of the loveliest views on earth. On another occasion we went from Torrione di Ponte alle Grazie up to Le Rampe, finally arriving at Piazzale Michelangelo which had unfortunately been invaded by coachloads of tourists, so we sat in the Colonne for a drink.

'What are you having, Nica?'

'One of those ... you know.'

'Campari? Vermouth?'

'No.'

What he wanted was a simple glass of white wine, but served in one of those short, squat glasses they had in the old days, which the innkeeper would fill to the brim. I enjoyed the time I spent with Nica. This was all we needed to make the last clouded dregs of his life pleasurable.

He never said anything on the subject of my chemotherapy, but when I told him I was to undergo an operation, he was furious.

'Never trust a doctor. They're all morons. And then, you're going to let them remove bits of you? No, you can't do it!' He even asked me for a sheet of paper and a pen to write a letter to the hospital in protest.

'Nica, you're worse than the officials of the Japanese Imperial Council!' I exclaimed. I amused him with a story of how the high-level court functionaries in Japan had to ascertain that the girl whom the prince and future emperor had chosen as his fiancée had all her bits, that her body was completely intact. During the last selection process, which had taken place when I was still living in Tokyo, a girl had been rejected for having pierced ears!

Nica was fortunate. Throughout his life, he'd never had to have a single operation and now he was going to die with all his bits present and correct. But he would die in New York, in this bed with its water-filled mattress to prevent bedsores, in a city he regarded as uncivilized and where, after mastering so many languages and delighting people by imitating their accents, the only language he now seemed to understand was his native Italian.

And what about me? Was this where I wanted to die? No. I had nothing in common with this country. Everything that was mine belonged to other places. Perhaps Asia or maybe, if I was to be really honest, Europe.

Preoccupied by these thoughts, I told Nica how in ancient times the Chinese would ask to be buried in the place where young women gave birth, thus establishing a bond between different generations. They believed their body was not their own, but belonged to the Chinese nation, from whose soil they had risen and to whose soil they would return. And then, hoping to make him laugh, I told Nica that when the first Chinese diplomatic mission was sent to the United States, each of the Mandarins took with them a set of special boxes in which to collect their 'business' to take back home with them. Nothing that belonged to a Chinaman, not even his turds, could be permitted to remain in this land of barbarians! Nica smiled.

The walks we took around Florence that day were to be his last.

THE MEMORY OF WATER

Memory, we often forget, plays strange tricks on us. It remembers and forgets what it likes and does so for no apparent reason, that is, no reason which is clear to ourselves.

Failing to remember the name of a person or object, the elderly become incensed, fall into despair. Noticing that something in them no longer functions the way it used to, they take it as a sign of their decline. They perhaps forget that since childhood, memories stow things away and retrieve them in their own distorted manner when we rummage around.

After sixty years of this drudgery, the drawer in my memory that was marked 'homeopathy' was nearly empty; all that remained was one basic notion – that the best way to cure a cold is with cold. Along with this there were a couple of anecdotes I had picked up from who knew where, when or whom.

In the first anecdote, a young woman suffering from depression complains that being around people makes her feel uneasy; all she wants is to be by herself, preferably somewhere high up. She frequently absconds to the roof of her house and says she dreams about flying away. Her doctors, not knowing what to do, refer her to a homeopath who sees her wish to fly as the symptom of a nature unable to express itself, the nature of an eagle. From the city zoo, he procures a drop of eagle's blood which he dilutes with a litre of water. He then dilutes a drop of this concoction with another litre of water and continues to do so until he arrives at a solution purified of all but the dimmest traces, perhaps the memory alone, of the eagle's blood. He tells the woman to drink a few drops each day. Within a few weeks she claims to be feeling markedly better.

The second story, if memory serves correctly, concerns a young boy from a country village who has been stung by a bee. His face swells up like a balloon and he falls seriously ill. The boy's parents call the local homeopath who tells them to procure a substance called Apis 200, dilute it in a bottle of water and give the boy a few drops. It seems impossible since the nearest chemist is miles away and the boy's condition is worsening. Time is running out. The doctor therefore suggests they write the words 'Apis 200' on a piece of paper, put the paper in a bottle of water, shaking it well and give this to the boy to drink. Gradually the swelling disappears and the boy recovers.

When my friend Ludovico told me he'd found an excellent doctor who might be able to help us both, though I recalled little or nothing else about homeopathy, the memory of these two stories suddenly made the idea of consulting a homeopath appealing, especially after the long months I had spent in New York.

Following chemo and the operation, my fixers had given me two weeks' leave. And so, with trolley case in tow to shoulder the weight of my heavy bags and with my stomach still stitched up from the surgery, I compacted myself as much as possible to avoid contact with passing bodies. I then took a plane to Florence.

The homeopathic doctor's practice was in the province of Modena. He received patients by appointment only and his schedule was packed for the next two months. I warmed up to him from the moment he answered the phone. 'Could I come late afternoon on Christmas Eve?' 'Certainly,' he said. And so off I went.

Exiting from the motorway, we turned off on to a little country lane that seemed headed for some mist-bound limbo. Though a thick curtain of fog had descended around the car, the doctor's faxed directions were extremely precise and we managed not to get lost. Before meeting him, I chewed over his name, Mangialavori, which sounded strange even in Italian, and decided to rebaptize him Mangiafuoco – Fire-Eater.

Physically, he bore no resemblance to the character I had imagined. A smallish man, with light hair and green eyes, he lived in an old farmhouse that had been recently renovated. Fields, plants, fruit trees, everything here seemed to be in hibernation, including the other inhabitants whom there'd been no sign of on the way.

Fire-Eater received me in his small studio, which looked deliberately dimly lit and had a nicely perfumed air. Pinned to the wall was a cheap Tibetan tanka, while on the desk, placed there like an ornament, was a large ginkgo leaf. He was warmly attentive as he asked me about myself: who I was, what I had done in my life, what I still wished to do, how I saw myself, what my dreams were. Feeling immediately at ease, I spoke freely. Only some time later did I realize that Fire-Eater had been discreetly taking notes on a computer keyboard concealed behind the desk. Not once had he taken his eyes off me!

About my most recent illness he wished to know little. The ones which interested him were those of my childhood, haemorrhoids in particular. On that subject he wanted to know everything I could possibly remember. He was intrigued by the fact that in New York

I had kept a piece of paper and a pencil by my bedside so that I could write down any dreams I'd had as soon as I'd wake up. Apart from my daily diary, I had also kept a nocturnal log and this was what Fire-Eater focused his attention on.

He had me undress and lie down on the couch where he gave me a thorough examination, asking, in the manner of older doctors, whether it hurt if he prodded me at a particular point. To my great relief, it did not include the stomach. Returning to his desk, he posed a question which I thought was extremely deft.

'What did you expect in coming here?'

It wasn't hard to give him an honest reply. What I didn't expect was that he could cure the cancer, convinced as I was by now that the phrase 'cure cancer' was a contradiction in terms. In any case I had already entrusted that mission to the fixers at MSKCC. All I wanted from him was to help me sort out something equally important: my emotions. The outside world was having too much influence on my mood. I was irritable, unstable, subject to alternating bouts of euphoria and depression. I told him I had the feeling of looking at the world through a kaleidoscope. The slightest twitch and everything went green; another and it would become red, then black, then gold. I wanted to bring this mechanism to a halt, for everything to remain a single colour, to put an end to the highs and lows. I wanted to be able to hear '*Jingle bells*' without wanting to run out of a shop.

We spoke for more than an hour and the impression he made was excellent. Here was a man who, in addition to being astute and open-minded, was extremely cultivated and passionate about his work. He had no illusions about being able to cure cancer. He believed mine had been caused by some imbalance in my system. His job would be to help me work on the life force we all had inside us, which he believed I myself possessed to a great degree to restore my equilibrium. I noticed that while speaking about cancer and related matters he never used the word 'illness'.

'Of course, illness,' he said, 'brings to mind the idea of being ill, which obviously isn't good. I prefer the word 'disease', though perhaps it would be more correct to say 'unease' because essentially that's what it is: the body is not at ease and the symptoms of it are a sign that the body is in some way trying to integrate it. Our task, yours and mine,' he was careful to underline, 'is to support the body in its efforts to do so.' I felt close to this line of reasoning. He and I seemed to be on a similar wavelength and I, more and more curious, gradually got him to open up to me.

After an adolescence devoted to music, he followed the family tradition of taking up medicine with the intention of becoming a surgeon specializing in children's operations. His true passion, however, was anthropology. At some point during a journey to Latin America, he had got lost, or perhaps it would be better to say he found himself. In Peru one day, mingling with the Indios, he saw a shaman who was curing people of their ailments and from that moment – as they say of the saints – he found his 'calling'.

What had begun as a short holiday became a much longer stopover. The shaman took him under his wing and initiated him into his art. When he returned to Europe, he realized he could no longer follow the path of traditional medicine and chose an alternative solution in homeopathy. 'It's a wonderful form of medicine,' he said to me. 'Even if the medical establishment doesn't see it that way. But the way their culture expresses itself isn't always the most suitable. Especially when you're dealing with people who, thankfully, are not subject to precise laws, assuming such laws exist.'

I had to agree. He saw how interested I was and continued. 'Our detractors say homeopathy is nothing more than a magic trick.

So what if it is? Magic is serious business. Often we use magic to describe something we don't fully understand. But it's so much more than that. I would say it's on the same plane as religion or even science.'

Once, he told me, he had asked the shaman what magic was for him. 'A state of mind,' was his answer.

'You could say magic is a different way of interpreting things,' Fire-Eater continued. 'A much more interesting and creative way than what we're used to, since it combines art with the pleasure of playing with matter. Magic is something which transforms us, which in turn gives us the capacity to help others transform themselves. It's like what you do when you write. Maybe a single sentence in one of your books has helped make somebody's life that little bit better. Wouldn't you call that magic? The important thing to know is what you're doing and to let that natural energy flow freely.'

After those months in New York under the sway of the body-to-be-repaired logic, these words were music to my ears.

'What we do in homeopathy,' he explained, 'is treat people with tiny drops. Just like if we were to consult a wise man for advice, his response would be a matter of a few words. And then, think how a life is created with just a drop of spermatozoa. Whether it turns out good or bad, it's still a life!'

The problem, he said, was to help an ill person regain their equilibrium. '*Their* equilibrium,' he stressed, 'not what the establishment defines it as. Often, it's more important to alleviate the person's suffering than to cure them. If we always had the power to cure everything, there wouldn't have been any art.'

The aim of homeopathy was to try to identify the particular stimulus in each case needed to trigger the natural processes that let a person re-establish their equilibrium. This was the function of the drops and the reason why they were described as a 'remedy' and not a 'medicine'.

During our long chat, Fire-Eater never said anything against orthodox allopathic medicine and didn't criticize my decision to go to New York. On the contrary, he said that since I had chosen that particular course I should follow it through to the end. He would simply help me limit the damage the treatment was doing to my body.

Writing out his prescription, he explained that in my case the remedy was Calcarea phosphorica, a mineral extract of calcium phosphate. I was to take a Q1, first-degree solution, that is to say, a drop of the substance for every fifty thousand drops of water. The instructions were as follows: after giving the flacon a good shake, dilute twenty-five drops in half a glass of water, stir well and drink every night before going to bed. With the following proviso: the drops should not be kept near perfumes and should be drunk only after brushing one's teeth.

I was to go on taking these drops until one of my previous symptoms or some other suspect sign made an appearance. This would be the signal that my system was sufficiently stimulated and from which moment I would be on the upward slope of a healing curve. If there was no change in my condition after forty days I continue the remedy, but this time in a more concentrated, that is to say, diluted, form: Q3, a third-degree solution.

In addition to this remedy, Fire-Eater wrote me a prescription for vitamins A and E and suggested that on my return to New York I procure some liquid chlorophyll – not easily found in Europe – and take twenty-five drops three times a day. Other than this, I was to continue with my spiritual (so I hoped) exercise regime, take lots of deep breaths and get as much fresh air as possible.

I had enjoyed meeting him. Fire-Eater seemed to me a fine addition to the human landscape that each of us composes in our lives, and I thought of all the people I knew he might have helped with his magic. Bidding him farewell, I told him how lucky I felt, having finally found the right doctor to which he responded, not without a certain amused irony, citing the words of an esteemed colleague, 'Also the doctor who finds the right patient should consider himself fortunate.'

Seeing I had nothing against his magic and that his profession interested me, Fire-Eater told me he was soon to fly to Boston to give a seminar on marine remedies, in which he was a specialist, and I was welcome to attend.

It was late. Outside it was pitch-dark, the night still blanketed in a fog that heightened my sense of disorientation. The impression I had was of having stumbled as if by magic on a place belonging to another world. Luckily Fire-Eater had the foresight to telephone the local chemist who was waiting in his shop to give me the prescribed remedy. And I must say, getting there, groping blindly through the fog in search of the familiar neon green cross indicating 'Pharmacy' was an adventure in itself.

Shaking the flacon and counting out the drops, I religiously took my daily dose and also began to pay closer attention to my mental state. But checking to see whether or not the symptoms had intensified was hard work; how could you really tell if a pain had got worse or not? Yet, perhaps the very act of listening to myself in this way, attentive to the slightest shift in mood, contributed to the change. Within a few days I was dreaming much more than I had been lately. Many were about my childhood which were a sign, Fire-Eater claimed, that the remedy was working. Slowly, each day, I felt my equilibrium begin to return. It was wonderful, gone were the irascibility and irritation. I would find myself laughing with joyful abandon once again. It was just what I needed. Fire-Eater had done his job magnificently and I too finally played my part.

His use of words like magic and 'life force' made my mind echo with thoughts that were oddly familiar to me. I found the idea congenial that I had to cure myself rather than wait for someone else to do it. I strongly believed there was truth behind this vision whose logic escaped my fixers in New York, but which I thought could not be ignored.

Such truth undoubtedly lies behind the story of how the historic American journalist and editor-in-chief of the *Saturday Review*, Norman Cousins, survived a potentially fatal illness for which allopathic medicine had no cure. The Romans called it 'vis medicatrix naturae', the curative power of nature. On learning of his illness, Cousins showed great courage in mobilizing all his resources, rediscovering the therapeutic value of laughter and stimulating the will to live that each of us harbours inside of ourselves.

The idea had actually come to him years before from the celebrated German philosopher, musician and doctor, Albert Schweitzer, whom Cousins had gone to Gabon to interview for an article he was writing. At dinner one evening, perhaps wishing to pay a compliment to this extraordinary European who had brought his science to the jungle, Cousins said to him, 'People here are lucky to have a real doctor and not have to rely on witch doctors.'

Schweitzer didn't take too kindly to the observation.

'And tell me, what do you know about witch doctors?'

Cousins had to admit he knew next to nothing about them. The next day Schweitzer took him to a clearing in the forest not far from his hospital and introduced him to his 'colleague', an old witch doctor. Schweitzer made the American journalist observe the doctor at work for two hours: there were several patients to whom, after listening to their complaints, the witch doctor gave a small parcel of herbs; in other cases he simply blew upon them, all the while reciting spells; others still he referred to Schweitzer who was sitting close by.

Schweitzer explained to Cousins that the first group of patients were suffering from a malady the witch doctor believed he could cure with herbs; the second group's illnesses, psychological in origin, he treated with his own brand of psychotherapy. Patients whose problems were clearly physical on the other hand, such as those with a hernia, an ectopic pregnancy, tumour or broken bones, he sent to Schweitzer's hospital. Cousins, however, remained unconvinced. 'I don't get it. How is it possible to think a witch doctor can cure you?'

'You're asking me to reveal a secret that all doctors from Hippocrates on have tenaciously kept to themselves.'

'What secret is that?' Cousins couldn't help but ask.

'That witch doctors cure their patients just like we do. The patients don't know it, but the real doctor is the one they have inside them. And our success mainly depends on giving that doctor the chance to do their job.'

A few years later Erich Fromm, the German physiologist, said the same thing to a student who came to ask his advice about a difficult case. 'Don't worry. After all, it's not really us who cure our patients. We just stand on the sidelines and cheer them on while they do it themselves.'

There is a lot of truth in this: it isn't really doctors who cure the body of its maladies, but the body itself when it makes use of the medicines it is given. The orthopaedist may put a broken bone in a cast, but the real healing is done by the body or by its life force.

Yet the fact is that today's doctors want to take all the credit and have far less respect for the witch doctor than Schweitzer.

I returned to New York in a decidedly calmer, more serene frame of mind. Though still volatile at times, more often than not my kaleidoscope bathed everything in a golden light. The drops had worked their magic and my curiosity about homeopathy was growing. I found it all the more fascinating. Above all I liked the fact that it rejected the aggressive nature of traditional medicine.

My mind was full of questions: could the remedy that had done so much to alter my mood have a similar effect on the cancer? Could the drops stimulate my inner life force and restore equilibrium and sanity to an immune system that had gone haywire? All the forms of therapy my fixers had recommended had devastating and dangerous side effects. Homeopathic remedies, on the contrary, were completely harmless.

I was about to undergo radiotherapy and I knew there was little time to mess around with magic. But doubts about the procedure suddenly began to assail my mind. Perhaps two hundred years from now even the fixers from MSKCC would be considered primitives, their therapies seen as forms of torture that produced more victims than recoveries. I had begun to look more deeply into the literature of homeopathy, whose beginnings at the turn of the eighteenth century were rooted in a growing sense of repulsion towards the treatment of the sick who were confined to their beds and subjected to an alternating regime of bloodlettings and purges.

For almost fifteen centuries, medical wisdom had been based on the conviction that disease was caused by poisons which had to be expelled from the body at all costs. If this couldn't be done through the normal organs of secretion, doctors would resort to artificial means, the most popular being leeches which would be applied to various parts of the body.

Medical science continued to rely upon this method until well into the nineteenth century. On the night of his death, George Washington underwent seven such bloodlettings which was not much considering the forty-seven Louis XIII had to endure. In the year 1827 alone, France was forced to import thirty-three million leeches to replenish its own depleted resources.

'He had so much bad blood,' Leopold II said of their sovereign, whom they had diagnosed with a rheumatic fever, 'that even the bleedings were not enough to save his life.'

It was around this time that, Samuel Hahnemann, a German physician born in 1755 in Meissen, Saxony, was to develop a form of therapy that wouldn't end up killing patients. He was a trained chemist who set out to change medicine's approach to disease. He was able to save the lives of countless patients, an achievement which, according to his detractors, was homeopathy's only real benefit. In reality, however, there was much more to it than that.

A true scientist in his close observation of nature, Hahnemann discovered that the emergence of a new malady in a patient was often sufficient in itself to cure an existing one. For this reason he wanted to study in more depth a principle that had been long engraved in the popular wisdom of numerous cultures: that like should be treated with like. Known to Hippocrates in 400 BC Greece and rediscovered by Paracelsus during the Renaissance, the principle had been applied for centuries by people as far apart as the Chinese, and Native Americans and in India it still forms part of the Ayurvedic tradition.

Hahnemann carried out his first experiments on himself, discovering that the sap from the bark of a cinchona tree, when administered to a healthy person, produced symptoms similar to those of malaria. When he gave small doses of this substance to a person suffering from malaria, he observed that the patient gradually recovered. The conclusion was evident: by administering a small dose of the malady and triggering it, the body could be induced to defend and heal itself. Vaccines today work on the same principle. As perhaps does the bizarre method by which tribal people of Gujarat in India treat rabies: by taking ticks from the rabid dog's fur and swallowing them down with a swig of water.

The solution, Hahnemann realized, lay in making use of nature's prodigious pharmacopoeia to study which particular 'symptoms' a given element – animal, vegetable or mineral – was able to induce and for which it might, therefore, serve as a possible remedy.

He was assisted in his endeavours first by members of his own family and then by a number of volunteers. Each of them, after being given a tiny dose of a certain extract, had to keep a detailed diary of their physical and emotional reactions. From these accounts, Hahnemann drew the momentous conclusion that each person reacted differently to the disease, whether spontaneous or induced. While it was true that every illness produced common symptoms, not all the symptoms were the same in each case.

'Every patient,' Hahnemann noted, 'suffers from a malady which has no name, a malady which has never before occurred and which will not do so again in manner or circumstance.' From this observation, he derived the first cardinal rule of homeopathy: to be concerned solely with the patient, their symptoms and perception of their illness and not with the illness itself. For example, if you are suffering from a headache, Aspirin can relieve the symptom but not the underlying reason for the headache, which will find other modalities of expression.

The paramount concern of homeopaths is to understand the patient, which requires close observation and the ability to listen.

The words patients use to describe their condition and symptoms are of much greater importance than the objective signs of illness. What decides a patient's homeopathic profile are factors such as their physical appearance, habits, food preferences and moods.

Reading about Hahnemann and his research, I saw how Fire-Eater must have treated my case. Regarding my way of looking at the world as though through a kaleidoscope as significant, he had adjudged me to be unstable, subject to great flare-ups and freezes. Like phosphorous, I could become suddenly enflamed and then fizzle out the next minute. At the same time he'd also taken my wish to control the kaleidoscope seriously. Although phosphoric, I had my feet on the ground and was, in homeopathic terms, also 'calcarcous'. In line with Hahnemann's system in which patients were classified according to the most suitable remedy, Fire-Eater's medical records had me filed under Calcarea phosphorica'. Generally speaking, once a person's remedy had been identified, it would remain the malady for the rest of their life.

The idea that each patient should have their own unique remedy was another remarkable contribution of homeopathy to medicine. Traditional medicine employed compounds made from dozens, if not hundreds, of elements each with its own function, not knowing whether these would clash, and in any case ignoring the eventual effect of the combination. Even now we often take combinations of drugs without knowing what effect the whole cocktail will have on us.

Hahnemann abandoned this practice of combining drugs and using only one remedy at a time. If the first failed to work, he would try another and so on, but always one at a time so that the symptoms they provoked could be studied. The fruit of this research, gathered from experiments made on healthy individuals using all manner of substances was collated in a volume called *Homeopathic Materia Medica* which still is the homeopath's bible.

The other major advantage of homeopathic remedies was, and still is, the absence of worrying side effects. The solutions are completely innocuous. Unlike allopathic medicines, all of which come with the warning to keep away from children, homeopathic remedies present no danger. A child who accidentally swallowed the whole flacon wouldn't have to have his stomach pumped.

Hahnemann's somewhat antiquated vision of humanity and its place in the world made him a New Age prophet before the New Age. Man was a composite, multidimensional entity made not only of matter but also intelligence and consciousness. 'The mind,' he wrote, 'is the keystone of man.' Disease therefore, being a biological phenomenon produced by an altered existence, should be regarded in terms of the person as a whole. 'It is the patient who is sick, not his organs.' Hippocrates had said something similar, as do today's so-called 'holistic' practitioners of 'alternative medicine'.

In Hahnemann's view the doctor's responsibility was much greater than simply restoring his patient's physical health. 'For man in his normal state,' he wrote in 1810, 'the spiritual life force animates the material body. This force governs the organism as a whole and maintains its various parts in magnificent harmony, such that the mind which inhabits it may make liberal use of this healthy, vital instrument to attain the higher goal of existence.' For Hahnemann, the body was much more than a machine.

Another important aspect of homeopathic medicine on which the remedies have been based has been its use in tiny doses or extremely diluted solutions. At its origin was a need to test actual poisons such as cyanide or arsenic, administered in infinitesimally small doses. Hahnemann discovered, however, that even in extremely diluted form the substances continued to stimulate the organism. Not only this, but the power of a solution actually increased or 'dynamized' as he put it, every time it was diluted and shaken the stipulated hundred times. From this observation, made in the last few years of his life, Hahnemann was to draw his final conclusions. The more diluted the remedy the more effective it became, even when the solution no longer contained any trace of the active substance.

It's because of this that homeopathy's detractors argue that in the end it is no more efficacious than a glass of water and it owes its successes entirely to the placebo effect.

A recent study published by the medical journal *The Lancet* showed that in an experiment carried out on two groups of patients, one treated with homeopathic products and the other with neutral substances, the group who received the homeopathic remedies had more successful cures, around two-and-a-half times more, than the group who received no treatment.

Nonetheless, traditional doctors continue to ignore all that happens beyond the confines of their tiny realms, adjudging it to be no more than the placebo effect, an expression they employ with a certain degree of contempt. By taking a completely neutral substance that they assume to be a highly effective medicine, a patient gets better. What more blatant proof could there be of the mind's power over matter? But this is a power the scientists are not yet ready or willing to accept, fearing the vortex it would open up beneath their feet which would obviously raise doubts about their whole conception of the human body.

How can one speak of the placebo effect, moreover, in the case of newborns or animals cured by homeopathy? There also exist homeopathic veterinarians. Fire-Eater told me about a number of them who worked with dairy farmers in his region. Apparently, to make good parmesan cheese, cow's milk must contain a form of subclinical mastitis, and so as not to kill this bacteria it is better to avoid using antibiotics in treating their diseases.

Following Hahnemann's death in 1843, homeopathy's fate became remarkably similar to that of today's alternative medicines.

People at that time were becoming increasingly disillusioned with traditional doctors whose methods they found barbaric. Their treatment of patients, as mere objects to be cut up, bled or pumped full of complicated medical concoctions, were regarded as dubious.

Homeopathy, like many other practices now becoming fashionable, appeared to offer a real alternative. These doctors were highly attentive to their patients and their remedies were neither aggressive nor destructive. The cholera epidemic that struck Europe in the early nineteenth century which lead to countless deaths contributed to homeopathy's burgeoning reputation when it became known that Hahnemann's disciples had an 80 per cent survival rate with their patients compared to the 50 per cent of traditional practitioners.

At the time of his death, Hahnemann was a celebrated figure with numerous disciples who could boast of having founded an entirely new medical praxis. It was one founded not on the diagnosis of an illness, but, much more complex and difficult, the diagnosis of the sufferer. It was a system that didn't limit itself to certain symptoms but which considered the entire symptomatology of the patient. In doing so, he had perhaps laid the foundations for the treatment of still unknown illnesses at the time, such as AIDS.

Initially it was the US which seemed to offer the most fertile terrain for homeopathy's development. American medicine had long been under the sway of figures like Benjamin Rush, a staunch supporter of surgical intervention, leeches and the administration of purgatives strong enough to fell a horse. He had little or no faith in the healing powers of nature and it had been said that he had shed more blood than an army general. Homeopathy represented a complete about-turn in medical thinking and for that reason alone it was highly popular. At the beginning of the twentieth century, it was being taught in twenty-two universities and practised in hundreds of hospitals. More than a thousand chemists stocked its remedies and around a fifth of American doctors had become specialists.

It had become so popular in the US that insurance companies were offering a 10 per cent discount to clients who made use of it. And yet, it was this very success that was the cause of homeopathy's decline. As traditional medical associations saw their members lose clients and pharmaceutical companies' profits plummeted – since remedies were cheap and were often prepared by homeopathic doctors themselves – they began to see homeopathy as a dangerous rival to be eliminated. The attacks were ferocious and relentless, and it wasn't long before homeopathy was relegated to the ranks of the non-sciences. University courses in homeopathy were shut down and its practitioners ostracized by the medical establishment. Much the same occurred in Europe, despite the fact that homeopathy had enjoyed the patronage of a number of esteemed figures from Mark Twain, Pope Pious X, Goethe, Dickens, Nathaniel Hawthorne and William James. Even Britain's royal family had frequented homeopathic doctors since 1830.

Another reason for homeopathy's decline in the West was the progress made by traditional medicine itself. The advent of the microscope and the resulting discovery of bacteria permitted doctors to investigate the cause of every single disease. Their attention was increasingly drawn to particular parts of the body rather than the whole. In India, by contrast, homeopathy which was brought to the subcontinent during the time of Hahnemann by German missionaries, was to have its own history and autonomous development. Gandhi described it as 'the most refined, least expensive and least violent way of treating patients' and advised the government to encourage its spread. Homeopathy was recognized as one of the official branches of medicine; 162 Indian universities currently offer courses, while some 150,000 doctors practise it throughout the country. It exists as the most accessible and affordable solution to the health problems of the poor.

In the West, where science has become a new form of religion, homeopathy has suffered greatly from its inability to scientifically demonstrate its efficacy. No chemist or biologist can prove that a cause-and-effect relation exists between the quantity of a substance present, or no longer present, in a remedy and its healing effects. And yet, why should this come as a surprise since it is precisely such a mechanistic, molecular interpretation of biological matter that homeopathy questions. How can we expect science and homeopathy to reach an understanding if they speak different languages?

During the post-war years this dialogue of the deaf was further complicated by the enormous progress made by scientific research. Medical practice accepted as an incontrovertible truth the notion that every illness was caused by an alteration in a molecular mechanism. This meant that the treatment had to modify or replace the molecule with pharmaceuticals introduced into a patient's body irrespective of their constitution. It was the exact opposite, in other words, of homeopathic thinking.

Homeopathy doesn't regard its remedies as a form of outside intervention, but as a stimulus for the body to heal itself from the inside. In its conception, it works from inside to out, higher to lower, and from the primary to the secondary organs, proceeding in the inverse direction to the disease's symptoms. The appropriate remedy, therefore, begins by dissolving the newest symptoms before working backwards through the others. For this reason, the reoccurrence of the patient's old symptoms is considered a good sign, as it means the treatment is working and the ultimate stage of the healing process has been reached.

This may sound fascinating, but from a traditionally scientific point of view it remains unacceptable. Doctors accustomed to normal medical practice find the homeopath's claim absurd that he can cure a patient simply with a solution containing a few drops of a dubious substance taken before bed. Such scientific doctors lump homeopathy as the kind of pseudo-therapeutic that runs from fakery to self-massage. Undoubtedly, homeopathy still suffers from its reputation as a kind of watered-down magic, or worse, witchcraft.

But what do we really know about water? Positivists as we are now, we find it absurd that water may preserve information about elements or substances it once contained, but which are no longer present. Yet are we any more aware of what remains in the wake of an event in the place it occurs? Or of what objects, substances or their respective molecules may be able to communicate? Despite all our claims of understanding and our contempt for everything unscientific, we go on making use of what serves our purpose without necessarily knowing how it works. Psychiatrists, for instance, have gone back to using electric shock to treat certain mental disorders despite the fact that they still don't know which of its effects are beneficial to the brain. And yet they apply it with the same faith as the housewives of old who spread their sheets out on the lawn during a full moon with the belief that it would make them whiter than washing powder. Likewise, Indians will take a glass of water in the morning that they've kept in a copper jug overnight, thinking this restores and balances the bodily constitution.

The first step in any form of knowledge is the awareness of not knowing. The most modern and open-minded branches of science have accepted, for example, the claims of chaos theory, or the butterfly effect, according to which an insignificant or minor event in one part of the world may have catastrophic repercussions in another. Scientists have even accepted that contrary to what they once believed, there is no such thing as objective observation, since not even the most inanimate object remains indifferent to being scientifically observed.

What we know about the world is only an infinitesimally small fraction of what we don't know. All things considered and notwithstanding the tremendous progress science has made, we are still surrounded by a whole range of phenomena that we don't understand any more than we know what they may mean or conceal.

Another area in which New York excelled is books. Whatever it was you wished to read, you would find it here and, more often than not, you would stumble across some fascinating volume you didn't even know existed. My favourite hunting grounds were the miles of book-laden shelves crammed inside the walls of Strand Bookstore on the corner of Twelfth and Broadway. There you could also procure half-price review copies of newly published titles as well as second-hand copies of out-of-print volumes.

One day, while looking around the shelves devoted to alternative medicine, I was struck by one particular book by an English biologist. According to the blurb the author, Rupert Sheldrake, after studying at Cambridge had ended up in India in the ashram of Bede Griffiths, a Benedictine friar, student of C.S. Lewis and author of several studies on the decline of modern man in the materialistic age and his possible spiritual redemption. It was in this ashram in Shantivanam in Tamil Nadu, that the young Sheldrake wrote his fascinating essay, 'A New Science of Life', combining his experiences and certainties as a scientist with the feelings and doubts of someone who has embarked on the path to spiritual enlightenment.

According to Sheldrake's thesis all living beings, and probably mineral life too, have managed to store facts in their memory relating to the experience of similar life forms without there having been any communication between them, at least not of a type familiar to us. In other words, when any member of a species begins to manifest a new form of behaviour or way of reacting to a given experience, this new action, provided it is repeated several times, will have an effect on the species as a whole, the implication being that all so-called immutable laws of nature are in the end simply changeable habits that depend on behaviours which have gone before and the frequency of their reinforcement.

Sheldrake recounts an experiment he carried out over a period of several years in London. Rats of different generations were placed in a tub with one exit route. This tub was then slowly filled with water. The rats, he discovered, gradually learnt how to escape. While as many as half the first generation drowned, the number was much fewer in the case of succeeding generations until a point was reached when all the rats were able to make it to safety.

But the astonishing thing was that when the experiment was repeated in Australia several years later, almost all of the rats of the first generation found their way out. It was almost as though the experience of the London rats had somehow been transmitted to them. The same phenomenon can be observed, Sheldrake says, when minerals and metals react to certain chemical processes. Crystals which became saline after a number of experiments in London did so immediately when the experiment was later repeated in another part of the world.

Sheldrake's conclusion is that a long-distance accumulation of experience must take place both temporally and spatially, a process which he calls 'morphic resonance'.

Could something similar occur in the case of water? Could it be that it somehow remembers the contact of a substance that has passed through it and retains the information? And yet to a more open-minded view of biology – one that doesn't see molecules as the only determining factor in the functioning of a living organism and accepts that other factors such as energy and bio-electromagnetic information may have an equally important role – such a theory would be more than plausible.

Recent experiments have shown how water treated with electromagnetic waves takes on properties that can be transferred to other biological systems. In other words, something is imprinted on the water in the same way it is on a piece of paper. This would go to show that water has a memory.

The homeopathic vision of medicine fascinated me, if for no other reason but that it offered an alternative approach to that of my expert New York fixers. I was now beginning to have serious doubts about these mechanistic methods.

Trudging back and forth between the hospital and my apartment, undergoing even more tests, undergoing anaesthetic for yet another operation, my thoughts increasingly turned to the memory of water, to Fire-Eater's remedies and the possibility of abandoning radiotherapy and its devastations. Back when I started chemo I'd had conflicting feelings about this country whose values

I didn't agree with, but to which I had nonetheless come hoping for salvation. The Americans had returned to torment me, now that I had glimpsed the possibility of an un-American alternative.

A culture's values are inevitably reflected in all its forms of expression. American medicine, without a doubt the most advanced on the planet, reflected an imperialistic aggression to which I was becoming more and more hostile. After the fall of the Berlin Wall and its victory in the cold war, the US no longer appeared to feel the slightest embarrassment about showing the world how much it thought of itself: humanity's finest achievement, the greatest power that had ever existed on earth. Such an extreme concentration of arrogance had produced a civilization without limits, which regarded its domination of others as a natural and divine right. And which it was not afraid of 'destroying to save', as a US general put it, after razing an entire village to the ground to liberate it from the Viet Cong.

Interventionist, aggressive, destructive – this was also the way of American medicine and has been since the time of the American Revolution. The vision of an apparently boundless country to be conquered in the gradual push to the Far West had given birth to a notion of medicine as ground to be conquered, regardless of the massacres committed along the way, whether the victims were Native Americans or patients. One article I read pointed out that as much as 40 per cent of all operations carried out in the US every year were pointless and that more Americans died under the knife each year than those killed in a single year of the Korean or Vietnam War.

On the other hand, though, it was thanks to American medicine after all and its perpetual willingness to try out new tools, techniques and drugs that a number of illnesses had plagued humanity for centuries were finally defeated, with a resultant lengthening of the average lifespan. But it had done so because of resources accumulated through its systematic exploitation of the rest of the world, resources of which I myself now had the advantage.

Such were the thoughts that churned around in my mind as I prepared to undergo radiotherapy. Having completed the tests and the trial simulations, I still had a weekend left to mull things over which, as it happened, was the very weekend Fire-Eater was holding his Boston seminar.

My relationship with America was in crisis, and Boston, with its memories of protest marches against the Vietnam War, was equally disappointing. Pretty, civilized and with a slight air of haughtiness, it nonetheless lacked genuine grandeur. Nothing about the city was in any way exhilarating or touching. I flew there on a small planes that departed hourly from New York, shunting back and forth between the two cities like the buses in Florence that ran from Porta Romana to Duomo. The landing approach took us over tracts of identical little houses whose snow-covered roofs afforded them some small allure. Everything was on time, slick and efficient. Only, if one looked closely, they would see that this efficiency was founded on what could only be described as a modern version of the caste system. As is the case of the untouchables in India, in the US it is the Blacks, Puerto Ricans and Latinos who handle all the 'dirty business'. From garbage to luggage, toilets to bus tickets, all working for a pittance of as little as seven dollars an hour, this work was mostly done by them. The odd thing is – and here, perhaps, lies the secret of the whole mechanism – they are all convinced that they are free citizens of the best of all possible worlds.

A rung above these untouchables is a quintessentially American caste: the losers. Though often white and fairly well educated, for some reason they can't make it in the no-holds-barred arena of all-out competition which, prizing aggression and ruthlessness, pushes them to the margins. Frustrated, somewhat pathetic, they too are victims. There were three taxi drivers who ferried me around on my first day in Boston and I believe they belonged to this caste, each writing the endless script of the American dream.

The seminar was being held in a hotel about forty miles outside of Boston. With its regulation synthetic carpets, fake wooden furniture and pointlessly enormous swimming pool, no doubt it had been plonked down on this particular plot of land because it was cheap, being out of the way.

Fire-Eater's seminar turned out to be mind-bending stuff, like landing on Mars and discovering that Martians were probably better-looking, more intelligent and warmer beings than most humans. It was one thing to read up on homeopathy in the few books I had managed to get hold of. It was quite another to find myself here among Fire-Eater's fifty-odd disciples who would huddle together in groups during the session breaks to discuss their patients and trade their mysterious remedies. Yet these Martians too, I soon discovered, were a part of a caste, of society's dropouts, aspiring to something higher than consumer society's humdrum material rewards.

The participants, many of them women, were all on the run from successful careers. Some were doctors, others psychologists. There was also a scattering of artists and ex-hippies. A number of the men had grown beards as though to mask their previous selves. I had the impression that for a lot of these people homeopathy was not just a profession, but a way of life. 'To help my patients,' a forty-something ex-librarian told me, 'I need to understand them and to do that I need to understand myself.' An ex-painter then said that for her, homeopathy was the most 'artistic' form of expression she had ever encountered. Many were of the opinion that homeopathy's growing popularity marked a crucial turning point in the history of humanity. All of them appeared to be highly motivated, each with their own sense of mission. In Fire-Eater's case, as he put it himself, this was to give homeopathy the scientific credibility it had lost and to restore dignity to the profession as a whole. 'We're doctors,' he repeated on several occasions, 'but if we want to be taken seriously, we've got a lot of work to do. We mustn't abandon our analogical method, which after all has been of service to humanity for thousands of years. At the same time, though, we have to accept that the scientific approach is not necessarily all that bad. We have to try and muster our forces.'

He remarked how homeopathy was currently going through a crucial phase in its evolution. Having become now fashionable, its reputation was being jeopardized by the claims and practices of myriad quacks. Equally dangerous were the big pharmaceutical companies whose former hostility towards homeopathy had gradually given way to a struggle for market position. It was producing remedies for every kind of illness which ran counter to one of homeopathy's fundamental principles: curing the patient rather than the disease.

Fire-Eater's plan involved a complete overhaul of homeopathic practice and training new practitioners to be recruited. *Homeopathic Materia Medica* was to be expanded and restructured in line with contemporary criteria. It was absurd, he said, to rely on tried-and-tested remedies when there were so many new ones readily available. The sea alone was a potential gold mine of substances homeopathy had so far made little use of. The aim of this seminar was to present a number of marine remedies that he had studied and successfully employed in treating his patients.

For the next three days, armed with an array of slides, diagrams and notes, Fire-Eater spoke of sepia ink, the shell of the *Homarus gammarus,* which is a European lobster, the sexual life of jellyfish and their poisons and, above all, starfish. The name 'starfish' was enough to set me dreaming. The ancients, believing they were actual stars fallen from the firmament, had given epileptics the task of fishing for them since they too were thought to be touched with something divine.

Fire-Eater's knowledge of these particular myths and literary texts lent his presentation a magical aura. He was keen to repeat how important it was when studying the effects of a certain remedy to also study the behaviour of the animal or plant from which the remedy had been extracted. 'Every creature,' he said, 'has its own way of surviving in its natural habitat, a system that would be reflected in the patient's reactions to the remedy.'

He described the *Homarus gammarus* as a unique species whose head had an organ similar to the human ear containing a small pebble-like orb that gave it a sense of balance. When the lobster grew, it shed its now highly restrictive shell. But doing so made it weak and defenceless and so it would bury itself in the sand until a new shell had time to grow. In the *Homarus gammarus*'s stomach is a liquid that makes milk coagulate and from which a remedy can be extracted to treat people allergic to dairy products. Fire-Eater went on to recount the experience of one of his *Homarus gammarus* patients. A boy of nine was brought to see him by his mother, a domineering physical exercise (PE) teacher and fitness fanatic. Her son, she said, was overweight and hated sports. Allergic to milk and all its by-products, he had frequent asthma attacks. She had decided to consult a homeopath because the boy had become dependent on a bronchodilator after seeing numerous allopathic doctors. Following a tonsillectomy, he had grown excessively fat and suffered from terrible bone aches. He loved prawns and ate them all the time even with fruit.

During the visit to Fire-Eater, his mother did all the talking, reading from a notebook where she had written down, point by point, everything she had to say to the consultant. The boy looked scared. Each time he opened his mouth to speak, his mother interrupted him. Nonetheless Fire-Eater managed to get him to talk about something his mother didn't know: his dreams, and it was there that he found the key to the problem. The boy told him he often dreamt of a huge shadow accompanying him everywhere he went. He wasn't afraid of the shadow, but regarded it as a guardian and protector. The remedy, Fire-Eater decided, was *Homarus gammarus*. But why?

In physical terms, Fire-Eater explained, the boy was allergic to dairy products. He was unable to rely on his mother for support, and to face the outside world he wanted to make himself fat, thinking this would give him a greater degree of consistency. He ate prawns out of an instinctive belief that this crustacean could help him. In the story of Peter Pan, it was the boy's shadow that protected him from the dark, not his mother. Hence, the prawns which the boy desired so much, and the doctor's further analogy with the lobster, whose shell could offer the protection of its own 'shadow'.

Fire-Eater prescribed the boy an extract of *Homarus gammarus* and after a few weeks he was no longer allergic to dairy products, began losing weight and was cured of his asthma attacks. Could this be called medicine? Why not? A doctor, after all, was so because of his ability to heal patients, not his degree certificate. And I had no reason to doubt the veracity of Fire-Eater's story. Could it be the power of suggestion or the placebo effect? It did not matter as long as it helped people get better.

For three days we listened to Fire-Eater's seemingly endless fund of stories about jellyfish, sepia patients and legends of other remedies from the deep. I found his descriptions of his various patients, their habits and mannerisms, their food preferences, even their tastes in music highly engaging. In the light of the strange correlations that Fire-Eater traced between people, animals and plants, maladies and remedies, the world seemed a more interesting place.

The audience hung on to his every word and I with them. Sometimes I would lose track of his reasoning, unable to see any logical connection between things, perhaps because there was none and to look for one was a mistake – as he himself was to remind us – but I was fascinated nonetheless. It was as though a gateway had been opened to an unknown world.

At the same time, however, stuck in my earthy Florentine rationality, a number of his fantastic tales escaped me completely. I thought I'd understood them, but in reality I understood nothing. Clearly, on such shaky grounds as this, woven from mystic echoes and portents, what counted more than the message was the messenger. With his combination of intelligence, learning, charisma and wit, Fire-Eater was just the man for the job. His was a convincing, sometimes simply dazzling, presence.

On the other hand he may just have been a particularly enchanting Pied Piper.

I fully enjoyed my three days on Mars, where the people, conversation and logic were refreshingly different. How strange this chain of events was, all that was happening to me or that I was causing to happen. In 1993, the advice of a fortune-teller had persuaded me to radically slow down the pace of my life and to begin looking at the world through a new set of eyes. Now it was cancer that had brought me to this seminar and to encounter all these strange people. Though my disease, or as Fire-Eater had called it, my unease, undoubtedly had its menacing side, it also had its positive, creative or one might even say luminous aspects. Through it I discovered homeopathy, a field I would have otherwise completely ignored. Perhaps there was something inside me that had a desire to grow, and now the thing that was growing was cancer … My God, I was already thinking like a homeopath!

The non-logic of homeopathy had somehow pulled me in, its topsy-turvy reasoning appealed to me. Perhaps this was what I had been looking for all along, even though sometimes the gaps in logic bothered me. I had the impression of seeing a circus acrobat twirling and spinning in the air between one trapeze and another until at some point he would fail to catch hold of the bar. My mind too would plunge into a void of incomprehension.

Yet, despite my enthusiasm for the delirium of homeopathic unreasoning, I knew I couldn't seriously consider giving up radiotherapy, no matter how magical the homeopathic remedy. Perhaps I myself was a victim of scientific prejudice, but that was how I'd been made, curious yet ultimately rational, an explorer minus the bold. Though I was certain Calcarea phosphorica had greatly contributed to improving my state of mind, I couldn't convince myself of its power to bring a halt to the production of haywire cells. And the more incredulous I became, the less the remedy would work.

Boarding the plane back to New York, I was happy to curl up once again in my New York burrow.

'Of every ten Americans,' the evening news declaimed, 'four will have cancer at some point in their lives.' It then went on to say that many people in the US are still dying of cancer because insurance companies refuse to cover the exorbitant costs of the newest treatments with the excuse that they are still 'at the experimental stage'. So too was the radiotherapy I was due to begin the next day: an experiment I knew was itself carcinogenic. But I had made my decision.

That night I had two dreams. In one I was flying high over a world that seemed so distant that it didn't interest me anymore. In the other I found myself walking along a beach where abandoned inert objects sprang to life as I passed them, each emitting a dim glow that assumed the form of a bird which then flew away to freedom.

I took all this flying to be a good omen.

IN THE SPIDER'S EMBRACE

'Are you ready, Mr Terzani?'

'Yes,' I answered.

At this point everyone present ran behind the protective shield of the armoured doors, while I lay bare-chested in the middle of a semi-darkened room, not moving a muscle and trying to breathe no more deeply than usual. I had to remain exactly as they had left me, immobilized, so that the black spots they had marked on my chest would coincide with the red light that beamed from the fiery eyes of the infernal machine overhead. It was a contraption I had dubbed the 'spider', feeling myself to be no more than an insignificant fly caught in her mysterious web. Her large round head observed me from above, then slowly began to move, never coming closer but pausing at my side, then moving again and positioning itself beneath me before coming full circle. With every shift in its orbit, it emitted an eerie hiss that would change to a whistling sound ending in a distant lament. And I, the prisoner at the centre of her magic web, was the target of a seduction that I had no desire to resist. I decided her embrace would be my salvation.

I had accepted this wager as I had done many times in the casinos of Macao where, after losing all evening at blackjack, I would turn to the roulette wheel and bet everything I had left but the return fare to Hong Kong. I would wait with barely suppressed trepidation to see where the skittering ball would come to rest.

Behind the darkened glass of the big porthole I could discern the figures of the nurses and technicians. They were following the spider's movements as she bombarded me for what seemed like an eternity with her murderous, precision-guided rays. I concentrated on my breathing, trying to keep it as even as possible, inhaling and exhaling so as to barely cause a ripple in my chest so that the bursts of radiation were sure to find their targets. I didn't feel pain. In fact I felt nothing – nothing, but a sensation of being at the mercy of a force, a real *presence* I had never previously encountered.

It's by now common knowledge that too many X-rays are bad for a person's health. The risk is that even a tiny dose of radiation might have the unfortunate side effect of causing some form of cancer. A chest X-ray, for example, emits three units of radiation – already a dangerous dose according to official estimates. In the course of our encounters – five per week over a period of six weeks – the spider would unleash upon me more than three thousand units.

The radiator, master and tamer of the spider, knew what he was doing: in my case as in the seventeen before mine, he had weighed the pros and cons of the bombardments and to limit the damage he relied upon the correct functioning of a special screen which minutely controlled the surface area and depth each charge of radiation was to reach. A three-dimensional computer-generated map showed the targeted organ; a second computer produced the model of the specific screen to be constructed in a heavy metal alloy and fixed to the spider's head, while another followed the trajectory and supervised the bombardment itself. Because my body had to remain as still as possible, a plaster half-shell had been fashioned for me in which I was laid out and immobilized.

The experimental treatment I had agreed to undergo consisted of destroying the concentrations of rogue cells in a specific body part without causing 'collateral damages' to use the euphemism military leaders commonly employ when describing the inadvertent destruction of a school or death of civilians during combat. In my case it was a question of bombarding one organ without affecting the surrounding organs.

My love affair with the spider was the most difficult period of the whole treatment. Maybe it was because I hadn't seen the inside of a hospital for two weeks, but I no longer breezed through its doors with the indifferent curiosity as before. The vivid-hued kingdom of homeopaths and their cornucopia of natural remedies made the white world of allopathic doctors and their medicines, radiation especially, look drably artificial by comparison. Though I never felt her touch, my sessions with the spider left me completely exhausted. I was sometimes unable to stand for more than a couple of minutes at a time. For several hours after the session I felt an odd burning sensation inside. Breathing too deeply gave me the impression of having inhaled a backdraft of flame, a feeling I'd never experienced before, but it was not a wholly unendurable one. With the help of conscious awareness I was able to douse it in a stream of reflection and soon had the blaze under control. Though the accompanying brochure had tried to reassure me that radiation wouldn't make me radioactive, in some ways I felt the spider had done me more violence than chemo. It had sucked out my will to live. I went out less, looked around me less. More and more focused on myself, I was less than where I ever wanted to be: on top of things.

It is all a matter of perspective. Each time the world seems to shrink, our own worries and concerns grow correspondingly larger. Our death seems a horrible, unthinkable thing. But if we are able to expand our vision and see the world in its magnificent totality, however miserable our personal situation, it becomes a part of that vastness, the unending yet entirely natural fever and fret of humanity.

I saw this every time I turned on the TV or went to the cinema. If the movie was particularly dumb, I became depressed and the pain in my stomach seemed unbearable. But if I happened to see a film that I enjoyed, like the restored version of Fellini's *Nights of Cabiria*, all that was happening to me seemed an expression of that 'great and terrible world' which the old Tibetan monk describes to Kipling's *Kim*: an episode from a fine story in which I was a mere minor character.

This is why art, the real art that comes from the soul, can be such an important force in our lives. Art consoles and unburdens us; it points us in the right direction. One might say it even heals us. We are not simply what we eat or the air we breathe, but we are the stories we have heard, the childhood fairy tales that have lulled us to sleep, the books we have read, the music we have enjoyed, the emotions that have stirred in us because of a painting, a statue or a poem.

One day when the spider had given me even more of a beating than usual, I tried to lift my spirits with a visit to the Metropolitan Museum of Art. I soon realized that despite all the various mutations I had undergone, one thing had been left intact: the loathing I had for museums, especially huge ones like the Met. It was all too much: too many paintings, too many people, too many statues, too much bustle, too many souvenir shops, guards, lights, postcards, pens, T-shirts. The Met was to art what

Balducci's, downtown, was to food. In both places you could find specialities from every corner of the globe. Renaissance paintings and pastas of various shapes, colours and sizes; Greek sculpture and Mughal miniatures and different kinds of cheese, olives and smoked salmon, you could find everything. Assailed suddenly by a cloying feeling of indigestion, I made for the exit.

The only museums I could stomach were the smaller, more human establishments such as the Mauritshuis in Ajax or the Lahore Museum, or the one in Peshawar. It was enough to fill my day with an inexplicable joy.

I added the Met to the list of places I found depressing. Luckily at the Paris, the rep cinema that was close to where I lived, a complete retrospective of the films of the Merchant-Ivory Productions was about to begin. I recalled how much I had enjoyed some of the ones set in India. The retrospective was my salvation. I watched those films with a mixture of pleasure and relief and my spirits rose and remained risen. The prospect of returning to the spider disturbed me less and less and I began to think of ways to extricate myself from the clasp of its deadly rays.

In my apartment was an old cardboard box I'd had for years into which I threw everything I thought I might need one day for a certain journey, and written on it was the following verse:

Healing comes from plants
and from the knife
from a righteous, holy man
and from the mantra that is sung.

The phrase dated from the sixth century BC when, in Iran, there lived a character whose life we know little of. His name was Zarathustra and he founded, or perhaps merely revived, a religion centred on fire: fire that purified yet remained forever pure. It was a fire that was impartial, for the heat it provided was the same for a wise man and a fool. The fire gave light, bestowed life, and in reducing all to ashes was a reminder to man of the impermanence of the whole creation. And that it was to destroy most of Zarathustra's own writings. The original manuscripts of these sacred texts disappeared in 330 BC when Alexander the Macedonian – who despite his misdeeds is still called 'the Great' – razed the library of Persepolis and all its collections to the ground. What remained was lost in the seventh century AD when the Arabs, who were recent converts to the Prophet Muhammad's Islam, put Persia to fire and sword, burnt its temples and forced the entire population to become Muslim, systematically erasing every last trace of the tolerant fire religion.

Of Zarathustra and Zoroastrianism, all that survived was what had been committed to memory by a few of the faithful who had escaped the slaughter along with what Islam had been unable to destroy, such as the maxim engraved on the rocks of a remote mountain range that eventually found its way to my box of odds and ends. Yet, this alone was enough for Zoroastrianism, with its Temples of Fire and Towers of Silence to survive as the official religion for thousands of people: the Parsis. Today the largest existing Parsi community live in Bombay (now Mumbai), in a country where those persecuted for their religion – most recently Tibetan Buddhists – have always found sanctuary.

Shortly after moving from Bangkok to Delhi, I became curious about the Parsis and went in search of them, at which point the phrase appeared on the box like a viaticum. I couldn't possibly have imagined then that one day I would have passed through all it suggested to heal myself. At that time I was interested only in plants, or rather the plant of plants: the mythical one, which according to various legends, contained the elixir of life.

People of all epochs, looking upon nature as a chest of hidden treasures, had ventured into deep forests or scaled the face of a mountain in search of some magic flower, root or grass that would save them from sickness, old age and death. Back then, I was planning to retrace such journeys in a more modern key and write a book about the search for something that in all probability didn't exist. Or perhaps it did, this salvation from drug addiction. I got the idea from a bizarre book published in Britain in 1935 written by James S. Lee, no doubt a pseudonym. The book in question, *The Underworld of the East,* was the story of the eighteen event-filled years the author spent working for the British government as an engineer in the coal mines of China, India and the Malay Archipelago at the turn of the nineteenth century. The story remarkable as the author accounted how, after ruining his health by becoming addicted to every drug from morphine to opium to cocaine and hashish, he eventually managed to find a way out. One evening, when Lee was staying in a small settlement in the jungles of Sumatra, a sampan, a kind of small boat, with several Malaysians aboard stopped at the water's edge by his wooden veranda. The men, who were from the Island's interiors, wanted to barter a sheaf of roots and grass for some opium. It was an offer Lee accepted, for among the cluster of plants was one he had never seen before: a shrub with small buds full of seeds.

Lee boiled the seeds in water and left the infusion to evaporate until all that remained was a deposit of white powder, which he added to the food of the rats that shared his home as an experiment. Noticing that the animals survived, he decided to try it on himself. The results were surprising. The white powder from the seeds seemed to cancel out the effects of all the various drugs he had taken, giving him instead a great feeling of vitality, both mental and physical.

It was because of that powder that Lee could cure his addiction and rid himself of the syringes, lamps, pipes and other paraphernalia that had sustained him for years. He had discovered something miraculous. He called this the elixir of life.

Whether or not Lee's tale was true was impossible to say. Yet the idea that it might be fascinated me. So many young kids would be able to haul themselves out of the black hole of drug addiction if somewhere on the island of Sumatra that plant really did exist! My plan was to go looking for it, using Lee's descriptions of the area as a guide. Who knew where that thread might have taken me?

As for Lee himself, his life remained a mystery. I wrote to the original publishers of his book for information about him but received no reply. It was as though for some reason they no longer wanted to have anything to do with the story. Meanwhile, the second volume of Lee's promised memoirs proved impossible to find. Perhaps it had never been published. And yet he couldn't have been a complete invention. His account of how, after contracting malaria in a remote corner in the Indian state of Assam, he was given his first injection of morphine, and how, becoming addicted, he moved on to cocaine and other substances, sounded wholly convincing. His disillusionment with the epoch too had the ring of authenticity. Having to descend into the earth's viscera where he saw countless workers killed by gas explosions or collapsing tunnels, Lee began to develop a world view that today we would no doubt call 'New Age'. In his view, anticipating the Gaia theory, the earth was a complex living organism for which human greed had no respect. All they did, on the contrary, was inflict the most terrible wounds upon her. And the earth, to defend herself, replied by unleashing on man her arsenal of diseases, earthquakes, droughts, floods, famine, explosions, typhoons and fires.

Man, Lee stated, would make great progress with his science, invent synthetic foods, live in artificially heated and ventilated underground cities, dig deeper and deeper into the earth in search of an energy source to replace the slowly dying sun. Yet, however much human beings tried to prolong their lives using every means at their disposal, in the end they would lose their battle. Despite the rhetoric, there was something truly sincere in Lee's *ante litteram* environmentalism. Could he possibly have lied about his 'miraculous' plant?

What intrigued me more was the response I got from an Italian chemist and plant specialist to whom I had sent a photocopy of Lee's book, asking if he was aware of the existence of such a plant. Yes, he said, it might be the Mitragyna plant: a small tree whose fruit resembled small melons and contained dark seeds. There existed twelve known species. An American scientist named Shellard, who had studied them in the 1970s, discovered that they contained strange alkaloids capable of producing the effects Lee had described. 'What surprises me,' the chemist wrote to me in conclusion, 'is that no pharmaceutical company has made use of this research yet and I have no idea why this is.' Bingo! That teasing 'why' provided the perfect beginning for a story, the first step in my intended journey.

We exchanged a few more emails, all of which ended up in the cardboard box together with various notes, newspaper clippings and old maps of Sumatra I had collected. I was deeply drawn to the idea of investigating to what extent Zarathustra and James Lee had been right about the healing powers of plants and why their findings had either been forgotten or deliberately hushed up.

But plants were obviously the first thing I thought of when I set out to find, if not a cure, at least a natural way to cleanse myself of the various poisons that the unnatural cures of modern science had inflicted upon me.

One evening, nearing the end of my course in Tarot reading at the Open Centre, I happened to see a flyer on the noticeboard for a course that was being held by a famous herbalist. Just what I needed, I thought. I called the woman up, briefly explained my situation and fixed an appointment. And so, I found myself setting off one morning, not for Sumatra, but for New Jersey.

It was raining and New York was as sad as a city can be in the rain. The umbrella-less did their best to shrink into themselves in the vain hope of avoiding a soaking, an unpleasant prospect since here there was no smell of water hitting dry earth, the joy that nature accompanies during the season's first rain. It was a perfect day to see how limited and partial my own impression of life in New York was, viewed from the privileged, cosseted perspective of my observatory in the heart of Manhattan.

The huge sanitized space of the bus station alone, with its crowds of lone, expectant passengers stooped over plastic plates heaped with equally plastic food, was depressing enough. So many people and yet such a vast hush, save for the sudden metallic blurt of tannoy announcements.

Passing through the darkness of Lincoln Tunnel was like crossing a border. Out of its mouth was another America, an unending realm of parking lots, prefabricated houses, chain restaurants and blank-faced motels, and all of it with the air of something provisional, semi-disposable, built to collapse after only one season.

Everywhere I looked, there were American flags: enormous, billowing outside gas stations, post offices and fire stations. There were slightly more modest versions at the windows of houses and on garden flagstaffs.

Even the bus driver, a genial fellow whose bulk belied his somewhat robotic mannerisms, had a tiny American flag sewn on the sleeve of his neatly pressed white shirt. Feeling slightly sleepy, I asked him to wake me up when we reached New Jersey.

I fell asleep thinking of herbs and of how my grandparents, who came from farming families, had been quite familiar with nature's healing properties. At the first sign of a stomach-ache, cold or diarrhoea someone would be off to the fields, returning with some herb or other and the words, 'Boil this and drink it tonight before going to bed.' Nature was always the first doctor we consulted. All that was needed was to be able to recognize leaves, flowers, seeds or rind, knowledge I was to see vanish before my eyes during my own lifetime. My mother refused the poultice my grandmother wanted to spread on my chest when I had a cough, preferring to go to the chemist's for a more modern, synthetic remedy. Being more expensive, there was a guarantee, or so she reckoned, of its superior effectiveness.

All ancient civilizations believed that aside from her obvious bounty, there was something rare, precious and miraculous hidden in nature. For the Chinese, before it was turned into an artificially grown industrial product, it was ginseng, the kind they regarded as the earth's essence in human form, like the fairies of legend to whom it did indeed bear a remarkable resemblance and which grew only on the highest peaks. It became a cure for all kinds of maladies, ageing especially. For the Indians, it was soma, the herb of immortality mentioned in the Vedas. It was a creeper that supposedly grew exclusively in the Himalayas above four thousand metres. By eating it the yogi claimed they could prolong their lives to up to two hundred years. Today it can no longer be found as though the knowledge of its whereabouts, if ever there was such knowledge, had also disappeared.

But now do we even know the reason why the mistletoe has for centuries been considered a plant of good omen, so much so that druids of ancient times would harvest it only with a golden scythe? Or why it became a part of the folklore of numerous cultures as a mysterious and sacred plant with the power to cure countless maladies? No. And yet we continue to hang a sprig of this strange parasite, which attaches itself to the tops of oak, pine and birch trees, whose lymph keeps it evergreen while the leaves drop off and die, above the door at Christmas as a lucky charm.

As a plant, the mistletoe serves no purpose. Neither its wood nor its leaves can be used for anything and its berries have no special properties. But in winter these same berries provide vital sustenance for forest birds. In Germany, meanwhile, a clinic has recently been opened where certain forms of cancer are treated with an extract from the mistletoe berry.

The likes of Erich von Däniken may have been right in their hypothesis that we human beings were once colonized by a civilization of space-ranging gods who, after a brief sojourn on earth and disappointed by our inability to make use of their vast stores of knowledge and wisdom, harrumphed and went back to their remote corner of the universe while we, so the story goes, forgot they had ever been here.

The bus driver didn't forget to wake me up. My head was still buzzing with the thought of those astronaut gods. I found myself on the main street of a small town that appeared as though it had been hastily assembled the night before to shoot a scene for a horror movie. Perhaps the film was being shot in that very moment, judging by the gaunt, shabbily dressed women shuffling up and down the sidewalks. Though it was only ten in the morning, a few were already drunk. The houses were all small, single-floored, wooden box-like structures, most of them abandoned, some with 'For Sale' signs on the door. On the two-hundred-metre stretch between the bus stop and the herbalist's studio, I saw a holistic health centre, a yoga and meditation centre and a chiropractor's studio. My herbalist lived in an old building made of rotting wood. Since I was early for my appointment, I sat on a plastic chair on the veranda, watching the rain cascade from the roof on to the carpet. From behind the door I could hear the herbalist concluding her session with the previous patient, explaining the importance of 'karmic relationships' and how these had changed her life. For years I had been planning an expedition to go looking for the elixir of life, and now, instead of hacking my way through the jungles of Sumatra, here I was under the leaky roof of some herbalist's studio in a working-class neighbourhood of New Jersey. Our encounter was pleasantly futile. She was an attractive woman in her forties, a fresh-faced girl-next-door type ceding to incipient obesity beneath her long, droopy skirt. Greeting me affectionately, she asked me to sit on the floor while she herself sat in the lotus position on a rug. She lit a stick of incense – it was for me, she said – on a low altar-like structure that held a small wooden Buddha. Her white-painted study was cluttered with bric-a-brac culled from various New Age shops and stalls. Though sitting on the floor was perfectly natural for me – I'd been reading and writing that way for years – I began to wonder how her other patients managed. She immediately launched into a feminist spiel: in the past, anyone with the slightest knowledge of the natural world had been viewed with suspicion. Many women who had healed people with herbs had been accused of witchcraft and burnt at the stake. Changing gear, she then moved on to a diatribe against modernity: religious and scientific orthodoxy together had suppressed all animist faiths and in doing so severed our ties with the world around us.

'And it's because of this that we've lost touch with the intuitive part of ourselves and with nature and all its powers. What I want, she told me, with the tone of someone explaining a vocation, 'is to rediscover all this and bring it back to life. I see plants as a way of restoring contact with our divine natures.'

She was a wonderfully charming woman and, as I was familiar with the territory, I agreed with most of what she'd said. But it was clear that my trip had been in vain. What I was looking for couldn't be found in words, however fine or noble or sincerely expressed they were. I guessed she knew this too, but we went on nonetheless, speaking about cancer, the immune system and the suggestions she had. Like Fire-Eater, she prescribed daily doses of chlorophyll along with two Chinese herbal extracts and a species of marine algae that I would have to order from New Hampshire. She advised me to drink lots of carrot juice and eat mountains of mushrooms, particularly shiitake mushrooms. Then, more embarrassed than I was by the absurdity of the situation, she said that the most important element of her treatment was the waves of positive energy she would send to me when I was far away. Trying to suppress my laughter and not wishing to offend the woman, I gave her a much greater sum of payment than she had asked for.

The bus driver on the journey back home was a beautiful black girl, again with an American flag on her sleeve. The passengers sat still, like sedated zombies, and I among them.

The road from the bus station in New Jersey to my burrow wasn't exactly the ideal route for anyone wanting to reconcile himself with the United States. The neighbourhood it passed through with its rows of below-bargain basement clothes stores, nighthawk cafes and 'adults-only' porn emporiums could only be described as ugly. To shake off its grimy clasp, I veered east towards Fifth Avenue where suddenly everything was just elegant boutiques, bookshops, chic bistros and drugstores. But as is said, my eyes seemed to notice only the shadow cast by every lamp.

While I was waiting for a traffic light to change to green, I was struck by a scene taking place in the mezzanine of the building across the road from me. Framed in large windows, dozens of men and women were running, but without actually going anywhere. Purple-faced and dripping with sweat they faced the street. Though it wasn't the first time I'd seen a fitness centre, the image of all these young bodies who had trooped in straight from the office to work off their frustration and fat seemed to sum up the entire logic of this civilization: running and running and going precisely nowhere.

I felt like one of the Tibetans in a story the Dalai Lama's brother once recounted to me. The year was 1950. A delegation of monks and functionaries who had never set foot outside of Tibet had been invited to London to discuss what Britain could do for their country. Coming from a land that though in many ways extraordinary, it was still poor, primitive even, the monks were accustomed to vast empty spaces with a variegated natural habitat, while they themselves were equally colourful in their vivid cassocks and hats. Finding themselves in the underground Tube one day, they saw a sight that astonished them: hundreds of people crammed on to the platforms, running to catch a departing train, or reading newspapers as they glided up and down the moving stairways. And through this commotion, no one spoke a word to his or her neighbour, no one smiled. The leader of the Tibetan contingent, his face stricken with compassion, turned to their English guide and said, 'What can we do for you?'

Certainly, Tibetans like those monks no longer exist. Many Tibetans too now dream of living the way people do in London. Nonetheless, the question remains: who is the more primitive?

With the herbalist's prescription in my pocket I went into a vitamin shop, hoping to find some of the items she had recommended. Among the endless rows of transparent plastic containers every possible combination of vitamins, along with extracts of garlic, onion and Gingko, the first thing I saw was a homeopathic kit: an attractively packaged box containing five rows of flacons each colourfully labelled with the name of the remedy in question. Including my own! But seeing this my heart sank. 'My' remedy had been worth something on account of the chain of people and events by which I had arrived at it, because of a drive through a fog-bound plain, the Fellinian chemist who had stayed open late waiting for me. Here, in its package with meticulously detailed instructions printed on the box, the remedy was completely worthless. Just like everything else: the qigong of Master Hu, the Open Centre and its Kundalini Yoga, the meditation courses in New Jersey, even my comely witch with her bouquet of herbs. Everything I saw around me somehow seemed perverse.

At the height of the Fiftieth street I noticed a man, a little younger than myself. Dishevelled and with a slightly sickly air, obviously visiting New York, he posed in front of a Vietnamese restaurant as his wife clicked a picture. Imagining this photo placed next to an older one, taken probably when he was a soldier in Vietnam, I had the sudden urge to hug this man with whom I might have at least something in common: nostalgia for Saigon, the smell of rotting vegetables, a time when our lives were rawer, more basic.

Weeks passed which blurred into months until the day arrived that, by way of life's strange paradoxes, cancer patients fear the most: their last day as a patient. For many it was the fear of relapse, but for me it was the fear of returning to a state before the illness.

'We've done all we can,' Doctor Goodluck said to me with the confident smile of a mechanic handing back the keys of the car he's just repaired. 'You can go back to your normal life now, and come back for a check-up in three months.'

A normal life? A normal life was the last thing I wanted. Go back to the way things were, slip back into that rigmarole of interviews, ambassadorial dinners, articles to write, conversations as tiresome and pointless as the one you might have, stuck in an elevator with someone for thirty floors when it would have been better to take the stairs? No. No more conversations like this for me.

If this was the reason they'd fixed me up, they needn't have bothered, especially as I was now convinced that my cancer was in some way connected to the life I'd led before and that the time had come to get a new one. I had a different life now to go with this different body, its enormous hernia stabbing at my belly that the junior surgeon had hastily stitched up after the operation, its sparse clumps of hair and its way of dragging itself around in amphibious slow motion. Never had I been so aware of my mortality. I thought and felt differently, my rapport with the rest of the world was different.

All of this was evident to me, but it wasn't so for others. The real battle for me now wasn't chemo or radiotherapy, but the desire I had to change my life. Around the sick there inevitably gathers a benevolent conspiracy of well-wishers who try to convince them that their illness is a temporary state, that the most desirable course is a return to the normality that preceded it. Doctors, family, close friends: the conspiracy is universal, all saying in their own way, 'Come on, cheer up. You'll see, everything will be just as it was before.'

So on the evening I bade farewell to the hospital, I found myself the guest of Kofi Annan, then Secretary General of the United Nations, and his wife. An old friend of mine who was writing a book about Annan had spoken to him about me, and as a surprise had asked him to invite me to dinner to celebrate my 'return to normality', an invitation I couldn't very well refuse. It turned out to be an extremely pleasant evening and Annan and his wife made warm and genial hosts. Only when I was leaving their Upper East Side apartment did I realize that I really was no longer my old journalist self. Maybe it was because I'd been living in silence for so long, but rather than ask him for his opinion on any matter, I had done most of the talking, repeating the same point over and over again from every possible angle.

I told him that it was his responsibility to place morality before politics or economics; it was up to him to use his uniquely privileged platform to say the things that everyone was waiting to hear, to speak from the heart and not merely from the head. The world could not go on being governed solely by greed and self-interest. We were responsible for more, something higher than our own families, companies or nations. Not only was he in a position to say these things, but he had all the right credentials to do so: his background, his origins, the colour of his skin, the fact that he would not have to stand for re-election. It was a great opportunity for the world, especially now when humanity was in such dire need of someone of his stature. It was up to him now.

Discovering that we were both born in the year of the tiger and we would both soon be turning sixty, he agreed that we had reached a moment in our lives when we could step out of the fray and regard the world from a higher vantage point, the moment when a man, whatever his position, must do what is right and not simply what suits him. We even spoke of death and I asked him if 'afterwards' we would wish to be remembered for our prudence. With an amused chuckle, as though letting me in on a secret, he added that prudence was what all his advisers were constantly recommending as the best course of action.

'Then why don't you just fire the lot of them?' I jokingly asked.

If he thought I was mad, he didn't show it. To be honest, I had a sneaking suspicion he considered this an excellent idea. As I walked home it continued to drizzle, but I didn't mind. I felt good in my new skin.

THREE

INDIA

RETURN TO THE SOURCE

Those who love India will know, they don't know exactly why they love it. It's dirty, poor, infected, sometimes thieving and lying, frequently malodorous, corrupt, merciless and indifferent. And yet, once you have met it you cannot live without it. To be away from it is to suffer. But such is love: instinctive, inexplicable and disinterested.

When you're in love you hear no reason, you have no fear, you can do anything. You feel you can embrace the whole world and that the world returns your embrace. India, unless you're immediately repulsed by it, induces this exaltation. It makes you feel like a part of Creation. You never feel alone there, never completely isolated. And this is India's peculiar charm.

Several thousand years ago, India's wise men, the rishis – literally 'those who can see' – had the intuition that all of life was one and it was the experience of this revelation, religiously renewed by every generation , that formed the kernel of India's great contribution to human civilization and the development of conscious awareness. Each and every life was simply one of the myriad forms composing a great whole that was life itself. To most Indians, such a philosophy is second nature, part of the very air one breathes in the country. Just being there gives the visitor an unconscious affinity with that ancient wisdom. Seemingly without effort, you find yourself attuned to a panoply of new sounds and dimensions of existence. You not only feel differently there, but you think differently too. Perhaps this is because Indians don't conceive time as a straight line but as a circle. There, the past, present and future mean something different to what they do in the West; progress is not regarded as humanity's ultimate aim, since all will be repeated. To the Indians the notion of forging ahead is a mere illusion. Perhaps this is because it doesn't believe that the 'ultimate reality' is that of the senses. India is able to instil a sense of detachment in even the most sceptical visitor. This detachment is one of the country's most unusual aspects: it somehow makes what is most terrible about the country seem acceptable. It is acceptable, because that's the way life is: both marvellous and cruel. And since life is inseparable from death, there is no pleasure without pain, no happiness without suffering. Nowhere else in the world will you find such a dramatic and shameless coexistence of opposites – beauty and monstrosity, fabulous wealth and dire poverty. This vision of the inevitable duality of existence was what incited the rishis to look for its hidden meaning, the meaning of duality, how and why it should be kept so. Today India is still a spiritual catalyst for those who venture there. You notice the change as soon as you arrive, beginning with a sudden feeling of being at peace with everything and everyone. In India, I had no need of any 'remedy' to get back my equilibrium. Though it existed in nothing specific, the remedy was all around me, in every detail of my surroundings.

'India is a life-shortening experience,' Dieter Ludwig, the photographer, had warned me when I arrived in Delhi many years ago. 'But,' he keenly added, 'it's also an experience that gives life meaning.'

An old friend of mine, Dieter had organized a welcoming party to introduce me to some colleagues who lived in the city. In his own way he put me on my guard, but equally congratulated me for deciding to write the closing act of my career as a journalist in a place where such careers normally began. From his barsati apartment, the terrace of which was a jungle of plants that Dieter nursed and talked to as though they were family, one could see the cupola of an old Mughal tomb silhouetted against the twilight, a vision whose beauty seemed expressly designed to console the miserable crowds thronging around its base. I had met Dieter in Indo-China during the war and he had been far ahead of me in his quest for the meaning of life.

After several months in the sanitized haven of New York, when I decided to return to Delhi, the first thing I did was pay him a call. Chemotherapied, operated and irradiated as I was, I now had to be even more careful to avoid falling ill. I was to stick rigorously to the litany of tried-and-tested rules every prudent visitor to India recites to himself: never drink water that hasn't been boiled and never eat raw vegetables or anything fried in oil of dubious provenance. I was weak and vulnerable to be sure, but if I had to be careful about what I ate and drank, my spirit that sought sustenance other than mere food and drink took wing. After having spent so much time in the US, going back to Delhi was like winning back a lost love. Coming from a world of blessed reason, efficient and perfectly organized in every way, I suddenly found myself in one where reason gave way to absurdity, sometimes to insanity. It was a world where all was precarious, where the only certainty was a universal uncertainty.

In India, nothing can be taken for granted. Telephone lines are nearly always dead, power cuts can last for several hours, the fax breaks down every five seconds because of a surge or loss of electricity. But in India one accepts, one adapts since such things have already occurred countless times before, always in the same way, and will continue to do so for a long time. Whatever happens, India remains the same, and this in itself is soothing knowledge. It makes you realize that you are, after all, just a mortal human, one of the innumerable extras in an endless, absurd spectacle that only we in the West have the presumption to think we can direct and decide how it should end.

Having spent the last few months in a luxury apartment building in the heart of Manhattan, complete with liveried doorman, automatic laundry and a Mr Fix-it on call twenty-four hours to mend whatever needed mending, I now found myself in a dilapidated old residential block at the entrance to which one of the many cows grazing peacefully amid the traffic had decided to set up its shed.

As in New York, here too were dogs, though not at all the well-groomed pure-breds I would see in Central Park, each with its retractable leash and metal tag, some with their collars embossed with the owner's name, address and telephone number. Here, there were lean, raw-boned mongrels that roamed in packs. My neighbour, Bhim Devvarma, looked after them. Approximately my age, he was a warm-hearted man of minute stature and nephew to the Maharaja of Kuchlehar. He had grown up in a palace surrounded by elephants and now, every morning, he would set off from his modest apartment accompanied by his servant-cum-cook to feed the hundreds of dogs that prowled around our neighbourhood. Come rain or shine, every morning he would get into his old banger to feed these dogs. In his marvellous documentary on India, Roberto Rossellini showed how in the countryside, relationships between man and beast are almost symbiotic. Even in the major cities where a natural awareness persists, little has changed. The human, animal and vegetable kingdoms are simply aspects of the same whole, different stages in a single existence.

Though I was still suffering from the effects of jetlag, my internal alarm woke me up promptly at dawn. My first morning there, I decided to go back to Lodhi Gardens, one of Delhi's finest parks, which was about a kilometre from my flat. For years I had gone jogging there, long, gruelling runs that left me drenched in sweat. Now I could only walk, but it was just as lovely. Everything was as I had left it: the vultures perched on the cupola of a small abandoned mosque, yoga devotees with their little mats spread out on the grass, people in a circle with their arms raised, splitting their sides laughing – a highly therapeutic exercise, some say, and in any case an excellent way to start the day. As usual, a mixed horde of crows, pigeons, parrots and even squirrels were fighting over the bread crusts some passers-by had scattered on the ruined tombs. There was still the scrawny old man with the white beard I had seen the last time who roved the grass plains drawing handfuls of flower and sugar from a cloth bag to sprinkle around mysterious holes in the ground. I even saw him feeding ants, something that could only happen in India! Anywhere else the response to everything would have been to exterminate the ants, a massacre with fire, DDT and boiling water being the most popular methods. In India, by contrast, people do unto ants what Lakshmana, one of the heroes of the Ramayana did for Sita, his sister-in-law, to protect her when he had to leave one day. Around her hut, he traced a line with the point of his bow, saying to her, 'This line you must never cross.' The Indians call it the Line of Lakshmana, or the Lakshmanarekha.

Everything in India usually refers to a myth or legend where Indians appear to feel much more at home than in what they do in the everyday world. Sometimes, the reference is to something as simple as ordinary common sense. One has no need to imagine ants as the reincarnation of a grandfather or uncle to understand that they are as much a part of creation as we are. So why exterminate them? Here too lies an important aspect of India.

What is inconceivable to Indians is the notion that humans are superior to animals and have the right to exploit and kill them at leisure. If they choose to exploit it for any reason, they must give something in return or at least offer thanks to the gods who created them. People are a part of nature themselves; they depend on it for their existence and as the Indians know well, the frog doesn't drink the water of the pond it lives in.

We in the West too are beginning to realize there is something deeply wrong in the way we behave towards the natural world, to the point where we sometimes have the impression that our much vaunted civilization, founded on scientific reason and domination of the environment, has led us up a blind alley. Nevertheless, we continue to hold on to the belief that the same scientific reason will help us find a way out. So we continue chopping down forests, polluting rivers, drying up lakes, depopulating the oceans, breeding and slaughtering animals of every species because in this way, the economists say, we generate well-being. And it is under this illusion that well-being means happiness that we invest all our energies in consumption, as though life were an unending Roman banquet at which one eats and then vomits so as to go on eating.

Surprisingly, we do it as if it were the most natural thing in the world, convinced we are acting within our rights. We regard ourselves as a separate entity, charged up with the notion of our own ingenuity, talents and above all, freedom. And yet it is exactly this feeling of freedom and disconnection from the rest of the world that causes the solitude and sadness in our lives. Concerned solely with our limited personal sphere, we are unable to feel the grandeur of the whole of which we are a part. The rishis would say we have lost our 'connection with the cosmos' that we have become like kupamanduk, the frog protagonist of an old Indian folk tale.

One day, in a small well where a frog had lived all its life came leaping and splashing another frog who claimed he was from the ocean.

'The ocean? What is the ocean?' the frog from the well asked.

'A big place, enormous and vast,' said the newcomer.

'How big?'

'Hugely, immensely, gigantically big.'

With its leg the frog in the well traced a circle on the surface of the water. 'This big?' it asked.

'No. Infinitely, colossally, prodigiously bigger.'

The frog in the well traced a larger circle. 'This big?' it asked again.

'Massively, exceedingly, superabundantly bigger.'

At this point, the bemused frog in the well traced a circle as large as the well. That was all of the world it knew.

'No,' said the frog from the ocean. 'Much, much, much bigger.'

'Liar!' yelled the kupamanduk at the other frog, whom it refused to speak another word to.

Indians believe they are free, if not from the cosmic spider's web in which we are all enmeshed, at least to freely think for themselves. Having lived in China for many years where the people still seemed to believe that having a single thought of their own was punishable by death, the Indians' mental liberty came as a relief.

And yet there was nothing particularly new in this. Perhaps what was regarded as true power in India was never of the short-lived, temporal variety held by kings or warriors but was that of the sages. No other culture had such a store of tales of wise men or hermits sought out in their forest retreats by humble kings wishing to pay homage or ask their advice. Only in Indian culture, no matter how rich and powerful the rulers may have been, were the sages who could 'see' beyond the deceptive world of appearances, a gift more precious than any amount of wealth.

The interests of the rishis, who weren't just mythical beings but actual historical personages, lay less in the world around them than in the being itself, which they studied by looking into themselves, operating on the mind rather than the body. The mind was their laboratory, and through the experiments they carried out, the rishis tried to understand its properties, how it functioned and how it could be controlled. They reflected on the mental states according to whether the self was asleep, awake or dreaming, asking themselves, for instance, what the difference was between a tiger encountered in the forest and one encountered in a dream, since both struck fear in the heart.

The great Indian mystic Ramakrishna recounted the tale of a woodcutter who, dreaming he was a king, was suddenly woken by a friend. The woodcutter was furious with him.

'There I was sitting on my throne, dealing with affairs of state with my seven sons, masters all in the arts of war, by my side. How dare you disturb me?'

'But it was only a dream,' his friend replied.

'You understand nothing,' the woodcutter said. 'Being a king in a dream is as real as being a woodcutter in one's waking life.'

In China there's a similar story about a monk who dreams he is a butterfly and on waking up no longer knows whether he is a monk who has dreamt he was a butterfly or a butterfly that has dreamt he is a monk.

Studying the mind naturally led the rishis to ask what lay behind it, what forces sustained it, and to look for the governing principle that gave meaning to life. While other peoples had set themselves goals of conquest, navigation, acquisition of wealth and discovery, the Indians, who in their two-thousand-year history had never invaded another country or conquered a foreign territory, had always pursued knowledge as their ultimate aim, not of the world but of the self. This, they believed, was the key to everything since amid the eternal mutability of all things, its essence alone was unchanging.

Perhaps this explains why Indians had never been particularly interested in history and produced relatively few books on the subject. For them, the succession of events was much like the sand raised up by a storm, whose form was as mutable as it is irrelevant. And because they considered what we thought of as the real world to be a dream, traditionally they hadn't shown much interest in changing or improving it. For that world was only a fragment of the whole, and knowledge of it was, at best, partial knowledge.

But had they, for all this, become great philosophers? No. Throughout the pages of India's history there wasn't a single Aristotle, Plato, Kant or Hegel. This was because in India philosophy, i.e., the love of knowledge, has never been used to construct abstract value systems but was regarded more as a means of support or guidance for one's life.

I remembered my own experience with philosophy, a subject I had studied in high school. Only now do I realize that actually I understood absolutely nothing. To me it had simply been an intellectual exercise, a subject just like physics or biology, but none of my erudite teachers managed to help me understand whether philosophy had anything to do with my life. In India, by contrast, there seemed to be a common awareness that philosophy, far from being mere mental gymnastics, was the exclusive province of the well-educated elite whose secrets were kept hidden away in the ivory towers of academe or confined to the 'philosophers' themselves, was part and parcel of life, the Ariadne's thread that would lead us out of the labyrinth of ignorance. For Indians, philosophy was the religion by which they hoped to attain salvation, which for them meant knowledge. Not the utilitarian knowledge employed to manipulate, conquer or otherwise dominate the world, but as the holy scriptures say, 'the knowledge that, once acquired, leaves nothing further to be known: knowledge of the self'.

To the Western ear this tune might sound somewhat old and hackneyed since the only knowledge which counts for us is that which is applicable or 'useful'. No longer asking ourselves who we are, we view others exclusively in terms of what they can do for us.

In the early 1930s, an intrepid Englishman by the name of Paul Brunton undertook a long journey through the Indian subcontinent searching for traces of that wisdom whose existence he believed was threatened by the irresistible rise of Western thinking. One of the charming characters Brunton encountered on his travels was an old yogi who in a conversation with him said, 'When your wise men in the West leave off trying to make engines run faster than those which they already have and begin to look within their own selves, your race may then find more real happiness. Can you say that your people become more contented each time they discover something that enables them to travel more quickly?'

More than seventy years have passed since then and one can still find many Indians who will ask the same question, but have we ever really asked it ourselves? Now that everything has become a race and we live life without reflecting over it much, we are running faster than ever before, trying to pass the time and postponing the satisfaction of our deeper needs to some undefined future date. In cities especially, life can go by without a single pause for thought or moment of quietude to counterbalance the endless rush of things to be done. No one, it seems, has time for anything any more: not for wonder or horror, or to be moved or become enamoured or simply to be alone with oneself. Already there are thousands of reasons not to stop and think whether we are any happier for this onrush, and countless more could be invented if need be.

There was one group of people I knew who always had time. They were the shepherds of Orsigna in Tuscany where I holidayed with my parents when I was a boy. Chewing on a stalk of grass, they would remain motionless for hours, recumbent on a mountain top from where they would observe their flocks in the distance, their minds free to think, dream, to compose the odd line of verse that they might scratch on a rock or else intone at the poetry contests they held on Sundays around a demijohn of wine.

In India, some people still have that kind of time. Like the man you might meet on a country road who offers you a cup of tea from his crude stall, often just to share a simple reflection with a passing wayfarer. Pouring the tea into a terracotta bowl, he will tell you that by throwing it to the ground after having drunk it one returns it to the earth from which new bowls will be fired. Which, if you think about it, is what happens to us all.

Encountering Indians in the bazaars of Asia Minor, the ancient Greeks were immediately struck by their inclination towards reflection and would say of them that they were not merchants but philosophers. It could be anyone, not necessarily a pundit or one who knows the Veda by heart.

Some of the greatest sages of the last 150 years were self-taught individuals of extremely humble origins. The highly respected Nisargadatta Maharaj who died not too long ago was a simple cigarette vendor who would sit in a wooden cubicle rolling tobacco into leaves. Celebrated in the writings of figures like Max Müller and Romain Rolland, Ramakrishna came from a line of peasant farmers as did Ramana Maharshi, a man who considered silence to be one of the most effective means of communication. With his silence, the echo of which is still felt today, Ramana was to change the lives of thousands of people. Another great rishi of modest origin was Kabir, one of the most revered of India's poets who lived in the sixteenth century in Varanasi where he earned his living as a weaver. Among his disciples were some of the most affluent and powerful figures of the time. Though he was offered the chance to quit his loom and the market stall where he sold his wares several times, Kabir refused, saying, 'weaving is my way of praying'. When he died, though Hindus and Muslims contended for the funeral rights, he left orders to 'cover my body with a veil and all will be decided'. When the veil that covered the body was lifted, the body had vanished into thin air and in its place was a mound of flowers that the two disconsolate communities could only divide equally.

In Delhi, I had my own personal sage, the jeweller of Sundar Nagar. He too was a man of the bazaar who could always be found in his old shop with its eternal half-light and walls plastered in portraits of ancestors and gods, the air filled with incense smoke. This old man was the only person I could confide in without being offered the usual words of commiseration. I was struck by the way he reacted when I first told him about my illness. With great tact and delicacy, he told me the story of a Muslim who, cast out from the mosque, tumbled all the way down the steps but, because he thought of Allah at every step, was sad when he finally came to rest at the bottom. From time to time I would call upon him. One day I arrived at his shop just as the imperious wife of a European ambassador was exiting to step into a waiting limo bearing the '01' number plate of the diplomatic corps whose door was held open for her by a uniformed chauffeur. At this I couldn't help but launch into one of my usual tirades against the arrogance of certain functionaries and their spouses who, instead of representing their country, regard it as a particularly exclusive item in their personal wardrobe. The jeweller offered no comment, but simply asked if I knew the story of the god Indra and, adopting a fairy-tale tone, commenced.

Charged with the task by the other gods, Indra killed the giant dragon who kept all the world's waters imprisoned in its womb, thus restoring life to the earth and happiness to its people. But Indra's pride for what he had achieved made him conceited and vain, and so he asked the god of the arts to build for him a sumptuous palace fit for a hero. The palace the architect built was truly magnificent, but Indra was not satisfied and demanded more rooms. The architect went to Brahma to complain and the latter took the matter up with Vishnu who decided to do something about it. So he disguised himself as a child and presented himself before the palace gates and asked to be received by Indra. At first Indra laughed at the presumption of this little runt, but in the end granted him a hearing. From the height of his throne he asked the child what he wanted. Drawing nearer, the child began to laugh and from behind him appeared an army of ants invading the throne room. 'Who are those ants?' Indra asked, a worried note creeping into his voice. 'Those?' the child asked. 'They were all Indra in previous lives.'

Indra understood at once what the child meant, as did I. This jeweller was a true master of diplomacy.

On another occasion our conversation turned to the subject of children. I asked him how many he had. Like myself, he had two. I asked him if he thought there was anything we could still give them.

'Give them? Give them everything you have, they need it more than you do. At our age we have to cultivate what is not perishable, the rest can go hang. You know the story of Guru Nanak?'

I knew that Guru Nanak was the founder of Sikhism but I wasn't familiar with the story and so once again settled back to hear it.

'Guru Nanak was always travelling. One day he arrived in a village where he saw a handsome house at the entrance of which were a great many coloured flags, fluttering in the breeze. The house, he learnt, was the home of the richest man in the village, a moneylender. Every time he filled another box of money, he would raise a new flag and hold a big party. Guru Nanak went to the house and asked if they could offer him something to eat. Instantly recognizing who he was, the owner ordered his servants to bring him a spread of things to eat and drink. When he had eaten his fill Guru Nanak asked the moneylender for a favour.

'Certainly,' said the moneylender, happy to perform a good deed and hopefully boost the credit rating of his karma too. 'Whatever you wish.'

From his bag Guru Nanak withdrew a rusty metal pin. 'Can you keep this for me? You can give me it back when we meet in the next life.'

'You have my promise,' came the reply, 'and I promise also that you won't have to pay a thing for it.'

As Guru Nanak set off, the moneylender ran to his wife to tell her what had happened.

'You imbecile!' she screamed. 'And how do you expect to keep such a promise? When you die you won't be able to take anything with you, not even that rusty old pin!' Struck by the truth of his wife's words, the moneylender set off after Guru Nanak and threw himself at his feet, begging to become his disciple.

The jeweller enjoyed telling these stories as much as I enjoyed hearing them. Coming to the end of this particular tale he went on speaking, as though to himself.

'Death strips us of everything we have. If we could only shed its weight before we die, we would surely feel more free.'

He was right. Why wait until the last moment to clear away all this clutter, to get rid of all the deadweight of objects and emotions which burden us as we struggle through life? Better to do it now while we still have the strength, while we are still fully aware. Now, that really would be liberation!

'Sure, death is going to come. If not at the market then in Samarkand. Why not be prepared for it? You know the story of Samarkand?'

I did know it and had reread it recently in a volume of Robert Musil's posthumous writings. It was an old tale from Central Asia, but I pretended like I wasn't familiar with it so I could hear it recounted by the jeweller.

One day a caliph sent his vizier to the bazaar to find out what the people in the village were talking about. The vizier set off to do his bidding and in the crowd noticed a tall, thin woman wrapped in a black cloak staring at him. At the sight of her, the terrified vizier ran back to his caliph, imploring him, 'Sirah, help me!' At the bazaar I saw death herself. She was there for me. I beg you to let me leave this place at once. Give me your swiftest steed, so that by nightfall, I will reach safety in Samarkand.

The caliph consented to his request and the vizier galloped off in a cloud of dust. Puzzled by what the vizier had told him, the caliph decided to go to the market himself. There in the crowd he espied the woman in the black cloak. Approaching her, he asked, 'Why did you frighten my vizier?'

'Frighten him?' Death asked. 'I didn't even say a word to him, only I was surprised to see him here, for our appointment is tonight in Samarkand.'

Such were my conversations with the Indian jeweller of Sundar Nagar.

And where but in India might one find a dentist like Dr Siddhartha Mehta who, in order to remove one of my teeth, after giving me a tiny dose of anaesthetic, took up a pair of pliers with the warning that I would hear a slight creaking sound. Summoning his powers of concentration, he gave the pliers a forceful tug and the tooth came out clean as a whistle. Laying it on the table, the dentist raised his eyes skywards.

'Thank you,' he murmured to his god, and turning to me added, 'He always lends me a hand, you know.'

THE LIGHT IN ONE'S HANDS

It was on the Open Centre's noticeboard that I saw the word 'reiki' for the first time, flanked by its two ideograms, on a leaflet inviting enrolments for a beginners' course to be held the following weekend. I was immediately drawn to these two Chinese characters whose literal meaning is 'universal energy', and not the 'therapeutic qualities of spiritual energy' to which the course promised access. But what put me off was the mention that reiki's founder was a Japanese man who had lived 150 years ago. I had lived in Japan long enough to know what facility the children of the land of the rising sun had in appropriating others' ideas and relaunching them into the market with 'Made in Japan' stamped on the label. In Hokkaido, I had visited the 'world's first pyramid' which had been naturally built by the Japanese, not to mention 'Christ's Tomb' and the 'House of Santa Claus'. So I wasn't interested in knowing what this Japanese gentleman from the Meiji era, a time when his country was determined to copy everything it could lay hands on in its rush to 'modernize', had managed to cook up with the ancient 100 per cent Chinese concept of 'ki', i.e., vital energy. I had already gleaned the wisdom of Master Hu and that was more than sufficient.

In Delhi, however, a course in reiki held by two Indian 'masters' was too bizarre a cocktail to pass up. I called the number and almost immediately the fax spat out instructions. Participants were to come dressed in loose-fitting clothes of the purest cotton or wool and reminded not to wear any perfumes as they could 'interfere with the free circulation of energy'.

The course was being held in a school just outside of Delhi, a stone's throw from the Qutub Minar, a tall sandstone minaret built over 900 years ago by Afghan invaders as a symbol of Muslim domination. It was a pleasant location, large and clean, the building's empty rooms overlooked a sunlit garden. In our room, there was a huge mat covered in white sheets. We students, or perhaps it would be better to say 'clients' in view of the not-so-insubstantial sum we had paid for the three-day course, sat in rows while the two masters, a man and a woman in their fifties, both recycled from who knows what previous life, assumed the lotus position on a slightly raised wooden platform, a natural and elegant way of sitting ... only if one can manage it. Extremely healthy too, as I knew from my own experience, having sat that way for years to read and write, curing a nasty backache in the process.

There were around thirty of us in attendance, again mainly women, and we each had to introduce ourselves. I restricted myself to a few words, only saying that I was a pensioner. It was during this 'getting to know everyone' session did I quickly realize that the human matter of which the class was composed, although entirely Indian apart from myself, was remarkably similar to the courses held at the Open Centre. They were odd individuals who had evidently reached a crisis point in their lives, educated but unsatisfied, each in search of some elusive otherness, a form of consolation or escape. Many of the women were middle-aged, some were single young females enjoying a spell of freedom, while the male participants included a radiologist, an advertising executive and a photographer. All were in some way victims of the same consumer society that had driven their counterparts in the US and Europe to seek solace in courses of meditation, yoga, Tarot or qigong, and my New York anaesthetist to become a Kashmiri Sufi.

They were Indians but of the 'new India' – urban, modern and well heeled. After years spent chasing dreams of Western-style modernity, they were now beginning to feel some of the symptoms of its spiritual sickness. This new India, which bore a marked resemblance to that colonized one or, as V.S. Naipaul once wrote, 'wounded' by England's disdainful occupation, now found itself marching to the tune of a new imperial power, the USA. It was the

India of the emergent bourgeoisies of Delhi, Bombay, and Calcutta who had turned their backs on the millions of villages where the majority of the population still lived and which continued to resist colonization. It was now the India that had given up being vegetarian, that drank alcohol, wore designer jeans and sent their offspring to study abroad. It was an India that had asserted its 'right' to develop its own nuclear capability and thus renounced its traditional quest for a power other than predictable force of arms, an India that had refused the teachings of Gandhi.

The two reiki masters had the profile of their audience down pat and their promotional spiel would no doubt have gone down just as well in New York City. Human relationships have been reduced to nothing; we live increasingly isolated and solitary lives. The planet we inhabit is menaced by the effects of pollution and the human race risks extinction. Even if it survives, society will have changed beyond recognition. The time has come for scientists and saints to join hands to save our world.

For most of India's population, all this was of course completely irrelevant. The problems faced by the hundreds of millions of people who live on the banks of the Ganga or in the country's interiors were somewhat different to those touched upon in this pre-course waffle.

'How can you still worship the sun and moon as though they are deities?' a Western traveller might ask an old Brahmin. 'The sun is nothing but a huge ball of exploding gases. And as for the moon, the Americans planted their flag on it there years ago.'

'Oh no,' the Brahmin would reply, beatifically calm in his remote little temple. 'The sun and moon that we venerate are not the ones you know. They are much, much further away, in the beyond. Those that you see are merely the disciples of the ones we worship.'

My course companions couldn't have been further removed from that old India, a place which is full of wisdom and surprise. They belonged to the India whose rapid change I had witnessed with my own eyes. Arriving in Delhi in 1994, Angela and I found the city plastered with signs that read: 'I'm back!' The 'I' in question was Coca-Cola, announcing its return to the Indian market after a seventeen-year ban. Giant cardboard effigies of bottles hung from lamp posts, disfiguring the streets, while a smattering of protesters had gathered outside the hotel where the great comeback was being celebrated.

Having renounced its experiment in autarky, India was now ceding to the temptations of the free market. In the absence of a contrasting ideology that was deeply felt, resistance to globalization's massive push had become impossible. That which was practised by Gandhi had died at the moment of India's independence. The ensuing wave of modernization had produced a gradual turn to the West and though pockets of resistance occasionally sprung up here and there, especially after Rajiv Gandhi took the reins, surrender was total. Together with Coke came mobile phones, cable TV with its diet of US police shows and sitcoms dubbed into various local tongues, the Enron Nuclear Power Station and an avalanche of junk food from Big Macs to Kentucky Fried Chicken. And this was merely the prelude which the cities greedily lapped up to a veritable deluge of the new: undreamt-of sexual freedom, a dramatic drop in arranged marriages, more divorces, more desires, even anxieties and insecurities.

India certainly did not need globalization to teach it the Kamasutra, but it had taken the Western-style individualism to unhook the 'joy of sex' from its social function: to keep marriages going. Women's magazines in India now proselytized the right to orgasm, infidelity, lesbianism and the latest urban fashion: key parties.

Founded on the philosophical principle of oneness, India now had its own 'holistic' magazines in which the concept, recycled in a mawkishly New Age key, was used to sell courses in psychophysical wellness and other such fakery.

Western characters were now landing regularly in India bearing gifts of ancient Mayan or Egyptian wisdom. There was an American who held courses in the 'Teachings of Lemuria', the mythical lost continent of whose secrets he claimed to be the depository, offering participants the chance to 'expand and fortify the psychic powers that keep them close to God'. At the same time, an Australian taught the Melchizedek, the 'Eternal Lord of Light' method, which supposedly enabled you to 'attune yourself to the heartbeat of the universe and attain a perfect balance between mind and body'. This method, so the leaflet said, was practised on earth at the time of Atlantis, its secrets passed on to the humans by dolphins and whales. Though long forgotten, it had recently been 'revealed' to the gentleman in question – a follower of Sai Baba – by the ascended master Toth. The course, for which one naturally had to pay a hefty enrolment fee, covered areas such as 'activation of orbital holographies, the Merkaba or light love-body, the new platinum, magical hermetic energies and redirectioning of the elements to suit each individual's lifestyle'. By practising the Melchizedek method, a woman suffering from breast cancer could apparently cure herself in two days. AIDS victims too were believed to greatly benefit from this.

And so, in India, where so many Western seekers during the twentieth century had hoped to find a secret balm for the soul that might prove vital to their society's survival, now finds itself reimporting those very secrets in pre-packaged, commodified form. We all know how things fragrant with the mystery of distant lands tend to be much more alluring than those under our nose.

'Reiki,' said our master on the first morning, 'is a spiritual medicine for many maladies. In our lives, there is too much stress, too much strain, too much tension. Its aim is to restore a sense of balance between the different levels of our humanity: the physical, mental, emotional and spiritual. Each of us possesses a force of divine origin. What we must do is learn how to harness this force and transmit it using our own hands. Reiki is the secret method that will permit joy to enter our lives and it takes only three days to learn.'

For its powers to be credible, reiki needed a story, a founder, a thread leading back to a mysterious treasure trove of secrets. Theosophical Society too had to invent for itself a pantheon of exotic-monikered 'masters' who from their unimaginable hovels in Tibet had issued instructions to its founders. Gurdjieff, the eccentric founder of the Institute for the Harmonious Development of Man, whose adepts included Katherine Mansfield and René Daumal, and who could list among his admirers figures such as the architect Frank Lloyd Wright, vaguely hinted at having learnt some important lessons during his travels in Central Asia and Tibet. The answers to his quest he had supposedly found in certain arcane Armenian manuscripts salvaged from the monastery of Sarnung between Urmia and Kurdistan.

Reiki too was in need of a pedigree. The one our female course master rattled off took more or less the same form as those employed in hundreds of other courses throughout the world reiki had now become the 'in' thing and was currently the fastest growing among the New Age practices. Already there was Rainbow Reiki, Yin-and-Yang Reiki and Transcendental Reiki to choose from.

Its story begins with the birth of Mikao Usui in 1865 to a Japanese family of ancient Samurai lineage. After completing his studies, Usui took up a teaching post in a minor Christian university where his students challenged him to explain the miracles of Christ, his power to heal the sick and restore life to the dead. Usui, not having the answers to hand, decided to go and look for them. His travels took him to China, India and Tibet, and eventually to the US where he lived for seven years, picking up a degree in medicine from Chicago University. On his return to Japan, Usui went into retreat on Mount Kurama, to the north of Kyoto where he planned to spend three weeks fasting and meditating. To keep count of the days he made a pile of twenty-one stones, throwing one off the mountain every day at sunrise. On the final day, however, on casting the last stone into the abyss, he was astonished to see it turn around and come back towards him, transformed into an enormous ball of energy and light. As the ball approached, Usui tried to take cover but was too late. Travelling incredibly fast, it hit him smack on the head. When he regained consciousness, Usui discovered he had the answer he was looking for all along. The source of all healing and miracles is this luminous, divine force, a universal energy that must be controlled and directed by the imposition of the hands. And the way to do this was reiki.

At this point, Doctor Mikao Usui tried out his method on Kyoto's beggars and the homeless people and was so successful that he was soon able to open a small clinic in Tokyo. During the disastrous earthquake in 1923, Usui joined the relief workers and with his reiki method healed hundreds of injuries. Following his death in 1926, Usui's disciples erected a statue in his honour in the Saihoji temple near Tokyo.

This is where the story would have ended, had it not been for a certain Mrs Hawayo Takata, a Hawaiian Japanese lady. Around 1970, after learning reiki from Chujiro Hayashi, one of Usui's students, she began teaching the method in the United States. Through the efforts of her twenty-one students, coincidentally the same number as Usui's stones, reiki was soon known throughout the world thanks to a gradual proliferation of students who became teachers who then had students who became teachers and so on. It wasn't long before reiki manuals started cropping up on bookshelves everywhere, each sporting on its cover a faded old photograph of a charismatic middle-aged Japanese man whose beetle-browed, bespectacled face, framed by his grizzly hair and beard, beamed with a benevolent, if slightly crafty grin. In other words, the classic personification of mysterious Oriental wisdom.

Before we could try out the method for ourselves, however, we had to first perform a set of exercises designed, so the course masters said, to focus our powers of concentration and enable us to 'look beyond'. For one of these, we had to sit down and close our eyes, imagining Usui's experience on the fateful twenty-first day of his fast. Another exercise required us to look up at the sky to try to see the 'little balls' of energy that swirled around in the ether.

Though all my powers of concentration were employed in trying not to laugh, my course companions approached these tasks with the utmost seriousness. Some claimed they could see light, others claimed they could see energy. One woman, as though possessed, spoke of being enveloped in a wondrous glow.

'Good,' said the course master in conclusion. 'Now you have an idea of the invisible world.'

From here to the miraculous was but a short step. He began to recount one such miracle that Mrs Takata had performed. Called to a friend's sickbed, Mrs Takata arrived to find her friend already thirty minutes into her eternal slumber. Mrs Takata didn't despond, however, and at once began performing a reiki manoeuvre on her friend's heart. Just as the woman was being laid in her coffin, she suddenly got up, stepped out of the coffin and went on to live another five years.

The master explained that it was all a matter of learning to use this universal force that existed in each of us. The method was simple: one cupped one's hands slightly and held them at a distance of ten to fifteen centimetres from the body to be healed.

To get the hang of it, we each had to 'treat' our neighbour and then let ourselves be treated in turn. It certainly wasn't easy to keep one's arms rigidly extended and still for around ten minutes, the time it took for the wave of vital energy to pass from our body to our neighbour's body. For a complete cleanse, meanwhile, the hands had to successively act on various organs, a process which would require a session of at least one to two hours.

'You must never perform reiki on the head,' the male master warned us, 'where the Corona Chakra is located, or on the belly button. And with people who have cancer, never perform reiki on the Root Chakra at the base of the spine.' This caught my attention. 'All illnesses,' he continued, 'arise from a physical or emotional imbalance. One famous oncologist has come to the conclusion that cancer is caused by a lack of love and for this reason has proposed a cure of at least three great hugs a day. Patients who have tried this therapy have benefited enormously.' Hearing these words, I could have got up, slapped him and left. But instead of indignation, it was again laughter that threatened to burst the floodgates. I had to control myself to avoid embarrassing the class.

Matters only got worse when it was my turn to proceed with joined palms to participate in the 'attuning ceremony', the ritual through which the master would attune the force that existed in each of us to that of the universe. Entering a semi-darkened room,

I saw him standing before a small altar that was lit by an oil lamp. Mumbling incomprehensible phrases, he struck a bronze bowl with a wooden stick. The sound, he explained, would awaken my inner force and tune it to the reiki's frequency. With this mystical connection established, I would be placed in contact with the universal energy source which I could then use to cure others.

As we stood facing each other, there was no way of avoiding him. My only fear was that I would laugh in his face; there was much to laugh about. Back in the classroom, describing reiki's properties, the master told us that it could be equally effective in treating a broken computer. 'The tools we use,' he explained, 'are extensions of our bodies. And have you noticed…' he paused meaningfully, 'how the machines we use and depend upon tend to break down when we are in a bad mood and everything seems to go wrong?' This point appeared to be of paramount importance to him: when not mentally attuned to the universe, everything around us seems to suffer, not just our bodies. He also explained how reiki could be performed on plants and animals and, as though addressing me in particular, he added, 'Plants and animals are not sceptical. They are more open-minded than most human beings.'

All this I endured, and at the end of three days I received the first-level diploma. Armed with this certificate and following a twenty-one-day reiki self-cleansing programme, I would be eligible to enter the second level. Here I would learn to perform long-distance reiki and be able to cure people on other continents, since I would then be able to tune in to a much clearer, more powerful frequency than the basic universal force offered in level one. At level three, I could learn the secrets of attuning others and so become a reiki master myself, something I soon realized, I had no intention of doing.

The course left me with a growing feeling of irritation. The spread of so much superficiality, with all its attendant dangers for people with serious illnesses who might take it for a cure, seemed an insult to the intelligence. And yet, reiki's worldwide success was undeniable. In Delhi alone there were reputedly more than 2,000 masters. And to think that it had all begun in Japan where, strangely, I had already been involved in a bizarre incident concerning the imposition of the hands.

In the mid-1980s, I was travelling in the northern region of Honshu, Japan's main island, with a fellow journalist from Tokyo whose family name – this time authentically samurai – meant 'true friend'. It was the middle of the night, we had reached the town of Takayama and were just turning in for the night in an old *ryokan*, a traditional Japanese inn, when I heard voices outside that seemed to be speaking in Italian. Listening closely, I realized they were conversing in Tuscan dialect. I sprang up, threw open the window and called down to them. They turned out to be a group of youths from Pistoia who had travelled to that remote corner of Japan for the big celebrations being held in honour of a 'new religion' that I'd never heard of, but back in Pistoia, they were apparently adept.

Revising my plan of the following day, instead of returning to Tokyo, I followed this group to an extravagant temple whose roofs were like the giant rolling waves of a shimmering sea. At the far end of the temple's main hall, decked entirely in red, was a stage built atop a huge aquarium in whose depths red-and-white carp were swimming solemnly. When the curtain was raised, amid a landscape of fake mountains and real waterfalls, there appeared wrapped in white veils the high priestess who extended her welcome to the various delegations of followers from parts of Japan and the rest of the world. Here, I had stumbled upon the Mahikari sect. Founded during the 1930s by a Japanese army officer, the idea for the sect had come to him after a fall from his horse in Vietnam. Enlightened by this, his calling was clear: he found a religion exclusively devoted to the alleviation of pain and to curing the maladies of humanity. The chord he struck proved to be the right one, and in no time at all his disciples began to multiply. Following his death, his daughter had taken the reins and Mahikari became one of the wealthiest and consolidated sects to have bloomed – and frequently wilted – in Japan each year.

Adepts now ran into the tens of thousands and were easily recognizable, especially in underground stations where they lay in ambush, waiting to accost hapless commuters with an abrupt hand placed to the forehead and a promise to cure whatever illness they might have.

Here was the secret of Mahikari's success: by simply becoming a member, one automatically acquires the power to heal with the imposition of a hand. The energy, once again of the universe, came from the sky while the sect itself served as a kind of power station. And here was the catch: in order to keep their powers, the sect's members had to pay a monthly fee, the spiritual equivalent of an electricity bill, to stay connected to the 'light'. Reiki worked in a similar fashion, with the only difference that one acquired its services with a single advance payment. Once attuned, there was no risk of being cut off at the mains.

I wrote to my true friend in Tokyo, wanting to know more, asking him to dig up whatever he could on Usui and his healing system. He replied within two weeks, saying that in Japan reiki had no followers, the market for healing hands having already been cornered by Mahikari while Usui's name was practically unknown. The only trace my friend could find of him was the statue in the Saihoji temple. Not only was Usui not listed in the nineteenth-century medical register, it was also highly unlikely that he had received his degree from Chicago, given that the university's medical faculty did not exist at the time. In all probability, my Japanese friend reckoned, there had never been a Doctor Mikao Usui; and his story, with its embroidery of sepia-tinted mug shots and whispered miracles, was no more than a cunning ad campaign for a new healing technique.

Whatever the truth may be, the whole operation had been an enormous success. Reiki had gone on to gather disciples throughout the world and several of its masters were making a fat killing with their websites and how-to manuals, not to mention the monopoly they held on divine descendance. In reiki, only those who had studied under a disciple or a disciple of a disciple of Usui could claim to be masters. Direct descendants alone gave their teachings the stamp of guaranteed authenticity and correct tuning with the force.

I later discovered that there existed another version of how reiki, again through Usui, had come to be born. This time, a more action-packed American version.

According to this scenario, Usui, who was interested in Buddhist scriptures from his early childhood, one day found himself in a small second-hand bookshop in Kyoto. The year was 1899. He purchased a bundle of old manuscripts including a text he's been searching for years, 'The Tantra of Lightning that Heals the Body and Illuminates the Mind', concerning the transmission of energy for therapeutic purposes. Originally from Tibet, the work dates back to the seventh century, supposedly brought to Japan via mainland China by the founder of the Buddhist Shingon order. From it, Usui learnt the rudiments of reiki and began practising. Following the Tokyo earthquake, sensing that his health was beginning to fail, Usui put all the material he had collected on reiki, including his own notebooks and diaries, in a lacquer box which he gave to his favourite student shortly before he died. At this point, the lacquer box turned into a kennel for a shaggy dog. Called up for military service at the outbreak of World War II, the student entrusted the box and its contents to a temple. In 1942, he was killed in Manila, the temple was bombed and the box was rescued by a group of monks who wandered through Japan until a young American officer with an interest in Buddhism bought it from them. The officer, swiftly promoted to the rank of general, took the box back to the United States and dumped it in his lumber room where it lay forgotten until 1994 when it was discovered by his son who, as luck would have it, turned out to be the reincarnation of a famous Tibetan lama.

According to the documents found in the box, reiki was supposed to derive from Buddha himself in his therapeutic guise as 'Lord of the Light of Lapis Lazuli'. In other words, the reiki you can now learn in a weekend is not 150 but over 2,500 years old. This is just what its prospective adepts want to hear.

So what was reiki on about? Should we have avoided it? Not in the least. Anything could trigger the healing process; whether it was meditation, belief in a saint, yoga, prayer – so why not reiki? The important thing to believe was its efficacy. The imposition of hands was an old religious practice and one couldn't deny the deeply consoling, even 'therapeutic' effect that a friendly approach towards another person and touching them with affection could have. I didn't know whether it could cure cancer or bring back the dead, but it certainly helped to reduce tension, becalm the mind and inspire positive thinking or healthy forms of expression, like laughter, which reinforced the immune system. In religious traditions, including Christianity, the effectiveness of healing hands had always depended upon the quality of the healer and not the act itself. Only a truly spiritual person who was pure of soul could have the 'magic touch'. Reiki had managed to topple this aristocracy, turning its magic powers into a method that anyone could learn, irrespective of their own psychic or moral fibre. What was once regarded as a gift from God had now become a buyable commodity.

But the question was, did it still work? No, the Taoists believed it didn't. If the right means were used by the wrong man, they were sure to malfunction. But who listened to the old Chinese sages nowadays anyway?

In any case, whatever the qualities or defects of my masters, the course, it seemed to me, hadn't been a complete waste of time. Certainly, it was better that another weekend of shopping and TV. One at least had the chance to get out of the usual routine, see themselves in a different light and perhaps bring home something new. I myself had learnt that chewing a mouthful of food thirty-two times results in a person eating less and receiving more nourishment in return. Or at least that's what my masters said.

One evening, when I was at the house of some Indian friends, I told them about my reiki experience and its accompanying frustrations. Having come to India expecting to find a strong culture, one that was confident of its ability to resist the onslaught of globalization, I had discovered in Delhi an India that was in doggish thrall to the products, fashions and ideas of the West. My host, a bearded, cultivated film producer whose modern views belied a deeply rooted attachment to tradition, didn't share my pessimism.

'Don't worry,' he said to me. 'India may run after everything, it's true, but at a very, very slow pace. You'll see. It will even be late for the funeral of western culture.' In his view, India would digest the ongoing process of Westernization just as in the past it had swallowed up the Muslim and English invasions.

For thousands of years, India, like the rest of Asia including China, had been guided by aspirations of a primarily spiritual nature, aspirations which, in one form or another, would continue to thrive. Here, nothing was ever dead and buried, nothing destroyed or replaced. India represented Noah's ark; on board it there survived things that elsewhere had long become extinct. Here, there were preserved the seeds of all of humanity's most noble thoughts, even in the field of medicine, as I was to discover when I embarked on my personal quest for a cure. This was the only country in the world which still practised Unani, the ancient Greek medicine founded by Hippocrates and brought here by Alexander in the fourth century BC. It was a country where the most diverse forms of treatment, from Western medicine to Ayurveda, homeopathy and naturopathy to Chinese and Tibetan medicine could coexist.

In my old days as a journalist, I'd kept a dossier headed 'Medicine' where I would put everything published by the Indian press on the subject. Over the years I had accumulated many stories, some of which were truly bizarre. For example, in the city of Hyderabad thousands of people queued up once a year to swallow sardines about five to six centimetres long whose mouths had been stuffed with a mysterious herbal composite, apparently a miraculous cure for asthma. The recipe had been the exclusive property of the Goud family since 1845, when one of their ancestors was given this formula by a holy man claiming to be a descendant of Ayurveda's mythical founder. Today, more than half a million people resorted to the treatment which, it was said, worked only in the first week of June when a certain astral constellation appeared in the sky, catalysing the reaction between the sardines and herbs. The flood of asthmatics was now so great that there was often a shortage of fish, at which point the government had to step in to guarantee the supply. Though the Goud family did not ask for payment for the sardine miracle, donations were always welcome.

Among my clippings were a number of equally outlandish cures, such as one based on music, for diabetes and hypertension. Then there was the ancient 'water therapy', a journalistic euphemism for drinking a glass of one's own urine on an empty stomach daily, a practice highly recommended for all sorts of maladies and whose most esteemed adepts included an a former prime minister. It was also believed that there were countless cures for cancer. Salvation was promised by various homeopaths based in Calcutta, while on the outskirts of Delhi there lived a doctor who claimed to have perfected a cancer vaccine based on potassium cyanide. 'Three drops of this vaccine administered to a three-year-old,' he declared, hoping to patent his discovery, 'are the best life insurance policy you can give a person. No matter how much he smokes and drinks, he will never develop cancer.'

While searching for my own cure, I realized there were a thousand different paths I could have followed, a thousand directions I could have chosen. My dossier bulged with names, addresses and telephone numbers. But I decided to start with someone whom no one had written about, a man yet to be discovered and one who made no attempt at self-promotion. He was someone several of my Indian friends had spoken of in the most glowing terms: a young Ayurvedic doctor who lived on the other side of the subcontinent.

THE PERSONALITY OF HERBS

Whenever a plane experiences turbulence, it occurs to me that flight is not man's natural state, and that I should have kept my feet on the ground and taken a train instead. Indian planes, with their inclination to rattle and creak, lend themselves to this kind of reflection more than others. The one I was flying on was supposed to land at Visakhapatnam, an important port city in the state of Andhra Pradesh on the Bay of Bengal, but cloud cover was so low and thick that the pilot couldn't find the runway. Rather than wait for a bright spell above the storm, he maintained his holding pattern in the middle of it, giving his passengers an excellent opportunity to ponder their destiny. From such a height, my destiny had a certain irony: in my quest for a cure, I was headed for a place that was practically unknown, a place 200 kilometres from the airport. It wasn't in any of the guidebooks I'd read, and yet, even before touching down, I was perhaps about to hit on the cure of all cures.

However, I was spared this solution. After being jolted and bumped around some more, the plane made an umpteenth heart-stopping plunge into the void and before we knew it we were on the ground, where the familiar, despairing yet somehow magnificent face of India rushed up to greet us. Barefooted taxi drivers and hotel touts pushed their way up to the front of the workless multitudes who in the absence of other attractions stood to gaze upon the planes landing into the city. From among the taxi drivers I picked the oldest, the one who looked most trustworthy and the only one with shoes on his feet.

Visakhapatnam is India's fourth largest port and one of its major development centres in the race to 'modernize'. An imposing new motorway now jutted from the airport, steering a wide berth of the dozens of little shops, shacks and fruit stalls that crowded the old roadside. To reach one of the yellow sties that passed for a phone booth, I had to traverse mounds of sand and construction rubble. From there I called my doctor to fix an appointment. My friends in Delhi had already told him all about me. The road to his place ran through alien hills. Only a few years ago, the driver told me, they had been covered with trees, but now it was the same old story. These hills were like hairless heads, the trees cut down, the earth left to erode and crumble, the climate altered and there were long spells of drought followed by tremendous floods. Equilibrium may have shattered, but modernity marches on, leaving more victims in its wake. This handsome motorway, still without either central reservation or crash barriers, was one of the fronts of its advance. After every three or four kilometres lay an overturned truck, its cargo strewn across the asphalt, or a mangle of twisted car metal from which it was hard to imagine anyone had made it out alive. 'Every day it's like this. A real slaughterhouse,' my driver said to me.

In each of the villages we passed through, we saw a typically Indian scene: clutches of idle men crouched down for a smoke or a chat, or simply to look on at the motorway atrocity pageant. As we paused at a crossroads, my gaze fell upon a group of workers; some were loading clods of earth on to a cart using their bare hands while others rooted around with their rudimentary tools in the pitted ground. One old man was hacking at an enormous tree trunk with a pitifully small axe. From the window of the taxi, moving my hand back and forth, I signalled to him to use a saw. Understanding, he smiled back at me, shaking both hands in the air in an Indian gesture whose meaning I immediately recognized: 'I don't have one.' Along the roadsides, vendors stood at their stalls, splitting coconuts open with hatchets or slicing mangoes with small sickles.

Looking at the countryside through Western eyes, one could only despair. Not a single well-maintained field, nor any sign of purposeful cultivation. Earth and plants were left to run wild. India's main industry seemed to be that of waiting. One waits until the earth produces something of its own accord, until the trees bear fruit that can be sold at the stalls. One frequently finds themselves asking if India's current misery is in part due to this indolence, the feeling that doing anything is pointless, that nothing will change, and everything has already been done, seen and tried but none of it was worth the effort. The world is *maya* – an illusion. The important thing is not to make a better life for yourself, but to avoid being reborn.

My driver wanted to stop for a drink of sugar-cane juice. A fog of flies enveloped the stall, but no one seemed the least bit perturbed by the thought of bristly black bodies being squelched in the rusty cogs of the two wheels whose job it was to squeeze the sap from the canes. A young boy absent-mindedly turned the crank handle while plucking some pieces of yellowing ice from a plastic container and stuffing them into a black bag, crudely fashioned from a car tyre's inner tube. After beating the bag with a stick, he added a dollop of the resulting slush to the glasses.

In the next town we drove through were hundreds of men and children with shaven heads. My immediate thought was that there must have been a lice epidemic. The driver then offered a better explanation. The local temple, he told me, had been built in honour of a goddess whose odd demands upon her worshippers were that they bring her half a coconut and cut off all their hair.

A good way to save money at the hairdressers, I thought, and perhaps an effective cure for lice too!

The further we wandered from the shining developed centre of the port town, the more we became mired in the India I knew: buildings left half-finished or abandoned, roofless houses, here and there the consoling presence of a village of bamboo huts whose roofs of woven palm leaves drooped down to the ground, leaving only the small aperture of the entrance visible with silhouettes of oxen-drawn carts in the distance.

Convinced as I was that the most interesting discoveries often came about simply by following a slender thread of possibility, the idea of going to see a doctor in a place no foreigner had reason to be appealed to me enormously.

Arriving in Kakinada proved to be a less than exhilarating experience, however. Despite the odd name, it was just another one of India's countless dirty old towns with the added attraction of two fertilizer factories from whose towering chimney stacks sputtered a miasma of greyish murk.

It had been raining and the roads, lacking proper drainage, were reduced to a muddy quagmire which staggered a procession of mango-laden carts, men in filthy dhotis along with others less fortunate in cheap Western polyester trousers and shirts and women of a magnificently untroubled regal bearing. In my hand-woven cotton kurta-pyjamas, the kind you can buy in any store, I appeared to be the only Indian in town.

The 'doctor' I went to visit, a small, spindly man in his early thirties, was waiting for me outside his house. I was struck by his eyes which glowed like welcoming hot coals. Here was clearly a remarkable individual with his own special 'charge'.

The house was brand new, modern in style, its grey cement walls still unpainted. He had moved in with his family only two months before and my first task was to flip through an album of photos taken at the inauguration. Following an ancient Vedic rite, a cow and heifer had been the first to enter each of the rooms of the house. On the roof the doctor had built a coir shed for meditation. There the vibrations were perfect, he told me, as they were bounced off an old tree that dominated the garden with its bottle-green trunk and broad, rain-glazed leaves.

From one corner of the garden jutted an ancient coconut palm with half-exposed roots which looked as though it might keel over at any moment. No, it wasn't dangerous, said the doctor. Quite the opposite in fact: it was extremely useful. Snapping off a piece of root, he informed me with a beatific smile, that it was the best cure for files? Or did he say piles? I had no idea what he was talking about. The doctor placed a friendly hand on my rump. 'Oh yes, for haemorrhoids. Now I understand!' I said.

'Piles, yes,' he replied, breaking off another length of root from the foot of the tree. 'You chop it very finely, grind it with a mortar and pestle and apply it … here.' Thankfully, this time it was his own rump he slapped.

The doctor shared the cement house with his mother and two younger brothers. His father, an employee at the local hospital, had died prematurely some years before. 'I remember he suddenly began vomiting blood, a reaction to British chemical products, especially aspirin,' he explained. For a doctor, this seemed to me an odd way to describe an illness, but it didn't take me long to figure out that this was no ordinary doctor. I began to think of ways to extricate myself from the situation as soon as possible without causing any embarrassment to either of us.

The arrangement made was that I would remain in Kakinada for at least a week to purify my body while he prepared the medicines I was to take thereafter. If I backed out now, I would disappoint him terribly. For although it had partly been my own curiosity, partly a small glimmer of hope in a cure that had fuelled me on this long journey, I realized upon my arrival that for the doctor and the townspeople I was the cure, the long-awaited miracle. A 'famous international journalist with cancer' who had come all the way from Italy to be treated in Kakinada, is no doubt the way he would have put it. The neighbours were already spying on me from their windows and kids were shamelessly walking in through the door as the doctor gave me a guided tour of his premises.

'These are all just herbs,' he said, indicating two large bales of hemp in a room he referred to as his lab, but which to me looked more like a dust-caked cubbyhole. From under the sink he produced a hefty stone mortar and pestle that he would use to pound the herbs he had ordered especially for my cure. His study, also covered in dust, was where he had his library where the shelves contained more bumps than books.

His mother asked if I wanted coffee, tea or water, while the doctor, proudly steering me into his new living room, moved to switch on an enormous colour TV. The images that blazed to life were those of an American movie on the Vietnam War.

The doctor's rudimentary English made understanding him difficult, but for this too he had made provisions. Help arrived on a Vespa in the form of a young man who described himself as the doctor's uncle, despite being only a couple of years his senior. He had taught English in a secondary school until he got married to a girl belonging to a lower caste but a richer family. Her expensive lifestyle he now supported by selling life insurance. At present, however, the thing he had to sell was his nephew, the doctor. From a briefcase he extracted a number of letters from the cured, entombed in plastic, along with various medical invoices, all the while regaling me with the litany of illnesses from obesity to asthma, arthritis to psoriasis that his nephew had successfully treated. To remove cataracts he had developed a special pack based on a mix of opium and honey that could resolve the problem in three days without the need for surgery. As for diabetes, within two weeks his treatment would make insulin completely unnecessary. One of this specialties was curing sterility.

'Here is a letter from the first female patient, cured in 1989,' the uncle said. 'After treatment she had three children. And all for just Rs 3,000. Obviously treatment of cancer and leukaemia takes considerably longer and thus it is only to be expected that costs rise accordingly,' he continued, masterfully introducing to his pitch the delicate matter of money. Though his uncle's spiel clearly made the doctor uneasy, there was little he could do. The man appeared to be in some way his master and insisted on playing his part to the hilt.

The uncle went on, telling me how theirs was a family of 'orthodox' Brahmins who had been snubbed by their more modernized, sophisticated brethren. He cited his in-laws as an example, who had made a lot of money by starting their own business. As for him, he too had broken with tradition, finding the complicated web of social relations imposed by religion both appalling and absurd. What mattered in his view was not caste but individual success. A self-confessed atheist, he was openly contemptuous of everything connected with the past.

'Rituals? Ceremonies? Pure Insanity!' he exclaimed.

To further illustrate his point he told me how every year for the Festival of the Snake, peasants from Kakinada's surrounding countryside would construct small burial mounds into which they would pour buckets of milk, inviting snakes to drink in the hope that, should they meet one day in the fields, as a token of their gratitude they snakes would refrain from biting them.

'What kind of attitude do you call that?' the uncle asked. 'Out in the fields they are afraid of snakes and try to kill them, but in the temple they venerate them like gods, genuflecting before the beasts and offering them massive quantities of milk. Wouldn't it be better to give it to the poor children on the streets? Brahmins are unbelievably selfish.' He added that when the doctor's father had died, not one Brahmin had turned up at his funeral, believing they might be pursued by spirits on the way home from the crematorium, spirits which would then have taken up residence in their homes. His own father had helped many of them when he was still working at the hospital but in the end, however, they thought only of themselves.

The doctor appeared to be greatly embarrassed by his uncle's yacking. After he left, the doctor and I strolled together towards the centre of Kakinada and he was able to tell me something of his own life.

Central to his story was the house in which he'd been born and raised and where till two months ago he'd still been living. More than 200 years old, this small, dilapidated, dimly lit building set off a dirt track looked as though it hadn't seen a repair man or a lick of paint in all that time. The roof slates had loosened and the beams rotted through. To keep the rain out of the main room where his grandparents lived, a blue plastic sheet had been fitted under the ceiling. The place was in complete disarray. With heaps of planks lying around the floor together with a bicycle without wheels, an old motorbike and a rickety armchair on which his grandfather was enjoying a quiet snooze. But when his grandmother opened the door to the puja or 'prayer' room with its statuette of Hanuman, portraits of other deities, piles of coconuts and oil lamps that were used to make offerings to the gods three times a day, I felt like I had walked into another world. It was a world held together by threads other than those of efficiency, a world of old, 'orthodox, pious' Brahmins whose only real activity seemed to consist of presiding with meticulous precision over these immutable rites.

'Fresh water,' said the doctor, indicating to an old well in the yard from which his family had drunk for generations. His eyes lit up. 'Very fresh,' he repeated, scooping some up in his cupped hands. Here too in a corner of the garden stood a tall, majestic coconut palm at least three times as high as the house itself, its half-exposed therapeutic roots entangled with the doctor's own past.

The eldest of three sons, the family had feared that his might be an abnormal birth since his father had married his own brother's daughter. As a child he was often ill and had spent much of his adolescence bedridden. Various allergies coupled with chronic asthma and repeated attacks of bronchitis had prevented him from playing with other children and from making friends. Unable to regularly attend school, he was more familiar with the hospital where his father worked and where he was regularly pumped with Western medicines, free of charge. 'Including,' he said, 'various hormones and steroids.'

Nobody, not even his grandfather's brother, a famous Ayurvedic doctor, was able to find a cure for his ailments. And so he grew up dreaming of how one day he would discover the perfect cure for himself. A voracious reader, he had devoured every book he could lay his hands on. Everything he read he could remember even several years later. Two Swamis, one from Rishikesh, the other from Varanasi helped him decipher holy scriptures and he told me that from the time he was a child he had collected texts on Ayurveda, astrology and herbs of every type, all of which, in his view, were aspects of medical science.

This collection was apparently held in the heaps of paper I had noticed on the knotted bookshelves of his study. By the age of five he had already begun to distinguish the different herbs, to 'speak to them' as he put it; they became his first toys as well as his first friends. He felt they were like real people, each with its own character, its own qualities and reactions. At sixteen he had identified eight separate herbs that he knew would be useful in treating his own condition. By combining them in the right measure he had managed to cure himself of all his ailments. At this point in the story a Western doctor would no doubt say that it wasn't the herbs but the onset of puberty that had done the job. But noticing how passionately he spoke of herbs and the various ways they could be combined, I believed that the rational explanation was not, as often happens, the fullest. Perhaps the disappearance of his symptoms was in some part due to his having taken his life in his own hands. Discovering his own path, he had gone from being a patient to being a healer.

Having cured himself, he had now set out to visit the various healers and doctors in the region, learning something from each one and constantly adding to his growing collection of herbs. Soon he had his own patients and his first treatment successes. One day, a public official from the state of Andhra Pradesh invited him to a five-star hotel to see if he could do something about his various aches and pains. It was from that moment that the doctor's name had begun to circulate outside Kakinada. His reputation had now spread as far as Delhi, which is where I learnt of his practice

At that moment, the uncle decided to rejoin us and together they gave me a lift to the Jaya Deluxe Hotel which, according to a roadside billboard, was the most elegant in town. On arrival, I wondered what the least elegant must be like. In my Indian garb, it was as much as I could do to obtain a room and not be shown the door like some impecunious hippie or backpacker who had got the wrong address. The bedsheets were wrinkled and grey which I covered with a sarong I took everywhere with me. Lying on the bed staring at the ceiling's asbestos tiles – a material regarded as among the most carcinogenic today – I started to laugh, imagining the faces of my fixers in New York. If only they could see me here in this deluxe hotel the day before I was due to be treated by their 'colleague'.

I was awakened by a sickening stench of fried onions wafting in through my hotel window. Evidently, it was the hotel's kitchen staff preparing their deluxe breakfast. I had to miss out on this treat, however, since I had to be at the doctor's by 8 a.m. sharp on an empty stomach for the clinical–astrological exam on which the finer points of my therapy were to be based. While in the vestibule, young waiters rubbed filthy wet rags across the grisaille floor, outside the hotel doors I could see that the heap of garbage had grown considerably since I arrived and a motley crew of dogs, pigs, goats, cows and crows – India's street sweepers – were already on the job.

I decided to go for the appointment on foot. Though the walk was short, it proved wholly unsuitable as psychological preparation for the encounter failed to instil in me the necessary faith in the doctor's cure. An indistinct grey sludge puffed and bubbled in the open sewers as though possessed of some malefic life force as a cow paused on its lazy way to sip placidly from the mire before clopping off again, dragging its nose along the ground as all animals in India seemed to do. Perhaps this was to ensure that no scrap of food slipped past unnoticed. I thought of the milk this cow would produce and tried to imagine someone actually drinking it. I thought of the average life expectancy in India – fifty-two years – and remembered the doctor's uncle telling me how no one in their family had made it past their sixtieth year, not even their grandfather's famous Ayurvedic brother – my doctor's mentor – who died at the age of fifty-eight. Though he was the victim of a massive heart attack, they said he had at least foreseen his death.

The doctor was waiting for me with a radiant smile, his gleaming eyes brighter than ever. Sitting me down on a stool, he stood in front of me holding my arms aloft by the wrists and with his eyes tightly shut began to auscultate the blood coursing through my veins. There was something wrong in the left side of my body, he said, an infection. He had me undress and lie down on a straw mat. On the left side was the enormous hernia that had appeared after the operation, but of this he seemed to take no notice. Instead he focused on the long incision that traversed my belly and disappeared around the back. I had three types of disease, I explained to him. That incision had been made to remove the one in my kidneys.

'The operation was done in India?' he inquired, looking puzzled.

'No, in America.'

'That's strange. In India, you reach the kidneys from behind, not from the front.'

He carefully examined my legs, knees, the area around my liver and finally my eyes. Then peering at the surface of my tongue, it struck him. 'There! There's the infection! Tell me,' he said, excited by his discovery, 'have you ever suffered from haemorrhoids?'

'Yes, for twenty years.'

'And have you ever had back pains?'

'Yes, quite often, in fact. Especially lately, before I fell ill.'

He looked overjoyed, as though he'd found the key to the mystery. In his view the haemorrhoids were the source of all my woes. 'You Westerners don't take notice of them, but haemorrhoids are a major illness, a sign that you must take very seriously.'

Fire-Eater too had been interested in my piles. According to my Indian doctor they were the cause of the 'infection' in the centre of my body, around the stomach, the infection that had then spread to the kidneys. The kidneys, he explained, contained a coiled spring which was so long it could encircle the entire globe. My spring had broken, but there was no cause for alarm. With the right medicine he could get it working again. But first I had to clean out my stomach, a process that would take a week.

'At this moment it is full of worms,' he claimed. 'In such a condition my medicine can have no effect.'

'Worms? In my stomach? I don't have any worms in my stomach!'

'And how do you know that?' he asked defiantly.

'Because my doctors in New York have been inside it several times, that's how.'

He smiled indulgently as though I had told him a childish fib and then proceeded without further ado to the second part of the visit: the astrological part. After looking at the lines, not on my palm, but on my thumbs, he began to meticulously examine my skin, keeping his eyes peeled for signs, moles, red or black marks. When he was done, he made some complicated calculations involving my date and time of birth, and after a few minutes of mentally adding, subtracting, multiplying and dividing, he arrived at the number 2,526, a number that would be extremely important to me and that I must not reveal to anyone on any account.

In his view, the constellations were aligned in my favour with Mars alone exerting a negative influence, which was why I had to be careful of its rays. There was no need to worry, however. He knew the plants and herbs that could counter them and would form part of the potion he would prepare for me. My disease was mainly in the blood, but in time it would heal.

Though how much time, I wondered.

If I began taking the potion in combination with certain metals – he suggested gold – six months would be sufficient for me to be cured. Without the metals, however, it would take at least a year.

Before giving me the gold he would reduce it to ash by applying heat. In any case, it was a matter of just a few milligrams. But a few milligrams would intensify the formula.

At this point the uncle who had been translating all through the visit picked up a piece of paper and a pen to work out some numbers. For all the doctor's cures the unit of measure was the mandal: a quantity that would last forty-one days. This meant that for six months I would need four-and-a-half mandals. Combined with the gold, the entire therapy, not including the stomach cleansing operations I was to begin that afternoon, would cost me Rs 12,000, that is, around 250 euros. By Kakinada standards it was a handsome sum, though not an outrageous one.

During the course of the treatment, the doctor told me I would have to be very careful about what I ate. Aside from onion and garlic, ingredients that would be good for me because they apparently helped to cool down the inflammation, I was to avoid anything that grew in the dark or below ground at all costs. This meant no carrots, potatoes or beetroot. I couldn't eat cucumbers, aubergines or pumpkins either. Instead, I was to eat various kinds of corn and rice, especially if it was more than six months old, not to mention green salads, cabbage, beans, chickpeas and all types of fruit. And gold, naturally. Such a combination, the doctor said, would guarantee me good health for the rest of my natural life, a warranty that without the gold, would slip to twenty years.

'Twenty?' I asked. 'That's already a bit excessive.'

He wanted to have another look at my hands. Asking me to join my palms, he observed the tips of my thumbs and my two little fingers, mumbling something which the uncle translated as 'radiation'. I had no idea whether he was referring to the radiation from Mars which was supposedly bad for me or the one from New York, of which he knew nothing but had probably detected some trace in me. For it too must have left its mark and was no doubt more tangibly malign than that of the Martian rays. I returned that afternoon to witness my medicine being prepared, after which I took the first dose to clean my stomach. Now I had decided to play along, or at least shift my perspective. Rather than cede to the crushing disappointment of not having found the cure I was looking for, I thought I might as well take advantage of the bizarre scenario I had stepped into to explore a world I would otherwise never have known. Once I had convinced myself that I wasn't simply wasting time, everything suddenly appeared to be much more interesting.

By the time I got back to the hotel I had worked up quite an appetite, but the sight of the restaurant with its closely drawn curtains, sealed windows, and tables still sticky from the leftovers of previous diners soon made it pass. Following the traveller's golden rule of sticking to boiled eggs and bananas, naturally after removing the extremities, I asked if they had something of the sort. Eggs? The waiter looked at me as though I'd asked him to boil his own hand. This was a strictly vegan restaurant where eggs were viewed as living things. If I insisted, however, I could eat them in my room.

That afternoon the doctor's house was abuzz with activity. A patient who was being treated for diabetes had been given the task of procuring a number of ingredients for my potion and showed up with a big bag of herbs which he proceeded to pour out on to the lab's dusty floor and began to sort through. Then there was a big, misshapen fourteen-year-old girl who had arrived from Visakhapatnam, accompanied by her mother. Every week they made the five-hour-long bus journey to treat the girl's obesity along with a nasty case of psoriasis. Now she even had nits, her mother complained. Like many other patients who came from afar, they would stay in the house overnight. To repay the doctor for his hospitality, they would crush handfuls of roots and herbs in the big stone mortar. All the work took place on the ground outside which clearly hadn't seen a broom in aeons. The rhythmic pounding of pestles was occasionally interrupted when a hand swept down to gather the stray herbs that might have popped out of the mortar, scooping them from the earth and returning them, dust and all, to its stone bowl. At one point I witnessed the mother extract what must have been a nit from her daughter's hair and crush it with her fingernail before plunging the same hand back into my herb mixture. At the end of the afternoon, the greenish paste was divided into several small portions and rolled up into little balls left to dry in the sun.

The only people seemingly unaffected by the hustle and bustle in the 'laboratory' were the doctor's two younger brothers who, after watching a movie on TV, turned to fiddle around with some electronic gizmo. One had just come back from Hyderabad where he had taken the written test for a job as a bank clerk. If he didn't clear it this time, he would take the test again and again until he was accepted. He was prepared to get his white collar no matter what it took.

Just as I was about to go back to my hotel, the doctor arrived. Grinning from ear to ear, he presented me with a glass of some green brew he had prepared which he wanted me to drink in front of the assembled company. It was a medicine for my worms.

Luckily I had a bottle of water with me. Emptying that out, I poured in the doctor's concoction and promised him I would take it before retiring to bed.

The uncle figured out my stratagem right away. 'Patients should never see how their medicines are prepared,' he said.

I asked the doctor to describe the composition of my anti-cancer potion which he said was made of twenty-nine different vegetable substances. Pulling out two dictionaries, he began to reel off their names beginning with *Anacyclus pyrethrum* and *Celosia cristata*, but he suddenly stopped. A look of worry began to creep across his face. Why was I so anxious to know the formula? Was I perhaps planning to pass it on to the 'scientists' as he called them? I swore to him I had no such intention, but he looked unconvinced. Rather than continue with the list, he told me that to produce a single mandal he had used twelve kilograms of roots and herbs, which he reduced in the end to a mere fifty grams of pills. Accompanying me to the roadside the doctor apologized for his reticence. Far from wishing to keep his anti-cancer formula a secret he had a plan in which, he said, I could be of valuable assistance. What he wanted was to place his formula at the disposal of the World Health Organization (WHO) so that it could be made available to anyone who needed it. I was supposed to write a letter to the general director informing him of my visit and requesting the necessary funds to enable the doctor to carry on his research. But since this was his plan, he preferred not to discuss it in front of his uncle.

Back at the hotel, I studied the bottle with its lizard-green liquid and thought I might as well drink the stuff, or at least have one tiny sip. Not doing so seemed a betrayal of the doctor's enthusiasm and good faith. Yet, equally, drinking it would be counter to my instincts. And so the slime finished up gargling its way down the plughole. Perhaps it really would have been effective, even pleasant, but in the end none of this made any difference. The point was that I didn't believe in it, though I naturally told a different story the following morning.

I stayed on in Kakinada for another two or three days until the pills had dried and took advantage of the wait to visit some of the region's old temples and see what remained of the harbour where two centuries ago the French had established a colonial settlement in an attempt to unsettle the English. Besides, I wanted more time to speak to the doctor alone.

He was an unusual character, a man of disarming sincerity. He told me he had recently become a Brahmachari, meaning that he had taken a vow of chastity, and therefore had no plans to marry, instead devoting all his energies to medicine. He believed that the shastra – the ancient holy scriptures – contained the explanation for everything that had happened in the universe. One only had to know how to read from the heart.

Though his world view, comprised of an odd mixture of science, astrology, religion and philosophy, no doubt would have appalled the Western mind which was accustomed to not only separating science from other fields of inquiry but distinguishing between the different branches of science. To a traditional Indian mindset it was completely normal, everything being interdependent and part of an indivisible whole. Because people were not merely bodies but had also a mind and a soul, their illnesses could not be treated purely in brute physical terms. In the mind of an Indian, the physical and the metaphysical were far from being opposites and instead complemented each other. Being the oldest of the known sciences, astrology remained a part of medicine. In daily life religion and philosophy too played an important role in combining physical exercise with ethical principle – yoga was a prime example – and thus couldn't be excluded when it came to diagnosing and treating illnesses.

Having his own roots in this tradition, the doctor spoke to me of the personality of herbs, the planets' rays, the spring in the kidneys and the therapeutic values of sounds. He added that 'cleansing of the body both inside and out is vital for our health, but more importantly, for keeping the mind and the soul calm.'

Though we the modern citizens of the West might find this rather hard to swallow, for an Indian the body's health is not merely self-serving. It is the way to ensure the health of the soul. Life is not just for living, but it must also be understood. To live is to attain the meaning of life for which the body's health is an important end, though not an exclusive factor. Illness can be a way of uplifting the soul. From this perspective of Ayurvedic tradition, our usual scientific reasoning no longer holds.

In Sanskrit, *ayuh* denotes the period between birth and death while *veda* means 'knowledge'. Therefore, by extension Ayurveda is 'the science of life'. In other words, it is everything we need to know about diet, respiration, exercise and medicines to keep our physical bodies healthy and in harmony with itself and the universe. Our other bodies – the mind and soul – can develop their powers to the best of their abilities. The ultimate aim is not what we call health, but moksha: the liberation from the cycle of life and death. The doctor told me that the Indian habit of greeting someone by joining their palms in front of their chest meant to wish them good health – a salutary salutation. This gesture united the points of energy transmission in a person. Greeting an older or more learned and esteemed person by touching their feet, on the other hand, was a way of charging oneself with their energy. This gesture was considered a sign of generosity on the part of the person whose feet were being touched since it sapped a certain amount of their strength.

'The feet keep the body upright,' the doctor said. 'That's where all the power is. The more powerful the person whose feet you touch, the more energy you receive from them.'

I listened closely as the doctor feverishly described the relationship between our health and sacred sounds like 'Om' between planets and plants. Enthralled by the bizarre connections he traced, I realized that the vision of humanity of this young man from Kakinada was much more vast, more magical and complex than that of any of my New York fixers. For him, the body was clearly not simply a machine, no more than illness was just a physical condition. Therapy could not be reduced to chemicals and his cure for my cancer had to take even the planets' influence into account.

I warmed up to the way he described herbs, plants and animals as though they were people. But I warmed up even more so to the man himself; pure of heart, he seemed crushed between the rock of tradition and the hard place of modernity, between an honest desire to understand life's mystery and the need to make a fast and easy living. Lacking friends or support and having to drag two insipid siblings along, he was torn between the pious orthodoxy of his Brahmin grandparents and the slickly sophisticated ways of his non-believing uncle. Probably feeling lonely and misunderstood, he thought that in this avid listener and his hastily scribbled notebooks, he had finally found his link with the outside world.

When time came for me to leave, he gave me the medicine he had prepared, holding both hands out to me in a religious gesture as though consigning some precious relic. For a moment I thought I'd take that medicine. But in the end the small, recycled, plastic containers and their cargo of little brown balls were to end up with the many lost and forgotten objects absent-mindedly cast aside after a journey.

The doctor, on the other hand, I haven't forgotten. Thinking of him standing there with his fiery eyes in that town in the middle of nowhere in the shadow of the fertilizer works, I can't help but feel a slight twinge of guilt. I did nothing to help him. I didn't even write the letter to the WHO.

HE WHO PASSED THIS WAY

Travelling. The joy of a lifetime. A teenage dream that had become a profession. It was a way of life that was always the same, yet always different: the preparations for departure, the going, the writing about it. But what the sense of it all was I, honestly, had never stopped to ask myself.

Now, as I sat on the terrace of the Ganges View Hotel in Varanasi, watching the endless flow of the world's most sacred river, and beside it the equally ineffable one of its ancient people, that sense was clear to me. The reason for all my moving, for that constant setting off in search of something outside was simple: inside, I was empty. Empty as a sponge, yet equally ready to soak up and be filled with whatever it encountered.

Travelling was my life's joy, a teenage dream that had become a profession. It was a way of being that was always the same yet different every time: the preparations before departing, and then going there and writing about it. But I had never bothered to ask myself what the sense in it all was.

Travelling excited and recharged me; it gave me something to think about. In other words, it made me feel alive. Arriving in an unfamiliar country kindled a new flame, like the start of a love affair. I still remember like it was yesterday: the first time I crossed the Swiss border to work as a dishwasher and years later driving across South Africa, or my first day in Saigon, the spectacle of Angkor Wat, arriving in Samarkand, Kashgar, riding on horseback into Lo Manthang, each time with the feeling of discovery.

Wasn't this what I was still doing, after all? In this respect at least, the mutations of chemo and radiotherapy hadn't changed me. On the contrary, they had led me to repeat myself. If I had previously gone in search of adventures and ideas, the quest this time was for a doctor, a wonder herb, a magic formula, a miracle, or a cure. But always in the same way: by roaming the world. What people had always done was hope to discover in some far-off land or time the key to all mysteries. It was simply a question of locating the exact place. Every now and again, someone had risked all in the quest for such a treasure, hence there existed the myth common to every civilization: the wandering hero, the child of the gods who loses his way but finally makes it home after a long and arduous journey. Gilgamesh, the Sumerian king who travels without cease in order not to die; Ulysses, determined to voyage beyond the pillars of Hercules, the then known edge of the world. We have always regarded travelling as a means of spiritual growth, as though it were a way to uplift the soul. In India, they say the sadhus, the beggar saints, must be like water continually in motion, otherwise they stagnate. If I had chosen to stay put in the past, I would probably have suffered the same fate. But what about now?

While in Kakinada I had begun to wonder whether continuing to travel would lead to a dwindling store of discoveries. I even had the impression that the old call to depart had begun to ring in my ears like the dull sound of a cracked Chinese vase. And where was I to go in any case? Every corner of the world looked promising. Should I go back in time to one of my previous lives, as Doctor

Brian Weiss and his 'retrogressive therapy' suggested, on the principle that my present malady was rooted in some trauma that had occurred centuries before? Or should I make an astral voyage of the type I had attempted with Nica, maybe to reach a place mentioned in one of the myriad New Age books that cluttered my shelves? Through a group of Brazilian healers it was possible to fix an appointment at the astral hospital, a psychic zone where the finest physicians and healers of all civilizations and epochs gathered to collectively devise a 'personalized therapy based on colours, scents, sounds and laser beams that has the power to cure all imaginable maladies.'

Maybe I was just tired and the time had come to end my wanderings. After yet another journey, I was in need of rest so I checked into the Ganges View Hotel, handing myself over to the care of its kind and considerate owner, Shashank. He would pay his early morning respects in the temple below the terrace to Hanuman, the monkey god, and then devote the rest of the day to looking after his guests. He offered them cultivated conversation, sound advice, simple but extremely healthy vegetarian meals and evening sitar concerts, all things I was in sore need of. I had come from Bihar, one of India's most beautiful states but also one of the poorest and dirtiest. It was a land that had once flourished under rich and powerful empires governed by wise kings, but today was among the most criminal and violent regions in the whole subcontinent. It was also the cradle of Buddhism, which was the real reason for my visit. I went to Rajgir, to the Hill of Vultures where the caves in which Buddha, his cousin and favourite disciple Ananda retreated to meditate could still be found. I stood on the ruins of Nalanda, the famous Buddhist university and sanctuary for the interior life of an entire epoch, through which between the fourth and thirteenth centuries, the greatest philosophical minds in Asia had passed. This was until the Muslim invaders came and razed it to the ground, slaughtering some 10,000 masters and students, thus forcing Buddhism to seek refuge beyond the Himalayas in Tibet, China and later Japan.

I also went to Bodhgaya where Buddha had attained enlightenment under the *Ficus religiosa,* a tree that exists even today. From there I took the road to Varanasi. My reason for visiting Buddhism's historic sites was to feel the spiritus loci, to see with my own eyes that tiny corner of the world – a single plain surrounded by seven hills – where 2,500 years ago a legend was created who like Moses before and Jesus and Muhammad after, would alter the course of human history. One by one, I wanted to retrace Buddha's footsteps. He too was one of those mythical voyagers whose journey had begun with man's most physical and material dimension – the body – to arrive at what was most spiritual; in Buddha's case it was the mind emptying void of Nirvana.

And this myth, perhaps because it contained what we unconsciously believed to be the truth, continued to hold sway over us.

Gautama Siddhartha was a rich and carefree young prince married to a beautiful girl with whom he had a son. His father was the sovereign of the small realm of Shakya and he was the natural heir. One day, however, while exiting the gates of the city where he had spent his childhood, sheltered from all evil, he bumped into three people in quick succession, one who was sick, one old and one dead. He then realized that the human body – even his own – was not merely a source of joy, but also a source of pain.

The revelation left an indelible mark on him, causing him to abandon his wife and son along with the realm that would be his one day. He changed his life completely by seeking an escape from suffering not only for himself, but for all of humanity. At first, believing everything was tied to the body, he attempted to detach himself from it, ignoring its demands for food, water or clothing. For six years he lived the life of a forest hermit, eating only one grain of rice or sesame seed per day. But then, having turned himself into a macabre skeleton, he was no longer able to stand or remain conscious and realized that by failing to take care of his body, his mind suffered as well which prevented him from meditating. And so he chose to nurse himself back to health.

Living hand to mouth on what people gave him, Siddhartha continued on his quest until one day he sat down under the tree which would later become the tree of Bodhi – enlightenment – where he decided to remain until he had found the answer. Many temptations presented themselves, but in the end Siddhartha's will prevailed.

At sunrise he pronounced his victory. 'Now I know all there is to know,' he said. 'I possess everything one can possess. There is nothing more I need.' He was alone with the earth as his only witness.

For seven weeks, Buddha – the Enlightened or Awakened one – stayed close to the tree to which he owed so much, then moved to Sarnath on the outskirts of Varanasi. There, for the first time, he set in motion the Dharmachakra, the Wheel of Law before his five assembled disciples. He began to teach them that between the blind fulfilment of bodily pleasures and the ascetic's denial of the body there lay a middle course that led to the detachment from these passions and an inner peace beyond all suffering. This was the way of dharma, the only correct way to see, to speak, behave, exert oneself, live, be inspired, attain awareness and meditate. What Buddha's enlightenment actually consisted of, however, remains a mystery. He never spoke of it with great precision, only saying that words were not always the best road to understanding. Everyone had to experience enlightenment for themselves. He had shown the way and it was up to the others to follow.

From the wealth of stories that surround the myth, Buddha emerges as an eminently sensible fellow, a man with no time for religious zealotry, dogma or occultism of any kind. To a disciple who pestered him with intellectual questions and who one day asked him whether the soul pre-existed the body, Buddha replied by recounting the story of the soldier pierced by arrows who was taken to a surgeon to have them removed in time to save his life, but who insisted on knowing who had shot each arrow and for what reason. The disciple's question was irrelevant because whatever the answer, what really mattered was to understand what it meant to be born, grow old, suffer and die.

Buddha didn't care much for definitions, knowing that like words, they could be a trap too. On one occasion his disciples asked whether he would still exist after his death, to which Buddha replied, 'By saying yes I will give rise to confusion, by saying no, likewise. After his death, Tathagata will be as limitless as the oceans.'

Tathagata was what he called himself and wished others to call him. It meant 'He who has passed this way'. This was the image he wanted to leave: not of the enlightened, nor of a god, but of a man like any other, one who had passed this way that others could follow. He died at the age of eighty, poisoned by food an untouchable had offered him in all sincerity. According to one version it was a dish of mushrooms and according to another, it was pork. His last words to his disciples were, 'Everything that exists rots and decays, so you must all work hard to attain salvation.' In the following centuries Buddha's doctrine began to spread throughout India. Numerous kings and their subjects converted to Buddhism, as did Emperor Ashoka the great who brought the doctrine of dharma as far as the island of Ceylon from where it became diffused throughout the whole of South-East Asia. With its rejection of rites and castes and introducing the idea of compassion, a notion wholly foreign to Hinduism, Buddhism was a true revolution in India and perhaps the only one to have occurred in the country's long history. Although primarily spiritual in nature, the revolution was also directed against the religious and political powers of the Indian Brahmins. The latter were slow to react and it was only in the eighth century, thanks to Shankaracharya, the great commentator of the Vedas who lived in Varanasi, that they managed to organize a counteroffensive, slowing down the spread of Buddhism among the lower castes. The Muslims completed the job and by the late thirteenth century, Siddartha's doctrine became practically extinct in the country of its birth.

Buddha has become a part of the vast pantheon of Hinduism. Granted official respect, Buddhism and its concepts like dharma, which are in any case of Hindu origin, are now deeply rooted in the common sentiments of ordinary people. The Indians have nonetheless forgotten that Gautama Siddhartha was once one of them and I found it amusing to ask souvenir stallholders in Bodhgaya why their figurines of Buddha were slant-eyed. Buddha could be everything: Chinese, Japanese, Tibetan, Indo-Chinese, Thai, Mongolian, but no longer – and this was especially true here in his native land – Indian.

Every day, from my hotel's terrace, I would watch the sun rise from the opposite bank of the river as crowds of people stood on one side of the riverbank, stooping to gather cupped handfuls of water whose shimmering drops they offered to the sun's first rays with a skyward sweep of the arms. It was the strangest of spectacles: for several miles thousands of people stood lined along the riverbank, at the foot of steps, temples, houses, palaces and amid chants, prayers and the clamour of bells, all facing the water. At the same time, on the opposite bank was nothing but an obscure veil of mist covering the deserted earth. Fullness and emptiness, light and shadow, sound and silence: metaphors of opposites that formed a whole truth as a harmony of contraries. For Varanasi was sacred but only on the western side. Only those who died on the western bank of the Ganga, the crowded, chaotic, sunlit bank where day and night the insatiable pyres blazed, would be saved from reincarnation. The other side was bereft of event, save for when the corpse of a child or sadhu was found washed up on the shore. There, nothing existed or became, and death was no liberation.

In what is one of the oldest inhabited cities in the world, it has been this way since time immemorial. For over 4,000 years millions and millions of Indians have come here to die. They believe the western banks of the Ganga is the only place on earth the gods free them from the cycle of rebirth. For this reason, Varanasi is a place that belongs to another dimension, another world. At times, it required the protective distance of the hotel terrace in order to try to understand or simply not to become lost. For a westerner, to think of the sacred in terms of filth, squalor and decay is an arduous task. I too was swept up in that holy fervour of death to which there clung not a trace of sadness.

Sometimes even seemingly insignificant detail reveal just how huge and complex the world really is. One morning, almost unconsciously, my eyes began to follow the meticulous gestures of a woman as she arranged and watered a beautiful corona of orange flowers around the neck of a small stone goddess on the riverbank below my terrace. Just then, a black goat wandered over and nibbled off a small mouthful of petals. It was about to take another bite when it was chased away by a cow which gulped down the bouquet of beauty and prayer the woman was offering to her goddess. None of the parties involved was in the least offended and the three of them, woman, goat and cow, went their separate ways.

Stepping out on to the same terrace years before, Angela had said, 'From here you can see the world the way God must see it … and you realize he can't possibly take care of everything.'

Could our Western unease have derived in part from the desire to do just that, to concern ourselves with everything that happened in the world and our attempt to try and change it? Perhaps there was wisdom in the Oriental view after all; all that existed outside us was immutable and that our only hope was to change our inner selves. This was Buddha's message too, though he believed such a change could only come with great and constant effort. Dying in Varanasi by no means guaranteed salvation and it wasn't an accident that Buddha went to Sarnath to announce the fact.

Walking north from the Ganges View Hotel, past numerous flights of steps that lead down to the river, one encounters two cremation grounds where the task of publicly disposing human remains is an unending one. There I passed hours watching the to and fro of the living and the dead, the continual bustle around the fires of staff and relatives. But what struck me was that nobody cried.

Here no one raged against death, whereas we in the West had such great difficulty accepting it. For us, death was always a defeat, something to combat with all the means at our disposal and even in extreme situations pray for a 'miracle' that would convince nature to alter her immutable laws for once.

There's a story of a woman who came to Buddha clutching her

dead baby who had passed away only a few hours before, and asked him for a miracle: to restore her child to life. Buddha agreed but on one condition: the woman must bring to him a handful of rice from a family who had never been visited by death. The woman ran from house to house, village to village, but everywhere she went there had been a death. Resigned, she returned to Buddha and 'he who passed this way' consoled her. But she had understood. Now they were together on the same road.

I regarded those bodies being brusquely set alight on the pyre and about how much we in the West identified with our bodies. It was difficult for us to conceive being separated from them. Even our hopes of immortality and resurrection were tied to the body. Unlike the Hindus or Buddha himself, we were unable to think of it as an instrument to be used and then unsentimentally thrown away.

On the streets of Varanasi, you see processions of people moving, almost without interruption, towards the cremation grounds. In each case, the body of the departed lies wrapped in a sheet on a bamboo stretcher shouldered by four men, its uncovered face turned towards the sun. There is nothing funereal about the cortège; nothing of the sombre shuffling one normally associates with such events. On the contrary it swiftly marches forward, almost breaking into a trot. There is no music, only the rapid, pounding cry of 'Ram Nam Satya Hai' – Ram's name alone is truth – to which a chorus of voices responds 'Satya Hai, Satya Hai' – it is truth. And on they march towards the pyre where the deceased's firstborn son, with his head shaved for the occasion, lights the pyre and watches as the flames devour both wood and flesh. Once the flame dies out, he pours a bowl of water drawn from the Ganga on the ashes. Then without turning around he goes down to the river to perform his ablutions before returning to the world's spinning wheel.

The funeral is not the father's but that of the body, and since no longer of value to anyone, it can be dispensed with. The West finds it natural to identify the deceased with their body, to make it the object of their sorrows. But when it comes to our own bodies the sense of identification is even stronger. The idea of it going up in smoke scares us and for this the Sufi vision of the great poet Rumi offers scant consolation.

I died as a mineral and became a plant,
I died as a plant and rose to animal,
I died as animal and I was Man.
Why should I fear?
When was I less by dying?[3]

One day, Shashank sat down next to me on the terrace and handed me a book about Varanasi, which he insisted I should read. He was right to do so. Among the many fine stories about this other-worldly city collected in the book, I found a passage from the *Brahmana*, a part of India's store of ancient sacred texts. It was the lines in which Indra, the god of travellers, encourages a young man by the name of Rohita to embark upon a life on the road:

'For a man who does not travel about there is no happiness, Rohita! Living in the society of men, the best man becomes a sinner. Therefore, travel!'[4]

---

[3] From *Selected Poems of Rumi*, translated by Reynold A. Nicholson.

[4] Quote from *Aitareya Brahmana*

In these lines, Indra had spoken to me too. A few days later when I returned to Delhi I wasn't yet ready to sit down, especially under a tree. Deep down I was still a sponge and my feet still dreamt of becoming flowers.

THE POWER OF PRAYER

At night, Old Delhi Railway Station is the kind of place likely to send Western travellers who are unaccustomed to India's ways into a panic. After the perfumed plush of one of the trompe l'oeil hotels where foreign tourists normally take lodgings, they might think they'd got the wrong century or even planet. They might even think they have fallen into the gaping mouth of hell, an animated reproduction of what for us would be the dark ages.

Nowhere on earth is there a scene to compare with it: the unending river of people pouring up and down the overpass in a flood of brightly coloured misery, the misshapen clumps of bodies huddled under platform roofs, patrols of police absently swinging their menacing-looking bamboo sticks, Sikh farmers in blue tunics with glittering swords dangling at their sides, trident-wielding holy men in orange cassocks, the station porters in their red dustcoats, each balancing a precarious tower of suitcases on their heads, plastic pickers rooting about on the rubbish-strewn platforms amid scampering rats, gangs of kids who live off petty theft and others' leavings in the station which is their only home.

From here depart all the country's major trains. These trains plump you down in the foothills of the Himalayas or the deserts of Rajasthan, on the banks of the Ganga or the plains of central India; the trains which derail, collide or explode causing dozens of fatalities and occupying the headlines for a few hours and resume normal service.

My train was headed north. At 6 a.m. it was due to arrive in Pathankot, the nearest station to Dharamshala where the Dalai Lama lived in exile, the spiritual and political centre of the Tibetan diaspora and a destination for thousands of young westerners like the English girl in the couchette below mine.

'Why are you going to Dharamshala?' I asked her.

'Same reason as everybody else,' she replied. 'Because I'm unhappy.'

I couldn't say the same about myself since I was going there to seek a cure for my illness. Yet, whatever our reasons, we were both drawn to Dharamshala by the same force, that of a myth of Tibet as a sanctuary, a realm of peace and serenity, receptacle for mysteries and miraculous powers.

The myth was an old one. Of all the countries on earth, Tibet, sheltered by the chain of the Himalayas, was the only land that was truly inaccessible. Its ruling theocracy, headed by the Dalai Lama in his dual role as king and godhead, barred entry to all foreigners. Those who risked venturing there would return bearing fabulous tales of its riches, its monks with magic powers who could run like the wind or survive for days naked in the snow.

Human beings harbour an innate need to believe that there exists an El Dorado somewhere, a paradise where people live at peace both with themselves and others; where, liberated from nature's laws, they can enjoy limitless freedom, perhaps even from death itself. Tibet, an immense plateau of rare beauty with its verdant pastures set amid imposing peaks, its arcane monasteries in their eyries and crystalline lakes in whose waters certain lamas, it is said, could predict the future, was the ideal screen on which to project such a dream. There, one could find Shambhala, the mythical kingdom of purity, the antechamber of nirvana and last stop on a Buddhist's way. There lay the Valley of the Moon and Shangri-La where whoever arrived vowing never to go back might hope one day to become immortal. Everything about Tibet was magical, and no one could escape its spell, not even a colonial official of Her Majesty's empire!

In 1903 when the first foreign military expedition penetrated the country's borders to arrive in the capital, its youthful commander Francis Younghusband, dismounting from his horse and clambering up the hill that overlooks the plain of Lhasa, was visited by an overwhelming spiritual experience.

He wrote that from that moment on, his life was never the same and the myth continued to grow.

In 1959, the Chinese invaded Tibet on Mao's orders, razing its monasteries and slaughtering thousands of monks, forcing the Dalai Lama to seek asylum in India. Tibet, the proud, independent land of mystery was finished, colonized, demolished and refashioned Chinese style. Its myth survived, however, and became the quintessential symbol of a civilization crushed by the clunking hand of communist materialism.

When the Dalai Lama, one of the few great men of our time, was awarded the Nobel Peace Prize in 1989, Tibet was at the height of its celebrity and Dharamshala, the town where his holiness resided, had become, in the minds of happiness seekers everywhere, the place to be.

Thousands of European and American youths, dozens of whom swapped their backpacks for a cassock, began to pour in. There even came a band of movie stars, writers and artists, and even a stream of young Israelis brutalized by their military service who hoped to rid themselves of the hate that had been drilled into them. Almost simultaneously, two Hollywood blockbusters appeared dealing with the vicissitudes of Tibet and the life of the

Dalai Lama. Everything Tibetan, whether it was art, Buddhism or medicine, was finished.

I too had always been fond of Dharamshala and had gone there on several occasions to interview the Dalai Lama and to write of the Tibetans and their hopeless plight. Normally, I would stay at the Kashmir Cottage, a bungalow the Dalai Lama had purchased for his mother when he arrived in India. The place where she had ended her days, it was now the property of his youngest brother, Tenzin Cheogyal, known to the world as TC, who had transformed it into a home for himself as well as a quiet, modestly furnished guest house. The last time I had stayed there was in 1996 with Angela and my old friend and travelling companion Leopold on whose account we had come. Leopold had not been well. After selling his jewellery business in Bangkok – he said he didn't want to spend his whole life producing useless trinkets – he had founded a review and began to write himself. However, he increasingly complained of feeling weak and run-down. The doctors in Paris said the problem was probably to do with his liver, perhaps hepatitis. Before pronouncing their diagnosis, though, they wanted to do some further checks. But Leopold had preferred to postpone all this and set off on another journey. He came to visit us in Delhi and we spoke about the hepatitis. I told him of two 'miraculous' cures I had heard about, the first was practised in Peshawar on the Afghan border. I got the recipe from an old carpet dealer who swore it had cured him. All you had to do is this: take a goat, skin it and wrap yourself naked in the blood-soaked hide and sleep in it for several nights. 'Within a week,' he assured me, 'the liver is completely healed.' The other, Tibetan in origin, was the invention of the Dalai Lama's own personal physician and liver specialist.

So there we all were, at the Kashmir Cottage. Thanks to TC's recommendation we managed to secure an appointment at the Men-Tsee-Khang – literally the 'Institute of Medicine and Astrology' – with its famous director, Dr Tenzin Choedrak. He was a lean man in his seventies whom twenty years of prison and beatings at the hands of the Chinese had left with a permanently dislocated jaw and somewhat cross-eyed expression. With his shoulders against the window, wrapped in a red blanket, Dr Choedrak sat cross-legged in a wooden rooftop loggia that was his consulting room by day and bedroom by night. We sat opposite him, accompanied by a young Tibetan woman who served as our interpreter. It was all very simple and modest, the man himself was of a warm and calm demeanour. 'Somewhere in our past lives,' he said, 'we Tibetans must have done great wrong to the Chinese. This is why they have made us suffer.' His own story was already legend. Born in a village that was a three-day walk from Lhasa, Tenzin Choedrak was just a young boy when he entered one of the region's great monasteries. At the age of thirteen, he was chosen to study at the capital's School of Medicine and when he turned thirty, by this time regarded as one of the country's most brilliant doctors, he was posted to Potala, the Dalai Lama's residence, to look after the God-king of Tibet, a young man eleven years his junior.

In 1959, when the Dalai Lama fled to India disguised as a soldier, many of his followers remained at their posts in Lhasa so as not to raise suspicion. Among them was Tenzin Choedrak who was arrested, imprisoned and subjected to every kind of violence imaginable along with thousands of other disciples.

The fact that the doctor knew the secret formula for several wonder cures was of no interest to the Chinese who despised all that was Tibetan and regarded anything to do with religion as an obstacle in their path of modernization to be cleared away. Tenzin Choedrak was sentenced to an extended period of hard labour and the Chinese requisitioned the Potala Palace, throwing out masses of old odds and ends that to them signified nothing but clutter. Among these were 200 kilograms of a mysterious black powder which, though apparently useless, the Tibetans had preserved for over three centuries.

With the passing of the years, the Chinese came to realize that Tenzin Choedrak, reduced to breaking rocks in an open quarry, was a special individual. Firstly because, unlike many other prisoners, he had survived his torturous ordeal and they reckoned he must have been in possession of some kind of secret that might be of use to them too. Then there was the question of the black dust which, after dumping it in a stream, the Chinese realized consisted of a precious mixture of gold and silver that had been intricately refined. They eventually discovered that it was this powder Tenzin Choedrak had used to create his treasured 'longevity pills'.

The Chinese had promised to set him free if he revealed to them the secret method of obtaining the black dust and the pills. At first, Choedrak refused, but after protracted negotiations involving emissaries of the Dalai Lama himself, in 1980 the authorities in Beijing allowed Choedrak to leave China to join the exiled Tibetan community in Dharamshala. Choedrak returned to his post as the Dalai Lama's personal physician – visiting him twice a week for check-ups – and took charge of the Tibetan Institute of Medicine and Astrology where he began the manufacture of three different types of longevity pill and oversaw the training of over 100 young Tibetan doctors.

This was the man who now sat before us asking Leopold to describe his symptoms as he examined his eyes and mouth, checking his wrists to measure his pulse. The visit didn't last long. In Dr Choedrak's view, Leopold's case was simple: yes, the problem was with his liver, but his pills could take care of it. He scribbled out a prescription, but we weren't ready to leave just yet since there were so many things we wished to ask him. I took the lead. How had he managed to survive his years of forced labour?

'By making a fire in my stomach,' he replied. 'With this, I was able to digest the inedible food which killed so many of the other prisoners.' The exercise, he said, had been taught to him by the lama of the first monastery he had joined as a child. But he told us he could say no more about it as he was sworn to secrecy by an unwritten pact between master and apprentice.

We went on to ask him what other illnesses he could cure. Disarmingly modest, he made no great claims, saying that many westerners, Americans especially, had come to him seeking a cure for AIDS. But this he didn't know. At most, he could help them improve the quality of what life they had left.

Back then I had no particular interest in cancer, an illness which I imagined only affected other people. I did ask him, however, for suggestions on how to combat depression, a request that was to lead to a strange occurrence which, even now, I find myself unable to explain. Choedrak replied by saying depression was primarily a Western condition. 'And the reason for it,' he continued, 'is that you in the West are too attached to material things. More than that, I will even say you are obsessed with them. Say, someone loses a pen. From that moment on, he thinks of nothing but his lost pen, failing to realize that it has no real value and that one can write equally well with a pencil.' As he spoke I automatically began taking notes with my old black Mont Blanc. The doctor went back to describing his years in prison, his precious pills and the various mantras that had to be recited during their preparation. Once our interview ended, we thanked the doctor for his time, proceeded to the chemist and returned with the pills to Kashmir Cottage where, back in my room, patting my pockets, I could no longer find my pen.

I immediately sent our interpreter back to Doctor Choedrak and asked the Dalai Lama's brother to telephone the institute. But there was nothing that could be done. The Mont Blanc was gone and I could think of nothing else. Not because I was particularly attached to it, but because I had a sneaking suspicion that the old doctor, detecting a note of scepticism in my question, had decided to demonstrate his powers and teach me a lesson. Could that really have been possible?

That very night Leopold began taking his pills. They looked like sheep droppings, and yet all three of us were convinced that there was something special about those little pellets. They were 'charged', charged with the vicissitudes that had led to our obtaining them, the mantras that had accompanied their manufacture and the meticulous procedure Leopold had to observe in taking them, squashing each pill before swallowing it with a swig of lukewarm water. Above all, they were charged with all the powers they had in the patient's mind, just where the magic lay. Even the fire in Choedrak's stomach had been kindled in his mind. The practice in question, called tummo – 'the mystical fire' – was part of an old exercise in yoga that the Tibetans had adapted to the climate of their own country. To survive the tremendous cold of Tibet's winters, monks were taught how to warm themselves up by focusing their minds on an imaginary fire in the pit of their stomach. Its flames, fanned by the mind and rhythm of breathing, would rapidly spread to other parts of the body. In the course of his instruction, the monk was made to sit naked on the ground wrapped in a cotton sheet known as a repa that had been soaked in cold water. The idea was that the heat generated by the monk would quickly dry the sheet. The great poet and holy man Milarepa, 'the man in cotton', got his name from drying three such sheets in quick succession.

That evening at dinner, we discussed all this with TC who told us that in 1981 his brother – 'His Holiness', as TC respectfully referred to him – had allowed several of his monks to perform the tummo before an audience of Harvard doctors and professors who were seeking scientific evidence of the mind's power over the body. It worked. Within a few minutes, all the monks had raised their body temperatures by several degrees.

Returning to the matter of my vanished pen, I asked TC if he believed the old doctor could have literally made it disappear. Deliberately vague in his response, he seemed amused that a sceptical Western journalist like me could entertain such a preposterous notion.

Perhaps as a reply, he told us the story of his own birth. His mother had already had fourteen children – the Dalai Lama being the fourth – when she was pregnant for the fifteenth time. The newborn did not survive long however, and his mother was distraught. But a lama came to see her and told her not to despair as the child would be reborn. Before the dead baby's body was removed to prepare it for the funeral, the lama took some butter with which he marked one of it buttocks. Shortly afterwards, the woman became pregnant again and when the baby was born, on its bottom was the very same mark. This was TC, the last of the brothers.

Leopold continued to consume his sheep droppings every night and within a few weeks he began to feel much better. Had it been the pills or had his liver, perhaps not as severely damaged as he thought, healed itself? It was impossible to know for sure. But the fond memories I had of my meeting with the doctor had been enough to convince me to go back to him again, this time to ask for suggestions on how to treat my own illness.

The train pulled into Pathankot station at dawn. Dharamshala was a four-hour drive away, so I took a taxi with my English sleeper companion and two other young backpackers. Though all first-timers, they already knew that the Dalai Lama was due to hold a series of special 'seminars' over the following days. Completely uninformed of the event, I hadn't thought it necessary to book ahead. So as soon as I set foot in McLeodganj, I saw my plans started to go awry. Dr Choedrak, it turned out, was ill himself and wouldn't be able to see me for several days. Like all the other hotels in town, the Kashmir Cottage was fully booked on account of the stream of foreign visitors who had come to hear His Holiness's teachings. I had nearly given up when, thanks to the usual fortuitous chain of circumstances and chance acquaintances, I met Prince Rupendra, a young scion of one of region's oldest, most eminent families. He offered me the honour of being his first guest in an old bungalow named Hari Kothi, which he had inherited from his grandmother and had just finished converting into a hotel. More than 1,000 years ago his ancestors, the raja of Chamba, had founded a Buddhist university in Bihar similar to the one in Nalanda, for Tibetans who came to study in India. Rupendra assigned me the king's bedchamber that had been his grandmother's room and where Vivekananda, the celebrated mystic and student of Ramakrishna, had spent the night 100 years ago. With its walls covered in old photographs of the prince's forebears, its liveried servants and the heraldic banner of the Raja flying from the flagstaff, Hari Kothi seemed far from the Dharamshala I knew. Nonetheless, the prince did everything he could to make me feel at home and one evening, learning of my interest in Tibetan medicine, he invited a Dutch doctor of his acquaintance to dine with us. She too, had been drawn to Dharamshala by its myth, wishing to do something for the Tibetan cause and learn what she could about their approach to illness and their treatment. For over a year she had worked at the local Tibetan hospital, but the experience had left her disappointed and embittered and she had now made up her mind to leave.

The Tibetans, she told me, had been spoilt by the attention they received from foreigners. But what of their medicine? The little that was of any use was derived from Ayurveda. Anyone seeking an alternative form of medicine had only to look there. Tibetan doctors, she said, were the first to doubt the efficacy of their own cures. The slightest cough or increase in body temperature was enough to send them running to her for antibiotics and vitamins. Sure, they still insisted their precious pills could cure hepatitis and transform hepatitis B positive, which can lead to cancer and could be potentially fatal, into hepatitis negative; but she never found any scientific evidence for the claim.

But had she ever seen anyone successfully cured by Tibetan medicine? Yes, there had been one young man from the West who had refused allopathic treatment, but as his hepatitis was of viral origin, he would no doubt have recovered in any case. But she had seen many die just because some lama, after a soothsaying session, had told them not to go to the hospital and let themselves be operated on by Western doctors like her.

But what about the Tibetans' miraculous powers? I hopefully asked. Was she certain they had no basis? Hadn't they, after all, made my beautiful pen vanish into thin air?

If their powers were indeed so magical, she retorted, how come they hadn't been able to defend themselves against the Chinese invasion?

These so-called powers were a trap into which the Tibetans themselves had fallen. At the time of the 1903 British colonial expedition, convinced they were invulnerable to rifle bullets, they had been mowed down by Colonel Younghusband's machine guns.

The Dutch doctor's impressions gave me pause. At the bottom they were a little different from those of past travellers. Back in 1900, an enigmatic Japanese monk by the name of Kawaguchi Ekai had managed to enter Tibet by pretending to be a pilgrim and spent three years there. In the account of his travels, written when he returned to Japan, Kawaguchi describes the country's terrible hygiene conditions and the complete lack of effective medical practice, boasting of how sought-after he was on account of the few elementary notions of doctoring he had gleaned as a young boy flipping through the medical texts of his physician grandfather. He recounts one episode when a fight broke out between two monks in the monastery where he was staying. Despite the collective wisdom of thousands of lamas, he was the only person able to fix the dislocated shoulder of one of the litigants.

How was it possible that today Tibetan medicine was generally regarded as one of the most valid alternative practices when only 100 years ago the Tibetans themselves had had such little faith in it, or as one of the maxims Kawaguchi had picked up from them put it: 'In Tibet, every Mongol is a doctor.'

Heinrich Harrer too, the Austrian author of the celebrated *Seven Years in Tibet* and one of the few foreigners who had lived in Lhasa during World War II, did not have a single positive thing to say about Tibetan medicine. He recounted how at that time people who fell ill would rather have consulted a fortune-teller or faith healer than one of the lamas from the school of medicine.

I too had been little impressed by this school when I visited Lhasa in 1979. One morning before dawn, bartering my Polaroid camera for a bicycle, I managed to slip free of my Chinese guide and made the arduous climb up Medicine Hill. From up there, as I watched the sunrise with Lhasa spread out below and the façade of Potala Palace before me, I realized that what I was standing on were the ruins of the old school of medicine. The Chinese, declaring it to be a resistance hideout, had reduced the building to rubble with their artillery. But it was still a holy place for the Tibetans. In the early morning light, dozens of people clambered up the hill to scrape clean its scattered stones and gather up the dust. The scene was incomprehensible to me until an old Chinese man explained its significance. The gathered dust would be dissolved in water and taken as a cure-all for several different maladies.

Perhaps the Dutchwoman had not been wholly wrong in her assertion that Tibetan medicine, even though its tradition had once had a solid foundation, was now reduced to mere superstition. 'If the patient enters the doctor's studio with his left foot,' I read in a book of medicine I had recently purchased in Dharamshala, 'the treatment will be successful. If the patient offers the doctor his left wrist rather than his right, the healing process will be faster.'

From the same book I learnt that there were in fact six pulses the doctors must auscultate on each arm and that each of these had its corresponding organ in the body. Then there were the 'special pulses': one of these reflected the condition of the family, while another was the so-called 'guest's' pulse. Could such 'logic' be trusted? The Dalai Lama himself seemed doubtful. Hadn't I seen him, after all, treat his sore throat with antibiotics even if he chased them down with one of Dr Choedrak's potions?

Was it all in fact just a myth?

In part, yes. There is no doubt that the West's interest in Tibetan medicine as an alternative form has grown hand-in-hand with its sympathy for the Tibetan cause and the Dalai Lama himself. In the United States, there has been a profusion of Tibetan medical centres in the last few years, while in every European country one can now find a whole troop of healers, masseurs and lamas offering their services and medicines at exorbitant rates. Numerous 'healing systems' and 'health programmes' are sold on the strength of the Tibet label. One such system presenting itself as a combination of philosophical, medical, astrological and tantric wisdom promises not only to cure every illness, but also rejuvenate the buyer, give them inner and even 'world' peace. Another system known as self-cure consists of denying the existence of one's illness. Cancer sufferers, for example, are gathered in a circle and made to repeat a mantra, 'I'm not ill, I'm not ill, I'm not ill', ten, a hundred, perhaps a thousand times. And yet, I'm convinced that in certain cases it must work because 'in certain cases' everything works.

The demand for Tibetan medicine has now increased to the point that Dharamshala's Institute of Medicine and Astrology recently had to open a special export office. Aside for the famous sheep droppings, the medicines now available include anti-stress tea, various beauty creams, incense for meditation – excellent too for 'states of imbalance provoked by sexual frustration, dry tongue, tinnitus, water retention and vertigo' – as well as a health tonic which the box assures us will 'optimize physical fitness, improve kidney function and boost sexual energy, impeding premature ejaculation and prolonging copulation time'.

If the Dalai Lama saw how these cure-alls were being packaged and promoted, I'm sure he would respond with one of his inimitable belly laughs. He is, after all, the first to realize that the

'Free Tibet' cause is no longer a question of principles, justice or international ethics, but simply a marketing strategy. Tibet sells, but only the way the consumer wants it – wrapped in myth.

'First we were victims of Chinese imperialism,' a Tibetan writer based in Dharamshala once told me. 'Now we are the victims of Californian neocolonialism and New Age culture that wants us soaked in religion and pacifism, riding yaks up mountainsides and meditating on snow-capped peaks. The West will pour money into anything connected to what it sees as Tibet, whether it be monks, dancers, artists or mystics, but not to help us get back our own Tibet.'

Dharamshala is the quintessence of this transformation. Once a centre for exiles determined to preserve their identity and return to their homeland one day, it has now become a theme park based on misconstrued idea of Buddhism, spirituality, magic, meditation, astrology and medicine. After having waited for more than forty years, the Tibetans no longer seriously believe they will return to the land of their birth and have by now adapted themselves to their displacement. McLeodganj is a shopping mall, specializing in New Age bric-a-brac, from Buddha-embossed bags and strings of beads to relaxation CDs and books on tantrism. The market fuels the myth of a Tibet that has little to do with the country's real past and even less with its present that has been swallowed up by China.

Yet, the myth remains. One evening, making the acquaintance of a group of foreign residents in Dharamshala, veterans of the Free Tibet campaign who had been here for years doing their bit for the cause, I saw that their need to believe in the magic of Tibet outweighed any other form of logic. An American man told me how he had once accompanied the Dalai Lama on a visit to Delhi for a ceremony that was being held in the park dedicated to Gandhi. When a swarm of wasps assailed the assembled participants, His Holiness had gone on with his speech without being disturbed by a single one. An eccentric English lady named Jane Perkins, who had lived in Dharamshala for almost fifteen years, complained that she had trouble sleeping on account of the fledgling monks in the monastery next to her house who were learning the art of levitation and who, unable to stay suspended in mid-air for very long, would come crashing back to earth with a loud thud that constantly kept her awake.

Jane told me of an extraordinary ceremony that was to take place the next day seven miles outside of town. How fortunate we were to be able to participate. The sixteen-year-old Karmapa who had recently escaped from China where he was being kept hostage as a possible successor to the Dalai Lama would make his first public appearance. Here he would bless the assembled crowd with the 'powers of longevity'. Just what I was looking for!

And so, I found myself the following day in a situation familiar only to the incorrigibly curious traveller. Set up in a remote and stony valley, the temple for the ceremony was still being built. The Indians, fearing reprisals from the furious Chinese, no doubt cursing themselves for having let the holy boy slip, had organized an impressive security cordon. Everyone present was instantly searched and their papers checked by one of the dozens of armed police officers and counter-intelligence agents who had been brought in for the occasion. Cameras and tape recorders were instantly confiscated. There was something absurd in this combination of Buddhist tranquillity and state-of-siege hysteria, old lamas and levelled sub-machine guns. Finally, after hours of waiting and spot checks, we were admitted into the temple's vast interior. In the front few rows sat the monks, around twenty of whom were Western converts and behind them a group of

Buddhists who had made the trip from Taiwan. Finally, towards the back were a mixed crowd of Tibetans, foreign residents and travellers among whom was the happiness-seeking English girl of the train. The Karmapa appeared, surrounded by a host of lamas and Indian bodyguards; a big, strapping country lad with ruddy cheeks, he looked surprised by all the attention he was receiving, though it was wholly understandable from the perspective of the Tibetans since in their eyes this boy was the thirtieth reincarnation of a great master, a reincarnation much more ancient – and therefore spiritually advanced – than that of the Dalai Lama himself who had chalked up a mere fourteen.

'Though I myself may not possess the power of longevity,' said the Karmapa, 'I can nonetheless, as tradition dictates, confer it upon each of you, together with that which will bring all your desires to fruition and grant you peace, harmony and happiness.'

He had great stage presence, this boy, helped in no way by the circle of monks who scraped and grovelled around him, bent literally double in deference. After all, here was a boy who might one day become the leader of the whole Tibetan diaspora when, following the Dalai Lama's own death, his people will have to wait for the child in which he was reincarnated to reach adulthood.

Reincarnation. I have always marvelled at the Tibetans' ingenuity in adapting to the contours of their own culture and using to their own advantage, the age-old idea that not everything in us dies with the body, but that some remainder which we might call the soul, for want of a better word, migrates to a new one. In this way, the Tibetans have managed to avoid the degeneration that is implicit in the notion of hereditary monarchy. As the son of the son of the son is unlikely to be of the same calibre as his illustrious ancestor, the safest way for a dynasty to ensure quality control each time is to choose as heir to the deceased an exceptional boy whom they recognize to be his reincarnation. In the case of both the Karmapa and the present Dalai Lama, the old monks' instincts seemed not to have failed them.

The Karmapa's blessing was not, as I had thought it might be, for all and sundry but was personal. Each of us was granted our own which made the whole business last much longer than expected. Patiently I stood in the queue until I found myself in front of him and we exchanged smiles. I gave him the white kata Jane had procured for me, which, after 'charging', he draped around my neck. He then gave my slightly bowed cranium a tap with the base of a small gold stupa that must have contained some kind of holy relic. After this one of the lamas handed me a small grey ball of tsampa – the malt flour Tibetans put in their tea with yak butter – which I gathered I was supposed to eat. Another lama gave me a knotted red ribbon, this too charged with blessings, that I was to wear to protect myself from harm.

I went outside and sat in the sun, observing the others as they left the temple. They seemed excited, happy, each convinced as Jane was, that they were truly fortunate to have received such a gift from the Karmapa. I, on the other hand, was sceptical and rational, maybe even arrogant. I was already thinking of how to get rid of the grey ball in my hand and looked at it sitting there. What if this was the medicine I'd been seeking, as it apparently was for the others to whom it promised long life. Couldn't it do the same for me? I popped it in my mouth and ate it, then carefully tied the red ribbon to my rucksack.

It can be useful to change one's point of view sometimes. It occurred to me then that I hadn't understood anything about Tibetan medicine and had got off on the wrong foot in Dharamshala, which is to say the right one. My reasoning up to that point had been of the kind I had so desperately wanted to get beyond in New York. It was the same as that of the Dutch doctor, founded on logic, the scientific view that saw me as a body and the illness as merely a physical phenomenon.

If what I had expected to obtain from the Dalai Lama's personal physician was the type of medicine prescribed by the fixers at MSKCC, a medicine which acted chemically on my body, I had obviously come to the wrong place. I had already tried that kind of medicine, the best money could buy.

Here the medicines were of a different order. They weren't designed to trigger any kind of reaction in the body, let alone a chemical one. They were cures for the mind and the soul. Back in Lhasa, I had felt only contempt as I watched the Tibetans scraping the sacred stones for a handful of dust to drink. It was an attitude, I realized, no different from that of a Chinese commissar. In reality the Tibetans knew what they were doing, invoking a power not of chemistry but of prayers and blessings. This, it was now clear to me, was the only power the cures in Dharamshala had. It was a power I could refuse if I wanted to, but I had no right to it for being unlike that practised by my New York fixers. Its value, if it had any, lay precisely in it being different and its difference derived from its religious roots.

Originally, Tibetan medicine was nothing but Indian Ayurveda, and the texts the Tibetans studied were mere translations from the Sanskrit of shastra classics. However, Ayurveda had been brought to Tibet by the same monks who had introduced the country to Buddhism. Like Buddhism, the way it was adapted to suit local conditions gave it a profoundly Tibetan character. Buddhism, which was almost forgotten in its native India, became in Tibet an almost wholly new religion with its admixture of the fundaments of Bon, the local animistic faith, while Ayurvedic medicine became more enmeshed with Buddhism, losing sight of its Indian scientific roots and assuming an increasingly religious, Tibetan form.

Buddha himself had been dead for more than 1,000 years when the Tibetans converted to the religion that bears his name, but the conversion was overwhelming and complete. Buddhism went on to influence every aspect of Tibetan society. In India too Ayurveda had a spiritual component from the beginning, but this was connected to philosophy, not religion, and the practice of medicine had never been confined to the priesthood. In Tibet, however, where Buddhism had taken over everything, including politics, only a lama could study to become a doctor. This was a tradition which went back to the rishis, the Tibetans preferred to think of their medical practice as something that had arrived at their doorstep far more recently – from the sky.

'Our medical science dates back to Buddha,' recited the various books I had purchased, words which I at first imagined were simply a manner of speaking, but were in fact to be taken quite literally. Rereading those books in the light of a purely Buddhist interpretation of phenomena, everything I had initially found absurd began to look more and more logical. From the Buddhist perspective all the various forms of evil, whether mental or physical, had a common origin: ignorance. Ignorance of the self was the cause of all the suffering afflicting man from the time he was born to the moment he died. It was the same ignorance that lay behind 'the mind's three great poisons' – desire, anger and dull-wittedness – that were responsible for all the maladies of the body. Only by a constant practice of moral rectitude and meditation could one free themselves from all evil. In this sense, Buddha truly was the founder of medicine: having identified the ultimate cause for human suffering and discovered the antidote to every kind of pain, he was the great doctor and one's only real cure was to follow his dharma.

In the Tibetans' view there was no difference between religion and medicine. Man, being a combination of mind, body and spirit, had only to be pious in order to be healthy. Illness was a disorder that took root in the mind long before it appeared in the body. This was why any therapy for the Tibetans had to be spiritual therapy first. Reciting mantras or executing a given number of prostrations was more important than swallowing a pill.

I was finally interested in understanding how adapting Ayurveda to their style of life and especially to their religion the Tibetans had transferred, sealed in Buddhist containers, the fundamental concepts of Indian medicine. Thus, Tibetan medicine was still roughly divided into the nine great sections of Ayurveda: illnesses of the body, children's illnesses, women's illnesses, illnesses provoked by the spirit, wounds inflicted by weapons, poisoning, rejuvenation, fertility and aphrodisiacs. It also employed the same range of medical herbs as Ayurveda especially those that grew in the Himalayas. Similarly, the Ayurvedic theory of the three types of individual constitution – vata, pitta and kapha – whose imbalances Indians believe to be the origin of all illnesses were translated as 'the mind's three poisons' in Buddhism. The four phases of Ayurvedic practice, moreover – diagnosis, cause, prognosis and treatment – mapped on to Buddhism's four noble truths: all is suffering, the causes of suffering lies in the passions, one can end all suffering, to end suffering one must take up the dharma.

To complete the Tibetification of Ayurveda, the Dalai Lama's followers added to the various manifestations of Buddha Sangye Menla, the Buddha of medicine to whom were attributed the sacred texts of *Gyu-Shi,* as well as the four tantras, which as we all know are translations of Indian Sanskrit texts, and the power to heal.

With his blue-painted body – the reason he is also known as the Lord of Lapis Lazuli – partly covered in a golden tunic, the Buddha of medicine is represented in the lotus position. In front of him sits a tray filled with fruit including aurora, the fruit of perfect health, which is impossible to find in today's decadent world but which will grow again when a new Buddha arrives on earth.

Another thing I read in one of my books was that meditating before a tanka on which this Buddha was depicted would make the nectar of health gush from his image. 'Rays of light emanate from the heart of Sangye Menla under whose influence man feels liberated from all negative thoughts and is cleansed of all ignorance. Maladies disappear and the mind's three poisons are placated.'

This is what I needed. I'd had many tankas over the years, but never one featuring the Buddha of medicine. So I decided to go with Jane to pay a visit to an old painter based in Dharamshala whose almost exclusive patron the Dalai Lama was. I asked him if he would paint a Sangye Menla for me. He said that for the moment it was impossible: he had to paint all the tanka for Karmapa's monastery. However, one of his disciples could do the job. Karma Sichoe, a twenty-seven-year-old orphan and Free Tibet militant – he had fasted for forty-eight days in front of the Chinese embassy in Delhi – promised he would send it to me in a couple of months. The only thing he needed to know was whether before mounting the tanka on its blue brocade, he should open the three centres of heart, word and mind on the Buddha's back. Knowing that the rays I needed came from there, I nodded.

I tried calling Choedrak's institute again, but was informed that the doctor was still unwell – he died shortly after my departure at the age of seventy-six. But by this point seeing him no longer seemed as important. Dharamshala had already given me more than enough: I had received the Karmapa's blessing and been given his red ribbon, charged with the power of longevity. I had ordered a Buddha of medicine which the painter would send me through Jane, plus I had stocked up on a supply of the finest incense, the fragrance of which stirred up memories of peace and serenity, which are 'powerful'of themselves and thus perhaps also therapeutic.

I took a taxi back to Pathankot and from there the night train back to Delhi. By dawn we had entered the labyrinthine tangle of rails that converge just outside the city. The train slowed down, its whistle signalling frantically to warn the lines of men crouched to defecate on the track of its approach. We then crossed the vast swathes of shanty town that lie on Delhi's periphery and which compose a suffocating expanse of filth, stench and misery. Children, goats, pigs and crows rummaged amid heaps of plastic and putrescent trash. From the train's cool and comfortable interior, the scene outside seemed unreal. The window was like a TV screen flickering with images from a horror film. Or so it must have seemed to the wealthy Indians who had been my travelling companions and who were now getting ready to disembark. I was struck by their apparent indifference and it reminded me of something that always seemed like the black hole of Hinduism – its lack of compassion. I could understand why so many Indians of the lower castes had in the past converted to Buddhism and why, later on, a much greater number converted to Islam.

FOUR

AMERICA

TERRA INCOGNITA

A certain Jerry was supposed to deliver me to the Commonweal, a retreat in California, where I was to attend a week-long seminar for cancer sufferers. Everything had been arranged on the phone or by email and I had no idea what to expect. The plan was that Jerry with a red jeep would arrive at 9 a.m. to pick me up from my hotel in San Francisco. And when I saw him, a pony-tailed forty-year-old with a drifter's beard, I realized it was better not to expect too much. As soon as I sat down in the passenger seat, he began to regale me with the story of his life. Sure, he was a driver, but that wasn't his real job. He was actually an actor, but 'since Hollywood only produces blockbusters with the major league stars', he preferred to stay out of it and stick to theatre instead, working with a small company run by some friends of his when the occasion arose. The last such occasion? Well, that was a long time ago …

Jerry was on his third wife who ran a drugstore near the place we were going to, but she too had another vocation. The store was just a way of getting by. She was really a 'visual artist'. I didn't even ask what this meant, by now being familiar with that peculiar, and ultimately harmless, vein of American madness: dissociation. No one is happy in their own skin, content to be themselves or satisfied with the job they do. No one wants to be where they are. Jerry rattled on, but I had already turned my attention to the landscape. After crossing the Golden Gate Bridge, we took a high road along the coastline where the city thinned and the houses fell away. The morning was warm and a pleasant breeze blew through the jeep's open windows. A distant haze blurred the line of the horizon, making sea and sky merge into a single plane. I was happy to be who I was and happy where I was.

I knew the Commonweal was off the beaten track, the nearest town being Bolinas. I looked for road signs indicating how to get there, but in vain. 'That's one battle we've won,' Jerry said. 'Signposts disfigure the landscape.' He then added as a clincher to his argument, 'Folks who live around here know their way around ... as for the others, well they probably got no business being here anyway.'

Around me the landscape was turning into a wilderness, barren and bereft. Though close to a major city like San Francisco, its natural beauty had been preserved – thanks to a disaster. In 1971 a stricken tanker had dumped its load of crude oil offered $50 a day to anyone who volunteered to help clean up the beach and save its fauna, especially seabirds grounded by oil-sticky wings. Hundreds of young hippies and surfers from all over California responded to the call, many of whom, bewitched by the landscape, decided to stay on supporting themselves by rearing cattle and pigs or by organic farming. Determined to preserve the area's natural beauty, several of these ex-hippies managed to gain office in local government, which was easy since they were now in the majority. Since their arrival the population of Bolinas had more than tripled from 600 to 2,000.

The road snaked through grassy dunes, climbing and pitching like a roller coaster. Jerry suddenly turned off on to a dirt track and within a few minutes we had arrived at an impressive cape that plunged vertiginously down to the ocean. It was as though for millions of years the waves had gnawed the land down to the bone of the cliff face. Scattered high up on the rocks, rhythmically pounded by the crashing surf, were a line of odd-looking cement blocks resembling sea-defence bunkers, surrounded by a forest of iron masts and enormous rust-eaten antennas. From a distance, the place seemed deserted, an alien outpost left by a group of disillusioned Martian explorers.

'Who knows, maybe they'll come back,' said an amused Jerry when I told him my hypothesis.

He then went on to tell me it had an equally curious history. It had been set up by the Marconi Corporation of America. It was from here at the dawn of the twentieth century that the first radio signals had been beamed across the Pacific. During World War II, it had been used to intercept Japanese radio transmissions. But with the advent of newer, more sophisticated communications technologies, the centre and its thirty-hectare site had become obsolete and in 1975 it was put up for rent. The then twenty-nine-year-old Michael Lerner took out a fifty-year lease on the place.

'I guess you could say it came along at the right moment,' he told me a few days into my stay there. 'I'd just got divorced, my dog had died and my dad had cancer.' With the help of some friends who had settled along the coast, Michael fixed up a couple of the buildings and transformed them into a centre for 'study, reflection and peace'. This went on to become the Commonweal.

I'd heard about the place from some patients at MSKCC and

had read Michael's book, *Choices in Healing,* on the various options – including medical – available to cancer sufferers. I contacted the centre while undergoing chemo, asking if I could attend one of their seminars. On the phone I had a hilarious conversation with a certain Waz who was in charge of the programme and was lucky enough to find a place for session number eighty-three.

My first impression of the place was of having stepped into some enchanted realm. Concealed in a forest of gnarled, knotted trees, bowed by incessant ocean winds, lay the absurd Assyro-Babylonian edifice that had once housed Marconi's generators and was now the site of the centre's offices and library. Further on were three houses with toilets, kitchens, seminar rooms and guest accommodation. I had a good feeling about the Commonweal. The elfin staff looked as though they'd stepped straight out of a fairy tale: middle-aged men with bushy whiskers and puppy-dog eyes, fresh-faced women with close-cropped hair. There, one whose head was completely shaved was the cook: a Buddhist monk with a strictly vegan repertoire. Waz, whom I knew only by his gravel voice, turned out to be a tall, lean African American. With his blonde goatee and silver earrings, he had the face of a friendly pirate, his pale green eyes set in a dark olive complexion. He had practised yoga for many years and written hundreds of poems, some of which were quite excellent.

'And where are you from?' I asked the cook's assistant whose full-moon face was impossible to place, though she might have been Korean or Native American.

'Me. Oh, in this life I'm, you know, from Ohio. But in my previous life I was Indian.'

'Really? How do you know that?'

'Uh, it's a long story, I can't go into it now,' she answered, skipping off to the kitchen.

Many of the participants were yet to arrive. At lunch I had the chance to get to know the Commonweal's founding members, almost all of whom had a history of illness, the wait for a cure, healing and occasional relapse. Michael, who had lost his father and sister to cancer had himself suffered a severe muscle disease from which he had only just recovered, while both leaders of my seminar suffered from cancer. Wasn't this the origin of the shaman, after all? The sufferer-turned-healer? People who had survived a major illness would obviously find it easier to help others. The shaman's scars were proof of his authenticity. Here at the Commonweal we all had our scars, which made it easier to talk.

The centre's staff told us about past seminars, friendships they had forged, funerals they had attended. They pulled out group photos, showing us who was still around and who wasn't. I was struck by the naturalness with which they spoke about death.

That afternoon Michael presented the course: 'A process designed to slowly get the body back on its feet and revive submerged or forgotten aspects of the personality'. The method? Group discussions, massages, meditation, sand therapy, drawing therapy, yoga and breathing exercises. The aim? To reduce the anxiety caused by the illness, present various therapy options, familiarize ourselves with various self-help strategies that could improve our physical and psychological condition and more importantly, enable us to face it with equanimity.

'The one thing you should never do,' Michael said, 'is hold yourself responsible for your cancer. We're all swimming in a sea of chemical products that didn't exist 100 years ago and there's no doubt at all that our health is connected to the health of the planet we live on.'

This was one of Michael's favourite themes and the one on which much of the Commonweal's work was based. He insisted greatly on the distinction between 'cure' and 'healing'. The former, he said, was a term doctors used that had to do with medicines and their eventual success or failure in beating the disease. It was a physical matter that depended on external factors. Healing, on the other hand, referred to the process by which the sufferer regained their equilibrium, and as such was more a question of their interior resources and of what they brought of themselves to their encounter with the disease. The Commonweal offered no cure for cancer, but could help in the healing process. This was the real function of the seminar.

After dinner – vegan naturally – it was time to introduce ourselves, recounting the stories that had led us here. There were nine of us in all, six women and three men, all with yellowed skin and a stubble of post-chemo hair growth and fear in our eyes. I was the only foreigner and from my angle, everything that followed was another chance to take a closer look at the America which had caused me so much anguish in New York.

An orthopaedic surgeon who looked a few years my junior recounted how his wife left him shortly after his cancer was diagnosed. What bothered him most, he said, was that she had taken all the furniture. The same had happened to a fashion designer, a petite, vivacious woman in her mid-thirties whose husband had presented her with divorce papers following her diagnosis. Ravaged by chemo, she was tormented by the fact that she couldn't take care of their child whom her husband was taking away from her. Other than one woman from San Francisco who had the emotional support of a loving husband and two wonderful kids, the position of all the others was unstable, marked by disappointments and conflict. Many felt abandoned by their families, saying how colleagues and friends had been more understanding. A lawyer from Denver was almost in tears as she told us how her secretary and assistant had both turned up at work with their heads shaven to save her from embarrassment.

The nine of us sat on the ground in a circle, together with a facilitator from the centre who was also in charge of the box of Kleenex that was passed around to whoever was speaking for them to dry the tears we all knew would accompany their tale. As soon as we noticed this strange yet oddly apt game of pass the parcel, the whole company burst into a fit of collective giggles. Even the young fashion designer couldn't help herself from laughing. I thought how the sadness and the rage that accompanied my companions' stories had more to do with their lifestyles and relationships than with the illness itself. Forget gross domestic product (GDP) or per capita income; here was the true criteria for measuring a society's development. But how to calculate the value of having in your life someone you could count on, with whom you could look both back and forward and share the joys and sorrows of the moment. What would the healing value of such a person be? Enormous, I would say. At this, the lawyer from Denver burst into tears: her oncologist had said there was nothing he could do for her and she would have to look for a new one. Another woman, a judge from Minnesota, claimed to have found the ideal doctor: he had never spoken in terms of healing or survival rates, years or months left to live. All his words were those of encouragement and she was determined not to end up a statistic.

A man in his early fifties who worked for a human rights organization based in Washington with a long history of cancer said he'd gone through two wives and several doctors to avoid feeling alone in his illness.

They were all angry with their insurance companies who would always find a loophole to get out of paying hospital bills. The orthopaedic surgeon had recently discovered a clause in his life insurance policy stating that his children would get nothing in the event of his suicide.

The most imposing 'presence' at the Commonweal was the ocean. Its vastness could be felt even when it couldn't be seen and whose breath was still audible when one wasn't consciously listening to it. Day and night, the ocean was always there. Maybe it was the true master here, the medicine we had all come to seek.

I slept well that night and woke up early at the first glimmer of dawn. Its meagre light was barely enough to see my feet by, setting out on the path that led from the guest rooms through the crooked forest, crossing the green dunes before plunging recklessly down the cliff side to the ocean; the immense, magnificent ocean that tumbled endlessly on to the beach, embracing the rocks on the shore. For billions of years, it had gone about its business, cancelling any traces left in the sand of footprints, a crab edging from its tiny hole, the mark made by a bit of wood.

I walked along the beach picking up small, odd-shaped stones: flat and pink, polished smooth by the waves with a black circle in the centre like the fossilized eye of some ancient sea creature. Here I could savour the planet's antiquity, the overwhelming vastness of nature. The surf threw up a vaporous haze that partly hid the rising sun, but it made me feel the infinity of the ocean more keenly. I thought of eternity then not as a time without end but as a moment without time. A moment when I felt I too was eternal, enveloped in a greatness which I know was within me.

On the way back, as the path flattened out, was an old wooden shack I hadn't noticed before. An iron hook held the door closed. I opened it and found myself in a space that, though tiny, was fraught with a presence. A low table served as an altar for offerings of dried flowers, seashells and a single ruined candle, left by past visitors. I decided to leave the small pile of stones I had gathered on the beach. The floor of the hut was partly covered by a straw mat and I sat there in silence listening to the breath of the universe along with my own breath.

Going down to the ocean became a daily ritual. I would go down for a walk to the beach every morning while the others were asleep, and then each evening before dinner, I would sit, sheltered from the wind, on the grassy plateau which dominated the coastline and watch as the water took on the burnished hues of sunset.

One such evening, during an exceptionally strong wind, the waves below battered against the shore with merciless abandon and I stopped to observe an old tree trunk that the ocean rhythmically snatched away and gave back. I thought of this trunk as my body, watching calmly from the slope as it bobbed on the tide before disappearing into the embrace of that benevolent giant. Two beautiful pelicans appeared in the sky, their massive wings outstretched to let the wind carry them effortlessly along the coastline. And might they not be my soul? I felt a great sense of peace then, wondering how many before me had a similar wish to fly away like the pelicans, swoop down over the rocks and out, out far into the sea. How nice that would be. I felt magnificently alone, without responsibility, without weight, without the burden of anyone's tears.

That evening at dinner, I discovered the centre's trendy vegan cuisine, despite its varicoloured allure, turned out to be dull as dishwater, insipid and tasteless. But so healthy, as the monk-cum-cook would say, presiding over a kitchen from which not a cup of coffee or even tea was to be had, only herbal infusions.

Mornings began with meditation and relaxation exercises led by Waz. He had a talent for creating a relaxed atmosphere and helping us construct the 'space of inner peace' where we could always take refuge, forgetting the weight of our head, arms or legs. He even spoke of a 'sacred place where the finite and infinite meet'. Though words like these had begun to irritate me, the exercises themselves were really useful and could easily be integrated into my daily routine, helping me keep my body and perhaps something else too.

After breakfast it was time for group activities and discussions. One I particularly liked was 'imagery': seated as always on the ground with a large sheet of paper and coloured pens, we each had to illustrate what was most natural to us, both our life at that moment and what we expected from the future. Once completed, each of us had to present our vision to the others in the group, explaining what we had wanted to express in the drawing. I found it curious that all my companions hoped things would get better in the future.

I had divided the sheet into four equal parts. At the centre, I had put a rosy-red sun rising – or setting – on the median, the horizon line of a blue sea. On the seabed, the area describing the present, I had drawn a sunken wreck of a boat on whose hull was the Chinese ideogram for life, as shoals of fish blithely swam through the algae from present to future.

When my turn came I explained, half-seriously and half to amuse the others, that on a universal scale my illness was of little account; whatever happened in future, the sun would still rise and set, fish would still swim in the depths of the cosmic consciousness.

The most disturbing drawing was that of the human rights worker from Washington. He had depicted himself in front of an organization chart showing all his appointments: his office, his children from his two wives, the hospital, the herbalist, the acupuncturist, the masseuse. He explained that to get from one place to another often required an hour-long drive and asked himself whether all these alternative medicines were really worth the effort. The future saw him climbing a ladder, finally free of appointments.

Throughout my life I've always had some difficulty with the concept of 'we': the attempt humans make to feel part of a wider community. The word has always made me uneasy. For thirty years I had a wonderful life as a journalist but never have I identified with the 'we' of the fraternity of journalists.

In some way I had a similar feeling about my companions here, though not out of arrogance. Almost the opposite, in fact. I couldn't see myself the way they did, as part of what Schweizer once called 'the community of those marked by suffering'. Let's face it, I wasn't marked the way they were. I couldn't compare myself with the orthopaedist who had lost both wife and furniture and who had a machine in his stomach to make his liver function. Nor I could with the woman from San Francisco who, not yet forty and with two small children, was now faced with the decision of whether or not to go through a second course of chemo with little chance of long-term survival. That kind of suffering left its mark. This woman's probable death, that was unfair. Not mine. I had escaped death on countless occasions: in Vietnam; in Cambodia where I was taken hostage by the Khmer Rouge; in the Philippines, when I insisted on climbing the fire-spitting volcano in Mount Pinatubo. I was lucky I was still here! And if my body's cells had run riot and had started aberrantly replicating themselves, there was nothing terribly unnatural or unacceptable about that.

And yet there was something profound that united us. Like my companions, I had never seriously thought about my own death. In New York I had felt death was possible, close at hand, but I had never consciously confronted the prospect. But I wasn't to blame. After all, that was the way humanity had always been.

An episode in the Hindu epic Mahabharata sums up the strange attitude we humans have towards death.

The five Pandava brothers, all exiled princes, spent several years living in the forest. One day, while hunting a deer that refused to be caught, the five brothers, tired and thirsty, stopped to rest in a glade. The youngest climbed up a tree and seeing a pond glittering in the distance, decided to go and fetch some water. After several hours when he had still not returned, the second brother went to look for him and he too disappeared. The same happened to the third and the fourth brothers. The fifth brother, by now alone, walked to the pond and was petrified by what he saw there: his four brothers lay dead at the edge of the crystalline water. There were no signs of struggle and the only footprints were their own. Distraught, but still thirsty the last brother scooped up some water to drink.

'Stop!' a voice said. 'This is my pond. Only by answering my questions can you drink from it. If you fail to do so and insist on drinking, you will die like your brothers.'

The voice was that of a stork and the bird repeated its challenge: 'Answer my questions and you may drink.'

The young Pandava accepted. The first questions were easy and he had no difficulty in responding. But then came the question of all questions.

'Tell me,' said the stork, 'what is the most surprising aspect of life?'

'That though man sees death reaping numberless lives around him, he never imagines it will one day come for him too,' the last brother said, touching one by one his brothers' corpses.

The answer was the right one and the spell was broken. The four brothers, none of whom believed death would come for them, were restored to life.

In the same sense, I was 'marked' like my companions. The death each of us referred to was not abstract or theoretical; it wasn't another's death, it was our own. My own. I soon understood that my real reason for coming here had been to speak about death.

'Okay, so how would you prefer to die?' the group leader began, striking the opening notes of that morning's theme. In no particular order and without fear of offending anyone or burdening them with our woes, we each took turns to respond, some clutching the box of Kleenex that was passed around the circle to those in need, others such as the orthopaedist in a more blackly comic vein. After telling us how his insurance premium would be annulled in the event of his suicide, he had spent a lot of time thinking and had finally decided not to use the gun he had bought for that purpose. He would take his boat out to sea and fake an accident, making sure his body was never found. Then the insurance company would be forced to pay up. More than a fine death, what interested him was tricking the insurance company. And this, our group leader said, was a positive sign, a sign of his will to live.

I was surprised to hear that suicide, with or without insurance fraud, was an option nearly all my companions had considered. Some were thinking of checking into an American institution whose name was unfamiliar to me: the hospices, homes for terminally ill patients where help was available to those who wanted to end it all. 'It's a question of waiting for the big wave … and then riding it,' said the group leader who had obviously been a surfer before her illness.

I spoke about death the way I had witnessed it when I was a child: not something unusual but a sacred, mysterious force that commanded respect and in whose presence you had to walk on tiptoes and speak in whispers. I had a vivid memory of those deathbed scenes, the hushed voices of relatives in the other room, the vigil that followed. We all stood around the corpse gazing upon it with wonder and acceptance.

In those days, if someone went to a hospital for treatment and the doctors said there was nothing they could do, they would be taken home to die in their own beds. And so, the last sensations of the dying would be those that were most familiar to them: the firmness of their own mattress, the smell of their own sheets, the creak of their door. Today, the opposite happens. Death is an embarrassment, something to be hidden from view. The terminally ill are shunted off to hospitals and sent to die behind a curtain, held immobile in a web of tubes and wires and surrounded by alien sounds, aggressive smells and unfamiliar faces. Though still here, they are already gone.

If I had the choice, I said, I would do everything in my power to stay out of the hospital and slip away the way my four grandparents had: in their beds.

Asking someone to pass her the Kleenex, the Denver lawyer thanked me. My description had convinced her not to go to the hospices.

The theme of death – the terra incognita from which no traveller returns – was much discussed that morning, though I don't know exactly what we were trying to do by talking about it in this way. No doubt a psychologist would be able to explain, but it wouldn't have helped in the same way that speaking to people who knew from experience what they were talking about did.

And this was a conversation that could only happen here. Again, it was the orthopaedist who spoke. One of the reasons for his divorce, he said, was his wanting to talk about his death, a subject his wife was desperate to avoid, constantly reciting average survival rates among people his age and with his form of cancer.

'She wanted to cure me with statistics,' he said.

The woman with the two young children spoke of how her illness was already an enormous burden for her husband, and she certainly didn't want to add to that weight by insisting on talking about her death. I had felt much the same way concerning Angela, which was why I was happy to be here where I could share such a weight with my fellow sufferers.

'Alright,' said the Denver woman. 'Let's say I accept I'm going to die and that maybe it's going to happen soon. Doesn't this contradict what we were saying earlier about the will to live?'

Having recently immersed myself in Zen parables, I felt I could contribute to this discussion with a story that in a way answered her question. I began:

There was an old monk who was about to die. Taking to his bed, he announced that by evening he would be gone. His disciples all rushed to his bedside. All except the most devoted who hurried instead to the market to look for a cake he knew was the monk's favourite. He couldn't find the cake anywhere, however, and so spent an entire day having one made. Hoping he was not too late, he rushed back to his master's cell and had no sooner stepped through the door when the monk suddenly opened his eyes and said, 'At last! Where's the cake?' He took a piece in his mouth and munched it with great pleasure. One of the disciples asked, 'Master, what is your last piece of wisdom? Tell us something by which we will always remember you?'

The master smiles. 'This cake is exquisite,' he said, savouring each bite.

With this tale, whose message was in a way similar to the wise words of the Delhi jeweller, I thought I was adopting a philosophical approach to the question. But then the charming mother of two young children said, 'Don't you think that all these stories, all the massages, the alternative medicines, the yoga whatever, all the scribbling, this talk about healing rather than cure, in the end it's all just bullshit?'

At this, we all laughed, except the mother of two who burst into tears, 'What I want … is a medicine that will just … get rid of this cancer. I want to get better. I want to see my kids grow up.'

She told us how she'd been brought up by a violent father who beat her when she was a little girl. Now she saw the same violence in her own young son and wanted to go on living to help him, so that he may not ruin his life. The group leader ended the session by asking us to remain seated in a circle and to close our eyes and hold hands to 'let our energies flow' between us. I found it all somewhat ridiculous and Californian, but recognized that this was me, the haughty European climbing up on his high horse again. Had he perhaps something better to offer?

Michael opened the after-dinner session saying we were going to talk about near-death experiences and about what we could expect from death, judging by the accounts of people who had journeyed to the threshold of the beyond and returned to tell the tale.

This topic I found particularly hard to take seriously. I had looked into it during the months I was in New York, figuring that UFOs and other such weirdness were a part of American culture. Though it might seem trivial and absurd, it undoubtedly played a significant role in shaping the nation's psyche. Hundreds of books had been written on such topics and dozens of conventions had been held around the country which brought hordes of people together to recount their bizarre experiences, even though the accounts invariably focused on the same details and employed the same imagery. But it was this very similarity of the tales that was seen as proof of their authenticity. I had read a number of these volumes myself and, oddly enough, had arrived at the Commonweal with one in my pocket whose title, *Why People Believe Weird Things,* said it all. So when the author, Michael Shermer who was with us then, began recounting the experience of a man who had made a return trip to heaven's gate like it was the most obvious thing in the world, I could hold back no longer.

'... The guy had a terrible car accident and was as good as dead,' said Michael. 'Then he found himself in a long dark tunnel, and in the distance there was this light that got bigger and bigger like it was pulling him towards it. And he heard a voice saying ...'

'In English, I presume,' I interjected, and everyone including Michael laughed.

The evening went on in this light-hearted vein. Speaking of somewhat more real cases of people who had been close to death but had managed to escape, Michael quoted from a book by a Jewish psychoanalyst who had been interned at Auschwitz. How had he survived when so many had perished? What kind of people were they, he wondered, the ones like him who had made it out alive? Were they more physically robust? Nothing of the kind. They were simply the ones who had had a more lucid grasp of life and death. This interested me.

To conclude the evening, Michael returned to the question of our inner space of peace, the place where we could take refuge. To open the door to this space, Michael pronounced three resounding 'Oms' before leading us in a collective 'transmission of compassion', which worked like this: Michael said Om, at which the person on his left pronounced their own name and prepared to receive the *metta* – the compassion and positive thoughts the others addressed to them. Then they would say Om and the person to *their* left would repeat the ritual and so on until the circle was complete.

At the end of this, my companions were all beaming, enthusing about the abundant stores of warmth, light and energy they had received. But all I had felt was growing anger. I was sick and tired of reason, sure, but the opposite horrified me just as much. This was my dilemma: only what I had discovered for myself or won through hard effort interested me and seemed to be of value; things I could grab from a supermarket shelf appalled me. *A Fortune-Teller Told Me* had been the book of a man who believed in the rediscovery of life's magic and mystery. But now that I was among the believers, I had returned to being the inveterate sceptic of old.

One afternoon, while strolling around an old building, I climbed up a wooden ladder and found myself in an empty room where the floor was covered by a groundsheet, depicted upon which, in shades of violet and black, was a labyrinth. Since it had obviously been put there to walk upon, I removed my sandals and stepped barefoot into the maze and gradually, after hitting several blind alleys and having to retrace my steps, made my way to its centre. I was alone and it felt good to be in the silence of the room, so much so that I returned several times. There was something magical in this idea of losing and then finding one's bearings, all the time moving towards the centre. A member of the Commonweal's staff I hadn't met before saw me on one of these occasions and came over to speak to me, saying it was she who had devised the maze and was planning to use it in one of the upcoming seminars. The idea of the maze interested her as a way of reawakening our spirituality, she said. It was a symbol of the sacred path each of us must take to approach their own centres. Here she thought it could help participants find something they had put aside, something which, though hidden, was attempting to express itself; something that could help us make sense of all that happened to us.

Borrowing a book on the history of labyrinths she recommended from the Commonweal's library, I learnt that the earliest ones dated from around 4,500 years ago: there was one dating from 2500 BC carved in a rock face, in Sardinia of all places. One of the first wall-carved labyrinths was to be found in Lucca on the façade of the cathedral. It had been put there so that the faithful could trace the path with a finger before going into the church. The labyrinth supposedly calmed the mind and made people forget their daily lives in preparation for their entry to the holy space where they would encounter God.

For centuries, the dream of Christians everywhere had been to make a pilgrimage to the holy city of Jerusalem, but from the twelfth century, because of the Crusades, the journey became more and more perilous. At this point several newly built cathedrals, each conceived as a miniature Jerusalem, became a substitute for pilgrims. For believers, negotiating the labyrinth on the cathedral floor was the conclusion of a symbolic journey they could not make in reality. Placed at the centre of this labyrinth was often a rose, the Western equivalent of the lotus flower, as a symbol of spiritual enlightenment. The most famous and perhaps finest of these labyrinths was in Chartres cathedral.

Another evening after dinner was a poetry-writing session, again led by Michael. Each of us had to write a poem that described our current state of mind. The following morning we would all be given photocopies of the others' verses, each of which would be discussed by the group as a whole. Michael once again encouraged us to express ourselves as freely as possibly, to jot down whichever words that came to us, and added as a warning, 'Don't wrack your brains too much. There's no word that rhymes with cancer.'

I remembered that when I was a boy I used to paint and at the age of sixteen I tried to write a novel. Once I even had a go at carving a piece of wood, but the poem I wrote that evening – if one can call it that – I believe was the first in my life.

Nobody ever told me,
I could fly.
Nobody ever promised,
I won't die.
Yet without wings,
I flew.
And now without regret,
For promises unkept,
For things undone,
Now without much pain.
I feel like flying yet... again.

Michael was quite a character. After studying developmental psychology, he had developed an interest in medicine, chemistry and ecology, but I doubted whether he was really a scientist at heart. Always deeply respectful of everyone's opinions, I had no precise idea where he himself stood. He, however, clearly thought he knew where I stood. Having seen more than a thousand people pass through the centre he had more or less grouped them into two categories: the mystics and the realists.

'You're certainly not in the first category,' he said, sitting beside me at lunch one day. 'Not that mysticism is necessarily a superior viewpoint to realism ...' He then paused for a moment and continued.

'And then, you've got to understand these are just labels.' He went on to point to his new wife as an example, who never discussed spiritual matters but who as soon as it started to rain would rush out to the road to scoop up the snails so they wouldn't be crushed by passing traffic. 'You see, she doesn't need to look for spirituality. Whereas I, I have to work on it a lot.'

And what about me? Was I just a realist? Or was I convinced realism and reason were no longer enough for me, fearing what Michael called mysticism and spirituality were ambiguous ideas that lacked any kind of objectivity or universality. I felt I was on a slippery slope. Sometimes the mere sound of words like 'energy' or 'vibrations' was enough to make my stomach cringe.

And yet, I too had begun to feel like there was something else, something more, and that one only had to change perspective for all the pieces to come together. The illness had come to teach me something. I needed to find my way through the labyrinth on my own to get close to my centre, devoting my energies to questions I would never previously have considered. Wasn't this what instinct had told me to do so as to be able to face my illness and live with it?

First of all, though, I had to overcome my arrogance, my intellectual resistance and my 'this-stuff-isn't-for-me' feeling. I needed to look at the world through a new lens. The one I had relied on up until now was perhaps no better, nor any less distorting. Regarding therapy, the Commonweal was definitely on the side of traditional allopathic medicine, which didn't mean it excluded alternative treatments. Michael strongly believed in the patient's right to choose and said the important thing was to safeguard their quality of life, especially from the therapeutic obstinacy of doctors or relatives. Though he had positive things to say about certain alternative therapies, he was particularly sceptical about a number of clinics that had sprung up on the US–Mexico border promising 'cures for the desperate'.

Michael believed it was crucial to try and involve patients in their treatment, especially psychologically, but at the same time completely rejected the New Age notion that it was the patient's responsibility or worse, fault, if they were ill. 'To me, that kind of thinking is both absurd and dangerous,' he said. 'Cancer is basically an epidemic type illness. Most of the reasons for it aren't in us, they're all around us.'

Michael and his colleagues had made a thorough study of the connections between cancer and the environment. Beginning with the most obvious correlations, they had reached a number of highly disturbing conclusions. According to one recent study, breast milk had become one of the most toxic of all foods. As the last link in the food chain, human beings were the natural receptacle for all the pollutant factors that had accumulated at each of its previous stages, multiplying their poisonous content by a hundred. Breast milk constituted a further link in the chain, which meant the suckling infant was the end-consumer of all the toxins its mother had accumulated during her life.

Breastfeeding, one of the most natural of mammalian functions, was gradually transforming into a subtle, indirect form of poisoning.

'In the last twenty-five years alone,' Michael said, 'tens of millions of Americans in urban centres have been drinking tap water that is in varying degrees contaminated by pesticides, defoliants and artificial fertilizers. They don't just drink it, they bathe and shower in it so their skin absorbs every small quantity of chemical components originally intended to be spread in fields.'

According to the Commonweal's research, breastfeeding was still the safest bet, however, as mothers tended to expel the chemicals inside them. And their kids, though undoubtedly ingested some of the poison, seemed to grow up healthier than those who were bottle-fed.

The relationship between human and animal health and the

health of the planet was another focus of the Commonweal's activities, which included promoting biodiversity and protecting the Californian coastline. This group of hippies who had originally rushed to the rescue of stricken seagulls and pelicans had recycled themselves wonderfully and they exemplified all that was good about American culture.

I kept contact with Michael for some time after the retreat. Though he told me he was continuing with his ecological campaigns, his most recent letters reflected a growing preoccupation with the planet's health. His experience with cancer patients had taught him that psychological awareness of living with an illness, which might at any point prove fatal, could be extremely positive. He asked whether a similar kind of awareness could be instilled in a country's population or in humanity as a whole. 'We humans have launched a ferocious attack upon every form of life on the planet and the resulting massacre now threatens to rebound on us. The time has come to recognize this once and for all, and finally do something about it.'

I agreed. If we wish to survive, we will have to develop a new awareness of ourselves, our being in the world, our relations with other people and living beings, and a new consciousness that will have to rediscover its spiritual dimension in order to counterbalance the obsessive materialism of our epoch. Only then can we hope to build a sustainable global culture and civilization. Our present civilization has led us up a blind alley and is sliding into barbarism. It is time to find a way out.

Michael's idea was to move from healing individuals to healing the planet. The earth, he said, was affected with a disease that threatened its survival, just as cancer threatened the lives of those who participated in the Commonweal's seminars. We had to create a movement that could raise human consciousness to what he called 'inter-being consciousness', awareness of the interdependence of all living things.

One morning, the 'imagination hour' took an unexpected turn when our whole took a walk across the fields to a cluster of seafront sheds. The largest one, somewhat dilapidated, had a ghostly aspect; the large room was illuminated by rays of sunlight that filtered through the roofing slats. Heaps of junk from fifty years ago took up most of the space: the skeletal carcasses of generators, antennas, electric cables and wireless sets. In one corner, still intact, was an old, red fire engine. It seemed like the perfect set for an execution scene, as indeed it turned out to be. Affixed to one of the walls, green from humidity, was a big white cardboard with the word 'cancer' written on it. In front of it, surrounded by piles of old bottles, sat a small table on which there was a set of marker pens. All of this had been laid out for the target-shooting exercise, the target in question being our illness, though we were free to add any other word that angered us or made us want to fling bottles at.

One of my companions wrote the word 'pain', another wrote 'bureaucracy' while someone else wrote 'insensitive doctors'. Predictably, the orthopaedist's word was 'insurance'. The sound of the bottles, as they shattered against the wall, was liberating. Everyone laughed, complimenting each other for a direct hit as they loaded up with more ammunition to hurl energetically at the target, delirious with joy. I, on the other hand, feeling no aggressive impulses, happily gave my ration of bottles to the lawyer from Denver. As we were leaving I took a black marker and over the now barely visible word 'cancer' I drew a moustache, a set of eyes and a laughing mouth.

On the way back, the group was in good spirits. They had enjoyed the game, with some saying it was the best thing they had done since arriving at the Commonweal. Undoubtedly, the controlled violence of bottles crashing against a wall had loosened the knots of pent-up rage within them.

During that afternoon's discussion the Denver lawyer offered us another piece of her life's puzzle. She had been married, she said, but her husband left her when their son was only four years old. There were huge arguments over who was going where with whom until the child spoke: 'You can both get out. I'm staying here on my own.' Eventually, it was the husband who left. At the age of eleven, the boy's behaviour became problematic. At school he would beat up other kids and insult his teachers, while in the house he was intractable, often hurling streams of abuses at his mother. On the advice of a psychologist, she got him a punchbag, which she hung in his room, saying he could do what he liked to it. Every time he had a grudge against someone or something, he wrote the name on the punchbag and beat at it with a baseball bat. The punchbag began to fill up with the names of schoolfellows, teachers, the boy's father, even his mother. 'That bag saved both our lives,' she said. When her son turned twenty-three it was time to sell the house and the removal of the bag was a solemn occasion. The two of them buried it in the garden like a relative being laid to rest.

Once you accept the fact that death is a part of life, you feel stronger. You feel no one has power over you any longer. This is what an old Japanese tale teaches. One of the emperor's young bodyguards, deciding he wanted to learn how to fight with the katana – the sword of the samurai – went to see a great master of the art and asked to become his disciple. The master, wanting to see what the youth already knew, exchanged a few thrusts with him. He was impressed.

'What school did you attend?' he asked the youth.

'I didn't attend any school,' came his reply.

'Impossible. You have already studied with someone, it's obvious. You've been schooled somewhere.'

'No, I tell you. I haven't been to any school. I taught myself. Since I entered the imperial guard, I've practised every day not to have any fear of death.'

'Ah, so that was your school,' the master exclaimed.

Overcoming our fear of death is a great step towards freedom. It helps a person live better just as it helps them to become a good swordsman. The odd thing is that while today people study and learns myriad different things, they learn nothing about death. Quite the opposite, they do all they can to avoid the subject, considered inappropriate topic of polite conversation as sex once was. So when that entirely natural, wholly predictable moment arrives, they find themselves ill prepared to deal with it and suffer terribly.

Eknath Easwaran, an Indian mystic who died in 1999 and who taught English literature and later meditation at Berkeley, recounted how his grandmother who was his spiritual guide had taught him a simple but important lesson.

When he was a child, he had been upset by the death of a relative. She had told him to sit down in a big wooden chair and to try and hold on to it with all his strength. He gripped the arms of the chair, but she managed to wrench him away from it anyway. Resisting her, he had felt pain. The grandmother then told him to sit on the chair again but this time without offering any resistance. The boy did as he was told and she lifted him gently from the chair and gathered him into her arms. 'That's just how it is with death,' she said. 'It's up to you to decide how you want to go, remember that.'

Grandmothers like Easwaran's are becoming rarer, especially

in the US where affluence, increased longevity and the myth of eternal youth have unsettled traditional roles. You can see the same idea beginning to set in in Europe. Grandmothers will increasingly lead 'their own life,' go on holiday with their boyfriends than worry about their grandchildren. People grow up with practical skills and the knowledge necessary for survival and material success, but can no longer count on the store of wisdom and experience of life and death that was once handed down by their elders. No one who can teach us how to die.

It wasn't always this way. Nearly all ancient civilizations, regarding death as a fundamental aspect of life, developed a culture of death which was their own way of facing its mystery. For thousands of years, the Tibetans have relied upon their sacred book *Bardo Thodol* – The Tibetan Book of the Dead – written, it is said, by Karma Lingpa, to cope with the moment of passing. When someone is about to die, the lama chases the bedside mourners out of the house and then tells the dying person not to resist, to let go, detach themselves from the things of this world and their loved ones. Every tie is being loosened, everything is becoming 'as empty as a cloudless sky'.

'Let go, my son of noble birth,' the lama says. 'The primordial light approaches. Become one with it. Go. Be on your way. Don't resist.' These are the words he whispers over and over in the ear of the dying.

The retreat, I increasingly realized, was a training course for illness. Michael even said as much one evening. 'A lot of people have to deal with cancer, but nobody is prepared for it. When they tell you you've got cancer it's kind of like being thrown from a helicopter into the jungle without knowing the first thing about how to survive. But if you had some kind of training you'd have a better chance.'

Michael believed strongly in the importance of support groups. A doctor from Stanford, following the cases of several women with metastatic breast cancer had made a surprising discovery: those who in addition to their normal treatment had taken part in regular meetings with other women sufferers had survived much longer than those who hadn't. A similar study carried out in Los Angeles had reached the same conclusion.

'But none of this made the front page, of course, not the way the discovery of a new miracle treatment would. It's all about the money and there's no money in support groups. Maybe it'll take another twenty years, but one day people are going to realize psychological support is a vital part of any kind of cancer treatment.'

And it worked. Completely cut off from the world and without the distraction of newspapers, radio or TV, the group became more and more united as the days went by, their discussions more uninhibited. Though concepts such as 'inner space of peace' or 'holy place' might have sounded flimsy, the week we spent in that secluded oasis by the sea was highly rewarding and had perhaps even helped us regain our equilibrium. It seemed to me that all of us had benefited, that the retreat had sharpened our awareness. Like the shack on the headland, whose name, I discovered, was Jennifer's Chapel, the Commonweal must have been a holy place after all. My companions had begun to believe there really was an inner space of peace where they could find shelter. We hadn't overcome our fear of death by any means, but it had become something we could calmly talk about, no longer a taboo subject.

One evening after dinner, we sat up late in the common room talking about funerals, last words, the things we would leave behind. Here too, the orthopaedist was ahead of us. He had already designed a memorial website and was compiling an enhanced CD that contained pictures and videoclips of his life, together with written accounts of the things he had done. His children, he said, had no idea of the person their father had been. This way, even though he was gone, they could at least download his memory.

Later, when the conversation turned to the subject of last words, I recalled Verdi's. Struggling with his ill-buttoned jacket, he had reputedly muttered, 'A button more, a button less …'

But when it came to writing down what I myself might say, all I could think of was this: 'I want to thank everyone who gave me a hand, and especially Angela who gave me two.'

Maybe we really are more than just a body, but this something is never fed or watered. While our senses get their fill of everything they desire, our putative soul is starved and wilts from thirst.

And yet each of us knows from experience that there are certain moments, a scene of great beauty, a particular word or phrase or a symbol in which we hear the echo of something familiar that we cannot recall. Moments when a voice whispers to us that we would love to stay and listen to but are distracted too quickly. The truth brushes past us and we pretend not to notice. The Mahabharata contains a wonderful image of such an encounter. A man out walking in the forest feels the tickle of a spider's web against his face. He has two choices: with a simple swipe of his hand he can remove it and carry on walking; or he can stop and with his eyes trace the web to its centre.

Such experiences happen often, allusions to something behind the world of appearances that we hurriedly decide to swipe past and move on.

Surely, it was time for me to stop and look where I was moving on to. Yes, this was my attitude now, but it still wasn't clear or obvious enough. Nothing is harder to remove than habit, the tried and tested ways we have of reacting to the world. Nothing is more difficult than liberating ourselves from what we know or who we think we are. I still had my repertoire of instinctive reactions, that ill-placed vanity, pomposity even, my presumption in thinking I had all the answers.

I couldn't deny that the United States possessed a vitality and variety, I might even say naivety and freshness. It had a spontaneity that an old European like me felt he had lost. But the ocean carried me back to it, to what was elemental, primordial.

Despite taking part in all the discussions, despite the benefits of talking about death, I noticed I clearly kept my distance, aloofly perched on my hill of European intellectual hauteur, staring down at something that in my eyes lacked sophistication. It might be all right for the Americans but not for me. I sometimes had the impression that much of what America had invented was simply hot air. But maybe that was what I needed to melt the pretentious, arrogant ice of my mind. This was the nature of the struggle taking place in me. I resisted; I didn't want to let go.

My reaction to the sandbox was typical. 'This is a wonderful way to help people express what they have inside,' enthused the leaflet. 'Every child knows how to play with sand. Now you can play too. But don't do it to prove or demonstrate anything. Just play. Let your unconscious mind be your guide.'

Hearing two women from my group raving about the sandbox was enough to put me off. The idea of playing with sand under the watchful eye of a woman my own age whose job it was to help me look inside my soul repelled me. I couldn't rid myself of the prejudices of the intellect, one who judges, interprets and has maybe read a book or two. Forever this obsession with self-control, it seemed absurd to have come all this way for things I'd never taken seriously before. So when I stepped into the room where I was supposed to 'let my inner child express himself', I was prickling with inner annoyance. The room itself was small and box-like. In the middle was a table with a big blue wooden tray on it, filled with a thin layer of white sand. The shelves that covered the room's walls contained a vast jumble of odds and ends: plastic figurines, crystals, bird plumes, bits of metal, wires, broken ornaments, different coloured ribbons, dried flowers, pebbles, masks, cardboard cuttings, playing cards, children's shoes and a myriad other objects. A big light hung from the ceiling, illuminating the sand tray as though it were a stage awaiting the opening act.

'I can't imagine what on earth I'm doing here,' I said, hoping to provoke the extremely kind woman who was waiting for me. 'Coming here I thought the best thing I could do would be to leave everything exactly as it was ... even that must mean something, don't you think?'

'If that's what you want, that's great, you're already done,' she said with a smile. She wasn't offended or annoyed in any way and that made me curious. She must have had to deal with countless know-it-all's like me and had no need to gas herself up to deal with my foolish swollen head. It wasn't the situation that was ridiculous, it was me.

I sat down and let her explain what I was supposed to do. She had a lovely way about her as she spoke, self-effacing even. I admired her ability to step back and blend in with the scenery. She was there, but her presence wasn't a weight. As though I were alone on a beach, I followed the instructions she gave me. With my eyes closed in meditation, I 'felt' the sand, letting my hands guide me. Then, opening my eyes, but still 'given over' to my inner child, I began filling a basket with items from the shelves: a red-winged angel, a piece of blue marble, a quartz pyramid, an old pine cone, a bunch of purple flowers, a toy pagoda, a plastic rainbow and counters from a game of runes. Flicking through a pack off Tarot cards, I was drawn to the Keeper of the Flame card and was about to add it to my cart when the woman said, 'In this case, it's better if you let your hand choose blind.' She told me to shuffle the pack and close my eyes. I chose a card; it was the Keeper of the Flame.

My finished composition, using less than half the objects I had picked, was a fairly simple one. With the sand I fashioned a mountain landscape that was dotted with two lakes. One of the lakes was made of marble and at the bottom of the other was an eye. From one corner of the tray, there sprouted the rainbow with the purple flowers placed diagonally opposite it. Through the valley I traced a path, first with one finger – myself, then with two – Angela and me. On one of the mountain tops, I placed the quartz pyramid, while on the ridge separating the two lakes I planted the three counters with their indecipherable runes. Then on one side of the tray, vertically so as to give it dominance over the whole scene, I placed the Keeper of the Flame. In a third corner, there stood a candle and beside it, on the tray's wooden edge, a half-open box of matches with one match stick popping out. Several times the woman asked me if I wanted to light the candle. Each time I said no. If I light the flame, I told her, it will die. This way, there remains something to be done. This way, I can slip free of time.

'And what about a title?' she asked.

'Eternity.' The word came instinctively to my lips.

'And those three runes on the hill. Are they supposed to be some kind of totem?'

'No, they're tombstones.'

'Which one do you like best?'

'The middle one.'

The woman made coffee for both of us. We sat facing each other, separated by the sandbox. She asked me to explain the reason for my choices and read to me from a book about what the Keeper of the Flame and the runes I had selected meant. Then, for ten minutes or so, it was her turn to speak about my rapport with cancer and my spiritual longings. What she said might have sounded obvious, banal, Californian. But, nonetheless it touched a chord in me I didn't know I had. Her readings of the signs I had left in the sand brought a lump to my throat. I got up, thanked her and went off for a long walk along the rocks on the beach.

Back in my room, I found photocopies of the pages explaining the significance of the Keeper of the Flame card and the runes. The woman had them sent along with a kind note. On the page from the book on Tarot it said, 'Choosing the Keeper means you are blessed with a divine healing presence. You recognize the strength you have in your hands to rekindle the flame in both your family and friends.' The entry on the runes, meanwhile, said: 'What you have chosen is the rune of the end and of a new beginning in your cycle of self-transformation. Choosing it means the life you have lived up to this point is over. You should let it die, let the energy be freed so that it can pass on into a new rebirth. Prepare for a great opportunity that will appear in front of you in the guise of a loss. When you hit deep water, that's when you become a great swimmer.'

Everything fit. But by now I was quite familiar with this type of message in which everyone finds the meaning that suits them. I could equally well have found something of myself in the runes or cards I hadn't chosen. And yet, a part of me had really warmed up to the woman, the sandbox and all we had said to each other. Had I learnt something after all? At least that I should be less arrogant and perhaps listen more to that voice, touch that chord, let myself go rather than remain trapped within the absurd boundaries we had unconsciously imposed upon ourselves and which were perhaps the root of all our suffering. We traced a circle around our lives that we believed to be enchanted and did our best not to step out of it. Inside it, however, we felt constricted, we suffered. Why couldn't we go back to being children again, curious about everything without limits or prejudices; free of the already known and taking nothing for granted?

The last evening, wrapped up in white blankets, we all trooped out to the headland to watch the sunset. There was a strong wind and we all huddled together for warmth. This was how we appeared in the group photograph they took which would be circulated, together with our comments, among the participants of future retreats.

When Jerry, the driver-cum-actor, picked me up to take me back to my own world, I showed him the lilac stuffed-toy heart I had been given as a grounding object to 'reconnect with myself', the Commonweal and the people I had met there whenever the need arose. And to think, I was almost going to leave it behind. But I still have it, and sometimes just seeing it there on the shelf among my books is enough to bring a smile to my lips.

CONCERTO FOR CELLS

'I've got the perfect yoga master for you,' Amrit Stein, a German friend of Angela's wrote to us. 'He lives in San Francisco.' Amrit was an habitué of India who learnt how to dance the Kathak, a traditional Indian dance form.

I could no longer go jogging but I still needed exercise, and yoga seemed like a good surrogate. An exchange of emails and an appointment after the retreat at the Commonweal later, I found myself once again caught up in a skein of new acquaintances, places and experiences that would take me far from my original aim – in this case yoga – but which otherwise I would never have otherwise encountered. Sometimes it's enough to take the first step in the right direction and everything else falls into place, well almost. Yoga didn't become a part of my life but, so many things followed from that first fateful meeting when I turned up at 10.30 a.m. at an address somewhere in the Avenues, a genteel San Francisco neighbourhood whose residents seemed to have been vacuumed away, leaving rows of clean white or powder blue houses. It depressed me to think anyone might have the misfortune to live in them! I rang the bell and the door opened.

'Tiziano!' exclaimed the man who answered. A bald sexagenarian with a white goatee, Ramananda was wearing black running shorts. I liked him, but immediately perceived a great sadness behind his smile. His face was scrubbed and shiny, his body lean with powerful shoulders. Only his legs seemed too thin, somewhat rickety. I thought, 'Strong house, weak foundation.' I followed him up a narrow staircase. The house was a kind of commune he shared with some of his students who lived on the first and second floors and the third floor belonged to him.

We sat on the floor; the room was neatly kept and everything in it was reassuring … everything except the photo of Sai Baba that peeped out from the corner of a mirror. I had always been deeply suspicious of these super saints, especially if they were multimillionaires; the blindness of their followers saddened me.

Though Ramananda had been born in Dar-es-Salaam in Tanzania where his father had emigrated to work as a teacher, it was his father who had given the boy his first yoga lessons and who had stuffed him with the ideas and values that for centuries were central to an Indian's identity. To do this, he had come up with an ingenious expedient: reciting the Bhagavadgita from memory, he would get Ramananda to check whether he had made any mistakes. This meant the boy had to follow the text extremely carefully and, therefore, ended up learning every line of it himself.

Following his father who was periodically transferred from one Indian settlement to another in East Africa, Ramananda grew up in a world similar to the one V.S. Naipaul describes in his novel *A Bend in the River.* He then went to England to study engineering where he met the famous yogi B.K.S. Iyengar who was visiting his university and whose student he became. Ramananda was a great admirer of Iyengar whom he considered a genius, but when I asked him whether I should go to his master, seeing as my house in India was not far from where Iyengar himself lived, he responded dryly: 'If you want to learn yoga, you should at least do it with someone who knows how to smile.'

We talked about the difficult relationship between master and student, how in India this rapport was further complicated by the fact that the disciple was supposed to surrender to the master and abandon himself completely. I found this kind of thinking dangerous. Sometimes the master in question – Sai Baba, for example – sprang to mind. Flattered by the absolute devotion of his followers, he would begin to think of himself as a god and the student would become entirely enslaved to his will.

Ramananda agreed, saying that while it was the guru's job to lead his students in taking their first steps, he should then allow them to find their own way. 'After all,' he added, 'what really counts is the method, not the guru.'

In his view the best method was Iyengar. His own rapport with his guru had been far from ideal, however. Now that he himself was a master, this role disturbed him. Years of teaching had led him to the conclusion that students, especially in the US, would invariably arrive already in a state of abnegation. Within a few months, however – on average six, he said – conflicts and tensions would begin to creep in. Everyone would want to be the guru's pet. 'Because yoga,' he added, as though wishing to rid me of every last illusion I might have, 'doesn't improve people, it merely brings out what is already inside them. If you're a thief, yoga can help you become a better one. Or if you're the envious type, yoga will turn you a darker shade of green.'

Ramananda refused to mythologize. It was easy at this stage for me to point to the picture of Sai Baba and ask if he was a follower. Not in the least, he assured me. If he'd ever had a guru, that had been Swami Dayananda Saraswati, a teacher of Vedanta, India's ancient religious philosophy and one of whose ashrams were in the US. Ramananda told me he went there every year to teach yoga.

I found Ramananda instantly likeable. He didn't try to sell me the illusion that yoga could cure illnesses or that it was the gateway to magic powers such as levitation or making oneself invisible, feats that as recently as the 1950s a number of practitioners of hatha yoga believed possible. Instead, Ramananda believed in perseverance and willpower and this put me at ease. I recounted to him the chain of events that had brought me here.

'Cancer! Aren't you afraid?'

'No,' I answered.

'We all have to die. It's just a question of whether or not you're able to enjoy the trip,' he thought for a moment and then commented. 'Yoga can help us keep the body and soul together along the way.'

Then, to lighten the tone of the conversation, Ramananda recounted an anecdote with which, he said, he liked to start his beginners' course.

A guy went to the dentist who saw he had magnificent teeth, but also that he had a fondness for chocolate.

'If you want to keep those teeth for another hundred years,' the dentists said, 'you will have to give up the chocolate.'

'If that's the case, I'll give up right now,' the man replied. Taking a bar of chocolate from his pocket, he dumped it in the wastepaper basket.

'Excellent! Now you will have perfect teeth for another hundred years.'

The man went out, but no sooner did he step on to the road was he hit by a lorry. In the moment before he died, he had the choice between two possible attitudes: he could tell himself, 'Damn that dentist for depriving me of my last piece of chocolate,' or he could say, 'Good job that before dying I finally did what I've always wanted to do: give up eating chocolate.'

Then Ramananda added, 'During our lives there are millions of things that can go wrong and they usually do.' I had the impression the life he was referring to was his own

We decided to start lessons the following day. Ramananda, meanwhile, invited me to have lunch with him and then made me a cup of tea. In this way I was able to meet the other members of the commune and among them was an elderly Indian gentleman who was Ramananda's patient. A car accident had left the man paralysed on one side, but Ramananda had promised to get him walking again. 'You really think you can do it?' I asked Ramananda, noticing how the man could barely drag his left leg while his left arm dangled uselessly by his side.

'Sure,' Ramananda said. 'It's just a matter of getting him to believe in his own mind that he can do it.' He invited me to watch as the man went through the exercises he had been taught.

Ramananda was a rigorous, not to say cruel, taskmaster,

barking commands at the suffering old man, ordering him to take small steps and keep his balance by thrusting out the right arm together with the left leg and vice versa.

Later he told me how Iyengar himself had managed to get the twenty-two-year-old cricket-playing son of a friend back on his feet again. On his deathbed the friend had made him promise to heal the boy who had been left wheelchair-bound after a car accident. With Ramananda supporting his weight, Iyengar had forced the youth to get up. Then positioning himself behind his shoulders and prodding him in the back with a cane, he began hurling insults at him, screaming at him to the point that both Ramananda and the other students thought he had gone completely mad. Finally he started pushing him repeatedly until, one laboured step at a time, he had managed to walk across the entire room.

'There. I've kept my promise,' the great master Iyengar said.

'The secret,' Ramananda explained, 'is to free the mind from the shackles of scientific truth.'

As for his own patient, he believed that in two months he would have him walking again.

The day we spent together was extremely helpful. I now had a good idea of what kind of person Ramananda was. I liked the man and he clearly liked me too. Though his sadness troubled me. The following day when I arrived for the first lesson, he greeted me saying I was over-tense, too judgemental and thought too much – the worst attitude one could have for yoga.

Perceptive, I thought, but what could be done about it?

The first thing to learn was a relaxation technique before each session. I had to lie on my back with palms raised and eyes closed. 'Sometimes, God will drop golden nuggets from the sky,' he said. 'You don't want to miss out.' Now every time I lie on the ground to do the exercise or simply to look at the sky, those nuggets come to mind.

The relaxation techniques Ramananda taught me were his most important contribution to my well-being.

'Lie down and relax. Empty your mind of all thoughts. Relax your muscles and let the knots loosen. Take deep breaths. Listen to your breath. Follow it as it passes into your arms, hands and legs; feel it cleansing, removing and healing. Imagine your breath sweeping away all impurities. Let every part of your body sink into the floor. Let go of your organs. Imagine your kidneys settling into the floor. Let the flesh slide from your bones and feel the deep joy as it rises in the inner corner of your eye. Let yourself go. You are cradled in the lap of mother earth. Just lie there in the space of the universe, without doing anything, without saying anything. Let the lump in your throat dissolve. Slowly feel it soften. You are happy even if no one else understands you. Summon all your energy and let go of everything that has taken up residence in your body that doesn't belong there. Slowly, slowly ...'

After fifteen minutes of these lulling words, there was still a part of my mind that clung stubbornly to thought and judgement. Ramananda began to teach me some of the asanas, the yoga positions he believed would be of most help to me, especially to my hernia. And so, I found myself upside down, head on the ground, suspended in mid-air from a belt or doing a shoulder stand against the wall. I soon realized that the Iyengar method which so enthused Ramananda was not for me. Iyengar's great innovation, he told me, had been in introducing gym apparatus into the practice of yoga. This meant that every asana required the use of belts, straps, harnesses, cushions, chairs or blocks of wood, the exact opposite of what I was looking for, imagining that yoga meant needing only one's body and floor on which to put it. Ramananda's apparatus repelled me. For more than thirty years I would run several miles every morning. It had been my way of meditating. On my travels all I needed was a pair of shoes and shorts. Wherever I was, I could go for a run. Sometimes it could be a real adventure as in Pyongyang where I had government agents at my heels, trailing me through the park in their dark sedan. Lumbered with all that apparatus I could never have stayed ahead of them, let alone done yoga. But I had signed up for a week of Ramananda's classes and so I stayed in the harness. Which was just as well, for had I decided to bail after that first hour I would have missed all that followed and this book would probably have taken a different turn. During that week, I was to witness the semi-paralysed man make remarkable progress, reinforcing my conviction that the mind, which for me was normally a source of great agitation, was also the source of great power in which I found myself believing more and more – the power to act on matter.

Ramananda also told me of a special seminar on yoga and sound that he and a musician from Calcutta were going to hold in his guru's Pennsylvania ashram. Their aim was to explore the potential therapeutic value of combining asanas with Indian classical music. It sounded interesting and I was excited at the prospect of meeting Swami Dayananda, the expert in Vedanta, and everything else which had somehow eluded me during all those years I lived in Delhi, which probably meant Indian thought itself. The seminar was to take place in a few weeks. Could I still enrol? I could.

From San Francisco, I flew to New York for my appointment with the fixers. The results of the various tests came back the following week: it seemed my lease on immortality had been prolonged, though I would have to go back for a check-up in three months which, as luck would have it, was just after Ramananda's seminar.

I took the intervening time out to rest and read up on yoga and music therapy, an ancient practice which, like many other forms of alternative medicine, had recently been rediscovered and was now becoming trendy. In the US, there were already more than fifty schools where it was taught and hundreds of centres were promising to cure myriad dysfunctions through music, from migraine to constipation and even obesity.

The notion that sound possessed an immense and mysterious power was as old as humanity. It had been placed at the origin of everything by various myths: 'In the beginning was the Word, and the Word was with God, and the Word was God,' begins the gospel of St John. For the Indians the magic sound was 'Om', first of all sounds and the one that incorporated them all, the sound by which Brahman the creator supposedly made his initial appearance before assuming physical form. For modern science too the world had begun with a sound: the so-called big bang.

Presuming sound to have divine origin, many ancient civilizations saw it as a link to the gods which perhaps explains why instruments like bells, cymbals and gongs played, and continue to play, an important role in religious ceremonies or why shamans from all continents use shells and horns to make contact with the spiritual world.

In various cultures there existed a number of similar legends in which sound, when its powers were harnessed, could be used to either kill, raise people from the dead, bring rain or hellfire, summon images from nothing or destroy matter, as in the crumbling of the walls of Jericho.

In ancient China, music was thought powerful enough to make the earth fertile or change a person's character. In Egypt, it was used to alleviate the pain of childbirth. In India, there were several texts written in Sanskrit which describe the therapeutic value of music. Similar treatises also existed in Arabic. Hippocrates himself sometimes resorted to music to heal his patients on the island of Kos.

The theory of sound's therapeutic properties was originally the fruit of mystical intuitions which science seems to have somehow confirmed. In its view, every living being and object, being an aggregate of parts in perpetual motion produced a sound that reflected its own particular nature. Every disorder or disharmony that affected the sound was regarded as a cause of illness, but the illness could be cured by re-establishing the original harmony, applying a 'just' sound that emitted the necessary assonance.

Mere foolishness? Perhaps not. Thinking about the way certain types of music can influence our mood or the way military marches were used to incite soldiers on the battlefield, it wasn't hard to imagine the effect of music whose sounds bypass our emotional responses, perhaps even penetrating our bodies directly and making the cells vibrate.

A number of contemporary Indian musicians had recently tried to identify which ragas could be used to help treat several illnesses and an extensive series of correlations had been established for pathologies from anorexia to rheumatic fever. The raga most suitable for insomnia was already known to Omkarnath Thakur who, during a visit to Rome, allegedly made a great impression on Mussolini in using music to cure *il Duce* of his insomnia.

From its earliest beginnings, yoga had always acknowledged sound's importance. One of the disciplines used to transcend the body and let the individual become one with the absolute was nada yoga: the yoga of sound. Returning to conscious awareness of the moment when God's thought became the word, i.e., sound and creation, the yogi would hear the divine sound not through his physical ears, but through the internal ear of his spirit, thus becoming one with the transcendental reality which was the ultimate aim of his practice.

The philosophy of yoga certainly seemed much more interesting than the contortions Ramananda had tried to teach me. I was curious to see how these different elements would be combined in the Pennsylvania seminar and whether it would be of any benefit to me.

The place where the seminar was to be held immediately made me think of Leopold and our conversations on the subject of 'deterritorialization'. In a forest of spruce trees at a freeway interchange in the midst of the typical Pennsylvanian plains, rose a white Hindu temple around which was a cluster of prefab bungalows. Once the property of a motel that had gone bust, these bungalows had been recycled and converted into an ashram. It was odd to think that in this compound, surrounded by flea-market stalls, a yoga seminar would shortly begin. Yoga is one of the oldest, most impenetrable of India's esoteric doctrines and one of its greatest secrets conveyed through arduous trials and initiation rites to the few who truly deserved to be let in on it. As recently as in the 1930s, a Western traveller in Varanasi trying to convince a famous yogi to give him lessons was met with the reply: 'Teach yoga to a westerner? Never. You would only turn it into a business.'

There were over fifty participants at this seminar, most of them women. It seemed as though they all knew each other and I was the only outsider. They had all been Ramananda's students before becoming teachers themselves, opening up 'businesses' all across the United States. They were all experts at the asanas and in using Iyengar's apparatus. It was the first time I'd found myself among such professional yoga practitioners. The experience only served to confirm my prejudices. Looking around me I saw not one serene face, not one smile or sign of inner peace. Everyone was focused on their own performance and on trying to perfect their contortions. The result was a gallery with expressions of sadness and solitude, rows of thin, pallid women with sunken eyes. Something wasn't right here, but I didn't know what.

Certainly, the ancient wisdom of India, where yoga had been practised for thousands of years, and the modern Western society to which it had only recently been transplanted made uneasy bedfellows. The former aspired to controlling what was most immaterial – the mind. The latter cared only about dominating matter through science and technology. The aim of yoga, which literally means 'union', was to free man from his illusion of being an individual entity that separated from the universe and to unite him with God. But how was one supposed to pursue such an end in a society such as ours, completely in thrall to the twin principles of individualism and separation. Perhaps even attempting it meant to court inner conflict, schizophrenia and the sadness I saw everywhere around me.

But no experience is completely negative, and my spirits were raised that evening when Ramananda presented a little man in a white kurta and pyjamas to the group that was gathered in the conference hall. It was his musical partner Mukesh Desai. Seated on a platform behind a harmonium and with a young tabla player on his right, he introduced himself by telling us that listening to his music should be like drinking water from a river: we could take as much as we wanted and stop when we'd had our fill.

'I sell water by the riverbank,' he said, laughing, as he tuned the harmonium to the tablas. Or maybe he was already playing. For that uninterrupted music continued for more than two hours and seemed to have neither beginning nor end: it simply flowed like water, like life. There was no sense to the words he sang and often they were merely the equivalent of our 'Do Re Mi' scale. But his voice, with its thousand modulations and its thousand colours, filled the whole hall with life and penetrated to the heart of each of us. Mukesh Desai was the true instrument and what issued from his lips was the magical sound we were to combine with our asanas. The evening left us all in some way elated.

During the following days, Mukesh Desai came to the gym every afternoon, and once Ramananda was satisfied with the positions each of us had assumed – I was exempted from such precision – he began to sing his ragas. I became more and more convinced they were actually entering my body, making my cells vibrate in a way to make them cease their mad replication. Was this the power of sound or the power of the mind?

Ramananda was an excellent teacher. He made no attempt either to rationalize the rapport between the asana and the music or to explain it in mystical terms, as most of the books that had been written on the subject did. In him everything was intuitive. Listening to our bodies he knew the music was influencing us in some way. He was aware of the experiments of the past and those of the current fashions, but wanted to try out his own experiment on his class of expert contortionists. With me it worked. By the end of the week, during the pranayama session, the breathing control exercise which involved neither contortions nor apparatus but was a question of simply lying on the floor, I felt the soothing vibrations of Mukesh Desai's voice enter every pore of my body. I was overcome by a feeling of joy I had never experienced at any concert before. Had the music awoken in me some latent force that might prove therapeutic? Or was it the mind which had associated those sounds with the sensations

I had begun to feel, giving me the impression that they were acting on matter? It made no difference. An explanation would have added nothing to the experience.

The other surprise was the Swami. Around seventy years old, tall, thin and slightly stooped, he arrived towards the middle of the week dressed in an orange tunic; and his opening speech, which was called the 'sunset speech' added a whole new dimension to the seminar. The man was sharp and extremely cultivated, but his serenity exempted him from any need to show off.

'Spiritual quest,' he began, 'is a quest for knowledge and the only kind worth pursuing is the knowledge of oneself. We think that we know, but we know only what we see, hear or feel through our senses. In truth what we perceive as reality is not real at all. Matter does not exist, it only appears to ...'

The Swami obviously knew his public. Quickly he moved on to the reason for our being here. 'Yoga? Sure, it's good for our bodies. It's a pleasant feeling to be able to bend down and pick up a leaf without needing help from others. But yoga isn't about the body. It means control over the mind, it means the union of mind and body, not so we can become athletes, but to keep the body healthy. It is a means of transport just like a car. If you want it to reach its destination, you have to keep it in good shape. The mistake is to confuse the end with the means.'

As he spoke of the West's obsession with property, its need to define everything in terms of 'me' and 'mine', one could see he had little respect for what yoga had become or for those who now practised it. He had an amusing way of explaining things.

'You say, "This apartment is mine," but if you look closely you'll see that what you call your floor is the ceiling of the people who live downstairs, your wall is yours but also your neighbour's. Nothing is truly yours, absolutely nothing – your body least of all. There are many who have a claim to it, your mother and your father, your spouse, the state to which you owe your duty as a citizen, the earth itself, even the fire that keeps it at the right temperature, water, the vegetables you eat: all of them can say, "This body is mine." You don't own anything. Not even your knowledge which you believe is yours. It has all come from books and your teachers. Yet you say, "This is my body." It seems so much a part of your identify. By saying "I", you think about your body. But if it is the "I" which identifies the body, it cannot very well be the body, can it? The subject that observes the object-body cannot be the body.'

To this he added: 'Yoga means being aware of yourself at every moment, being aware of every thought or gesture.' Those who failed to pay attention to each moment of their life risked the fate of a character in a tale the Swami proceeded to recount with wonderful expressiveness.

A man knew of the existence of a stone capable of turning iron into gold at the slightest contact. Determined to find it, he strapped an iron chain around his waist and set off on his quest. Every stone he saw he picked up and taped the chain with it. But the iron stayed iron and he would throw the stone away. This went on for weeks and months. More and more distractedly he repeated the gesture until one day he was stopped by a child who said, 'Hey, old man, where did you find that fine gold chain?' The man looked at his chain and saw it really has become gold. But which of the thousands of stones he has tossed away was the one which performed the miracle?

The Swami was highly critical of Western values, American values especially. He remarked how everything in the West had to be of some use and if it wasn't, it was considered worthless.

'This is the mentality of the vulture who flies high but whose eyes are always turned to the ground in search of something to sink its claws into.'

But everything he said referred to yoga in the end; he wanted us to understand much more than what asana and pranayama were about. These were only two of its eight aspects, he said in a challenging tone, and then went on to describe the other six: abstention from violence, detachment from material things, renunciation of falsity, detachment from the senses, concentration and lastly meditation.

Only a combination of all these elements deserved to be called yoga.

'Yoga is the way by which man unites his limited self with infinite being. The path is an interior one. The ultimate aim is to reach a state of perfection, though one which is not physical. Yoga is not designed to cure a malady, but to free yourself from all the suffering of the material world. Suffering which is born every time our "I" detaches itself from the self to focus on the senses or the objects of the senses. That is why yoga aspires to unite the I with the Absolute, which is a cure for everything because it is the liberation from everything.'

The yoga experts at the seminar didn't seem greatly interested in this grandiose vision of what for them was mainly a job. They were here to learn some new techniques to add to their course ads in the hope of attracting new students. This was the way of our world. For them the seminar was nothing more than an 'investment'.

For me, however, it was a completely different story. In search of something whose exact nature I didn't know, I found myself fascinated by this man who seemed to have dropped out of the sky, maybe from another planet. One day he recounted how as a child his mother had sent him to the fields to speak to the paddy so that there would be a good harvest. He still recalled his excitement on seeing the plants bowing to the wind as though they answered him. The Swami had a holistic vision of nature and the universe.

His world view interested me and I asked if we could talk. He replied with a handwritten note: I could pay him a visit on Saturday after breakfast.

The Swami's bungalow, though prefabricated like the others, was the only one with two floors. At the entrance was a pile of shoes, sandals and slippers. Obviously, I wasn't the only one to have sought a personal interview. Most of the visitors were Indians residing in the US who had come to ask him for advice or for a letter of recommendation or a blessing or simply to gaze at him in awe. He sat snugly in an armchair while the group squatting on the carpet included some fellow westerners. I stood to one side, observing the comings and goings of people who approached him devotedly, kneeling at his feet which were 'charged with his holiness' and touching them with a hand that they then brought up to their chest or forehead. There were many who wanted to talk to him and, gracious and attentive as he was, he answered with a smile, reaching into a basket by his side to give everyone something to take away with them: a grape, sweets, a tangerine.

Then he got up and summoned me with his hand while gesturing for the others to wait. He led me into a small, bare room in which the only items of furniture were two chairs: a comfy recliner and an ordinary wooden chair. It was clear which of them was mine, but at least I wouldn't have to sit at his feet. Imagining his time was precious, I told him in a few words who I was, how I had moved to India in the belief that there I could still find a civilization with the strength to resist the lure of Western materialism, and how I was now beginning to have my doubts.

I wanted to know if his country really was a treasure house of wisdom as so many westerners believed and whether in the long run it would be able to maintain this precious difference.

The question interested him immensely and we spoke about the myth of India as the guru of nations, a myth propagated in the West more than a century ago by the great mystic Vivekananda. Then the conversation turned to India's nuclear testing. I told him I had covered political affairs for years and had enough of that. Now I wanted to devote my remaining energies to seeking out what wisdom remained in India that could benefit the rest of the world.

This was also the task he had set himself, he told me, which was why he taught Vedanta, the fount of all the wisdom I sought, and then added that Indian spirituality was not bound to one person or nation; having remained true to its essence, it could appeal to everyone. Unlike other religions like Christianity or Islam, it had not been strangled by theology. He was curious about my reasons for attending the seminar and asked what had led me here. I told him everything in reverse, the chain of events that led from Ramananda to yoga to hernia to cancer. At that word he stopped me, wanting to know more, wanting me to be precise. Where? When? What treatments? I saw he was making some mental calculation. Then he said that every spring in his ashram on the hills of Anaikatti near Coimbatore in southern India he held a three-month course in Vedanta. If I wanted I was welcome to study with him.

'At your age, with the experience you've had,' he said, 'you could benefit greatly from it. Then I can put you in touch with an Ayurvedic doctor who might be able to help you.' He stopped and, as though in a trance, picked up a piece of paper and a pen: 'Tell me your date of birth, and the exact time and place.'

He immediately saw the doubt creep into my face. 'I'm not

really an astrologist, but I am interested in spiritual astrology,' he said.

'Spiritual what?' I asked. I was disappointed. After the journey of *A Fortune-Teller Told Me*, I had decided I was done with that world and had since steered clear of seers and astrologists and had no intention of going back.

'It's a way of understanding people's spiritual disposition,' the Swami replied. 'You know, it's not enough to have good intentions, and seeing as you've begun this quest it would be a good idea if we took a look at your spiritual horoscope.'

Clearly this was some kind of entrance exam. I remembered how meticulous Ramakrishna, the saint, had been in selecting his students and even Vivekananda had no doubt been put through his paces. This was the tradition, after all, the potential disciple had to be studied carefully. His way of walking, eating, even digesting had to be analysed, his body examined for signs of divine predisposition.

The Swami's test method was the horoscope, but the aim was the same: to see if it would be worth his while devoting his tutelary energies to a subject like myself. The idea of him considering taking me on as a disciple was amusing. What a résumé I had. From studying law at Pisa Normale to Leeds University to Columbia and now here I was, a candidate for the ashram, but first I would have to pass the astrology test.

The Swami summoned an assistant and gave him the paper with my birth details. When the door opened, I could hear the voices of those waiting in the next room. I stood up to leave but he hadn't finished with me yet. He wanted to continue talking about India and the political situation, he wanted to know my opinion on China, Pakistan, even the conflict in Kashmir. But I felt uneasy. I could sense the pressure of his disappointed faithful and I asked him how he managed to be so available, so willing to listen, having noticed how he would spend hours receiving people, all of them vying for his time and attention. He answered with a phrase that was to determine our future relations: 'I no longer have need of time, I've already done everything I want to do. What time I have left is public time. You too are approaching the age when you can dedicate your time to others.'

How I wished I could do just that, but it was so far from being the truth.

'You'll see, believe me. It will happen to you too. It's a question of pure mathematics. When you realize this nothing can be taken away from you.'

Could he really teach me this? If so, I really had found my master. He then added a few words on the subject of inner peace and concluded with: 'Let's meet again tonight after the music lesson.' As I gingerly crossed the waiting room I saw that it was now packed with people. It was the weekend and many Indian families had driven hundreds of miles to get here. They were all relieved I was finally leaving, but equally curious to know who this foreigner was who had managed to wrest so much of the Swami's time.

That evening, I waited until all the other participants had gone to bed before slipping out of my bungalow to walk to the Swami's. The spruce forest was alive with the sound of frogs and crickets and it was funny to think that I was going to see my exam results, to find out whether I had passed or failed.

At the foot of the wooden steps where I left my shoes, there were no others. The Swami was alone. Sitting in his armchair, he was leafing through a pile of papers.

'Perfect. Yours is a wonderful horoscope,' he said, seeing me standing at the door, pointing to the computer printout on which year by year was plotted my whole life in relation to the various planets. He smiled, delighted to be able to give me this good news.

'You were born without shadows, without any burden from previous lives, which makes you ideal for the life of the spirit. You could even become a guru yourself! It all adds up. You have never done anything for material gain, so now you are free to pursue the definitive liberation.'

He was excited as he leafed back and forth through the pages on his lap, retracing the history of my decisions, my turning points, my illness. Not wishing to make too much of it, I took no notes. He said that until March 2006, I would be fine and that I might cheat death even. I refused to think about that appointment, preferring to focus on the one I had in a few months' time at his ashram in India.

When I left the Swami's bungalow, it was a clear night and the air was cool. Before returning to my own, I took a long walk through the woods between the two freeways.

FIVE

HONG KONG

IN THE MUSHROOM KINGDOM

It was a story I couldn't afford to miss – or at least that's how it seemed from a distance. An old Chinese billionaire from Hong Kong had decided to use his wealth to leave an exceptional gift to mankind before he died: a cure for cancer.

After years of research and experiments, the drug was finally ready. It was the extract of a mushroom to which the Chinese have always attributed miraculous powers, and from ancient times which appears in images of some of their gods, especially the Eight Immortals.

I wrote to the Fire-Eater to ask him what he thought. He was enthusiastic.

'Do look into it,' he wrote back. 'Mushrooms are a fascinating subject. Many of us see them as a separate kingdom – they're not really vegetables and are obviously not animals; they are mushrooms, a realm of their own, with great therapeutic powers which have been known to man for centuries. Each of them has its own features and properties. After all, the first penicillin was a mushroom extract.'

Hong Kong was like a second home to me. I had lived there for eight years. I still knew lots of people and had lots of friends there, but when I arrived I decided to concentrate on the mushroom and steer clear of all the rest. So I didn't call anyone or show my face at the Foreign Correspondents' Club. Instead, I took lodgings in students' accommodation at Hong Kong University. This part of the city has changed rather little as compared to the rest, and retains some of the romantic charm of the old Hong Kong, like in the novel and film *Love Is a Many-Splendored Thing*.

In the mornings, just before dawn, the alleys in the quarter rising up to the peak were filled with wonderfully calm old men and women who seemed to have found in the various forms of t'ai chi, the struggle against the shadows, the perfect form of exercise for both body and mind. It was the moment of greatest peace in the whole day.

Getting to see this old Chinese billionaire was easy enough. He had me come down to one of his offices in Central, the commercial heart of the island, from which he ran various other commercial interests. The place was as bare as a monk's cell, with no sign of those ostentatious fripperies which billionaires usually find so hard to resist. He was around eighty years old, tall and thin, and had an unremarkable face, but was clearly sincere.

'We're not in this to make money; we just want to make people better,' he said, as if refuting an accusation I hadn't made. 'Life is all about give and take. I've taken a lot from society. Now it's time for me to put something back before I go.'

Basically I got him to talk about himself. The details of what exactly he had taken from society and how he had taken it, made the story of his mushroom sound even more impressive. He had been born into a poor family in the Yangtze delta region of China at a time when the country was beset by internecine warfare and scourged by warlords. He grew up in Shanghai during the Japanese occupation and worked there during the World War II and then the civil war. His whole life, like that of millions of other Chinese, had been one long struggle for survival.

He just got lucky. He had made his first fortune by importing needles for industrial sewing machines, then importing the sewing machines themselves. In 1949, as Mao's communist troops advanced, he escaped to Hong Kong with virtually nothing and had gambled everything he had on two products which he reckoned would have a great future: detergents and instant noodles. It was the noodles, which he talked about as though he had a great steaming bowl of them right under his nose, which made him his fortune.

The billionaire was basically a salesman, but an honest one. When I asked him, in talking about the mushroom, how his extract could possibly be a cure for all the different types of cancer, his answer was blunt and to the point. It wasn't a cure, he said, it was an aid, something to strengthen the immune system and which could be of use during radiotherapy and chemotherapy.

In other words, the story of the miraculous cure for cancer had been deflated as soon as it was subjected to closer scrutiny. Still, I let him continue, and in the end it proved to be no less interesting, probably because he was as passionate about his mushroom as he was about his noodles. Both were basically products which made life a little bit better for the rest of mankind.

The extract was the result of two parallel stories which happened to converge. One of them involved him personally. In the mid-1980s, the daughter of his best friend – another of Hong Kong's great tycoons – fell ill. They took her to various hospitals around the world, but each time the diagnosis was the same: incurable leukaemia. The billionaire promised his friend he would not rest and would move heaven and earth in order to help him. He was sure that, somewhere in the vast treasure trove of the ancient Chinese medical tradition, there had to be some herb or plant that could cure illnesses like cancer, which was likely to have been forgotten by Western medical science. He sent his emissaries to China and went there himself on several occasions to look for the answer, but to no avail.

At the same time, another series of events were unfolding in Shanghai. An elderly biologist who was a professor in a minor university, was rushed to the hospital, one reserved for party officials, with a suspected kidney stone. There were two beds in his room, and on the bed next to him was a high-ranking communist official who had just undergone surgery for cancer. This man told the billionaire that the only people who had a cure for his illness were the Japanese, who had used a mushroom native to China to develop an extremely effective form of medicine. Quantities were limited, however, and the formula was still a secret.

A Chinese mushroom? Which mushroom could that be?

Once released from the hospital, the biologist set to work to try and find out. There were more than 1,300 different types of mushroom in China. It would take years of research along with massive amounts of funding to find the right one. The biologist wrote a letter to his university, one to the government of Shanghai and one to the central office in Beijing, but no one took any notice, and even less showed any willingness to offer him money … until the billionaire from Hong Kong came to hear of his project and met up with him, deciding to back him with his riches.

The results didn't take long. Soon, they identified the mushroom with the highest degree of what was thought to be the anti-cancerous substance. It was the *yunzhi*, or cloud mushroom. The billionaire, convinced he had found the solution, encouraged the biologist to develop an extract and gave it to his friend's daughter for whom by this stage all hope was lost. She appeared to have been miraculously cured and she survived.

So the billionaire and the biologist embarked on a long-term project to gain scientific credibility for the extract, produce it on a large scale and make it available to the rest of mankind.

As he spoke to me, the old man put a great deal of emphasis on the philanthropic aim of this mission, which was fifteen years old now. However, it was clear at the same time that there was also a major nationalist agenda at work. Both the billionaire and the biologist felt that the ancient Chinese medical tradition had suffered greatly as a result of Western influences, and they wanted to restore hope and pride to that tradition by means of the anti-cancerous mushroom extract.

Streams of foreign missionaries had arrived in China at the end of the nineteenth century. Great American foundations like Rockefeller had built and operated their own hospitals in Beijing and other countries, soon marginalizing the localities where traditional medicine was practised. The Chinese elite became more and more dependent on Western doctors, and even the government of Chiang Kai-shek had ended up virtually banning local medicine on the grounds that it was too primitive. It was the communists who rediscovered it and Mao who, in one of his pithy, memorable phrases, said that in this area China had to learn to 'walk on its own two feet'.

Hong Kong had been a colony for over 150 years, and right from the start official medicine was put in the hands of doctors who had graduated from English universities. The cloud mushroom project no doubt contained an element of wanting to restore prestige to the research and work of the 'un-colonized'. This was something the old billionaire felt very strongly about and he also mentioned, far from coincidentally, another minor but significant project of his, namely, setting some of the poems of the Tang dynasty to music, so that young people had something more substantial and meaningful to listen to during their evenings at karaoke bars.

It was clear the old man did not like the rate at which things were going in Hong Kong or China. Even his business world had lost all its scruples, he claimed. In order to protect his mushroom extract, he had to set up a health association to which he had formally granted a monopoly on his product. He was afraid that speculators would buy up his extract, dilute it, increase quantities and sell it at exorbitant prices. At this moment the only way to get hold of it was to become members of the association – some 20,000 people had signed up already – and buy it through that channel.

The association had already opened three consultancy centres for cases which Western medicine had diagnosed as difficult or incurable while consultation for less needy cases was free. The old man had looked for a good traditional doctor in Beijing to run the three centres, but it had not proved easy to find one. In China too, nothing and no one was to be trusted as people pursued money without heed for anything else, he said. There were those who called themselves acupuncturists after just a few years of study, rather than ten years apprenticeship with a great master, which should ideally have been the case. As for the doctors themselves, many of them had qualifications that were dubious, and very few devoted themselves to the lengthy study of the classical texts with the correct, monk-like attitude. However, he had been lucky in the end. He had found a woman who had been trained in the old school in Beijing and brought her to Hong Kong for a couple of years. It was she who saw the patients, and decided the right doses of the mushroom for each individual.

I told the old billionaire that I would very much like to meet her as my interest in the mushroom was personal as well as professional. He understood; he himself took a dose each day and said he would arrange an appointment for me the next day.

Before saying goodbye, he called his secretary and made me a life member of his association. My membership card entitled me to priority in buying the extract and a special discount of 10 per cent at any time.

The health association's headquarters were just down the road from the Tsim Sha Tsui MTR station, the secretary had told me. Thus, I was forced to submit myself to that modern, and I find rather uninspiring, form of transport which carried me under the stretch of sea separating the Hong Kong Island from the mainland in under three minutes, rather than the breezy, airy crossing that the Star Ferry would have offered.

For those of my generation, Chinese or non-Chinese, the Star Ferry with its green-and-black ships, its old-fashioned crew with their blue uniforms and white collars, its wooden benches with back rests to be adjusted according to the direction of the crossing, the smell of the ocean, the view over the bay and its wax-sailed junkets, will forever symbolize the charm which this former English colony has now lost. The underground railway that has replaced it is much swifter and more efficient. But it's precisely that: an underground, stifling, with not a whiff of nature or view of the world, one of the countless examples of how man impoverishes life while thinking he's improving it.

The Hong Kong MTR is so perfect that the mobile phone signal works even when the trains run underwater. As every phone on the train kept ringing, I couldn't help but laugh to myself. I felt like I was listening to an orchestra of crickets at two o'clock in the afternoon.

The secretary had told me to take the B2 exit and that I would see the clinic building right in front of me as I came up the stairs. I followed her instructions dutifully, but the first thing I saw right in front of me as I came up to the street were three huge tortoises, strung up – still alive – above the steaming cauldron of a Chinese medicine shop.

Once upon a time this would have made no impression on me. I might have even found it exotic. Living among the Chinese, I had learnt that you could eat anything that moves. In seeking to imitate them, I had not balked at anything – dog meat, snake meat, and on one occasion during a trip in the province of Yunnan, a pangolin or scaly anteater, which I watched being flayed before my very eyes. How one can change in the course of one life!

After many years in India, when I had become a vegetarian almost by default, I now found it disgraceful that those three poor beasts should be kept in such suffering, simply to publicize the black soup that would be made out of their boiled counterparts, poured into glasses and lined up on the shop counter. People passed by, stopped, drank, paid and walked on. One glass cost around seventy-five pence. Not so much a rare pick-me-up or an instant cure for haemorrhoids, as – almost certainly – an aphrodisiac, like all other Chinese remedies.

The building in which the association's clinic was located was actually on the other side of the street. A tiny lift took me up to the fifth floor. The billionaire's secretary was waiting to introduce me to Doctor Li Ping.

She was one of the last products of socialist China: plain, no make-up, round head, slightly greying hair with a rather masculine haircut. She wore a jumper and black trousers beneath her impeccably starched white coat. As a student she must have worn Mao's blue uniform and had her hair in plaits. All the pieces of the jigsaw appeared to fit. She was around fifty, so must have been a 'little red devil' during the Cultural Revolution and entered the prestigious Institute of Chinese Traditional Medicine in Beijing when the Great Helmsman was still alive and only the best and genuinely communist young people were admitted. Her bearing and the modesty of her appearance retained that world. She had a gold band on her ring finger and a watch on her wrist that was not an item of jewellery, but merely an instrument to tell the time.

She received me in a small consulting room. The air was pleasantly thick with the balmy smell of herbs and bark which three young girls were cutting and grinding in chemists' mortars behind a dividing glass wall.

We sat on two stools: one was right in front of the other, close enough, it seemed, for our bodies to communicate. She asked what was wrong with me and how I felt while she took notes on everything I said. She was very interested in how I had responded to the chemotherapy and the radiotherapy. Had I a temperature, itching, vomiting? Had blotches appeared on my skin? She then took my right hand, placed it on her knees with my palm facing upwards, and began examining every detail using a magnifying glass.

'No, I'm not telling you your fortune,' she reassured me. 'I'm examining the state of your health. Every change in your body brings about a change in your hands.'

'My hands?'

'Yes, look here,' she told me, using a paper clip to point to the mound between my thumb and my lifeline. 'See, there are some formations here which look like tiny tofu cubes. This means your stomach is weak.'

She looked again, and showed me that my lifeline ended up in a triangle. 'There, that means you've had problems with your kidneys,' she said.

'Which one? Left or right?' I asked her, surprised by this detail I had not mentioned to her.

'I cannot say. I only see there is something wrong with your kidneys,' she answered.

'But how can that be? These are the same lines I was born with, but it's only recently that I've had the kidney problem,' I insisted.

'Some of the changes which take place in the lines of your hands occur in the space of seven days; others are slower and take months, sometimes years, to become visible.'

Then, still pointing with her paper clip and looking through her magnifying glass, she said, 'If the lifeline finished at this point, it would mean your life had already been lived in full. But it doesn't, it carries on. This means you still have much life left. Yes, much life.' She turned my hand over, looked at the back of it, and told me I was beginning to have problems with my coronary arteries. 'Nothing serious yet – nothing that Western medicine would detect – but something you need to prepare for. Your coronary arteries are beginning to harden.' She spotted a tiny wart on my index finger that even I had not noticed. 'Every time there are problems with the teeth, even with just one tooth, these signs start to appear.'

She took my pulse and concentrated for a long time. She said the pulse was weak, as was my *qi*, my life force. Then she looked at my tongue and said there were two cracks beneath the white film which was another sign of 'imbalance in the stomach'. She looked hard at my ears, and here too she saw signs of what she called 'stagnant blood in my stomach', though I have no idea how.

She examined my neck, following the line of the lymph nodes as a Western doctor would, and reached her diagnosis: I was generally in good shape, but I had weak *qi* and an imbalance that needed to be corrected.

She was convinced that what the Western doctors had done to me so far was right. Now their treatments needed to be complemented with other medicines. The mushroom extract would be ideal for raising my *qi*, she said. I could take three tablets a day and carry on like that for years since there were no dangerous side effects.

She wrote out a prescription in beautiful Chinese calligraphy and gave it to the chemist. The whole examination had taken half an hour. For that, and the first batch of medicine that would last me a month, I paid the equivalent of just over eighty pounds.

I saw the billionaire again a few times, and he introduced me to two scientists working with him on the project. As always, I learnt something from each of them, but that didn't change the impression I had formed about the mushroom extract basically being a nice story, especially from a distance. The billionaire also introduced me to the young Shanghai biologist's son, who told me something important about the mushroom: an old folk tale.

Once upon a time, there was a white snake that wanted to become a beautiful lady. For it to do so, someone had to fall in love with it, which was clearly far from straightforward. However, one day, a young man saw the snake, took it with him and told it that he loved it. Immediately the reptile turned into the beautiful woman it wanted to be, the two of them were married and lived happily ever after. But a Buddhist monk jealous of their union decided to separate them and went around telling people that the woman-snake was, in fact, the devil. When the young husband was seriously injured in an accident, the monk told him it was the woman-snake who had wanted to kill him. She was desperate and was the only one who could help him. She knew that a miraculous mushroom, the cloud mushroom, grew in heaven and it could cure everything. However, as a woman, she was not allowed into heaven. So out of love for her husband, she returned to her original form, and in a flash the snake darted through the clouds into heaven, managed to get hold of it the miraculous mushrooms, and carried them back down to earth with her. The young husband was cured in an instant and the mushrooms reproduced themselves and remained available for the rest of mankind.

This made the monk more jealous than ever, so he set a trap for the woman. He imprisoned her, shut her in an alms box and buried her in the city of Hangzhou. To ensure that no one could set her free, he built a pagoda on top of it, which subsequently became famous: the Lei Feng Pagoda.

When the Jade Emperor came to hear of how spiteful the monk had been, he issued an order for him to be arrested. So the monk sought refuge where he could never be found: in the belly of a crab that lived in the rice fields. And there he stayed, hated by all the Chinese who even today, look inside the shell of these crustaceans and beneath the membrane that remains when the meat has been taken away. They still see him in a small excrescence that looks like the image of a small, frightened monk.[5]

In the period when I had been involved with fortune tellers and seers, I had met a Chinese man in Hong Kong, a stock market broker, who had told me how to read people's fortunes from their

---

[5] The famous pagoda of Hangzhou collapsed in 1924. Lu Xun, the renowned author from Shanghai who remembered the legend being recounted to him by his grandmother, published a short commentary on it in which he said he liked the fact that the woman-snake was finally free, while the evil monk remained a prisoner in the belly of the crab until this entire species eventually became extinct. Served him right!

facial features. I still had his phone number saved on my computer and tried to ring him. I was surprised when he answered and even more surprised when I heard that he was no longer interested in physiognomy and instead, like me, had begun to investigate the cure for cancer.

I asked him about the billionaire's mushroom. He said he had heard of it. 'One of the many.'

He suggested we meet to go on a tour of the old herb and flower market in the Mongkok quarter, which turned out to be an enlightening experience. At every step, we were besieged by someone offering us something from China that could cure certain illnesses. One man, who mostly sold roses, also had a strange item among his many plastic plant pots. They produced something that looked like small ears of corn, each with a beard made of bright green strands that he said were excellent for treating diabetes. Another was selling shiny black seeds, like tiny buffaloes' heads with large horns, which were excellent for lung cancer. Someone else had a little plant with round, beehive-shaped roots, which were supposed to be excellent for breast cancer. He said the plant only grew near waterfalls.

But the strangest thing my friend took me to see was a half-worm, half-fungus, whose name in Chinese meant 'winter insect, summer herb'. This worm hibernates underground during the cold months in a mountainous region in China. A fungus grows alongside it, enters the worm, feeds off its flesh and germinates in spring with green leaves which turn black. My friend said this parasitic combination was believed to have magic powers and in his view its leaves were an excellent remedy for kidney cancer. He had had been operated on for precisely this illness, and after studying some ancient Chinese medical texts, discovered that centuries ago, this plant had been seen as an instant cure for all kidney diseases. The problem, though, was the cost: a pound of its leaves cost over £300, and had to be taken in large quantities to be effective. He himself had got up to almost two ounces a day, with around thirty plants which he slow-steamed in sealed earthenware pots. The infusion was to be drunk and the remainder was to be eaten. He said that to begin with, the potion had given him a bad cough, but only because 'it was cleaning my lungs out'.

A group of his friends now used the plant and helped each other out by ensuring that a regular supply arrived from China. He had also heard that the plant grew in the kingdom of Bhutan and that even the royal family used it.

One evening, the old billionaire invited me to dine with him and his family, at one of the most famous restaurants on Wellington Street. It was the kind with the suckling pigs strung up in the entrance to drain the fat, and aquariums which were visible from the streets where the best fish, prawns and lobsters would wait for a passing client to say, 'That one!' before being fished out and cooked to order.

I watched those lovely fish as they moved through the water, and then looked up at the pigs strung up on the hooks. It made me think of how man, apart from cases of hardship and famine, has always found odd ways of justifying the carnivorous violence which he perpetrates against other living creatures. One of the arguments still used in the West to justify the annual massacre of millions of chickens, lambs, pigs and cows is the fact that we need protein to live. What about elephants? Where do they get their protein from?

A friend of Gandhi's tried to persuade him to give up the orthodox vegetarian tradition of his family by using the same argument. He said the English had been able to dominate millions of Indians with just a few men because they ate meat, which made them so strong. The only way to combat them was to start eating meat as well. So one night, the two men went down to a riverbank, and for the first time Gandhi ate a mouthful of lamb, thus betraying the faith of his parents and his ancestors. But he felt awful. Each time he tried to go to sleep he could hear the bleating of the animal he had eaten, as he wrote in his autobiography.

Never again in the rest of his life did Gandhi touch meat, not even during his student years in England, where everyone said he would never survive the cold without it.

As a result of my upbringing, I had never really asked myself whether or not I was a vegetarian. At home we always ate meat if we could afford it, usually on Sundays. So when Angela and I arrived in India in 1994, we were both still meat eaters and for a while continued to be.

Once a week, a Muslim would come to our door with an immaculate suitcase from which he would pull packs of beef filets and steaks dripping with blood. Then one day, my German photographer friend, Dieter, pointed out a herd of cows to me that had gathered around a rubbish dump, intently eating plastic bags, paper cartons and newspapers. He said, 'That is what you're eating when you eat that Muslim's lovely meat. Just think of all the lead in those printed pages!'

Dieter was right, of course. Despite allowing himself to butcher cows, which for Hindus are sacred, our Muslim certainly did not have any fresh green pastureland he could despatch his victims to. What he was bringing us, in fact, were bits of the sickly street cows that nourished themselves on refuse.

This was what spurred me to give up. Then, as time passed, I noticed that since I had stopped seeing animals as food, I began to treat them differently, and saw them more as living beings and somehow part of the same life which populates and goes to make up our world. Now even the sight of a steak disgusts me, the smell of one cooking makes me feel sick and I find the idea of people raising animals simply for slaughter thoroughly distressing.

But vegetables are living organisms too, the meat eaters tell me, deaf to every form of argument. They act as though picking a tomato causes a plant as much suffering as strangling a chicken, or as if you could replant a lamb's leg in the same way that you replant a cabbage or lettuce. The most natural food for man is the kind that the earth and the sun produce.

I kept looking at the pigs hanging in the restaurant and imagined myself asking those who would eat them, 'Have you heard the screams that come from a slaughterhouse?' Everyone should be forced to listen to them before they tuck into a steak. The atrocity of that terror, the poison of that sudden last fear of the dying animal is contained in every cell of that meat. My grandmother, like everyone else, ate meat when she was able to, but I remember her telling me once never to eat freshly slaughtered meat, but to wait. When I asked her why, she told me that perhaps our forefathers, like her, understood the problems that could be caused from putting someone else's agony into our own stomach. Because what we euphemistically refer to as meat is in fact bits of dead, murdered animals. Why on earth would anyone want to turn their own stomach into a graveyard?

Angela still eats meat if the occasion presents itself. I just cannot bring myself to do so. It is no longer a health issue, but a moral one. It is one small but effective way of doing something against violence: choosing not to eat other living creatures.

Eventually the billionaire, his two daughters and some other guests arrived, putting an end to my solitary and pointless defence of the fish which were unlikely to be swimming in that tank much longer.

The manager came to greet us and accompanied us to a private room where a large round table had already been laid. I whispered in the manager's ear that I was a vegetarian. He understood and told me not to worry. As we sat down, the billionaire's youngest daughter who was sitting next to me, appeared to be dissatisfied with the equipment that had been provided for us, as she instantly complemented the ivory chopsticks and porcelain spoons with two mobile telephones that she kept switched on and which occasionally joined in the conversation. I noticed that the old man was not pleased with this, but even he, and all his riches, was unable to hold back the tide of innovation.

He told me that the first traditional Chinese medicine fair was being inaugurated the next day at one of communist China's shopping centres in Hong Kong. He recommended I go and have a look, but warned me against products which were not genuine and the experimental items which were bound to be on sale.

When I reached there I saw dozens of stalls in several rows lined up in a huge well-lit hall, which contained old party officials that had reinvented as businessmen (some rather awkwardly), young Shanghai yuppies and officials in the service of the liberation army who had introduced some new pharmaceutical product of the armed forces and their various commercial ventures. The entire hall was a fine example of everything China had now become: profiteering, deceitful and, like the old billionaire had suggested, untrustworthy.

Within the space of an hour, my pockets were bulging with visiting cards and samples of dozens of different types of medicines, all of which seemed to address two basic problems: cancer or male infertility.

I thought I was the only foreigner in the room when I spotted another, busily collecting everything imaginable. He said he was an expert in Chinese medicine and taught at an English university, but I reckon he was a spy working on behalf of some large Western pharmaceutical company which didn't want to lose the chance of getting its hands on a potential genuine discovery.

We chatted for a while and eventually I asked him if he believed the Chinese had invented anything close to being a cure for cancer that Western medicine was currently able to offer.

'Nothing whatsoever,' he replied. 'But it does have some excellent supplements.'

As I left the fair, I saw a group of Chinese swarming out of a nearby building who looked very different from the ones I had just left behind. They were pale and thin, and looked as though they had been taken over by something.

'Who are you?' I asked automatically.

'Falun Gong, Falun Gong,' they replied in unison. They had just completed a two-day international retreat to 'share their experiences'.

I had read about the Falun Gong; it was a mystical movement founded by the former communist party official Li Hongzhi in north-east China in 1992, which already had several million followers throughout the country. I knew the Beijing government had targeted them for one of its most severe repressions, that the communist security services had accused its followers of belonging to an 'illegal organization' and then a 'diabolical cult'. Tens of thousands of them had been arrested, tortured, several of them were assassinated and others shot in criminal asylums. But I had never had any direct contact with them before. I asked to speak to one of them who could explain their position to me.

They told me to come to the public gardens in Kowloon the following morning to 'do the exercises with them'.

I left my room at the university at 5.30 a.m. the following morning. It was pitch-dark, but the voices and sometimes the laughter of those who were going up the hill to do their exercises could be heard in the silence. They were the lovely dawn people who would later disappear into the anonymous crowd of the day that was breaking.

A taxi took me to the Tube station, where the train sped underground and then undersea until, in the space of fifteen minutes, I was at the entrance of the park in Kowloon. The followers of Falun Gong met up in a concrete area that was surrounded by several large flower pots. I remained to one side and observed them first. They arrived, took off their shoes, laid down a small plastic sheet or some newspapers on the ground, sat in the lotus position, shut their eyes and concentrated.

One woman, evidently appointed by the group for the task, put a tape recorder down on one of the flower pots and played a track of Chinese music with a voice-over directing the slow, graceful movements. The woman noticed I was there, brought me into the group and set about teaching me the various exercises; first those to be done standing up, then sitting down. They were very similar to the qigong exercises: hands on the head, then at eye height, then in front of the stomach, all the while holding the imaginary ball of the earth.

The exercises lasted for more than half an hour, then the roughly 200 participants, many of whom were women and some foreigners, split up into groups to read the works of Master Li. Each group had its own language: Mandarin, Cantonese or English. One small group even read in Swedish. There were twelve Swedish delegates who had come from Stockholm to 'share the experience'. Their leader was a mechanic at a nuclear power station and had first heard of the Falun Gong from an acupuncturist. He converted and had all of Master Li's works translated, and said there were already several hundred followers in Sweden.

While the various groups were discussing what they had read, the woman who had obviously been selected to help me understand the Falun Gong came and sat down beside me. She was like all the others: simple, modest and undemonstrative. Mrs Hui was forty years old. Her husband was an engineer who worked for the Hong Kong government. She started off by giving me two of the Master's books and when I tried to pay her, she would not let me. 'There must be no exchange of money between us,' she said.

Mrs Hui had been practising only for a couple of years. She had heard of the Falun Gong from a friend of hers. She had got hold of a book, read it and it had changed her life. Suddenly she had far more energy, far more spirit. She had previously been a Christian, but had never been able to practise what the religion preached: Love your neighbour as yourself. She had found this impossible but now with the Falun Gong, she found it easy.

'Why?'

'Because to be a practising member of the Falun Gong means first and foremost to incorporate all of the world's characteristics into oneself in order to get in tune with it.' As she said this, she made a pyramid shape with her hands and pointed to its summit as the point of arrival where everything is concentrated. 'Our strength lies in our simplicity. This is why we are able to progress so much more rapidly than those who follow other ways. We have no organization or membership list. No offices, no officials, no priests. We communicate by word of mouth or mobile phone if absolutely necessary. Everyone is free. Everything we do, we do of our own free will. The Chinese government says there are already 100 million of us. I don't know whether or not it's true, but even this doesn't matter to us. We are not attached to anything.'

I asked her why she thought the Beijing regime singled them out for such harsh treatment.

'The communists persecute us because they understand that what we do is more than just physical exercises. They understand that we're interested in the mystery of the universe and that we want to leave time and space. The communists only believe in what they see and they hate us because they understand that we see beyond things and live in other dimensions.'

Mrs Hui explained that in all their demonstrations – often improvised and silent – what they are asking for is the freedom to perform their exercises in public and to print Master Li's works. They had already moved their publishing house from Hong Kong to Singapore, after the former English colony was returned to the control of communist China. But not even this worried them, she said. Nothing would stop them.

'Human civilization is going through a period of great crisis. The only way to escape from it is for as many people to practise *fa*, the law of universal harmony. We who already practise it believe we can attain illumination in this life so that we do not have to be born again. We do not speak about this in public, however, otherwise people will think we are mad. And yet, the truth is that if we are here today, it is because we have sought and tried in our previous lives and have now finally achieved our objective. Master Li helps us so much in this respect. He has given us the tools and he identifies the solution.'

I pointed out to Mrs Hui that Master Li was a former low-ranking communist official who had fled to America in 1996, possibly alarmed by what he had started in China. He now lived there peacefully with his wife and daughters off the earnings from his books, which were a mixture of ancient Taoist ideas, old esoteric practices, Buddhism and a load of claptrap. He never appears in public, never gives interviews or dispenses instructions to his followers. It seems as though he himself has given up on the Falun Gong.

'We aren't interested in Master Li as a man. We're interested in him as a master,' Mrs Hui replied, not offended in the slightest. 'His books are just the starting point. What really matters is practice – regular, daily practice. The aim is to cleanse ourselves from all negativity.' In saying this, she made a gesture as if to indicate something dirty seeping out from her skin and rising towards heaven. 'The aim is to raise the moral standards of humanity.'

There was something pathetic, but also very touching about this woman. There was an anxiety about her, one which by now I had learnt to recognize, like that of the New York anaesthetist-turned-Kashmiri Sufi. It is the anxiety of those who want something great to add to their small lives, something which cannot be bought but only achieved, which does not belong to the realm of matter but to the realm of the spirit.

Moreover, in today's modern society where everyone lives more separate and divided from their neighbours, there is something attractive about belonging, about being involved along with others in a project which has global proportions. Regarding the Falun Gong movement specifically, one should also bear in mind what in my view is one of the greatest tragedies of our time: the demise of Chinese civilization, first mortally wounded by Marxist materialism, then wiped out altogether by the even more devastating materialism of predatory capitalism.

Ancient China was a complex society that was held together by Confucian values of order and hierarchy. A man could always flee from it by pursuing the mystical paths of Taoism and Buddhism. The China of today knows no values, save those of money and selfishness. Even those few socialist values which Maoism sought to embed have withered away now. The Falun Gong is in part a reaction to all this, and it is no coincidence that the example Mrs Hui gave me of improving as a person through practising this religion involved a value which in China had been treasured for many centuries: filial love.

'In Chinese society,' she said, 'the old have always lived alongside the young. But I was westernized, I wanted my own freedom and didn't want my mother to come and live with me when she was widowed. I believed my private life was something valuable that I had to protect. But one day, after having started to practise Falun Gong, I realized this treasure was in fact worthless and that I shouldn't seek to cling to it. So I decided to take my mother in with me. This forces me to reanalyse myself each day.'

One of the many aspects of Falun Gong I was interested in was the relationship which those who practised it had with their bodies and with illness.

Li Hongzhi had become a master through holding qigong courses, and during his first lectures in 1992 had 'touched and healed' various people from different diseases. Then, however, he had said he would not do so any more. To seek healing was the wrong way of approaching Falun Gong. It was a form of 'attachment', and had to be controlled.

'Yes, the master teaches us not to attach importance to illness,' Mrs Hui explained. 'Even if we have symptoms, he teaches us not to take notice of them. In all sick people, the symptoms are the same, but our attitude towards the symptoms is different and this is what matters.'

Mystical sects such as Falun Gong have always been a part of Chinese life, especially during times of change and upheaval. Such sects, which are usually esoteric and clandestine, have always played an important political role. They were also behind some of great rebellions, such as that of the Taiping in the nineteenth century. These rebellions have always been feared by the authorities in power, precisely because of this force which does not recognize reason. For example, the Golden Flower sect became so influential that in 1891, the imperial government in Beijing had 15,000 of its initiates massacred as a warning to others not to interfere in state affairs.

The sacred text of the Golden Flower sect, which Carl Jung was so fascinated by and which was certainly the inspiration for several of Master Li's theories, was supposed to have been first brought to China by the earliest Nestorian Christians. It was subsequently embellished with Confucian, Buddhist and above all Taoist elements. 'Everything is transitory,' the novices were taught, 'save for the Golden Flower which grows in the inner terrain of detachment from the things of this world.'

At each of their moments of great crisis, the Chinese have seen something flourish in their midst which has revived hope in spiritual values. The Falun Gong appeared to have the same sense of the current, confused situation of the country. I watched those who had been doing their exercises in the park in Kowloon fold up their plastic sheets and pack them away into their rucksacks. I watched them turning their mobile phones back on, setting off for another normal day in the life of today's Hong Kong. They were simple souls, a bit lost perhaps, but determined to the point of martyrdom and for this reason feared by the communists who believed only in the power of matter.

At the end of my visit to Hong Kong, what had got under my skin more than anything else – and stayed there – was not what I had been looking for. It was the Falun Gong. I had been moved by their determination to the point of folly. I had gone too far into the mushroom business, asked too many questions and received too many answers. I had spent far too much time socializing with the billionaire and his people. From close quarters, the miraculous mushroom looked like one of the many excellent Chinese things that can be useful for something or nothing.

But it had not been a total waste of time and the cloud mushroom extract had not been completely useless. When I got home, I gave my three months' supply which I had bought with my health association life membership discount to a friend of mine. He was in need of hope at that time.

I told him the story as I had heard it from a distance, along with the legend of the snake-woman and her love, and I'm sure those red capsules in all the little sealed bottles covered in Chinese writing did him good.

As for me, I had had quite enough of searching for new medicines and was now looking forward to spending three months in one place, far away from everything.

My next appointment was with the Swami at his ashram in Coimbatore.

SIX

INDIA AGAIN

MR NOBODY

I knew that when my turn came to speak, it would be my chance to rid myself of a huge burden.

I didn't have anything terrible to confess. All I had to do was introduce myself, but I had decided to do so without referring to my former self. This seemed like a form of release to me. My name, profession, nationality, everything which I would have turned to in order to define myself at one point, somehow no longer seemed to be me. I did not recognize myself in those fragments of my identity but felt trapped by them. Certainly they were part of my life that I had lived and enjoyed, but also one that had taken me first into depression, then all the rest. It was a relief to leave it all behind and launch out into something completely new.

In fact, this new thing had already begun and was certainly different to everything that had been me in the past!

I was a shishya, one who has earned the right to study, at an ashram – a kind of monastery – in southern India. I was sleeping in a bare bedroom with a put-me-up bed, a table and an iron stool.

Meals were eaten sitting on the floor in the large refectory, eating with my fingers from a stainless steel plate into which large dollops of strictly vegetarian mush were doled out from huge vats. I was studying the sacred Indian texts and taking lessons in Sanskrit, the language in which those texts had originally been written and handed down over thousands of years. Despite being tone-deaf, I was trying to learn how to chant ancient Vedic hymns and mantras, the magic formulas used to invoke divine aid in order to overcome the obstacles on the path to knowledge.

Now I had to explain to my fellow shishyas how I had come to be here. There were around a hundred of them in front of me: people of all ages, most of them dressed in white and sitting quite still in the lotus position, each on their own small mat lined up in parallel rows, all staring at me. Next to me was an old, very thin man completely swathed in an orange tunic which even covered his head, framing his dark face and long, white beard – the Swami whom I had met several months ago at the yoga and sound course in Pennsylvania. He was curled up on an armchair facing the audience, smiling as he played with his feet. The warm evening breeze wafted in through the wide open windows and doors of the large auditorium where we shishyas spent most of our days. There was a microphone to prevent the metallic sound of the rustling leaves of the trees from drowning out the words of those whom the Swami invited to speak.

I had thought about what I was going to say and knew that it is impossible to pinpoint the precise reason why things happen to us and why we do what we do. There are thousands of necessary, untraceable coincidences behind every individual occurrence in our lives. Some of the more immediate reasons why I had ended up in that ashram were my illness, my desire to know India better and to somehow put myself to the test. More than anything, however, it was my conviction that the lives we lead are one long constraint. We constantly move within the limits of what is unquestioned, permitted or acceptable, and that basically all we do is act out parts on the stage of life, even to the point of believing we are actually the characters rather than the actors. I needed to try something different.

Although I had led a more unusual and adventurous existence than most, I too had lived within the self-imposed limits of what was expected. For thirty years I had been a son, husband, father, friend, journalist, traveller – and a good one too. These were the roles I had fun playing, the masks I had enjoyed wearing. But who was I? And which of the several possible 'I's was me? The young, shy one who blushed and struggled to hold back the tears and emotions? Or the mature international journalist, always slightly bemused to find himself taken seriously by the grown-up world of which he had never really felt a part of? So many 'I's, all of them changing and highly unstable and not one I could feel truly comfortable with.

I wanted to escape from it all now. I wanted to break out of the enchanted circle of what I already knew, and jump off the pedestal of conventional certainties. I wanted to remove my mask. What once had been important to me no longer mattered as much, and the fact that I had pursued it with such determination now merely made me smile.

I had been successful as an 'actor', but I could not stop there. I had to press on, to carry on seeking, even if I didn't really know what I was looking for. Perhaps that's the point: if we knew what to look for, we would always stay within the confines of what we already know and never discover anything new.

At the time I was only vaguely aware of it, but the real reason why I had come to the ashram was that I had wanted to go on another kind of journey – an inward journey, rather than an outward one – the destination of which was not geographical but mental. Now what I craved more than anything else was a certain state of mind, a condition of being at peace with myself and the world. I understood instinctively that it was in this peace that I would find the real cure for my illness, and maybe others too could find the cure for the various physical and not-so-physical ailments which beset them.

So I took the microphone and managed to say my piece in a couple of minutes. I said that if it were true that the river you put one foot in is no longer the same as the river you put the other foot in – because the water has moved on in the time it took you to do so – neither was the man they now saw before them the same as the man who had arrived at the ashram a few days ago. That man was no more. So there was no point trying to talk about him.

I said I no longer wanted to rely on who I was or had been, on what I had done or had not done as a measure of my worth or respectability, like some form of foreign currency. I no longer wanted to speak of myself in the past tense, only the present. I had spent my entire life trying to make a name for myself and now I wanted to try and live my life without one. I was trying not to repeat myself, but to become someone else. I appreciated that this was no small task, and that I would have to work hard on myself. To start with, I had decided to take a vow of silence: I would not speak for one week and I was counting on them to help me. I said they were to call me 'Anam': no-name, Mr Nobody.

As I handed the microphone back to the Swami, I burst out laughing. He too laughed, and I felt a wave of sympathy from the shishyas sweep over me. This merely heightened the feeling of lightness with which I departed the stage. I felt as though I had got rid of the baggage I had been carrying around for ages –

baggage which I now realized contained rocks rather than precious stones. What a pointless burden this self-image had been! I was tired of the figure I would traipse around with and show off to the public. How many times had I had to recount the same amusing anecdotes that made up my life – how, as an Italian, I ended up writing for a German weekly newspaper, why I had been arrested in China, what I thought of the country I now lived in – on flights, on trains, at dinner parties at some diplomat's house or ministerial reception, out of a sense of duty, it was impossible to ignore, all just to entertain someone or to come across as being friendly.

How I had laughed at the Japanese whose identities were so closely bound with what was written on their *meshi* or business cards: name first, then much more important, their title and the position they occupied within their companies. But I had behaved in exactly the same way. To get myself noticed and avoid being sidelined, I too had been handing out business cards – acted out more than written – with their version of my identity on which so much depended.

However, like an intricate mechanism, an identity requires maintenance; it needs to be polished and oiled regularly. I had worked hard on every aspect of mine: my hair, my clothes, the way I introduced myself, made phone calls, kept in contact with people, replied to invitations and even the way I wrote my articles. Martin Woollacott, my friend who writes for *The Guardian*, had said to me back at the time of Vietnam, 'You're only as good as the last piece you wrote.' Keeping up with the 'I' of my last article had become an obsession. All for the purpose of maintaining a name. How many things in life depend on a name! Getting on to a list of people invited to attend a party, a list of people who have got in or passed, a list of winners or passengers, or on the front page of a newspaper. Always the same name, always the same identity. To hell with the stress of it! In New York, several parts of my body had been removed at the hands of the surgeons, without me dying as a result. Now it was me who was removing other, less physical parts. What did that leave? What would be left without my name and my history, all that I had worked on so diligently all my life to achieve?

Deep down this was the question we were all there to answer. And right from the first lesson, the Swami had assured us that there was indeed an answer which we would find in the Vedanta, the last part of the Vedas, devoted to the self which is not born and does not die. It is a self which remains unchanging when everything else changes, the self whose existence does not depend on anything else.

When I went back to my place, the man who was sitting to my left got up, threw his arms open wide and embraced me tightly, calling me 'Anamji', 'Anamji.'[6]

He was lovely, around fifty years old, small, fat, completely bald and with very dark eyes and a long grey pointy beard that reached his chest. Like many other brahmacharis, those who had taken the first vows, he was dressed all in white with a long shirt and dhoti. Like me, he carried a white sheet over his shoulders which he used as a shawl, cushion, towel or whatever else he needed it for. During the first lesson, when everyone had to choose their own little folding wooden desk to be responsible for, and the place we would then keep for the three months of the course, I had studiously avoided all the rows in the centre of the auditorium, which would have provided no support for

[6] In Hindi, the suffix '-ji', when added to a name, is a mark of respect. For instance, in India when Gandhi is spoken of he is usually referred to as 'Gandhiji', and the Swami was always addressed as 'Swamiji'.

my back, and had gone to sit against one of the walls. He had followed me and stationed himself right next to me. But he appeared not to be happy, and after a while asked me if I would mind moving a foot or two.

'You see,' he said, looking up towards one of the concrete beams that held up the auditorium ceiling and passed right over his head, 'all the negative cosmic energies are striking at this point and are falling on me right here; so I am not able concentrate or meditate.'

Was he mad? I didn't think so. He further explained by pointing out that the Swami always entered the auditorium via the northern entrance where the positive energies come from, whereas we, the shishyas, used the western door where the neutral energies come from, and there were no openings at all in the eastern wall, which was the one we were sitting against.

So naturally I moved, and thanks to this episode, Sundarajan and I became firm friends, like classmates sitting at adjacent desks. We helped each other with our translations from Sanskrit and sometimes skipped the odd group activity to climb to the top of the steep hill in the centre of the ashram and enjoy the view.

Sundarajan's story was unusual to say the least. He had been born into a south Indian family living in Malaysia who had moved there at the end of the nineteenth century to build the British colonial railways. While still very young, he had fallen in love with a statue in Kuala Lumpur – the statue of a goddess in his local Indian temple. It had been his first and only love and he had remained faithful to her. He had taken a vow of celibacy when he was still young and would have become a monk if family responsibilities had not prevented him from doing so. Instead, he had been forced to study engineering and worked for more than twenty years in a company that installed electrical systems. He had even worked at the Petronas Towers, one of the tallest buildings in the world, but now he had decided to 'devote himself to another kind of light', as he put it. After spending a year in a yoga centre in the state of Bihar, he now aspired to take sanyas, the vows of total renunciation of the world, from the Swami.

The India he had come to was not that of his father, but of his goddess. He was not looking to trace his own roots, but rather to find spiritual union with her and study the Vedanta with a view to returning to Malaysia to teach it to others.

I too, in coming to the ashram, had ended up in a different kind of India. It was not the India tourists come to take photos of, nor the one usually described by journalists. It was the seekers' India, the India of the great myths which gave mankind the idea of God and that of zero, as well as everything that lies in between. I had lived in Delhi for years, but I had always moved in political or cultural circles, and always felt I was missing out on something. This was doubtless because I had never taken any serious notice of what is really Indian: the spiritual dimension. It was like being a Martian who landed in Florence in the time of Dante and expected to understand it just by visiting the odd church without studying the Bible. Now I felt I was coming closer to the real heart of India in the most typically Indian manner: by going to live with a guru.[7]

Guru is a beautiful word, which unfortunately has lost a lot of its meaning these days through the way we have abused it in the West, where we speak of fashion, health and even sex gurus. *Gu* in Sanskrit means 'shadows' and *ru* means 'to put to flight, dispel'. In

---

[7] 'Guru' is not a title or qualification, it is a relationship. Hence a person may only be a guru to his disciples, not to everybody. Only a disciple will address him as 'guruji', in the same way a husband addresses only his own wife as 'wife', and not the wives of others.

other words, a 'guru' is one who dispels the shadows, who brings light into the darkness of ignorance. His orange clothing recalls the colour of the flame which burns in the darkness, the force of fire which consumes matter.

This was the real India. My guru was called Dayananda[8] Saraswati, and I was a member of the Arsha Vidya Gurukulam, literally the 'family of the guru of true knowledge', the knowledge which comes from the rishis or the seers. The location was beautiful, around twenty miles from Coimbatore, the capital city of the textile industry in the state of Tamil Nadu. I'd taken a taxi from the airport in order to get there. It was a lovely day and everything seemed to bode well. On the way to the ashram, I had stopped by the centre of Coimbatore to buy some pens, exercise books and a couple of kurta-pyjama in white khadi, the cotton fabric still favoured by Gandhi's followers. On the pavement I saw a man squatting in front of two bamboo cages which contained sparrows. He was waiting for someone to buy them and set them free so as to earn good karma. I bought all the birds he had and released them, delighting in their chirruping and basking in the approving comments of those around me.

The journey to the ashram, which I had spent in conversation with the taxi driver who had a degree in mathematics, was the usual Indian mixture of joy and despair, beauty and squalor. For several miles, the road crossed a plain which was dotted with suffocating rubbish and brick factories surrounded by filthy shanty towns that had sprung up, with lots of hungry, dirty people around. The ground was parched and liberally sprinkled with piles of plastic bags. There was no scope for even weeds to grow here.

---

[8] The names of all sanyasis end in '-ananda', signifying that their only goal is ananda, or joy.

The outline of the Anaikatti Hills could be seen in the distance – clear, blue and majestic. There was a time when the whole area had been covered with dense forest and even to this day in the little woodland that remained, the taxi driver informed me, there are primitive people who dress only in leaves and have a king as their leader. The tribe survives by gathering wild herbs for Ayurvedic chemists. The king is the only one who is entitled to talk to people from outside the tribe and anyone who comes into their territory without permission is sent away. These areas are still full of wild animals and many elephants. Even the domestic animals were impressive: as we drove along the road, which was rising and falling as we went from one hill to another, we saw herds of beautiful oxen with huge horns.

The taxi driver pointed out an estate in a valley to me which was completely barren. Until recently, it had been a beautiful forest. A foundation owned by the great Indian ornithologist Salim Ali had bought it with the aim of turning it into a bird sanctuary. But as soon as the owner of the estate pocketed the money, he razed it to the ground, cutting down and selling every single tree that had grown there. This was India!

We drove past an Ayurvedic medical college as well as an engineering institute. We finally reached the ashram which stood alone in the middle of a beautiful, lush green valley surrounded by rocky mountains and several peaks. It consisted of a group of white bungalows set amid eucalyptus trees, an auditorium, a refectory and a temple situated at the edge of a spacious lawn. The whole scene was presided over by a hill on top of which stood another temple.

I was lucky enough to see my release of the sparrows receiving its immediate reward: I had been assigned a single room, the one that was furthest from the centre of the ashram. It was at the edge of a wood with a brick furnace and a view of the mountains. Right in front of my room, a washing line hung between two trees for me to hang my clothes to dry.

I got used to life in the ashram – and to being Anam – with no effort whatsoever and my vow of silence helped me immensely. There was no chance of falling into the trap of having to making casual conversation. Instead I was free to concentrate on observing and listening to everything around me, allowing my thoughts to remain just thoughts without the need to translate them into sounds or words. Writing a few sentences in my diary every evening before falling asleep was sufficient.

My week without talking went by in a flash, each day the same, marked out by precise rhythms, the regularity of which meant that there was little scope for the anxiety of having to make decisions. Everything for me was planned and organized.

We were awoken every morning at 4.15 a.m., by the ringing sound of an iron triangle dangling from a tree, breaking the silence of what was still deep night. Half an hour later, two vats full of tea and boiled milk were laid out on the patio in front of the refectory.

At five o'clock, the great puja, or ritual washing of the statutes to the sound of mantras being chanted, began in the temple. At 6.30 a.m., the Swami led a meditation in the auditorium for half an hour, and at 7.15 it was breakfast, which usually involved boiled chickpeas. At 8 a.m. lessons began: Vedanta, Sanskrit, Vedic chants and the Bhagavadgita. The only interruptions to this routine were the lunch hour – again usually boiled chickpeas and rice – and two breaks for tea. At 6.30 p.m., as the sun set gloriously behind the mountains, *asati*, the ceremony of fire, took place at the temple.[9]

---

[9] The five elements which make up the universe are offered to the gods during this ceremony, i.e., fire, water, earth, air and ether.

At 7.15 p.m. it was dinner, once again boiled chickpeas and rice or semolina, plus occasionally yoghurt.

At 8 p.m., in the main auditorium it was time for satsang, literally meaning 'being with the truth', a meeting at which everyone was free to propose the topic for discussion. This was the only time in which the Swami was not 'up in the pulpit', that is to say, not sitting cross-legged on his small podium, but on a chair down with us in the audience.

At 10 p.m. the iron triangle sounded again. All the lights were turned off and the entire ashram was plunged into darkness and silence, and for the most part, slumber. This was the hour during which I would lay on my bed in my room, the two windows flung wide open, delighting in the rustling sounds and scents which the tepid breeze of the Indian night lavished upon me.

It took around ten days for all the shishyas to introduce themselves – there were 110 of us in all – and this took up most of the after-dinner meetings. It was one way of getting an idea of who my companions were and the reasons that had brought them to this isolated location in the Anaikatti Hills.

There were also young people of between thirty and forty years of age, from good families and academic backgrounds. There were engineers, a nuclear physicist and a pilot with Air India. There were also university assistants who had already taken the vow of celibacy, and having thus been released from every possession and material desire, now aspired only to wear the orange habit of the sanyasi, the renouncers, or spiritual beggars. After a few more years of living and studying in the gurukulam, they too could become swamis, or teachers.

Then there were the older people, with ordinary professional lives behind them, who had come to the ashram to become better acquainted with the idea of death, convinced that after this life they would come back to live another, not necessarily as humans, each with their own burden of merits and demerits to deal with.

Others, especially the female members, were there to give more of a sense of meaning to their lives, which had been spent in a network of family, social rituals and duties, or in exercise of professions such as medicine, which left little room for anything else, especially spiritual searching. Indeed the medical profession was particularly well represented, I noted. It was as though having to deal with so many bodily facts had merely strengthened their desire to look beyond the veil. Much the same as had happened to me, after having to deal with world facts.

Some of the shishyas were there for a sense of therapy. Others were there because it is part of the tradition in India to withdraw from life, and with the help of the Swami they hoped they could be free of the eternal cycle of life and death.

All the people who had come to the ashram had decided to start looking inside of themselves and go 'to the forest' together, as the sacred texts put it.

The forest was a storehouse of herbal remedies, of medicine for the body as well as the soul. 'Going to the forest' is a concept as old as India itself, and which continues to make it a place unlike any other; at least until the rest of the trees are cut down!

According to the traditional Indian way of looking at things, the life of a person is divided into four separate and distinctive stages, each with its own fruits, rights and responsibilities.

The first season is that of childhood and adolescence, the time to study and learn everything that will be of use for what is to come. The second season is that of maturity when a man becomes a husband and father, takes up his role within the family, and thus helps maintain and perpetuate society. This is the period in which it is right and proper to pursue wealth, pleasure, fame and knowledge of the world. Thereafter, when the children themselves become husbands and fathers, there comes the season of retirement and of 'going to the forest'. In retiring in this way, man leaves behind all his joys, worries, successes and disappointments – everything that is transitory and illusory in life – in order to devote himself to something more real and permanent.

The last season is the one in which man is free of all ties, and having become a humble beggar, he can become a sanyasi if he chooses. Dressed in the colour of fire – the fire in which he has symbolically burnt everything, including his desires that belonged to his temporal self – he may devote himself exclusively to moksh, the final release from samsara, the changing world, the ocean of life and death.

Moksha is the final destination of a sanyasi's journey. Nothing can distract him now. Certainly nothing from his past, which is burnt symbolically at a 'funeral' where he himself lights the pyre, emerging as a new person. Now he is not tied to anything – neither his caste nor his family or his name, not even his religion or any of its rituals. The orange tunic he robes himself in after this funeral is deliberately made out of just one piece of material, with no stitches or knots. When he dies, his body will be thrown into a river rather than cremated, for he, the sanyasi, has already passed through the flames.

Every season of life is formally marked by a ritual during which, like in any kind of initiation ceremony, life is born out of symbolic death and the new comes forth from the old.

In its own way, Western society too, in its pursuit of objectives, now solely materialistic, has institutionalized this passage to the final stage of life in the shape of retirement. Once you reach the age of sixty or sixty-five, you stop working and get paid to go fishing, paint, or get bored while regretting whatever it was that you once used to be: a manager, head of a department, lawyer, or cashier. Many such people end up having heart attacks, and in this way stop being what they were, once and for all.

I myself had stopped working – journalism no longer held the attraction it once did – but rather than simply enjoying my retirement, I had begun to look for something that was no different from what my companions were seeking: some kind of inner peace. Cancer had helped me in this respect, by finally giving me an opportunity to do so. I could finally be me without having to use the business card. I could abandon myself to my true personality and enjoy it. For there is no doubt about it: the closer we get to who we really are, the happier we are as a result. The key to it lies in knowing who we are.

Unfortunately our culture – or rather the industry which now determines our culture – has idealized youthfulness and turned old age into some kind of illness, pushing the elderly into being something other than what they really are – into pretending to be young people. But old age is not necessarily a bad thing, nor does it have to be a time for regrets.

For many, losing their sex drive is a tragedy, a humiliation. For me, it was merely another part of my becoming 'lighter'. I had spent so much time debating, kidding myself, making distinctions, controlling everything there was to be controlled, even attempting to spiritualize it, that I now worry that what came afterwards would be a disappointment. But all this was behind me now. What a wonderful thing old age is! It is an opportunity to reflect, to do what I had never had a chance to do, including thinking about life. It is possible to view physical decline, our bodies slowing down, illness and even death through different eyes. It was a time to understand new things, open other doors, discover and experiment.

The world continually pushes us into standardized forms of behaviour. If you can't sleep, take sleeping pills! But why should you? Maybe it'd be helpful, perhaps important, to stay awake at night every now and again and have the kind of experience that those who sleep never have. The night is the time for visions as well as nightmares, and this is exactly why we should aspire to know it, as the sun itself did in an old Indian tale.

A man from the earth goes to see the sun.

'How are things down there?' the great star asks him.

'Well, my lord, everyone worships you.'

'Everyone? Really?'

'Well, there is one lady, just one, beautiful lady, who never turns to you in devotion.'

'And who might that be?'

'She is called Night.'

The sun was very intrigued by this.

'Where is this lady?'

'In India,' the man replied.

So the sun hurried to India, but the lady knew he was coming, and decided to flee to the other side of the world. The sun followed her, but by the time he got there she had already returned to India. The sun continued to pursue this beautiful lady without ever catching up with her.

Was I mad? No, just old and no longer under obligation to anyone. I just wanted to be what I had always wanted to be: an explorer. But no longer an explorer of the outside world, I knew what that looked like now. Instead, I wanted to explore the inner world, the world wise men of all cultures through the centuries have said we have inside.

Modern man seems to have less and less of this world. He just does not have the time nor does he get the chance. The lives we lead, often in cities, do not help us to think of the big picture. We are continually chasing after details, minor things which mean we miss the wood for the trees. I understood this eventually with respect to my own profession. My job had been to tell people about wars. It wasn't to ask myself why, with all the progress man can boast of, wars continue to be a part of our existence or why the more civilized and progressive a country becomes, the more they invest in new weapons that are able to kill more effectively and in larger numbers.

Up until a few years ago, telling people about a war could still have some effect: people wouldn't stand for it, news of a massacre could still produce an emotional reaction. Now such things are useless. Every day there are new stories of massacres, injustices, torture, but no one takes any notice. We've become inured to it. We have all become accomplices in the simplest crime of all: indifference.

No one has the right answers any more because nobody is asking the right questions. Certainly not science, which in the West has become enslaved to large-scale economic interests and placed on the altar instead of religion. Science has become the opiate of the people, with its false pretence of sooner or later being able to solve every problem. It has reached the stage where it can clone human life, but it cannot tell us what life actually is. Medicine has got to the point where it can put off death, but it cannot tell us what happens afterwards. Do we know what it is that enables our eyes to see or our minds to think?

And yet, with our faith in science, we now take all these things for granted. We think we know, but we don't. So we're happy, confident in the fact that one day we will. After all, someone somewhere must be working on it! The world's population is increasing, its resources are used up, water in particular. It does not matter; soon science will be able to solve these problems too. Millions of human beings are dying of hunger in most parts of the world, but no worries; we can genetically modify different types of seeds, which should soon be able to produce miraculous bumper crops and along with that new forms of cancer.

We live as though this was the only world possible which seems to promise some kind of happiness. Happiness which is to be achieved through progress, which consists of more and more education – and what education! – more prosperity, and of course more science. In the end, everything seems to be reduced to a question of organization and efficiency. How wrong we are! We have allowed the wings of our imagination to be clipped, and reduced the whole world to just our senses, completely denying the other half of our existence.

For the wise men, the Indians in particular, the visible world is only part of – and not all of – reality. It's not even the most important part, for it is continually changing, prone to the destructive passing of time.

And yet, sometimes very little is required to make us take note of the rest. The great Bengali poet Rabindranath Tagore made this point by means of a simple comparison. One evening he found himself on board a floating home on the Ganga, reading a book by Benedetto Croce. He snuffed out the candle, and in a moment the room was flooded with moonlight:

> Spirit of Beauty, how could you, whose radiance
> overbrims the sky, stand hidden behind a
> candle's tiny flame? How could a few vain
> words from a book rise like a mist, and veil
> her whose voice has hushed the heart of earth
> into ineffable calm?

Our daily life is full of small lights that prevent us from seeing the greater light. Our minds have shrunk most incredibly and all we do more than anything is react. We react according to predetermined cultural and social models. And increasingly, we react automatically. We don't have time to do anything else. The path has already been trodden; all we can do is walk on it.

In the ashram, however, it wasn't like that. There was the time to live life paying attention to every moment. We practised acting as opposed to reacting, keeping our minds alert and being aware of each movement. The mosquitoes buzzing around my ears? Nothing simpler than to react without thinking, swatting them away with my hand. Instead, I forced myself not to kill them. And I liked it.

The ashram was certainly a strange place in many ways. Especially for someone like me, who all his life had been used to being around people and racing all over the world to tell stories and recount hundreds of problems, and who now, all of a sudden, found himself all alone, isolated from everyone, and just one problem to think about for hours on end, day after day, week after week: 'Who am I?'

Only man, the Swami says in his introduction to the Vedanta, has always asked questions regarding the nature of his existence, and has always been upset by the uncertain nature of the response.

The question is born of experience. Man looks around himself, looks at the world and then makes his observations. The world appears to him to be distinct from itself, like something from which he feels separate. Since everything he sees is infinitely greater than he is, he feels wretched, isolated and vulnerable, like a small wave intimidated by the vastness of the ocean, one which dreams only of being larger and more powerful to avoid being overcome by the other waves. It is in this perception of two distinct entities – the one who sees and the one who is seen – that man's eternal dissatisfaction and sadness are rooted.

The second observation man makes is that the world already exists when he comes to see it. It has been assembled in such an intelligent fashion that he himself cannot have been its creator. Who is it then? Thus man begins to search for his creator, for a god, who must then also be outside him since he is capable of creating the entire universe, including man.

'This is how religions are born,' said the Swami.

This Swami had been a sanyasi for more than half a century and so was looking in from outside the world and organized religion. Even Hinduism – a term which had been invented arbitrarily by the British, he said – was not a genuine religion, he believed, but a philosophy of life, one that had not been invented and had no sacred text in particular. It was a form of wisdom that had been deposited over thousands of years. The Swami did not consider the Vedanta to be a religion, but an instrument of knowledge, a way of understanding reality.

According to the Swami, in religions man always ends up having a limited view of himself precisely because all that the Self perceives is outside the Self. So man takes the distinction between himself and that which he perceives and knows as an unquestioned reality, just as the wave sees the ocean as something apart from itself. And yet, as soon as the wave realizes that the other waves and the ocean are made of water too, its feelings of inadequacy and separateness disappear.

So it is for man as well, the Swami says. As soon as man understands that he himself is the whole, and that there is no duality – between creator and created, between the one who sees and what is seen, between himself and God – he also understands what looks to him like a separate existence is in fact nothing of the kind, for nothing exists independently of its whole. I am the problem, but I am also the solution. Understanding this means true freedom from the illusion of existing individually. Individuality means only limits.

The important point, the Swami continues, is that the wave does not need to become the ocean. It only needs to understand that it is a part of the ocean. You are what you are. It's not a question of changing, but merely of appreciating who you are.

But how can you make this step-up in terms of self-awareness? How can the essence of man come to recognize itself in the whole? He needs someone to help him, to show him the way. It cannot know itself on its own. This is why a guru is needed, one who can dispel the darkness of ignorance. There is a classic story used for centuries in India to explain this.

There were ten students in a gurukulam. One day they decided to go on a pilgrimage, and one of them was appointed as their leader. They came to a place where they needed to cross a river and the leader asked if they knew how to swim. They all did. When they reached the other side, the leader counted them and discovered, to his horror, that there were only nine of them. He counted again, and yet again the total came to just nine. In desperation, the students began to look in the water. Where could the tenth one be? There was no trace of him, no body, no clothes, and not even a sound. They wept, and were at a loss as to what to do when an old man who had been watching the scene from afar stepped up and said to the group:

'There is no reason for you to be sad. The tenth man is not lost, he is here.'

'Where? How?' one of the students asked.

'He is here, now, with you.'

The students were sceptical.

'He is here, and you can find him without even taking a step,' the old man insisted.

The leader tried one last time. He counted the students slowly, prodding his finger into the chest of each of his companions. 'One, two, three ... eight, nine.' At this point the old man prodded his own finger into the chest of the leader. 'Ten! You're the tenth man!' he exclaimed.

The old man was merely pointing out the obvious: the one seeking is also the one being sought. He is the problem, but also the solution to that problem. The solution lies simply in discovering himself.

We do not know ourselves when we are born. In the course of our lives, we acquire a great deal of knowledge, but this knowledge does not help us understand who we are for it is derived from our senses, from inferences based on sensory perception. All scientific knowledge is of this kind – from our senses. What branch of science has ever asked who man really is? What microscope or telescope has ever looked into the recesses of the human minds? Since it cannot reach us through our senses and therefore may not be the subject of any branch of science, knowledge of ourselves eludes us. The old man in the story is the guru who shows how the self can learn to recognize itself. But it is not enough just to have a guru.

Right from his first lesson, the Swami made it clear that the issue, which lies at the heart of the Vedanta, is not religious. It is not about finding the answers through faith and even less so through the intellect.

Rather, it is a question of understanding that, just as the eyes cannot see themselves and require the help of a mirror to do so, the self cannot know itself without the help of a suitable cognitive instrument either. Such an instrument cannot be any of our senses, for these are capable only of seeing, hearing, touching and smelling the material, sensory world, and not the actual self.

This cognitive instrument, the mirror in which the self is able to contemplate itself, are the Vedas[10], or rather the final part of the Vedas known as the Vedanta and consisting of the Upanishads and the Bhagavadgita[11], the Song of God, which summarizes the substance of the issue in the form of a dialogue. By means of a series of reasoning which derive from both experience of the self and the world, the shastras or scriptures, if read with the help of a guru, demonstrate – just as the eyes see and the ears hear – that there is no duality between the one who knows and the one who is known. There is no such thing as distinct entities – the self, the world and God. All is one single, unique existence and this fullness is none other than the consciousness, one that has no limits and is outside time and space, pervades everything, sustains everything and is made to manifest in every form.

Such consciousness is pure and a witness to all, the reality which lies behind ordinary consciousness. It is Atman, Brahman,

---

[10] There are four Vedas: Rig, which is the oldest, and then there are Sama, Yajur and Atharva. They are collections of hymns and or mantras. Tradition attributes the Veda to the rishis, or 'seers'. Their date is uncertain, but they certainly date back to at least the second millennium BC. They were handed down orally for more than a thousand years, and thereafter in written form. Some believe the *Rig Veda* is the oldest book in history to survive in complete form. It is certainly the oldest text in any Indo-European language.

[11] Upanishad means 'to sit near', and refers to the shishya who would sit at their guru's feet listening to him. There are around a hundred Upanishads, but ten main ones. Most are in verse and some in prose. Many are in the form of a dialogue, say between a sage and his wife, a king and an ascetic, or as in one of the most famous which is titled *Katha Upanishad,* between young Nachiketa and Death, whom he has chosen as his guru.

Ishwara, Bhagawan, God; it is Fullness, or whatever else you want to call it, for as one of the most frequently quoted Vedic verses puts it: 'The truth is one, even if the wise men call it by a thousand different names.'

So the answer to the question, 'who am I?', is the magical phrase which resounds throughout the Upanishads, namely *tat tvam asi* – 'you are all this'. You are God, the creator of the whole universe, where *tvam*, meaning you, is clearly not to be understood in the sense of one's identity, the self we are all so attached to, but rather in the sense of that unchanging self revealed in the Vedanta. The Self in the sense of pure consciousness was never born and can never die.

This is where the wholly Vedantic idea comes from that God is in every form and every living being, in everything, even the humblest of things; an idea that has now passed into the common Indian world view. There is neither a plurality of god nor one sole God, but rather everything is God.

The self which each of us tends to become is confused in this because man aspires to free himself from his limitations, from his sense of being separate and distinct from the world. As the river, which too has a source and moves inexorably towards the ocean, tends to be confused and become one with it, losing its own identity, form and name in the process, so too does the self aspire to merge with the whole. This is its nature. The true goal of human life is to recognize this self and its divine nature.

The Swami appreciated that it wasn't always easy for us to follow his reasoning. Does it not say in the Upanishads that 'the road which leads to reality is as narrow as a razor blade and difficult to travel'? However, as if to lighten the atmosphere, to make things more accessible for us, and to provide a kind of bridge by which to help us remember his teachings, he used to recount some of the classic tales of the Indian tradition.

One such tale about the importance of understanding the self was this:

There once was a Brahmin, learned in the sacred scriptures, on board a boat which was crossing a river. He asked the old boatman: 'Do you know Sanskrit?'

'No,' the boatman replied.

'Without Sanskrit, one quarter of your life is wasted,' the Brahmin said. 'Do you at least know classical literature?'

'No,' replied the boatman once again.

'Then that's another quarter of your life wasted, for there are many beautiful books and reading them is a source of immense joy. Can you at least read and write?'

'No,' came the response.

'That's another quarter of your life wasted.'

At that moment, the Brahmin noticed that water was seeping into the boat and his legs are already soaking wet. The boatman tried to plug the leak, but to no avail. The water continued to rise and the boat was about to sink.

'Can you swim?' the boatman asked the Brahmin.

'No,' he replied in trepidation.

'That's all of your life wasted,' concluded the boatman.

The moral of this story is that it is pointless being able to read and write, to understand Sanskrit and read classical literature if you do not know yourself.

Lessons began exactly ten minutes past the hour, but we shishyas took our places well before that.

As we waited for the Swami, we began chanting a hymn to our guru: 'Om … Oh lord, I send my reverential greetings to my guru and all his predecessors. I call upon his grace to remove the veil of my ignorance and to him I offer my prostrations. Oh lord, protect us, nourish us, help us to study and understand the scriptures. Help us not to quibble over details. Om … Peace, peace, peace.'[12] We were directed in our chanting by two old ladies dressed in white, possibly widows, who were our singing instructors and whom I nicknamed the 'Vergers', because of the way they presided over every detail of the ashram's liturgy.

Then we recited some of the most famous and beautiful mantras of the Upanishads, using the same tonality, pronunciation and rhythm that had been used for centuries. One which I loved to sing at the top of my voice, and which invariably earned me disapproving looks from the Vergers and made my classmate Sundarajan laugh with amusement because of all the notes I missed, was the mantra from the *Brihadaranyaka Upanishad*:

Asatō mā sadgamaya
tamasō mā jyōtirgamaya
mr̥tyōrmā amr̥taṁ gamaya

which loosely translates to:

From the unreal lead me to the real,
from darkness lead me to light,
from death lead me to immortality.

As I uttered the word for immortality, which consists of the privative prefix *a* plus the word *mrita*, meaning death, I felt the

---

[12] All the Upanishads begin with the sound 'Om' and end in 'Om shanti', 'shanti' meaning peace. It is an invitation to attain to that state of serenity which knowledge of the self is able to bring about, a state of peace that transcends all understanding. Virtually all the Vedic hymns begin and end this way.

beauty of the Sanskrit language, which I realized provided the word for love in my own language, 'a-more', that which does not die.

The Swami would come in through the northern entrance, accompanied by a young brahmachari who would walk alongside him, shielding him from the sun with an open umbrella. The Swami would take off his sandals, mount the wooden platform, climb the three steps up to his podium, wrap the edge of his orange tunic over his head and sit down cross-legged behind a low table covered by a coloured throw. From under that tablecloth, in the course of a lesson, the Swami would produce all kinds of good things with which to illustrate the points he would make in his teaching, as all gurus have done for centuries in their teaching of the Vedanta. He would take a clay dish and explain how its existence depended on the existence of the clay. Without clay the dish would not exist, just as creation would not exist without consciousness. He took out a crystal ball and a rose to illustrate the illusory nature of the rose's colour when seen through the ball; it is the same confusion created by the self, when it attempts to distinguish between itself and what it perceives. He produced a rope with which to make the classic Vedantic comparison between the rope and a snake: to mistake a rope for a snake is exactly the same as to mistake the world of the senses for the real world. It is confusion of our own making: could the rope be mistaken for a snake if the snake did not exist?

One prop the Swami did not need was a copy of the Upanishads or the Gita. He knew them by heart and had given away his extensive library many years ago. He said he didn't need it any more, that he no longer wanted to depend on anything that was written down. This is what the Indian tradition has believed right from its origins, especially when the holy texts were still considered a mystery that could only be handed down orally, from the lips of a guru to the ear of a disciple. Even if he lost his memory as he got older, the seventy-year-old Swami said, he could carry on teaching from only a couple of verses. And he then told us another story.

Towards the end of the nineteenth century, an English teacher arrived in Calcutta, at that stage the Indian capital of the British Empire. He said he was interested in understanding India and its philosophy, and asked to meet a famous pandit who was a great expert in Sanskrit. He also wanted to take lessons on the Vedanta from this man who spoke perfect English. The pandit began by chanting the first lines of the first Upanishad, the *Isha Upanishad*:[13]

> Oṁpūrṇamadah pūrṇamidaṁ pūrṇāt pūrṇamudacyate
> Pūrṇasya pūrṇamādāya pūrṇamevāvasiṣyate
> Oṁ sānti, sānti, sāntih.

This he translated into English as follows:

> That is full, this is full;
> Fullness comes forth from fullness.
> When fullness is taken from fullness,
> Fullness remains.
> Om shanti, shanti, shanti.

The Englishman clapped his book shut, stood up and ended the lesson on the spot. In his diary he wrote, 'The Upanishads are

---

[13] The *Brihadaranyaka Upanishad* also begins in the same way.

the incoherent ramblings of an infantile mind.' According to the Swami, however, these two verses summarize the entire vision of the Vedanta, and this mantra alone is sufficient to keep the tradition alive, and provide food for thought for whoever was willing to try and understand them. We were to spend weeks meditating on them.

'These two verses contain subject, object, cause, effect, experience, totality. They contain the truth about us,' the Swami explained. 'I am purnam, fullness, a whole ocean which no one can disturb. Nothing can limit me. Waves and breakers may dance on my surface, but they are merely forms of myself that have manifested fleetingly. Waves and breakers appear to be many and diverse, but I know them only insofar as they are appearances. They place no limits on me: their stirring is merely my fullness being manifested. The waves are my glory, which resolve themselves in me. In me, a full ocean, all is resolved. All that remains is me, purnam, fullness.'

It wasn't always easy to follow him. On occasions, despite thinking I had understood, I realized that all I had done was grasp his words intellectually rather than 'experience' them. It wasn't an intellectual matter or an article of faith, he insisted. Nor was it about reaching logical conclusions, but was of going on a journey of 'discovery', step by step, as the Upanishads describe it. It was like submitting one's own consciousness to a kind of alchemy, allowing it to be transformed by the words of the sacred texts. But even these could be jettisoned once they had acted as a mirror to the self, like a boat used to cross a river may be forgotten, once it has served its purpose.

The Swami had been born into a traditional Brahmin family in Tamil Nadu. He had been an outstanding student and had started to work as a journalist in Madras. Soon, however, he realized this wasn't his true calling. He had withdrawn from the world, taken sanyas and become the disciple of various gurus. Eventually, one of these gurus, who lived in a forest and clothed himself only in ash, helped him make the step-up in terms of knowledge that gave him the confidence to take on another major challenge – that of reinstituting the classical oral tradition of teaching the Vedanta, and of bringing its vision of life back within the reach of everyone, not just in India.

The tradition had been established in the eighth century AD by Shankaracharya, the great Vedic commentator, but soon died out. Centuries of Muslim domination, when entire populations converted to Islam, had driven the teachings of the Vedas further and further underground. Later, the two-century-long British colonization proved even more devastating, introducing a new set of social values among the higher classes especially, and above all an education system intended to churn out little officers for the Empire to use, and to promote knowledge that was 'useful' – which knowledge of the Self clearly was not.

The Indians were lucky that their vision of the world rooted in the Vedas was not entrusted to a structure such as a church. It had not been handed down centrally as Buddhism was, for example, and this enabled it to survive. Hinduism had no monasteries that could be razed to the ground, nor did it have a religious capital that could be wiped out. Rather, a guru would pass on his learning to a group of five or six shishyas in some hermitage in a forest orally. And there were lots of such gurus throughout India. However, tradition insisted that only children from the highest Brahmin caste could be instructed.

The task the Swami had set was to break this monopoly and

to teach the Vedanta to anyone who was interested, whether or not he was a Brahmin or even an Indian. 'The desire to be whole is common to all human beings on all continents and at all times. The problem is universal and so too is the solution,' he said.

It had been fashionable among westerners at the end of the nineteenth century, inspired by Vivekananda in particular, to believe that the Vedanta could become the 'universal gospel', as Romain Rolland called it. There was something profoundly modern in the avowedly ancient vision contained in the Vedanta, which seemed somehow to fill the spiritual void created by man's new pursuit of individualism and materialism.

Unlike other religions, which set metaphysical targets that are usually deferred until the next life, possibly even heaven, the Vedanta has only one spiritual objective: to realize one's own fullness in this life, now.

The Swami believed that today, more than ever, this had to be the main objective of all mankind. He was doing what he could to promote the knowledge of the *Vedanta*. He had already instructed around a hundred swamis who were now teaching others in India and abroad. This was a huge task as traditionally, a guru had to look after each of his students individually. 'There's no such thing as mass liberation, just as there's no such thing as mass education,' he used to say. And he never tired of walking the path prescribed by tradition, day in day out, 'step by step'.

'My karma is to teach you; yours is to be my shishya. We both need each other,' he once said in order to lighten a long philosophical disquisition, as he was accustomed to doing.

At the start of the course, for example, he explained that his ashram was not one of those which guaranteed illumination or gold Rolexes, causing us to laugh at this allusion to Sai Baba, who people say is able to make watches or glasses of water appear out of thin air, or cause vibhuti[14] to rain down from his fingers on to the outstretched hands of his initiates.

'Of course, I too can do miracles, and if you want, I'll do one sooner or later,' he said, leaving us all holding our breath. He was joking, of course, but everyone loves a miracle and occasionally someone would remind him of the promise he had made.

The Swami was a great storyteller, and he used every rhetorical trick and device in the book to make his audience laugh and hold its attention. Once he went up to his little podium with a letter in his hand. He had just received it from a young man who had asked to become his disciple. Unfortunately, the young man's grasp of English wasn't quite perfect and he had ended his letter by offering the Swami his 'prostate' as opposed to his 'prostrations'!

Another time he arrived for the first lesson of the morning, which he began by telling another story.

A guru was giving one of his disciples some instructions: 'This evening, when you meditate, imagine I'm sitting on top of your head.'

The disciple departed and the next day he found his guru so full of aches and pains that he could hardly manage to stand up.

'How did it go?' the guru asked the disciple.

'Very well, guruji. I meditated in the way you suggested, imagining you were sitting on top of my head. But then after a while I got tired, so instead I began to imagine that it was I sitting on your head!'

'One evening, when it was time for satsang, the Air India pilot,

---

[14] Vibhuti is a term used to signify both the mark made on people's foreheads with ash derived from burning cowpats, and glory, as all glory turns eventually to ash. Vibhuti is used during pujas, and to make the sign of Shiva on people's foreheads, if one prefers not to use ash from a funeral pyre on which a corpse has been cremated.

who had taken three months' leave from his work in order to decide whether or not he wanted to become a sanyasi, took the Swami to task for this habit of telling stories, and asked him why he insisted on doing it.

'Haven't you noticed?' the Swami asked by way of replying. 'When you laugh, you open your mouth wide. That's when I can fill it with something useful.' Then he himself guffawed out loud, mouth wide open, and added, 'When a person laughs, they manifest a wholeness that would not be revealed in any other way. This is true if the person who is laughing is mentally handicapped, if they're stupid, or even if they're just a swami.'

The time of satsang in the evening after dinner was always one of the most interesting times of the day because anyone was allowed to ask whatever question they wanted. The questions the young brahmacharis used to ask tended to be philosophical in nature, concerning textual exegesis or metaphysical niceties. Those asked by the 'pensioners' brigade', as I used to call the group of elderly people headed by a former bank manager from Gujarat, tended to focus on the issue of death, how to view it and how to prepare for it. The Swami's method of replying to these questions varied. On one occasion he merely quoted some verses from an Upanishad:

> As a caterpillar reaches the top of a blade of grass,
> And gathers itself around as it passes to the next stage,
> So the self, as it reaches the end of this life,
> Gathers itself up and passes from the old to the new body.

Another time he said, 'When a man dies in Madras, people say, "He has departed." When a child is born in Coimbatore, they say "He has arrived." The traveller is one and the same. It is Atman, the self, unlimited consciousness which is not subject to becoming, never departing or arriving, always present.'

When he was asked if it was possible to have a life without any problems, he replied that no such thing existed; games were like that, life was not. Anyone looking for a life with no problems is like a country bumpkin who goes to a football match for the first time in his life and gets angry with the referee because he has given the twenty-two players only one ball to play with, meaning they have to run around chasing it all the time. 'But those are the rules of the game. Life is like that too. Without problems, there wouldn't be any glory. Problems are the trigger which cause us to begin our spiritual search,' he added. 'If we don't feel so lowly and so limited, we won't even ask ourselves what to do. Through conflict, man becomes both adult and mature.'

I watched the Swami with interest. He was patient, tireless and imperturbable. He never judged anyone. He did his duty, which was to teach us, without expecting anything in return, not even that we understand everything completely. He was sure he belonged to a great tradition, that he had a great truth to communicate, and that sooner or later that truth would be plain for us all to see.

'Truth is not the opinion of the majority. The majority may be able to vote for a government, but it cannot decide what the truth is.'

He was good at explaining difficult concepts, such as jiva, the individual which is in every living being and which is passed on from life to life, sometimes human, sometimes not; jagat, the world, a manifestation of, but not separate from, the Brahman, as a web is not separate from the spider that spins it; and samsara, the world of becoming, of desires. He said the concept of dharma should be comprehensible to us all: what I expect from others is what I should give to others.

The first time he explained karma to us, he did so as follows. Every action produces effects, some of which are visible, others not. It is the invisible effects of our conscious actions which constitute our karma. The effects of a positive action, such as helping someone, saving an animal, or even watering a plant, our merits that is, produce punya, or credits; those of our negative actions, or demerits, produce papa, or debits. When the jiva is in dharma it accumulates punya; when it is outside dharma, it accumulates papa, which then have to be reckoned with in the next life.

'Primitive man was aware of the existence of karma,' the Swami said. 'He left his cave to go hunting and came back home in the evening having caught nothing but a miserable squirrel. "Ahhafst annllsghahsnna?" his wife screamed at him (translation: "Is that all you've managed to catch, you idiot?"). In his defence he replied: "Naggasfsrgg snnsgshh" (translation: "I was unlucky"). Another day he came back with a huge beast large enough to feed the entire family. "Naggasfsrgg sgrggrisas," (translation: "I was lucky'"), he said on this occasion. What are good and bad luck, if not karma? We all understand that there is something which conditions our life in one way or another. But some, like primitive men, believe that things are linked to chance, or to some evil spirit, whereas others are convinced that only we ourselves are responsible for all that occurs to us, for "good" and "bad" luck are the fruits of our own actions in this or a previous life. This is called karma.

'Some religions attribute everything to God,' he went on. 'A son dies and people say to his mother: "God gave him to you, God has taken him away from you." But God doesn't come into it. He has nothing to do with all this. It's just a question of karma. It is the huge net we're all tangled up in; each of us has our own freedom of choice, so each of us also has our own measure of responsibility.'

He was particularly sarcastic about the word 'I', which we use all the time, and forms the basis on which we make our judgements about the universe. Yet, at the same time, it is a word that our minds are unable to objectivize and which is incapable of awakening any precise image in us. 'If we say "bowl", for example, an image forms in our minds. More or less like this ...' He then continued, 'But "I"? We say "I am tall" and we think of our bodies; we say "I am depressed" and we think of our minds. So what is this "I", which is present in so many different roles? The common denominator of all these different "I"s is the consciousness of all the other "I"s. Everything depends on that consciousness, but that consciousness does not depend on anything.'

He pulled a clay bowl out from underneath his table and said, 'Now, we are all conscious of this bowl.' He then put it back under the table, and showed us his empty hand. 'Now what do we have? We are conscious of its absence! So whether or not the bowl is there, what we have all the time is consciousness.' And so he went on, for hours on end. We all understood that at some point everything would become clear to us, obvious ... like in the lovely story which the great Ramakrishna used to tell.

A lioness died while giving birth and the orphaned cub was adopted by a flock of sheep. It grew up with them, ate grass with them, learnt to bleat with them, and to socialize as a sheep. One day, an old lion that had been watching him from a distance came and attacked the flock with a great roar. The lion cub was as scared as the sheep were, and tried to run away, but the old lion caught up with it, grabbed it by the scruff of the neck, led it to a pool and forced it to look at his reflection in the water.

'So what are you then? A sheep?' the lion asked him.

And for the first time, the cub let out a roar.

The lion cub in this story is us, for we don't know who we are any more than it does. And the water in which we see our true selves reflected is the Vedanta.

Without a guru there is no knowledge, which is precisely why a guru is so important. 'Why go from city to city, and from temple to temple looking for God? God lives in you – you are God. So stop looking for him and instead look for a guru who can help you discover yourself,' Shankaracharya wrote twelve centuries ago. This is the source of the absolute dependence between disciple and guru, which is so incomprehensible to us westerners.

In the ashram, I was often startled by the expressions of adulation the Swami would receive.

'Every human relationship has its limits,' a woman said one day during the evening satsang when this topic was being discussed. 'Between brothers, it is relationship with the father that is missing. Between father and son, it is the relationship with the mother. It is only in a relationship with a guru that there is nothing missing at all. The guru is a father, mother, brother, teacher, neighbour and doctor. The shishya has no problem that the guru does not take on because the guru does not have any problems. This is the reason for my devotion to my guru.'

Another woman said, 'When I met him, for me it was like I was born again. My parents gave me my body, but Swamiji gave me my soul.'

I was shocked, but I understood why people said that the guru wasn't a human being and that he was to be respected for his knowledge rather than as a person. However, such blind devotion, people throwing themselves so ostentatiously and literally at his feet, disturbed me.

After each lesson, the most devout of the students – there were perhaps a dozen of them – rushed to follow the Swami to his residence where he would sit himself down in a comfortable armchair, and they would line up in front of him to touch his big toe and simply gaze at him.

Right from the start I had decided I didn't want any part of this. So rather than follow the Swami, I would just go back to my bedroom. One day, however, Sundarajan pointed out to me that all the shishya who went to his residence came back with some kind of gift, usually a banana. It had been a while since there had been any fruit at the ashram and I was tempted. But as soon as I put my foot inside his house, I realized I would embarrass myself by throwing myself at his feet, but that if I didn't do so, I would embarrass everyone else instead. So I did abruptly turn around, rather surprising the lady who was waiting in the queue behind me.

As far as the rest of it was concerned, this monastic lifestyle was extremely pleasant: absolute peace, no responsibilities, each day marked by rituals and routines; and it gave me the chance to engage my mind on the most unusual – and at times quite extraordinary – subjects. It was such a joy to wake up each morning and think of Bhagawan without getting caught up in the detail of everyday life! The ashram was like a desert island, isolated from the world's hustle and bustle and the waves of its desires. This was part of its attraction.

I came to understand the appeal of the great traditions of monastic orders. I also realized why the Chinese communists had built a museum at Lhasa to show visitors like myself what the 'horrors of Tibetan lamaism' had been like. They described the monks as idlers who were escaping the rigours of life, from family responsibilities and hard graft in the fields, just so as to sing hymns in monasteries while being 'maintained by the sweat of the brows of those outside'.

I too at times had the impression I was like one of them, having left other people behind to deal with my problems. I thought of Angela, my friends who carried on working to keep the world running for me. I saw them going to the office, making phone calls, looking at their computer screens, answering emails, writing out cheques ... while I was doing none of this. Instead, from morning to night, all I was doing was thinking about Bhagawan.

'Leave everything outside that is external, whether it is people or things. Circumstances are what they are. That which worries you is outside the self. The self must desire nothing, nor must it judge. It must only be an object of meditation and leave everyone free to their own destiny,' the Swami said during his meditation at dawn. 'Retreat from your senses. Be like the tortoise, which pulls its feet and its head into its shell. Look at your body from the outside. Look at yourself as though you were a statue that breathes. Keep listening, take note of what happens to you and be aware of it ...'

The Swami was leading this meditation from high up on his little podium; the auditorium was swathed in complete darkness. He spoke quietly, uttering just the odd sentence. One of his most frequent themes was objectivity.

Meditating at dawn was like making a plan for the day. The fact that so many people were involved in it together, all ecalming their minds in silence, increased the sense of intensity and concentration and thus created a feeling of strength. It basically meant becoming aware of yourself. It is not easy to do because the mind is naturally restless, at times turbulent, and is easily distracted. Moreover, to try not to think is like 'trying to catch the wind with your hands, then make it go where you want it to,' as it says in the Upanishads.

Yet the ability to concentrate, to focus the mind on itself, appeared to be a question of willpower and strength of character, something it was worth investing every effort in. Ultimately, to be able to control your own mind means to be able to control your life.

The mind is the source of all of man's problems, but it is also the centre of many of their solutions. It is a hidden treasure; we go about our daily lives without realizing how much it is actually worth. All we have to do is take possession of it and learn to master it, by teaching ourselves to do what we do more consciously, rather than absent-mindedly, as we increasingly do now.

The Swami put this across very well one evening during the satsang. One of the pensioners had asked him what life was and the Swami replied quite simply, 'Life is a series of little steps. It's only by taking them one at a time, consciously, that we can hope to stay in control.'

I agreed with him: lots of little steps – sometimes even the odd one that seems a little further than we can cope with – but none of them to be taken lightly.

The ashram was an excellent place in which to think everything through, to review all judgements of the past in order to appreciate the value of the former things, to add new aspects to a vision of the world that seemed more and more limitless and to free oneself from taboos with each day that passed.

When I was a child, my mother had forced me to be an altar boy and to take part in the mass at our church near my home. It was the way things were done back then, but it wasn't really for me and after a while I rejected it – my first act of rebellion. From then on I don't think I took part in another religious ceremony. At the ashram I had another go, partly out of curiosity to begin with, but after a while I almost began to enjoy it.

I would leave my room just before 5 a.m., take a deep breath, smile and say hello to my stomach, which I imagined being filled with the clear fresh dawn air, and then I set off. All around me nature was peaceful and serene. The smoke from the brick factory mingled with the mist, created a veil of mystery that separated me from the mountains that were still damp with the night-time dew. The silence was broken by the cocks crowing in the distance, then the persistent cry of a strange bird that seemed to be calling out 'Help! Help!' and the petulant cawing of the crows; then by the ashram's necessarily vegetarian dogs, which were beginning to gravitate towards the refectory along with the shishyas. There was a tremendous feeling of peace in this slow procession of my companions, who in the still uncertain daylight were filing past like white silhouettes, solitary and silent at the foot of the palm trees, banana trees, the great rain trees and the forest flames with their orange manes.

After a mug of tea in silence, I would then head to the temple. It was a modest building, set above ground level and exposed to the elements: a flight of stairs, a concrete landing and a roof held up by some ten pillars. The focus of all attention – and devotion – was a great tabernacle in inlaid stone which contained a statue of the goddess Dakshinamurthy, the protector of the Vedas. In a smaller tabernacle to the side was Ganesh, the elephant god who helps his followers overcome their difficulties.

The first to arrive would sit in the rows at the front of the tabernacle, while the latecomers would gradually fill up the rows behind. The morning ceremony consisted of performing the statue's ritual ablutions and preparing it for the day ahead. Three pujaris or priests went about their tasks in and around the holiest of holies. The eldest of them began by removing the previous day's garments and flowers from the statue, while the others went backwards and forwards with bowls and buckets. Two widows began chanting the hymns that accompanied the entire ceremony, and their imperious stares ensured everything

– incense, flowers, oil lamps – was in the right place and that the bell, which even I was occasionally entrusted with, was rung at precisely the right time.

The statue, which was in black stone and life-sized, was first of all washed with water, then coconut oil, then water again, then with milk, yoghurt and stewed banana, then water again, and after being dried and polished, was sprinkled with a fragrant powder made of sandalwood. These actions were marked by regular invocations from the Vergers and the priest to which the congregation responded. It was enchanting to see this sequence of actions and sounds being followed so closely. After half an hour of beaver-like activity, the head pujari drew the tabernacle curtain and remained on his own with the statue for several minutes. The choir went on singing, then the curtain was drawn back – serious ringing of the bell here – and the statue was revealed in all its glory, decked out in colourful throws and decorated with flowers.

At this point the second part of the ceremony began. A large reed basket full of flower petals was brought before the tabernacle, the head pujari recited the goddess's 108 names one by one, and respectfully threw a handful of petals at her feet: 108 names echoed by the whole choir, 108 handfuls of petals.[15] The curtain was drawn again, then the ceremony moved towards its conclusion. When the curtain was reopened, the temple was in pitch-darkness apart from a single lamp suspended from the ceiling to illuminate the face of the statue, which in this low light looked as though it had acquired a life of its own. This was the moment of darshan, a Sanskrit world meaning 'to look', but also 'to be looked at'. Everyone got up from

---

[15] The number 108 is sacred in India. There are 108 classic Upanishads, 108 main devotional prayers and 108 beads on a mala, i.e., the Indian rosary.

their places, walked slowly towards the entrance to the holiest of holies, looked respectfully towards the door, put their hands on their chests and stopped for a moment to look at the goddess, and feel themselves being looked at by her.

In the eyes of many of my companions, I could see a joy that I myself did not have and which I envied. I was struck by the emotion with which people of all ages and social conditions prayerfully and longingly approached a stone statue in which they sensed a divine presence. Their faces bore the same lost, ecstatic expression of the small stone bull which knelt before the tabernacle, and which too was bowing in worship before the deity. One of the pujaris even used to give it a spoonful of milk to drink, with a mawkish hand gesture. Unsurprisingly, the milk ended up on the ground.

A bronze plate filled with the same burning camphor that had illuminated the statue while it was being dressed was passed round among the congregation, and with both hands everyone would cup the air around the fire and bring it to their faces and heads. As we left the temple, one of the pujaris blessed us by sprinkling copious amounts of water on us from out of a shell, while another put a spoonful of the banana compote that had been smeared over the goddess's body, into the right hand of those who passed by. This was prasad, food offered to the gods, which we too were free to eat now that it had been blessed. So as not to offend anyone, I put it in my mouth like everyone else, but spat it out afterwards while no one was looking.

Maybe because my mother forced me to take part in religious ceremonies when I was a child, I've always hated genuflections, making the sign of the cross, bowing and scraping before sacred images, or worse still, human beings. And yet, somehow, I didn't feel there was weakness in this hour of random comings and goings, dressing and undressing a lump of stone, in that drawing near with reverence, which I had long forgotten. It was quite the opposite. My companions seemed to draw strength from that ritual; it recharged them. I could sense its attraction and realized there was something profoundly comforting in that incredible sequence of actions.

All attempts to deny the force of rituals have done nothing but create horror, desolation and emptiness. China lost much of its marvellous ancient soul in the communists' attempts to repress and wipe out traditional rites. After seventy years of Soviet regime had erased this aspect of Russian life, this nation too became an easy market of souls for all the US Protestant denominations and their own form of rituals.

What about my world – the West? In our lay, iconoclastic drive towards a wholly materialistic understanding of individual liberty, we have rejected a long-standing tradition, ridiculed every form of belief and eradicated every form of ritual, removing all mystery and poetry from our lives in so doing.

Nowadays people are born, live and die without a single ritual to mark the most important stages of our lives. No act of reflection now accompanies the birth of a child, apart from possibly registering the birth in the public records office. Young couples now live together without getting married, the only rite they take part in being the removal of remains. They don't even mark the start of their new life together by putting on a clean shirt. Without such ritual or initiation, no one is aware of the passage that has taken place; if there is no symbolic contact with the sacred, there is no real commitment either. Often the only thing that is shared now is sex or the telephone bill. Even death is now experienced without the awareness and comfort that rituals bring with it. There is no longer a wake for the dead and the final farewell; and even if there is one, it is no longer handled by a priest or shamanic figure, but by experts in public relations.

In my lifetime I have witnessed the death of all these rituals, and now, when I look back, I regret having contributed to their demise, enthusiastically at the time. When I was young, newborn babies – even those like me born to communist parents – were still christened, wakes and proper funerals were still held for those who passed away, and weddings were a choral feast to be celebrated not just before God, but also before dozens of relatives and friends who implicitly became guarantors of that union.

I rebelled. I didn't want to get married, and when I did finally give in, principally for reasons to do with health insurance, it was a hurried and almost secretive affair. There were only the necessary witnesses present, and with a mayor presiding, who was from outside Florence, as I didn't want to be married by anyone who was a Christian Democrat. I didn't have my children christened and I wasn't there when my mother or father died.

And yet, when I was young I used to quite like all these rituals. I still remember how one of the great joys in my life was the first rite of passage I ever experienced at the age of fourteen when my parents, to mark my entry into manhood, gifted me my first pair of long trousers which they bought on credit since they were so poor. But the winds of time were blowing in a different direction and I went along with them, helping to destroy something that has not been replaced by anything, and leaving a wretched void in the process.

In India that wind of change has only just begun to blow; and especially in the countryside where the majority still lives, rituals remain a very important part of life. A peasant will not leave his house in the morning without touching the lintel of his door, a woman does not start her day without offering up a few drops of water to the sun.

To Indians, life is a ritual. The first is celebrated even before a child is conceived, the others at every passage thereafter. A ritual is celebrated when the child is weaned, when he is taken outside at night to see the stars for the first time, when his hair is first cut and when he becomes a brahmachari: he eats with his mother, then leaves home and returns with his first bhiksha or alms.[16] On it goes like this until he dies when his corpse is entrusted to the flames of the pyre which his eldest son kindles, using the same fire with which he himself was first initiated into the way of the Vedas, and with which the puja for his wedding ceremony was performed. Not even death can release him from the cycle of rituals. Twelve days after his passing, another ritual takes place in which the soul of the deceased is requested to leave the house, to cut every tie with the family and take his place next to his father and grandfather, among the ancestors who are to be remembered and respected.[17] The mantra recited on this occasion is quite beautiful, with every trace of sadness gone. Whoever wanted to cry will have done so already in the preceding twelve days.

Rituals are the great theme of the Vedas. They prescribe the actions, times and words of the rituals, and list the results one can

---

16* Bhiksha is the offering of food made respectfully to all those who devote themselves to moksha, or liberation. It cannot really be compared to what we refer to as charity, which is usually given without any respect for the beneficiary. Once the Swami recounted how even recently, an orthodox family he knew had refused to marry their daughter to a man in their village who had become rich and owned a hotel in the city. His crime was that he sold food and food was sacred; it should be offered freely, not sold.

17 His great-great-grandfather accordingly loses his place when he arrives.

expect if these are performed according to the rules. No detail is left to chance: from the length of time a mantra is to last, to the offering to be made to the pujari who recites it, from the number of days a pilgrimage is to last, to the method in which a house is to be cleaned. A ritual is an action that is expected to produce an effect. For this reason, the Vedas belong to the samsara, the world of desires, and are intended precisely for those looking for results in that world. Does a woman wish to have a son rather than a daughter? The Vedas tell her what she should do and how she should do it. Does a man want to be rich or go to heaven? The Vedas give him precise instructions on how to proceed. Cause and effect are the logic of the Vedas. Theirs is also the logic of becoming and change, of time and space, of the self.

But what about those who are looking for something else? Those who want to escape from the world of becoming, and break free from all of it?

Herein lies the truly original aspect of Indian thought. At the end of the Vedas, they reveal that their true aim is to render themselves obsolete. With the Vedanta, man finally escapes from all the rituals and their rules, from the slavery of the Vedas.

The Vedas are the religious part; the Vedanta releases from everything, including religion. It is no longer in the sphere of becoming but rather that of being. It has nothing to do with having children, or one's wife remaining faithful, with getting rich or going to heaven. The Vedanta is all about the self and unlimited consciousness, outside time and space.

Do you want to pursue the normal desires of this world? Then there is nothing wrong with that. Stay in the Vedas. But at the same time beware, the Vedanta explains, that even the paradise of the Vedas, however wonderful it is, is just another place and is still in time and space, and cannot last forever. One can attain it on the basis of one's own punya, or merits, but once that capital has been eroded they have to go back to the beginning and start all over again.

'You can't obtain an indefinite residence permit for heaven,' said the Swami. He himself could take part in the ceremonies, but was no longer either their subject or object. I noted how he allowed people to bow at his feet, but never performed any act of devotion before the statues of the various deities. He had nothing more to ask of them; he was now outside the world of desires.

This form of thought seemed to me to have grandeur to it, which I found attractive. Was I becoming religious now? Certainly not in the sense of the Vedas!

For a couple of weeks I didn't miss a single morning prayer session. Then, when it all started getting repetitive, I chose instead to climb to the top of my hill and enjoy the sunrise, rather than the ritual clothing of the goddess.

Even eating at the ashram was a ritual in itself. At half past twelve each day, the entire community, including several meowing cats and the usual band of vegetarian dogs would converge on the refectory and form a long queue that snaked from the main lawn all the way back to the entrance. The queue moved slowly. Once we had reached the top of the stairs, we took off our sandals, collected our glasses and plates from the piles set up on the two tables outside, and went into the great hall where, from a great battery of steaming cauldrons, the five or six shishyas on duty that day would serve us while singing. Each of us would hold out our plate with both hands, thank them and join the choir chanting the passage from the Gita where Krishna speaks of himself in the following terms:

I am the fire in the body of those who live,
I regulate breathing and digest food,
I am seated in the heart of all living creatures.
Everything comes from me: memory, knowledge and error.
I am the one who is known through the Vedas,
I am the one who knows them,
And the author of the Vedanta.

As we carried on singing, we would look for a free place on one of the straw mats which covered the refectory floor, and those verses from Chapter 15 of the Gita continued to echo throughout the hall until the last one of us had been served. The sound of Sanskrit is delightful. So too is the rhythm of the hymn in which Krishna, the Incarnation of Wholeness, manifests himself in some of his forms to Arjuna. Then we all put three fingers of our right hand into our glasses, which were full of water, and in a circular movement sprinkled several drops on to the food in front of us. In this way, the food became an offering to Agni, the fire god, the god of the stomach – an act of devotion and thanksgiving.

I liked all this. In my family we used to make the sign of the cross when I was young, but this too, like so many customs, has been lost in the frenzy of life. We now take everything for granted. We think we have a right to everything, although no one knows where this comes from and why. We think everything is owed to us and are no longer surprised to find something as pleasant and necessary as food in front of us, even though most of the time we haven't actually earned it.

Having something to eat has become a routine, at least in the West. It's no longer something out of the ordinary or to be thankful for. So we eat and eat, stuffing ourselves like morons, often in front of the television or while reading a newspaper propped up against a glass.

Everything at the ashram was given to the shishyas for free. The Swami taught us without receiving even a penny in wages, for this was his karma. Our food and lodgings were paid for out of the bhiksha, or offerings, made by some rich Indian who was probably earning merits for his own karma by means of this good deed.

Sometimes a businessman from Coimbatore or Madras would give us a treat to mark a special event or a festival – fruit, perhaps, or something sweet – so that his name would be written up in chalk on the blackboard along with the others to be thanked at the end of the hymn. On one occasion, the blackboard announced a bhiksha made by Anam to celebrate his wife's birthday, so before plunging their fingers into their rice and chickpeas, the entire refectory responded to a brahmachari's invitation to wish Angela every good thing in this life and her other lives by singing several Vedic hymns in her honour.

How she deserved those good wishes! She had let me stay there without once admonishing me, burdening me or making me feel guilty. She really was the best kind of medicine. And not just since I had been afflicted with this illness. Right from the start ours had been a shared life, with instinctive agreement on how to look at the world and where we wanted to go. What could be better now than to grow old together? Each in our own way, even at a distance, it was still just the two of us, forever.

However, these good wishes were still not sufficient to relieve me of my debt. One day the Swami explained to me that according to the Vedas, a husband who abandons his wife for a long period of time acquires papa or demerits on his bill of karma. How wise the old Indians were. Marriage was seen as a way to spiritual growth from which there was no escaping, not even for a short time and with the best of intentions, without there also being a price to pay.

To begin with, I was reluctant to eat with my fingers – you were supposed to lick them clean afterwards too – but soon enough I got used to this as well. I remember a comment made by a lady from high Indian society on this subject: 'Eating with a knife and fork is like taking a shower while wearing a mackintosh.'

The food at the ashram was not particularly enjoyable. No eggs – which are 'life' – garlic or onions, which according to tradition are supposed to stimulate sexual desire, and very few spices, also deemed to encourage frivolous distractions. This meant that the chickpea, bean, cauliflower and rice dishes were excessively bland. However, for several of my fellow shishyas this was still too much.

One day I noticed that a brahmachari sitting next to me was not using his plate. He was throwing the three or four courses we were given into a bucket, where he mixed them together with his hand 'so as not to be able to distinguish the flavours'. This was one way of controlling his desires, he explained. Eating was a necessity, but that was no reason to turn it into a pleasure that you could then became enslaved to.

'When all the desires that dwell in our hearts are abandoned, the mortal becomes immortal and attains the Brahman, here, now,' he proclaimed, quoting one of the Upanishads. He felt it was vital to overcome our continual distinctions between what we like and do not like.

The thing I liked most of all about this was the idea of putting oneself to the test, even in the little things. So I decided to do this by means of something I've always disliked: washing up.

I've always done my bit in the house when I've had to, but I have always avoided washing dishes like the plague. I hate it. But in the ashram, where what had been used had to be washed up straightaway once we had finished eating, I made myself do it, with love. I forced myself to do the washing up consciously, to do it for the sake of doing it rather than while thinking of something else, as the Vietnamese Zen Buddhist monk Thich Nhat Hanh recommends you to do to help you concentrate.

It worked. Even washing up, which I had so detested once, became a pleasant enough ritual after a while. In a long line with all the others, in front of a kind of trough with lots of water fountains, using ash and soap I carefully washed the high-sided metal plate, and glass that I had used, rinsed them and rinsed them again just as carefully, hoping that everyone else was doing the same, given that what I had washed would be used by someone else at the next meal, and I would be eating off a plate that had been washed by goodness knows who.

I know not many other people appreciated my singing, but I thought it was great. And there were plenty of opportunities to sing too. We sang at the morning puja, at the start of every lesson, before every meal, for a whole hour in the course on Vedic hymns and in the evening at the end of satsang just before going to bed.

Singing was a part of our days, and I realized it had an effect on my state of mind. Perhaps it raised my consciousness levels. This happened especially when we chanted the mantras. 'The Sanskrit of the Vedic hymns and mantras act upon our minds,' the Swami said. And I had no reason to disagree with him.

Perhaps it was their rhythm, or the regular breathing they imposed on me, but repeating the mantras chanted by the two Vergers gave me a sense of lightness that at times approached joy. As I sang, my Self seemed to become smaller and more remote, its destiny increasingly irrelevant.

Healing comes,
From a person who is upright and holy,
And from the mantras that one chants.

Was the Swami, the 'person who is upright and holy', who could heal me? Were the mantras I was singing the ones which Zarathustra spoke of in a fragment that I had happened to keep with me for years, from the time when I didn't have a clue what the word 'mantra' itself actually meant?

Someone who had blind faith in the power of what he, with his Tamil–Malayan accent would refer to as *mandram,* was Sundarajan. He had various secret mantras, which had been given him by an old sadhu when he was a boy, and on which his survival, he said, depended. He recited them out loud as soon as he woke up and then recited them silently to himself, concentrating all his attention on those mantras as he meditated. According to Sundarajan, the mantras were magic formulas, a bit like saying 'abracadabra', which had the power to influence spirit and matter. In his view, the words themselves created a vibration, which as it became attuned to each object or body's characteristic vibrations, generated a healing or destructive influence on that object or body. In a similar way that music was supposed to act on the cells, I guess.

He personally swore by all this, conveniently forgetting his studies in engineering in so doing, as I reminded him.

To begin with, I stuck with the explanation of breathing. Clearly, there is a close relation between the way we breathe and the way our minds work: one influences the other and it is not hard to notice when this happens. When our breathing is irregular, our mind is restless. When we get angry, we get out of breath. If our mind is taken up with beautiful thoughts, our breathing becomes deeper and more regular. This is true for even when we sleep.

By reciting the same mantra all the time, linking the last and the first syllables and so forth – this is called japa in Sanskrit – our breathing acquires a particular rhythm and brings about a change of mental state, or consciousness, of which the Swami spoke. Clearly one aspect of the mantra is the fact that the mind does not have a chance to wander, as it is forced to remember the precise sequence of words. There is no uncertainty regarding the next thought and this creates a distance between the Self and the mind, which allows the Self to observe it and keep it under control. At least, that's what the Swami said.

There was certainly something special about these sounds, which had been handed down from generation to generation for millennia, along with the same pronunciation, rhythms and hiatuses. If the mantras had not served some purpose, they would have been long forgotten and shelved. Instead, the tradition goes on. The guru who has complete faith in his disciple gives him a mantra, thought to be a precious gift that will unite them forever. And one of the many rituals is the one where an eight-year-old child is given a mantra which they may use for the rest of their lives.

As I saw it, what made these sounds special was the same as what made medicines special: the power of the mind. The idea that these formulas were magic, that they made something happen, whether a healing or something else, was what made the mind actually contribute that something else. I was convinced that the red chemotherapy liquid was effective, so it ended up being so, just as Sundarajan was convinced that the mandram kept him alive.

It isn't the thing itself which is powerful, but the power of the mind that believes that the thing is powerful. The Tibetans explain this through the means of a story.

After many years, a monk decided to go and visit his mother

who was very old and who he imagined was at the point of dying of hunger. But a surprise awaited him when he reached the village: his mother was fine. An old sadhu had given her a mantra, which enabled her to turn stones into potatoes if she put them into a pan. When the mother used her system to prepare his dinner, the monk, who by this stage was extremely learned in sacred matters, noticed that she mispronounced the words in Sanskrit and corrected her. The mother was proud of her son's erudition, and chanted the new version. However, it yielded disappointing results: the stones in the pan remained just stones, and the two of them had nothing to eat. The monk began to get the idea, asked his mother to go back to using her version of the mantra, and hot, steaming potatoes miraculously appeared once again in the pan.

Neither my mother nor my grandmother, who lived with us when I was a boy, knew any mantras. But they too recited prayers and sang hymns, which might not have transformed stones into potatoes, and goodness knows we could have done with them! But nonetheless it added something to the rhythm of their days. That was what it was like when I was young: the farmers sang in the fields, the craftsmen sang as they laboured in their workshops and we sang while we were at school. When I think of the sounds that accompanied my childhood – the bells, for example – and compare them to those my grandson will be treated to, it makes me despair.

We have given up on singing, and replaced it with listening to others singing, on some kind of a hi-fi system. This could not have been healthy. The Benedictine monks in a French monastery in the 1960s realized this, when they were all afflicted with the strangest disease. They suddenly began to feel tired, depressed and absent-minded. They had a meeting, and decided to sleep more. But this only made things worse: they were more tired and depressed than ever before. So they consulted their doctors, one of whom suggested they start eating meat, which they hadn't done for 200 years. Still no improvement. Finally, a very bright doctor from Paris noted that following the introduction of the new regulations brought in under the Vatican II council, an enterprising abbot had significantly reduced the number of hours spent singing, in order to increase the amount of time devoted to more productive activities. This had changed the routine of the monastery, the doctor said, and the treatment he recommended was merely to return to their former ways of doing things. After several months, the monks were once again in good health and good spirits. Singing attuned their breathing, which in turn increased their energy levels and vitality. The high frequencies produced by their singing recharged their cerebral cortex, creating a feeling of euphoria which meant the monks felt blessed all day and all night.

I felt the same kind of thing at the ashram – even for someone as out of tune as I was.

One evening, the Swami invited me to dinner. Like many Indians his age, he suffered from diabetes. So his diet was even more bland and basic than that of the refectory. We ate in the kitchen, attended to by the two Vergers.

He had not forgotten his promise to introduce me to an Ayurvedic doctor he knew and trusted, who could be of help with my illness. He had just spoken to him on the phone and arranged for me to be admitted to his hospital. They were expecting me.

THE HEALING PROPERTIES OF THEATRE

The thing that struck me most on arriving at the hospital was an elephant. From a distance it looked like it was painted on the white wall of the enclosure. Then I saw it flap its ears and slowly shake its enormous, pathetic head. Then I realized it was well and truly alive. But at the same time I realized that the elephant, which lived in the courtyard which all the patients' rooms looked out on, was much more at home there than I was. No one was taking a blind bit of notice of him, whereas lots of inquisitive looks were being cast in my direction. I was a foreigner who had come from a long way away, not a passing tourist, but a patient like them.

There are always surprises in store for when you reach your destination on a journey you are making for the first time. For me on this occasion, however, the surprises were considerable. I had reached Kottakkal, a small town in the state of Kerala, in search of the Arya Vaidya Sala, or Institute for Aryan Medicine, the oldest and most celebrated centre for Ayurveda in India. But rather than the tranquil place of rest I had been expecting, I found myself in the midst of a noisy circus being assembled. Dozens of men were labouring away to erect a huge thatched tent around the elephant; groups of bare-chested musicians were busy tuning their odd instruments; dancers were dressed in colourful costumes and actors whose heads were crowned with huge headdresses and whose faces were painted with grotesque masks, strutted around a wooden stage that others were putting the finishing touches to with bamboo shoots and thick ropes. Everywhere I looked, there was much toing and froing of people and objects. As I moved closer to the elephant, I saw its right leg was chained to a pole stuck in the ground and noticed a beautiful arabesque of flowers painted on its forehead.

As for the hospital itself, one of the men who was looking at me as though I were some kind of apparition, pointed me in the direction of the door marked 'Reception'. They were expecting me since they didn't ask me for any form of ID, or check if I really was the Anam referred to them by the Swami. They did not ask me to pay an advance on the tests and treatments I was to undergo, as the staff at the MSKCC had done with smiling efficiency. Money did not appear to be the driving force behind the Arya Vaidya Sala. A sign was displayed behind the reception desk which was advertising free consultations to anyone who turned up from nine o'clock to midday each morning. Other signs politely requested the patients to refrain from smoking, for the good of all. A list of the doctors appointed for each section was pinned up on a wooden panel. The surname was the same in virtually all cases: 'Varrier'.

The room reserved for me was number 502, on the top floor of the new wing of the hospital, with a view of the courtyard and its attendant circus. Behind this, I could see the luxuriant manes of the coconut palms, towering like fireworks above the masses of corrugated iron roofs. Everything was simple, but well thought-out and logical. There was no air-conditioning despite the tropical climate, but there were fans suspended from the ceiling. For patients unable to manage the stairs, a gently-inclined external corridor connected the various floors.

My room was clean and basic: a bed and a wooden bedside table, a thin kapok mattress, a pillow and two white cotton sheets. On the wall there was a photo of the hospital's founder, a man with a very serious expression and iron-rimmed spectacles wearing a black suit and tie, a gown over his shoulders and a yellow beret on his head. It was an old-fashioned image with the caption: 'Vaidyaratnam P.S. Varrier 1869–1944'. I did some quick calculations in my head. That meant he died at the age of seventy-five: not a bad advert for his medicines! Underneath his photo there was another smaller photo of his successor, also named Varrier. The Institute of Aryan Medicine at Kottakkal had begun as a family business in 1902 and had remained to this very day.

A young Sikh who saw me arrive came to my door and led me to the room opposite, where his father was. They had brought him there from northern India in the hope of finding a cure for him. The old man's table was full of bottles and phials. The young Sikh told me to let him know if there was anything I needed.

I had just enough time to put down my bags and look out of the window, when an old man, tall and distinguished-looking, came into my room. He was the hospital's administrative director who had come to greet me.

'You are in luck,' he said. 'The week of celebrations for the god Vishwambhara is beginning today.' He clearly thought I understood what he meant, and then continued: 'We are offering music, dance and representations to our Lord in the presence of the elephant. You know, the elephant occupies a very important place in our mythology; it is the god Ganesh who helps us overcome all our difficulties. Even your cancer ... you will see.'

I didn't want to embarrass him by showing my surprise at this unusual medicine-elephant-theatre combination. I mumbled that I too had a Ganesh at home: a plaster copy of the famous Angkor one.

'You will be benefiting much from these days,' the director added. 'For all of us, doctors and patients, the festival is a way of approaching the profound reality which is the Supreme Reality, that is, Brahman.'

It had been a long journey. The taxi from the ashram had taken more than five hours, through the hills of the state of Tamil Nadu, then down towards the coast of the state of Kerala. My young driver had been introduced to me as one of the few who spoke English, but once he had sat down behind the wheel, the only thing he appeared to be able to say was: 'Urine ... coming.' Hence our conversations never got much further than deciding when and where to stop for a pee.

I spent a long time silently thinking about what I saw, the typical little villages of low-roofed houses succeeding one another along the roadside, the typical sight of men and animals almost touching the ground as they sloped by. The houses were poor, the people were poor, but nature at least was rich. Every market boasted mountains of fruit, banks of vegetables and enormous bunches of bananas hanging from their squiggly stems, as beautiful as the letters of the Sanskrit alphabet I was seeking to learn.

Tamil Nadu is an ancient land with an ancient culture, wonderful literature and a very popular theatrical tradition. Politics has paid the price for this; since the seventies, the state has mostly been governed by famous actors. This is very typically Indian. People here do not distinguish between an actor and his role, and once someone on a stage acts out the part of a king, a hero or a wise man, the public assumes he is that person in real life too, and treats him as though he really were Krishna, Shiva or Rama. If he stands against the state minister in local elections, they all vote for him. After all, who would not want to be governed by a god, a hero or a sage, especially these days?

All this merely made me even more diffident regarding what we loosely term as 'democracy', where citizen participation seems to have been reduced to voting once every four or five years, and which everywhere in the world seems to bring all the mediocre, corrupt or inept to power. Democracy has become a system that primarily rewards banality and the lies of advertising, rather than wisdom and moral rigour. It was the absurdity of this system, for example, which made it possible for a respectable housewife from Piedmont in Italy such as Sonia Gandhi to become a prime ministerial candidate of 'the world's largest democracy', as India likes to describe itself. Did a country of over a billion people really need an Italian who did not even speak the national language properly to govern it? In the free electoral economy, her marketability consisted of the fact that she was the widow of the former prime minister Rajiv Gandhi – who was assassinated – the son of former prime minister Indira Gandhi – also assassinated. Indira Gandhi was the daughter of the first prime minister of India, Jawaharlal Nehru.

Poor Gandhi, dressed as a peasant, lived off nothing, and dreamt of a country that was free and independent, neither capitalist nor communist, a country that was the expression of its millions of villages which for him represented the true eternal soul of India. He was in favour of the small, not the large, on the side of men rather than machinery and the natural as opposed to the artificial.

'When a tractor can be milked, when its dung can be used as manure and as fuel, that's when I'll start preferring it to a cow,' he used to say. He had travelled far and wide, and he knew his country and its people well. Only in India can a hole in a wall be a bidi factory; only in India can a wooden cubicle on four legs be an ironer's workshop by day and his bedroom by night. Only in India can a gamchha, the coloured rag which a boatman or rickshaw driver uses to wipe the sweat off their brow, also double as a blanket when it is cold, or a turban when the sun is beating down.

Gandhi was convinced that small is beautiful, and the economist Franz Schumacher, a great admirer of his, developed this idea into a full-blown theory of economics that seemed very well suited to India. Schumacher argued that small local industries had to be protected against large companies and multinationals which would swallow them up. Like Gandhi, Schumacher said that the economy should be based on what is most important for man rather than the amoral principle of profit. Gandhi and Schumacher: both now forgotten.

Nehru was the complete opposite of Gandhi; he was in favour of the big as opposed to the small: big industries, big dams, big factories.

The same desire for the 'big' has formed the basis of virtually all post-independence Delhi governments' aspirations. The more time passes, the more India becomes like any other country: big army, big weapons including atomic, and the dream of becoming a superpower. India is less rooted in the villages whose purity constituted Gandhi's ideal, and more taken up with the global village instead, the only pure thing about which is the purity of its greed.

The difference between the states of Tamil Nadu and Kerala was obvious. I realized I had crossed the border when everything along the roadside suddenly became slightly cleaner and tidier. Kerala is not dominated by actors-cum-politicians, but by two forces, communism and Christianity. These have turned it into the state with the best schools in India.

As I gazed out of the window at the brilliant green rice fields, the mud houses painted red, the cows with garlands of flowers between their horns and the thin men clothed in their dhotis, one word came back to me: contentment. To be contented is rather less than to be happy. It means to be satisfied, to not desire anything more. This is what the Indians are like: content. And one is content if one choses to make do with what one has. The German word for it is *zufrieden,* literally 'to give oneself peace'. And for this, one must place a limit on one's own desires, as both the Upanishads and the Gita advocate.

India may be a poor country, but it is also a country in which the people have fewer needs, fewer desires; this is why, deep down, it is also a happier country than many others. But not for long: globalization is bringing the rest of the world's desires to India too, and eroding its contentment and its peace in the process.

The suspension system of the car – another old Hindustan Motors' Ambassador – was on its last legs, and every now and again it bounced over the holes in the road and threw me around in the most terrible fashion. If I had had an attack of some kind or my hernia had erupted, I imagined the young taxi driver dropping me off at one of the many hospitals or rest homes I saw along the roadside. None of them inspired a great deal of confidence: even the letters in their names, such as 'Shakti Nursing Home' or 'Lord Krishna Hospital' were falling off. And the treatments they offered were mostly for haemorrhoids and fistulas!

In the end nothing major happened to me, and I was spared the experience of being a genuine Anam, a Mr Nobody, in the middle of nowhere without the protection of my former identity. We arrived safe and sound in Kottakkal. The Arya Vaidya Sala was well known and everyone knew how to get there; it was the only hospital with an elephant parked in the courtyard.

I didn't manage to stay in my room for long. Every time I visit a new place, I feel the urge to find out where I am, to see what's around me and get the measure of it all. Perhaps it's just an instinct, like an animal that won't go anywhere until it's absolutely sure it'll be able to get back again.

It wasn't yet dark and the circus was still being set up, so I decided to go for a walk round the little town which I had seen only from the car so far. There was nothing special: lorries full of coconuts were unloading their merchandise in the main square next to the bus station and bazaar, which had the usual combination of little shops selling plastic shoes and clothes; small goldsmiths' workshops lined with red velvet; workshops where pots, pans and crockery were manufactured; and lots and lots of chemists, little hospitals and nursing homes. Kottakkal was evidently a town that lived off the health industry.

High up on the third or fourth floor of a building, I noticed a sign that said 'ICT computer', and thought it might be somewhere I could go and get Internet access. To get there, I had to go through a kind of obstacle course, which involved clambering over piles of rubble, going up a dark and dusty staircase and walking along a concrete landing with various small rooms off it. Inside one of these rooms, I spotted the silhouette of a man with a long black beard sitting with a woman on the floor around a lit candle. 'ICT computer' was in the room next door. It was an office, painted white, and with neon lighting; and there sat a young electronics engineer in a manager's chair behind an important-looking desk.

'Here you can see the two opposite sides of India,' he told me. He then explained that his neighbour was a 'local doctor' who chiefly treated women from the province by offering them remedies in some way connected with magic.

I told him that I too had come to Kottakkal in search of a cure.

'Tangalis?' the young engineer asked me.

'No, the Arya Vaidya Sala.'

'People from here don't go near it. It's too fashionable, too expensive. It's mostly people from outside who go there. Here people mostly go to the Tangalis – they're magicians.'

I had never heard of them.

The young man, a very polite, smart Muslim who let me use his computer to send a couple of emails, seemed to enjoy surprising me. The Tangalis, he explained, are Muslim healers who practise their medicine in the region between Kerala and Tamil Nadu. They exorcize illnesses, pains and other misfortunes by going into a trance and taking upon themselves everything that afflicts others. Usually they work in groups: some play instruments, sing and call upon Allah, while one of their members performs the exorcism, sticking needles into his cheeks and arms and wounding himself with knives, until his clothes are stained with blood. According to the young engineer, everyone in Kerala – irrespective of their religion – went to the Tangalis.

'There's nothing strange about it,' he said. 'Wasn't Christ supposed to have been nailed to a cross to take upon himself the sins of the world?'

Of course the Tangalis asked for money – they too had to live!

Did he himself believe in magic? No he didn't. He was an engineer, he was modern and he used a computer. But he wasn't surprised that so many people did believe in it.

It was dark by now, and coming back down the stairs of the building that housed these two 'opposite sides of India' wasn't easy. But it was even harder finding the road back to the hospital. All of a sudden the lights had gone off, as happens so often in this country, and the entire town of Kottakkal had been plunged into darkness. Gas and oil lamps were being lit here and there, but the little road which led to the Arya Vaidya Sala, with its open sewers giving off blasts of the customary Indian stench, was pitch-black and rather worrying. Along a wall I saw people squatting down in the light of tiny flames; they were fortune-tellers, waiting for clients. For a moment I felt uneasy. I felt as though I had ended up in some medieval miracle court. Here was I, also hoping to be on the receiving end of a miracle!

The sight of the hospital was comforting. The generators there had come into operation, the entire complex was happily lit, and the Arya Vaidya Sala appeared like a reassuring oasis of modernity.

The courtyard had filled up with people. The doctors and their families were the last ones to take their seats, gathering up the corners of their dhotis with both hands almost like they were wings, so that they did not have to touch the ground. The elephant had been decked out in an embroidered blanket, a golden mask had been placed over his head and covered his whole trunk. Actors and dancers moved around the stage, while the musicians tuned their instruments one last time. The spectacle was about to begin, but I headed straight to bed.

I was tired. Not just from the journey, but also from continually finding myself in new places, having to work out the new sounds, the new people and the new customs. I was tired of casting my nets into the sea, merely to catch something I had caught a long time ago. In 1993 I had travelled the world in search of fortune-tellers; this time it was doctors and alternative medicines I was looking for. I was no longer interested in exploring the outside world. Maybe I had been wrong to leave the ashram.

A great din of cymbals, trumpets and cries entered my room through the open window. I understood none of it, save for the fact that it would continue until dawn.

In the end, it was the silence that woke me. I had slept all night amid the incessant din and my ears had got used to it. Then all of a sudden, that part of us which continues to remain alert even while we are asleep suddenly realized that something different was going on and began to get worried. The noisy, unusual spectacle, which had been put on for the gods had now come to an end, and the peaceful, everyday spectacle that the gods put on for man was about to begin. A magnificent orange sunrise was taking place in the distant horizon, broken by the outline of the palm trees, slowly bringing houses, streets, alleyways and people out of darkness. White smoke emerged from the roofs of the nearby medical factory, bringing its balmy scent to me.

Down in the courtyard below, the stage was emptying, the groups were dispersing and the musicians were putting their instruments away. The patients were being helped back into the hospital by their relatives. They had been there all night! I saw several stop in front of the elephant, cross their hands and make a slight bow, as one would to say goodbye to the host at the end of a party. The elephant no longer had on its golden vestments. What it did have was a large bundle of twigs and grass rolled up in its trunk: breakfast.

I got up to have mine too. There was a sign up saying the food was strictly vegetarian. Everything was simple and clean, but here too someone had not been able to resist the lure of modernity, and a treacherous, phosphorescent lamp cracked like a whiplash every time some unknowing fly was enticed by the bluish light inside it, and burnt to a cinder.

At 9 a.m. sharp, a young doctor sent by the hospital director came to take me the short distance to the free consultation clinic: a row of long buildings with red roofs, light blue walls, concrete floors and white-painted dividing walls. The thresholds of the doors had been blackened by many years of patients and their relatives trudging in and out as they went to hear their verdicts. A tropical breeze blew through the open rooms, causing the yellow curtains at the windows to flutter. There were the usual silent groups of people congregating on the unpaved square outside which made me think of the provincial hospitals in Cambodia, where I had been to count the victims of the various American battles and bombings: same heat, same atmosphere, same dark faces, haggard and fearful. All that was different this time was my role. This was brought home to me the moment the young doctor said he wanted to examine me. He got me to take off my shirt and lie down on the bed which was covered in a black plastic sheet. As I did so, the window was filled with wide open eyes staring at me.

He listened to my breathing, took my blood pressure and asked me various questions about my previous illnesses, especially those I had as a child. I answered and he took notes. At the end he asked me, 'How did you react when they told you that you had cancer?'

'Well, I didn't panic,' I answered.

'And what do you think are your chances of being cured?'

'It's not easy to be cured of cancer,' I said. 'But I do at least hope to find some way of living with it for a while. That's why I'm here.'

He smiled, looked at me as though I had just passed an exam, and quoted an Ayurvedic saying to me, first in Sanskrit, then in English which I mentally translated into Italian:

The length of life is dependent
On the inner strength of the patient
And the order he displays
In the living of his days.

I asked him what Ayurveda had to say about cancer, given that it was a form of science dating back thousands of years, whereas cancer was a thoroughly modern illness.

He instantly disagreed with me. 'Time makes no difference. Man is still man and his problems are still the same,' he said to me. 'There is no such thing as ancient and modern illnesses. The only distinction is between a curable illness and an incurable illness. Cancer belongs to neither of these categories. The holy writings speak of it as *adbhuta roga*, an unusual illness.'

I was intrigued, but he didn't elaborate since he was not an expert in this field. The only person in charge of this area at the hospital was the director himself, he said. His own field of specialization was snake bites.

This also interested me, and he was delighted to take me to his own department and explain to me the names and characteristics of the dozens of cobras, vipers and other reptiles which he kept in lots of glass jars full of formaldehyde on his wooden shelves. He said each of those snakes could kill a man in a very short span of time.

'How short, exactly?' I asked.

'Half an hour. If a patient is brought here within half an hour of being bitten, we can save him. We have Ayurvedic herbal remedies which we can put on the wound or administer orally. These can neutralize any snake poison.' Each year they treat an average of 1,500 cases. Usually all the patients survive.

'Do all of them arrive within half an hour? Are all of them healed with just Ayurvedic remedies?' I asked.

'No, but what Ayurveda cannot do, allopathic medicines can,' he admitted frankly. As far as he was concerned, the two types of medicines were complementary. Ayurveda was simpler, cheaper and more environment-friendly. But if he and his colleagues could not find an Ayurvedic solution, they often referred their patients to allopathic doctors – usually in cases where they thought surgery was necessary. Surgery had originally been part of Ayurveda, the young man explained to me. There are ancient texts in which surgical instruments very similar to those used today are described with great precision. However, the practice had fallen into disuse, he said, possibly due to the lack of proper anaesthetics in the Ayurvedic repertoire. This is why it no longer has any form of surgery of its own.

Finally, the consultant P.K. Varrier arrived. He was over seventy years old, with white hair and a large nose, and deaf. He was polite, but cold. Looking at my records, which the young doctor had just made out, he said that in his view cancer was caused by a combination of dietary imbalances and the environment. A wrong diet paves the way for many diseases, including the one I had.

'For those of us who practise Ayurveda, food is of the utmost importance,' he said. 'Poor digestion can create a wide variety of problems. This is why we recommend the simplest of diets. The most expensive food is usually also the most harmful. People who fall ill have to change their lifestyles and above all learn to eat smaller quantities and more regularly if they want to get better. For example, dinner should always be taken early in the evening, long before going to bed.'

The idea of changing a lifestyle in order to get better was what I had had in mind from the outset, and I liked the fact that he placed so much emphasis on it. The rest of it all seemed a bit simplistic to me, but I wasn't there to argue.

'We can't promise anything. We'll do our best. But we can certainly improve the quality of your life,' he concluded.

He said he would prescribe a treatment for me that was still at the experimental stage. It was tailored to the individual patient and I was to follow it for a period of three months, after which he would see me again.

I asked what the initial results of this experimental treatment had been like. Good, he said. Some patients whose days were thought to have been numbered lived for another couple of years, and in some cases the tumours had disappeared altogether. Unlike Western medicines, these cures did not treat one or another illness in particular, but merely sought to re-establish the balance between mind and body. But I was made aware that there were no guarantees. It was an experiment.

By now I was used to experiments, and at least this one seemed relatively innocuous. He himself said as much: their medicines would have no side effects, as they 'do not enter the blood', but are absorbed via the digestive system.

He set great store by diet. In my case it was vital. I was to be strictly vegetarian and not eat fish. According to Ayurveda, he said, all animals which live in water increase the risk of inflammation. I was also to avoid coffee, tea and spicy food. It would do me good to eat lots of fruit and vegetables, but the latter should never be fried. Cabbage was excellent, both the white and savoy varieties.

At the end, Varrier turned to the young doctor, who, like a waiter, was waiting to take his order, pen and paper at the ready. They spoke in Tamil and uttered words which to me sounded like the names of herbs. Then he turned to me and explained that the treatment consisted of two types of medicine: a gelatine or a preserve, one intended to increase the moisture in the stomach and the other, which was more specific. The gelatine was likely to be unpleasant. I was to take a quarter of a teaspoonful, followed by two teaspoonsfuls of the other medicine diluted in eight teaspoonsfuls of warm water.

I asked him what the ingredients were of the treatment he was prescribing for me. 'Herbs, herbs,' he said. But I detected a note of reticence in his reply. The meeting lasted a total of twenty minutes.

I had to wait two days before the medicines were ready. I took advantage of this delay to visit the various departments of the hospital, and read some of their publications. One of these was a biography of their founder. I was intrigued to discover P.S. Varrier was described not just as a good doctor, but above all as a 'great patriot'. This interested me because it had much to do with the history and current state of Ayurveda.

Together with Chinese medicine, Ayurveda is one of the oldest forms of medical wisdom still practised in the world for which significant documentary evidence remains. Unlike Chinese medicine, however, Ayurveda has suffered long periods of decline over the centuries, and at one point became so marginalized that it nearly disappeared. The renaissance it is currently enjoying is the result of a particular anti-colonial form of political–surgical operation, whereby one of the limbs of this body of ancient Indian wisdom has been sewn back on, after having been severed almost completely.

Like all things Indian, Ayurveda has its origins in a myth. Brahma, the God of Creation, established the rules whereby life would be preserved. This wisdom, or Ayurveda, was brought to earth via his assistant demigods and was collected by the rishis. Finally, around 700 BC – here myth finally becomes history – a character named Atreya began to practise and teach Ayurveda throughout India. One of Atreya's immediate disciples was the first to set its basic principles down in writing. The majority of those writings date back to the sixth century BC, with additions and commentaries up to the fourth century AD. According to some historians, Ayurveda suffered its first crisis as early as the arrival of Alexander the Great in India, who brought several of his own Greek doctors with him. The Muslim invasions also certainly played a part in its decline, but the coup de grâce was administered by British colonial rule.

The imperial administrators, who arrived from England with their superiority complex and conviction that they were involved in some great civilizing mission, had no respect whatsoever for the natives' 'primitive' practices. Soon the natives themselves, especially those from the upper classes, became increasingly anglicized – Indians who effectively became 'dark-skinned Englishmen' – and ended up abandoning many of the aspects of their own tradition, including their own form of medicine.

The colonial regime was explicit and unswerving in its policy of repression. In 1805, the British barred every form of traditional vaccination against smallpox in India. In 1835, they shut down all schools of Ayurveda, banned all medical associations that registered Indian doctors, and outlawed every form of government aid to traditional medical and pharmaceutical practices. All medicines to be used by Indians had to be imported from Britain.

Even as recently as 100 years ago, the word 'Ayurveda' was uttered with contempt, while the Indians were becoming more and more fascinated with the 'miracles' of Western medicine. Clearly, Ayurveda survived in its own way in the villages where many of its practices had been part of the popular wisdom for centuries, and where many of the traditional herbs and plants had become a part of the families' diets. But the bulk of the tradition was lost, the chain of scientific transmission broken.

Ayurveda was rediscovered at the end of the nineteenth century as a part of the Indian rebellion against colonial power. The return to using cheap, local remedies rather than expensive British medicines became a symbol of the Swadeshi, the great anti-British, movement for home rule.

P.S. Varrier, the founder of the Arya Vaidya Sala, was one of the leading lights in the nationalist reincarnation of Ayurveda. He wanted to help the poor in his region and realized that the only way to do so was through local means. Therefore, in 1902, he set up the nucleus of what is now the Arya Vaidya Sala.

The fact that the Ayurvedic tradition had been broken and had been saved only when all hope had been lost, continues to have a bearing on its destiny, especially in India, where, ever since Independence, this practice has failed to receive the kind of government support it might have expected. Only 5 per cent of the Indian health-care budget is spent on Ayurvedic medicine, virtually nothing is invested in research and there is still no form of government control over the quality of Ayurvedic medicines produced in this country.

But the world is round, and life, they say, is a roller coaster. Therefore, while the majority of Indians prefer Western-style medicines, and those who can afford it choose to be treated in the best hospitals in London or New York, many westerners who have grown disillusioned with the form of medical care offered at home turn to Ayurveda instead, venturing into the bowels of India in search of 'ancient cures'. I was now one of them.

Factories usually excrete noxious fumes or bad odours, but the one attached to the hospital was an exception. It filled the air with the pleasant smell of aromatic herbs at all hours, for the work never stopped. When I arrived, accompanied by another young doctor – not a Varrier this time, but one of Varrier's sons-in-law – a group of girls dressed in beautiful yellow saris were emerging from the main gates after one of these shifts.

The factory had been one of its founder's great doings. He had realized that a large part of the problem with Ayurveda's poor reputation lay with the quality of its medicines, which were no longer prepared by the doctors themselves. The patients instead had to do it all themselves, or entrust the task to some inexperienced herbalist. Thus, it was that the ayurvedic medicines were assembled with such imprecision and in such unhygienic conditions that they ended up being the cause of new illnesses rather than the cure for existing ailments.

With the factory annexed to the clinic, P.S. Varrier was able to control the quality of his remedies, experiment with new ones and guarantee round-the-clock quality production.

As it was born of hermits' and rishis' observations of nature, the Ayurvedic medicine cupboard was comprised almost exclusively of herbs and plants, especially the ones that grew wild. The forest was the great treasure trove for such remedies and the young doctor accompanying me knew the Indian tale often told in this connection.

Once a great master told his pupils, 'Go into the forest and bring back anything you think is useless there.' Each of them returned with something: a herb, a root, a piece of bark. Only one student came back empty-handed, but he was the one who earned his master's praise. He had understood that anything in the forest was useful and could not bring back anything. That student became the court doctor and one of the great rishis of Ayurveda.

To ensure the quality of the herbs he needed, P.S. Varrier at the start of the twentieth century elected to set up his own network of gatherers, some in the Himalayas who were responsible for supplying the factory with the required amounts. Each family specialized in various products of nature and the work was handed down from father to son.

Today, 100 years later, the system is still in operation, and the factory is able to produce around 500 types of medicines, each containing more than fifty different ingredients.

For every sack full of medicines that we walked past, the young doctor told me where it came from – Punjab, the Kullu Valley or Karnataka – and how much the herbs it contained cost. The most expensive, at just under Rs 4,000 – around £40 – per pound, was a particular species of coconut that grows only in Sri Lanka.

We popped into a room where a series of large wheels activated electronically was grinding herbs and other rare items which the doctor said came from the animal kingdom, including stags' horns and various seashells.

The most remarkable part was the room where the herbs were boiled in huge cauldrons, of which there must have been around twenty. Standing in front of each of them were bare-chested men, their dhotis pulled up to their knees, who were using long wooden ladles to stir a black liquid which gave off dense, acrid fumes. Every concoction was for a different type of illness.

The illnesses they treated most successfully, according to the young doctor, were arthritis, osteoporosis and problems with joints and/or skin complaints. In many cases, the medicines were administered along with special massages using particular oils, some of which were produced in the factory.

As we walked, the young doctor explained to me that in Ayurveda, the medicines are classified according to nine different categories based on how the herbs are treated and what form they are to be used in, i.e., oils, powders, creams or infusions. I confess I wasn't paying much attention at this point, but it was then that I heard him say, '... because some medicines are diluted with water, others with alcohol, and some with cow's urine ...'

'Including mine?' I asked jokingly.

He looked somewhat embarrassed. 'Yours are made of herbs,' he said to reassure me. But a seed of doubt had been planted in my mind.

Every room, every office we walked into, contained a photo of the founder. He was the hero everyone looked up to. The rules he had imposed on this institution 100 years ago were still valid today. For instance, if any one of the 1,600 employees made a mistake, he or she was sacked on the spot, but their place was to be taken by that person's spouse or their child, so that the family as a whole would not suffer as a result.

We went into the dispensary where a long queue of patients, each with a prescription in hand, was awaiting delivery of their own medicines. They then showed me into a smaller room where special medicines were prepared.

'Here, this is part of your prescription,' the head chemist said to me as he fiddled with a bottle.

It was the gelatine. I asked if I could taste it, and before putting it in my mouth, I instinctively brought it up to my nose to sniff it. Disgusting. Now I could put a definite smell to my seed of doubt – cow's piss.

Again I asked what went into my medicine, I wanted to know the truth, but it was like getting blood out of a stone. They all insisted the gelatine was made out of herbs, that it had been prepared especially for me on the consultant's specific orders, and that it wasn't for commercial use.

I was quite taken in with the idea. A medicine tailor-made for me, one that was completely natural. As natural as cow's piss?

Once the factory visit was over, I walked back to the centre of Kottakkal to send another email to Angela. I also took advantage of the Muslim engineer's kindness to drop the Fire-Eater an email, to tell him how far I'd come: this time all for a remedy made from cow's piss!

The young engineer was pleased to see me again and wanted to tell me more stories about Kerala, which he said he was very attached to. He told me of a very ancient school of martial arts that trained warriors to use long, flexible swords with which one man on his own could keep several enemies at bay on the battlefield.

Another feature of this school was the body-to-body combat. They were able to paralyse an opponent with just the touch of a hand or by applying pressure with just one finger to a delicate spot on the opponent's body. In his view, some centuries ago, it was in this school that several Japanese students introduced karate and katana, the swords used by the samurai. Unfortunately, this tradition too had been lost, he said; a mixture of martial arts and magic had been overtaken by the introduction of gunpowder and bullets.

He was a bit like me, this young Muslim: modern, but nostalgic for the past. We talked for over an hour and before I left, he let me check my messages one last time. There was one from the Fire-Eater, who was amused by my questions, and offered some answers.

'Isn't it great?' he wrote. 'A humble cow takes a slash one morning and you get better ... anyway, cow's piss is nothing. Homeopaths use tuberculosis sufferers' sputum, gonorrhoea secretions, skin that has flaked off psoriasis sufferers, syphilitics' rubbers and the saliva of rabid dogs! And you believe that this is worse than what they put in antibiotics?' He reckoned I should give it a try.

I went back to the hospital the following morning, still mulling over his choice of words: '... you believe that ... Ah yes, the little matter of faith. I too thought it was important and I wasn't even Niels Bohr, the great physicist and one of the most important scientists of our time, who kept a horseshoe over his desk. Once a colleague who went to see him asked, 'You don't actually believe all this stuff, do you?'

'Absolutely not,' he replied. 'But I understand that it brings me luck even if you don't.'

He was wrong. As such an accomplished scientist, he should

have known that it wasn't the horseshoe that brought good luck, it was his believing in it. This much in my view is scientific fact – for want of a better expression.

Attitude is incredibly important in combating illness, cancer in particular. No one can explain it in scientific terms, but I feel it is possible for the mind, once it has been quietened and is at peace, to send the right signals to the immune system ordering it to do its duty properly. At times I had the impression that this was exactly how it worked. In New York, I had 'felt' that the red phosphorescent liquid they had used in the chemotherapy was doing me good. But cow's piss?

The day was drawing to a close and preparations were beginning once again for the night-time spectacle in the hospital courtyard. Under the great straw tent, a large crowd was gathering again around the stage: families with children, elderly people barely able to stand, dignitaries who someone would invariably be polite enough to offer a seat to. Some of the actors were rehearsing their parts; one man sat motionless at the foot of a tree, lost in meditation.

Two beautiful, freshly cut banana tree trunks still full of bunches had been placed at the entrance to the small temple devoted to the god Vishwambhara, to function as doorposts.

Some elderly people were going around lighting the wicks of the hundreds of oil lamps scattered round the courtyard: small stone ones on the walls and large brass ones shaped like trees with many branches typical of southern India. The smell of burning sesame seed oil mixed with the sweet scent of the medicines continued to waft from the factory next door. Above the noise of children playing, one could hear the warbling of a pipe which an old man, mawkish and dapper, was playing with skill and delirium as if he himself were entranced by the melodies he was playing in honour of the elephant. A little further away, a woman wrapped in a dark shawl was squatting against a wall, telling a young man his fortune as she read his palm.

Sounds, lights, smells and images: the world of a bygone era. In everything I was surrounded by, there was something profoundly authentic and genuine, a strength which I truly felt could be helpful to others. But was it helpful to me?

This doubt made me sad, as did not having faith and realizing there wasn't much more for me to discover in the outside world. Going backwards in search of lost wisdom was pointless too, for I realized there was no golden age to provide us with solutions to today's problems or medicines for modern illnesses. There is no shortcut for attaining wisdom. The only solution – here the Swami was right – is within us and the only discovery still to be made is that of being ... the tenth man, as the story he told us shows.

The Arya Vaidya Sala was right for Indians: it was unpretentious, inexpensive and offered hope and relief from suffering. People came from far off to find a place that was clean, had a good doctor, and where in the end and in some cases without paying for it, they received a form of treatment which they were able to believe in because it was a part of their lives. And even if it was cow's piss, at least the cow was sacred as far as they were concerned! This was their world, with their herbs and their gods. I'd have loved to believe in it all too, but I just couldn't bring myself to believe that I would find the right medicine for myself here.

The old Sikh man I was sharing a room with seemed to have found his own medicine all right. The previous evening I had seen him motionless in bed behind a curtain of bottles and phials. Now he was sitting happily next to his son in the middle of the crowd, following the spectacle as if in a trance, possibly seeing the Supreme Reality in it. Lucky for him if he did.

When I returned to my room I found a note from the head of the hospital inviting me to dinner with his family.

One of the consultant's grandsons, also a Varrier and a doctor, came to collect me. To begin with, he took me on a tour of the house. We went in through a doorway that was dominated by symbols taken from various religions, including the half-moon of Islam and the Christian cross. More than a home, the Varrier residence was a kind of medieval manor with lots of rooms and courtyards in which all three generations lived.

The group of buildings had grown up over time around the original wooden structure that the founder had erected in 1926. His ashes were kept in a small temple in a bed full of flowers. There was a marble statue of him in the courtyard. His presence was ubiquitous.

The shared sitting room of the house was filled with children playing around two large tables. The women were sitting on a sofa that ran the length of a wall, which was covered in black-and-white photos of the founder and his descendants.

The kitchen was like a long, grey entrance hall. Twelve cooks, who had come to reinforce the family's usual retinue of three, were busying themselves around the old iron cauldrons in which our dinner was cooking. The fire was made out of old tree trunks, which young helpers tossed into the burning embers as and when these were consumed.

The sitting room opened out on to one of the house's inner courtyards, in the midst of which stood a great ceramic vase containing tulsi, the plant which throughout India is held to be sacred as well as medicinal. Once upon a time, us Italians used to worship it too, but we have forgotten all about it.

Tulsi is related to basil. The Ayurvedic texts describe it as 'the plant which opens the heart and mind, and arouses the energies of love and devotion'. Tradition has it that tulsi contains mercury, the sperm of Shiva, which is supposed to make the plant able to confer the power of pure knowledge on whoever eats it. In India, tulsi is a part of everyday life. It is supposed to purify the home and bring good fortune to the women who water it regularly.

In the West too, especially in Italy and Greece, basil was considered a venerable plant at one point. Legend has it that it grew on Christ's tomb and had hidden powers. Women used to put it in cupboards to ward off moths, and a leaf of basil eaten every day, as millions of Indians still do, was meant to provide protection against illnesses. In the Greek orthodox tradition, basil was meant to bring good luck. A record of the special place held by basil among other plants survives in various European languages. In French and German, for example, basil is referred to as the 'royal herb'.

The loud bang of a gong reverberated from somewhere; this was the signal for us to take our places. The men sat with the men and the women sat with the women. I was placed next to the consultant, halfway down a long wooden table. The places were set not with plates and cutlery, but banana leaves and copper goblets. Some very elegant, lithe elderly people dressed only in dhotis moved around with gleaming buckets, into which they dipped their ladles to serve everyone their portion of rice and lentils, along with a coconut and mango raita. The food was vegetarian and we were to use our fingers to eat it. The water had all been filtered and boiled, the consultant assured me, and herbs had been added too.

I was surrounded by both the past and the future of the Arya Vaidya Sala: former doctors and great-grandsons of the founder were present, along with their own grandsons and great-grandsons, many of them were still children who themselves would become doctors in the same house, the same hospital one day. An enviable provenance.

Close to the kitchens, there were two rows of tables reserved for the actors and musicians who were also attended to by the same servants from the same buckets.

The consultant had heard I had been very insistent in wanting to know the ingredients of my medicines. No problem; via his grandson he would let me know the Latin names of all the ingredients. Then, as if he was replying to a question I hadn't in fact asked, he said: 'Yes, the gelatine is a compound made from a herb named sahadevi, plus the dehydrated solids of cow's urine.' He then paused. I could only smile and he continued to explain that each animal's urine has its own particular properties, and those of cow's urine were exactly the right ones for my symptoms. I was to have no worries over the quality of the product, he said. The Arya Vaidya Sala had its own cattle farm, the sole purpose of which was to collect cow dung and urine. They had also recently launched their own herbarium because they had realized that certain plants, which were important for them, were beginning to vanish as a result of pollution and indiscriminate deforestation.

P.K. Varrier was courteous enough, but in his own way rather gruff. I had never once seen him smile and I didn't really feel it was appropriate to carry on talking about urine, especially while we were eating. So I asked him instead how he saw Ayurveda, and this seemed to put him much more at ease.

More than a medicine, he said, Ayurveda was a philosophy of life because it has an ethical dimension, and its aim is not so much to help man remain healthy as to help him achieve his spiritual goals. This is why Ayurveda prescribes a form of discipline that is moral as well as physical. In his view, the inner strength of a patient was the only guarantee of a healthy life.

Returning to my case, he again emphasized that 'correct regulation of the appetites for food, sleep and sex' was of utmost importance. I was to be extremely disciplined and to pay careful attention to the quality, location, company, time and mental attitude with which I devoted myself to eating, sleeping and the other.

He knew I had come from the gurukulam and that I was a student of the Swami – who they held in the highest esteem – and he felt he could speak to me without fear of being misunderstood.

'What is the aim of knowledge,' he asked, 'but to understand nature so as to follow its laws and live better? We have to understand the place that we human beings occupy in the universe and what relationship we are in with the various cosmic phenomena, so that we may behave in a way that is disciplined, avoid disasters and help contribute to the well-being of all other creatures. If we do not know ourselves, there is no point in trying to get to know the world.'

I said nothing and wanted him to go on.

'This has always been the meaning of knowledge in the East. It used to be so for you in the West too. But only until the time of Michelangelo. Since then, your science has sought to understand the world solely with a view to using it for materialistic purposes. This is where you have gone wrong. Yes, a lot of research goes on today, but for what purpose? To discover the riches hidden in nature, take possession of them and transform them into merchandise. This is the reason why the Western world's progress is so unbalanced and the reason also for your spiritual decay.'

I felt as though he were thinking out loud rather than talking to me.

'It was industrialized society,' he continued, 'which introduced assembly lines to produce more and more, quicker and quicker, and then combine the various articles manufactured into one end product. This led to medicine being seen as the sum of its different parts, and of no importance any longer being attributed to that mysterious, invisible force which apparently comes into an organism at birth and leaves it when it dies. It was only the industrial revolution that gave rise to the absurd claim of being able to explain the universe in mechanical terms.'

Excellent stuff, all this. I agreed with every word he said. But did this mean I could bring myself to drink his cow's piss?

Here I was again, still on the horns of the same old dilemma. On one hand I was curious, fascinated by this way of thinking and seeing things; on the other, I was still tormented by a doubt that had appeared spontaneously with the 'doctor' at Kakinada, that it was talk that was effective in India, not medicine.

The old servants kept coming around, obsequious and meticulous, offering us more and more from their bright, shiny buckets. The shimmering oil lamps outside the window, the sounds from the courtyard and the aromas wafting over from the factory all helped to create an atmosphere from days gone by.

Once dinner was over, we all went back outside to watch the spectacle. They wanted me to sit in one of the seats left empty in the front row, but I thanked them, said goodnight, and with the excuse that I was going to bed, mingled with the crowds who were watching the play.

The show had just commenced. After some performances by dancers and singers, the Kathakali troupe arrived on stage. This troupe also owed its existence to the hospital's patriotic founder. Having founded the hospital, P.S. Varrier began to worry about how his employees would spend their spare time. To prevent them from indulging in 'sinful and wicked activities, which would also have sullied the name of the Arya Vaidya Sala', he thought of relaunching Kathakali, the old Kerala form of theatre which combined ballet, opera, pantomime and magical comedy, and derived from the old dances in which stories of gods and heroes were recounted to people in the temples.

Kathakali had been one of the traditional vehicles for transmission of popular culture in Kerala, but it too had begun to decline. P.S. Varrier contributed to its renaissance. He trained young actors, funded writers to re-establish the old texts and compose new ones and put together an itinerant troupe which visited every corner of the region with its shows. For almost a century now, the most important date in the troupe's annual calendar had been at the beginning of April in the hospital courtyard, for the festival held in honour of Vishwambhara, the divine protector of Ayurveda and the Varrier family too.

On the left-hand side of the stage sat the drummers who were able to create with their hands or with drumsticks the sounds of a battle, the rushing water of a torrent and the dripping sound of water as it falls on to a leaf. On the right-hand side were the singers. With the help of cymbals, a gong and an orchestra of around twenty men lined up behind them, all naked till the waist, the singers told the story and uttered the words of the various characters, for in Kathakali all the actors are silent and at most emit guttural sounds. The actors 'speak' via their movements, express their thoughts and states of mind by means of their hand gestures. They 'talk' with their facial expressions and the way they roll their eyes, which appear much larger than normal as a result of the way their faces are painted. Characters from the superior universe, the devas, or divines are painted green; the faces of women and wise men are their normal colour; and the characters who come from the infernal world or the asuras have their faces painted in red and black.

Ample, brightly coloured skirts, each made with more than fifty yards of material, lend weight and majesty to the movements of the actors who have bracelets inlaid with jewels on their arms and legs, golden chains around their necks and long fingerstalls on their fingers to make their actions seem even longer.

The stories enacted are all taken from the Mahabharata, the Ramayana, the Gita and the Puranas. It so happened that the one they were acting out that evening was one I was familiar with. Shiva married Sati, but her father is not pleased with the marriage. His new son-in-law doesn't appear to him to be very respectable: long-haired, his body covered in ash, he goes around with a snake around his neck and a half-moon on his head. As his father-in-law, he is ashamed to have such a relative and refuses to invite him when he organizes a great feast-cum-sacrifice in honour of the gods. However, it is Sati who is the first to take umbrage, and when her father piles on the agony in making a speech to all present in which he is critical of Shiva, she cannot bear the shame any longer and throws herself on the sacrificial fire.

Shiva hears about this and goes mad. He runs to the place where the feast is being held, cuts his father-in-law's head off, takes the dead body of Sati, puts it over his shoulder and runs through the world like a madman, destroying everything he finds. The other gods are concerned and approach Vishnu, whose responsibility it is to maintain order in the universe, and ask him to intervene. Vishnu manages to persuade Shiva to calm down by suggesting to him what to do with the corpse of his beloved bride: using Vishnu's weapon, the chakra, a kind of lethal discus, a bit like a boomerang, Shiva cuts Sati's body into fifty-one pieces, and wherever these fall on the earth a great temple is constructed.

Thus today there are fifty-one sanctuaries in India, each dedicated to a different part of the fair Sati's anatomy; one to her tongue, another to her feet, while the one dedicated to her yoni, or 'female reproductive organ' as the foreigners' tourist guides coyly refer to it, is in Guwahati, the capital of Assam. Remarkably, this temple dedicated to the vagina is located on a rock set on the banks of the Brahmaputra, a great river of India that is considered to be masculine![18] I visited it in the company of the last descendent of the maharajahs to whom in theory the temple, the Kamakhya, belongs. It was a feast day and hundreds of pilgrims had come to perform their puja, bringing with them their goats to be sacrificed, their children and childless women to be blessed. It was like something out of Dante's *Inferno*. From inside the temple, a fine tenth-century stone structure, a dark, slippery staircase led into the bowels of the earth where the vagina was – a damp, gloomy hole, Sati's mons Veneris, was covered in a red cloth which the people had strewn with water, money and flowers. The stench was overpowering, the devotion close to hysteria, the litanies chanted by the priest vaguely obscene, obsessive and potent.

The story of Shiva and his bride, who after being chopped into pieces comes back to life as Parvati, the daughter of Himalaya, and marries him again, is one of the most famous in India and plays a significant role in the country's collective psyche. Dozens of other stories derive from this. One such story involves the decapitated father-in-law. Vishnu, in an attempt to restore some semblance of order to the world, orders Sati's father's head to be placed back on its shoulders. The instructions are carried out, but at the last moment someone makes a mistake, so instead of his old head, Sati's father ends up with a goat's head.

The episode in which the father-in-law comes to realize the mistake that has been made was the one being acted out on stage

[18] Rivers like the Ganga and the Yamuna are deemed to be feminine.

at that moment. A tiny figure of a man with an animal's head was kneeling before a green-faced god, quaking and begging for help. The music and actions expressed the emotion, and the audience was rapt, hanging on to every word from the two narrators'. There were rows of children sitting open-mouthed on the ground in front of the stage; behind them were the dignitaries, then lots of women, and finally the crowds of spectators which extended right up to the perimeter walls. Dozens and dozens of other heads were peering out of all the windows. No one was sleeping: doctors and patients, musicians and actors, servants and masters, cooks, nurses, guards, mothers and children, all together involved in the same magical comedy of men and gods.

I too was taken with the beauty of the play and the world of fables it represented. It was a world that we in the West have less to do with. Just after WWII, not far from my home in Florence, there was a clearing – now a car park – where acrobats and strong men used to perform on Sundays, and every now and again a magician or an itinerant group of actors would pitch their tents there. Those spectacles and the emotions they provoked in me touched my heart for the first time and left an indelible mark on my memory.

How much I had changed! I had become so sceptical, so rational. I had always liked to pretend that I was somehow immune to all beliefs and superstitions. But now I was left with nothing, unable to feel what these people were feeling. Those sights and sounds had so much meaning for them, but none whatsoever for me. What they saw and heard with their spiritual eyes and ears, the eyes and ears of their souls, was so much more real than what they saw and heard with their physical organs. But physical organs were all that I had.

This was a sensation I had often had in India. Like years ago at the Kumbh Mela in Allahabad, where the largest crowd of Indians and holy men I have ever seen gathered to bathe at the sacred confluence of three rivers: two of them real, the Ganga and the Yamuna; the third one mythical, the Saraswati, the invisible river of wisdom which is meant to flow underground. There were hundreds of thousands of people on a sunny strip of sand. The difference was not in where we were, but in how we were there. I was in the sun, walking on the ground scattered with excrement; they were ecstatic and took no notice of what was going on around them, as though somewhere else, hovering in some gateway to heaven.

Perhaps it was like that because every place and every event has its own psychological meaning, over and above its apparent meaning. Perhaps for every external image there is also an internal image, which awakens in us a much truer, deeper reality than the one experienced by our senses. The meaning of symbols, myths and legends help us to go further, to see beyond the visible. This is also the true value of the store of fables and fairy tales we accumulate as children and draw on during the difficult moments of our lives, when we are looking for some form of direction or comfort.

We have fewer and fewer of these eternal myths in the West, myths that can lead to the soul or are symbols of something else. This is because we are artificially bloated with the modern myths of show business, fashion and sport, which end right where they begin and hold no secrets of their own.

Yet it is only by looking at things with a fresh set of eyes that the reality of daily life and of matter gives way to the reality which cannot be perceived by the senses, but which is no less true for that reason: the psychic reality, the only one in which 'miracles' occur, in which nails may be painlessly inserted into people's arms and swords into their tongues.

This was how the hospital at Kottakkal appeared to me that night. It was as though the stories being acted out on the stage, the music, the dance, the lights, the smells, being there all together, perhaps also the tiredness, helped people manage to lift the veil which prevents us from seeing 'everything else', to cross the threshold into another dimension and enter the world of another reality.

I myself had not made that final step, but I was happy to be there, and in fact couldn't tear myself away.

I was attracted by some strange music coming from the temple. Two men standing in the corner were accompanying each other, one with a drum, the other with a great bronze cymbal, and had struck up a plaintive chant. They were swaying to and fro, shaking their heads, to the slow rhythm of their mournful lullaby. Both were in a trance, with their eyes closed and their faces radiant every time they repeated the chorus. I sat on the ground, lost in the melody, and thought how easy, how light it would be to surrender my own body to the sound of that rhythm, and those wonderful musicians who continued to play and sing without pause, keeping the thread I felt I was holding on to unbroken.

The women made gestures with their right hands as they entered the temple, to their heads and their breasts, as though making the sign of the cross. Children were bowing with their heads to the ground before the holiest of holies, where one of the pujaris was chanting his mantras and continually throwing rose petals at the foot of the white marble statue of Vishwambhara.

I tried to make my way back to my room, but every detail prevented me from doing so: a dwarf who came to place two beautiful bronze oil lamps (both bigger than he was) before the god; the elephant, who at a word knelt down, and at another offered his legs and tail for six men to use as a ladder with rungs, so that they could climb up on his back and take a golden quilt bearing the likeness of the god, which had been outside in the courtyard all night, into the tabernacle.

I stayed until everything was lulled and then eventually silenced by the first light of dawn; everything, that is, apart from the mournful lullaby that continued to hover, distant and plaintive, over the crowd as it dispersed, and the elephant as it was disrobed of its vestments.

I felt like I was caught between two stools, still commuting between two different worlds: an old world, which I didn't want to be lost in and a new world, which it seemed to me ridiculous to ignore. One magical, with its ancient potions; one rational, with its modern chemotherapy.

I went to have breakfast with the other patients in the refectory, which was already open. My head was whirling and I don't even remember eating. Then my eyes fell upon a fly which kept buzzing around my plate. It was cleverer than the others which were continually getting burnt to cinders in the blue lamp. Instead, it was trying to obtain its own share of my semolina and coconut dip. I remembered Nur and her greengrocer beetle. What if that fly had been my Doctor Bringluck from New York, who had come to see how I was intending to be treated with cow's piss rather than her phosphorescent liquids?

I often thought of her: upright, strong, precise and warm. She spent every single day of the week in that hospital, with the same patients, the same problems, in those box-shaped, air-conditioned, neon-lit offices with their phones ringing, their computers, their letters and meetings. They were so unlike me, who despite all my ailments was once again – thanks to her – back on the merry-go-round, riding the white horse.

Which of the two of us was more 'ill'?

The grandson doctor found me there, talking to the fly. He had come to give me the Latin names of the herbs that had gone into my two potions. The sahadevi in the gelatine was *Vernonia cinerea*. The other potion, called (wait for it) nimbamrithadipanchathikthan contained five herbs: *Azadirachta indica, Tinospora cordifolia, Adathoda beddomei, Trichosanthes lobata* and *Solanum surattense*.

The medicines were ready, so I went to the factory and paid the bill: Rs 610, around £8.

I left Kottakkal in a taxi by mid-morning. On the back seat of another old Ambassador, a large cardboard box sat proudly by my side, containing nine bottles of the medicine made especially for me, each of them wrapped and protected with newspaper. My head was asking whether or not I would ever take it, but inside I already knew the answer. Not so much because of the smell whose origins I wasn't sure of, but basically because I didn't 'believe' in it. That elephant, who was still shaking its head pathetically in a corner of the courtyard, might have fascinated and attracted me, but as far as I was concerned it would always be – unfortunately, perhaps – an elephant, never a god.

A MIRACLE JUST FOR ME

The gate of the ashram swung shut behind the taxi which had brought me back. The world with all its noises, problems, desires and joys – all the externalities which the Swami used to speak of – remained outside. I put the cardboard box in the shade under my iron-framed bed, and returned to the tranquil, disciplined rhythms of the life I liked so much: the lessons, meals, pujas and hymns of the gurukulam, and the cawing, chirping, twittering and cheeping of nature that surrounded it.

At times I asked myself how I could ever bring myself to leave this bubble of peace and go back to living in a family other than that of the guru. But in the end, it never came to that. Perhaps simply because I knew the time would come sooner or later, and that when it eventually did come, somehow I would be more than ready for it. I imagine this must be what it is like when you die: your body weakens, your mind starts to think differently and when the time comes, everything seems more agreeable and less terrible than it had appeared.

As a man leaves an old garment,
and puts on one that is new,
the Spirit leaves his mortal body
and then puts on one that is new.

This is what Krishna said to the young Arjuna in the *Gita* to explain to him what death is like. And regarding the jiva, the 'he' that lives in the body, but is not to be confused with the body, Krishna adds:

There is no weapon that can sever him,
No fire that can burn him,
No water that can soak him,
Nor wind that can dry him.
Unthinkable, unchangeable, not manifest
Is the Self, and You, knowing that you are such, have no
Reason to suffer.

The Swami could speak for hours on just one verse or at times even just one word. After introducing the Vedanta through the Upanishads, the second part of the course dealt mostly with the

Gita, which summarized the entire Vedantic vision in the form of a dialogue between Krishna and Arjuna.

The mere sound of Sanskrit in some of the passages was sufficient to give me immense joy. Sometimes when we recited the verses together before the lessons, I almost felt like I was levitating, like the time when I smoked opium at Phnom Penh, or breathed in the history from atop the temples in places such as Angkor Wat or Pagan. I liked the vision of the universe expressed in these verses and also that of the people: great and small, cowards and villains, all caught up indiscriminately in the same destiny:

As myriads of moths throw themselves in the fire,
Only to perish,
So mankind throws itself in the flaming mouth
Of time, which leaves the world desolate.

Not because men are indelibly marked by some form of sin or because some distant god condemns them, but because:

All that is born will certainly die,
All that dies will certainly be born.
So much is inevitable; there is no reason to suffer.

The god of the Gita has no chosen people, he does not condemn them to hell for all eternity or reserve for some what he denies to others. This is the kind of god I like: a god who is everywhere, who requires no mediators, who doesn't need to send anyone down to earth, be it his son or some prophet, to do his bidding for him and to tell people: 'This is what he said to tell you'. A god that anyone can see in whatever way they like: in a lowly rock or on of the loftiest, most beautiful mountains in the Himalayas such as Kailash. It seemed to me to be a vision of free men deriving from a form of seeking all that was pure, without racial or social interests, in the name of humanity.

In this vision put forward by the Gita, I liked the fact that, unlike in Buddhism, the world of the senses was not seen as maya, or illusion, an obstacle to true knowledge. The Vedanta does not deny the world, only that the world has independent existence. But it is precisely in departing from our own perception of the world that we are all able to discover what the world actually depends on. Once this step has been taken, the world is of no more use and is left behind – in this sense it is 'illusion' – just as the eighteenth elephant in the following story is an illusion, a story told to illustrate this concept of maya.

A man dies, leaving seventeen elephants to his three children as their inheritance. In his will, he stipulates that half the elephants should go to his eldest son, one-third to his second son, and one-ninth to his youngest son. The children are at a loss as to how they should divide the elephants and are worried that they may eventually have to cut one of them up. They end up arguing. 'Our father was mad,' they said. 'He should never have left us with a problem such as this.' At that moment one of the king's ministers was passing through their village on his way to the capital, riding on the back of an elephant. He came to hear of their problem and said, 'Do not worry. Take my elephant, add it to your seventeen, and divide them up accordingly.'

The three sons were stunned at the minister's generosity, and did as he suggested. Now there were eighteen elephants: the eldest son took half the elephants, i.e., nine; the second took one-third, i.e., six; the youngest took one-ninth, i.e., two. This made a total of seventeen. The three brothers were delighted and thanked the minister, who took back his elephant – the eighteenth – and continued his journey in the direction of the capital.

This is what the world is like: not an illusion, but something to help us do our sums by and recognize that the entire universe is sustained by that consciousness, reality or fullness, by the self on which everything else ultimately depends. Hence, everything is within us – hell, heaven, happiness, sadness, joy and even the world.

Above all, I liked the fact that in the Vedantic vision of the world there was no concept of sin and no sinners either. Desires? Nothing wrong with them – they are part of life too. Among the many delightful definitions which Krishna gave of himself in the Gita, was one where he said, 'I am the desire in the hearts of men.'[19] However, we should be aware that desires tie us to samsara, the world of becoming, and that the only way to be truly free is to sever all such ties.

The Vedanta is modern because, as a form of knowledge it never contradicts science. Indeed, it considers science to be sacred, for as everything is god and there is no distinction between sacred and profane. 'All that scientists do is look into the mind of Ishwara,' said the Swami, who was not the slightest bit dogmatic or fideistic.

When he invited me back to dinner to ask how things had gone at Kottakkal, he was not surprised to discover that I had misgivings over the effectiveness of the cow's piss and said he would continue trying to help me. He said a young man would soon be coming to the ashram about whom he had heard very good reports – again

---

[19] Other definitions include: 'I am the taste in the water, the light in the sun and the moon, the word *Om* in the Vedas, the sound in the air, the virility in men. I am the fragrance of the earth and what shines in the fire. I am the life in all beings, and the ascetics' austerity ... I am the seed of all being, the intelligence of the intelligent, the heroism of heroes. I am the strength of the strong.'

an Ayurvedic doctor. He wanted to see him about his diabetes and said he would introduce me too.

I liked the fact that the Swami had an extremely rational, modern mindset, despite his dressing as a wise man from 2,000 years ago. For him it was all a matter of logic. He didn't see the value of intuition, he didn't leave much scope for the heart, and one day it struck me that in all the weeks I had been listening to him, I had never once heard him utter the word 'love'. I agreed that there was a level of reality which our eyes cannot see, our ears cannot hear, our tongues cannot taste, our hands cannot touch and our noses cannot smell. But in the end, that reality as he described it, came across as profoundly cold. One made up entirely of words. Sanskrit words translated into English maybe, but words nonetheless. He himself had said several times that 'salvation does not come from words alone', that it was also necessary to experience the meaning of those words. But I didn't feel as though I had done that. I had listened to the words, but I hadn't 'heard' them. I enjoyed listening to the poetry of the texts, but I didn't feel like they had opened a third eye for me.

I was having a crisis. I got an inkling of this – a premonition, if you will – one evening as I sat on the little patio in front of my room after all the lights had been turned off. It was a summer evening, like those of my childhood years in Orsigna, with distant voices of girls laughing, stars shining in the moonless sky and the headlights of the odd lorry passing by on its way to Coonoor, the old English hill station in the Nilgiris. The mountains were clothed in a magic halo of blue light. Along the ridges, the odd fire was devouring the little scrubland that remained. I missed the world. After so many weeks in the ashram, the isolation was beginning to feel unnatural. I sensed my concentration beginning to wane and there was a growing desire in me to slip away, to find out what the girls were laughing about or to see if those fires were not perhaps a part of some tribal ritual.

At the end of the day, even with all my inquisitiveness and my attraction to the 'other', I was and would always remain a European. Increasingly, I keenly felt the fundamental, delightful and fascinating contradiction between ours and the Indians' way of being in the world: for us, the supreme value of life is life; for them, it is non-life. Moksha, or the release from having to be reborn, is what this civilization aspires to. As a shishya, I too was being taught to aspire to this negation of life, whereas I in fact continued to quite like it just as it was. I saw much joy in it. I understood that for every form of joy there is suffering and I could see the value of battling against my desires. But while I liked being detached from things, I didn't want to be indifferent to them.

I was sure that the best way to enjoy a river was to stay out of the tide, especially at my age, but at least I had to be able to sit on the bank, to look at the water and listen to it flow past. All this seemed to me to be a long way removed from the ashram.

One day, during the lunch break, one of the older shishyas, the heart surgeon from Hyderabad, came and sat down next to me.

'Anamji, what do you know about pyramids?'

'Pyramids?' I asked. He went on, encouraged by my surprise. He could barely eat in his excitement as he explained to me that pyramids, not just the Egyptian ones, but all pyramids, large or small, in stone or any other form of material, anywhere in the world, have their own mysterious force which is still largely untapped. He, for example, had shaved using the same razor blade every day for months on end, which had never become blunt because he put it underneath a small iron pyramid after using it every time. He also had a plastic pyramid, which he put on his head like a hat when he meditated and a special mask for his eyes – like the ones you get on aeroplanes – made in the shape of a pyramid to help him sleep better.

He told me there was a very powerful pyramid just thirty miles from the ashram that had been built a few years ago. We could go and see it together and share the cost of a taxi. As a doctor, he was especially interested in the pyramid's therapeutic powers.

Therapeutic powers? I was interested in them too! I remembered that the Fire-Eater had said something along these lines once: how his faith in classical medicine had been shaken while he was in Peru and Columbia, where he had seen the Faculty of Agrarian Studies carry out research into the powers of the pyramids in the course of their struggle against various plant parasites. He had thought it was a joke, but in reality it worked, it didn't cause pollution and cost much less than a protective product for spraying crops.

I told the surgeon I was certainly up for such an expedition. He was delighted to have found another follower, and pulled a book out of the bag he carried over his shoulder, which he said I should read to prepare for the visit. The book was in the shape of a pyramid.

Some days passed, then one evening at satsang, the Swami announced that there would be no lessons the following day. He had to go to Bombay to give a talk to a group of businessmen who were helping to support us. His subject was to be: 'How to avoid stress in modern life'. We took advantage of this opportunity to set off on our trip. I knew that anything to do with powers would be of extreme interest to Sundarajan, so I invited him to come along too. Thus, the three of us made our way to the pyramid, once more aboard an old Hindustan Motors' Ambassador, which, with its high-backed, white-cloth-covered rear seats, will always be the symbol of luxury travel in India for me.

The pyramid too was just as Indian. Hidden-behind some palm trees that had been planted around it to make it look more Egyptian, it was made of simple stones and located at the edge of a private school bearing the name 'Perks'. The pyramid's distinguishing feature were the two large pipes wrapped in aluminium foil that stuck out just underneath its pinnacle, destroying all its natural balance and mystical structure.

'They are pipes for the air conditioning, which we had put in for the visit of Master Choa Kok Sui,' said the man who greeted us.

'Who?'

'Master Choa Kok Sui, the founder of pranic healing. He is a great healer. He has invented a system of treatment that has been having great success. He lives in Manila in the Philippines.'

Healer? I made a mental note of this to myself.

The pyramid's power, our guide explained to us, resided in its ability to gather and retain 'cosmic rays'. These rays made it possible for a series of things to take place inside it that would otherwise be impossible, from the sharpening of razor blades, to food being kept for unusually long periods of time, to the ability to enjoy perfect concentration in meditation.

As all three of us had come from the ashram where meditation was a part of the daily routine, this was the aspect of the pyramid we immediately wanted to test. But the results were underwhelming. The air conditioning, which had been installed when the famous master of pranic healing had passed through a few weeks ago, had already broken down and the heat on the wooden landing beneath the pyramid's summit at its exact centre was stifling. The cosmic rays, which according to the literature on pyramidology were supposed to have had such a great effect on so many characters in history, starting with Napoleon, had no effect on me whatsoever.

The man who had built the pyramid was also the school's director and author of the pyramid-shaped book, which the heart surgeon had given me to read. He was waiting for us in his office, and like all important people, was sitting at this desk signing papers intently. The school's slogan was displayed in capital letters on the wall behind him: 'I am proud to be studying here. What this school cannot give me, India will give me. What India cannot give me, the world will give me.'

'Was the school founded by the English?' I asked to start the conversation.

Not at all; he had founded the school himself thirty years ago on land owned by his family. The name 'Perks' was made up of the initial letters of his five children's names.

Rama Ranganathan was seventy-three years old, but looked younger, thanks to the powers of the pyramid, he said. Once on a trip to Europe, his ship had docked for several hours at Port Said and he had hurried off to see the pyramids. Since then they had been his passion. He had read up on them, written about them, and in 1992 built his own to record an exceptional event. The event in question was a drought that had lasted seven years, which he himself had brought to an end via an act of puja. Non-stop for three days and three nights, hundreds of people had come from the entire surrounding region to recite the magic mantras invoking rainfall, and at the end of the third day the heavens had duly opened. He built the pyramid on the precise spot where the puja had been performed, 'the holiest place in the school'. Plastic bags had been cemented into its foundations containing thousands and thousands of sheets of paper. On each sheet the word *Ram* – the name of the Lord, he explained to me – had been written one million two hundred thousand times. 'I am merely the driver,' he chuckled, pointing heavenwards to indicate God, 'he is the one who is telling me where I should go. After all, he is the boss of everything.'

The director was also an expert on the subject of Vaastu, the Indian version of Feng Shui, the Chinese art of arranging a building or furnishing a room in such a way as to be in tune with the forces of nature to make it more propitious.

He had certainly managed to make his building propitious and lucrative. Over the years, the pyramid had become something of a tourist attraction and the school's fame had grown – the number of students had increased from just a few dozen to over 2,000 – and in the museum-cum-shop, which now appeared to be more popular than the pyramid itself, various types of pyramids were on sale for personal use. The one my heart surgeon friend was particularly interested in was made of wood and could be disassembled into four separate bits. The idea was that you slept with it in order to be 'cured of various illnesses', as the director said.

I didn't think it could help with mine, but the heart surgeon insisted. What illnesses, exactly?

'My brother-in-law, for example, was on a waiting list for a heart bypass operation,' the director said. 'But he wanted to try the pyramid first. He felt better immediately, and now does not need to have the operation.' For a moment the whole thing felt like a set-up: a heart surgeon visits the pyramid, and as luck would have it, they tell him all about this miraculous healing of a man with a heart condition.

'So, where is your brother-in-law now?' I asked, with a touch of the old journalist's arrogance, one who thinks he has a right to know everything.

His brother-in-law was just a mile or so away, and as though the set-up was continuing – but it couldn't be! – we went to see him and found him lying down reading a book on a bed with the pyramid he had erected in front of his porch. One side of it was built in such a way that it could be pulled up and down to function as a door.

The man, who was around sixty-five, did not look like he was ill at all. He recounted his experience to the heart surgeon, answered many questions, and eventually pronounced that he had been 'miraculously healed' by the power of the pyramid and would never put himself in the hands of the surgeons. He had also recently read a study by some Americans which found that heart patients who had undergone surgery said they were no longer able to love or feel loved. In other words, a bypass operation could have negative effects on the part of the brain that registers those emotions and he wanted to die while still being able to love.

Who could argue with that? He quoted a phrase that each of us could have made our own: 'The measure of a man is not in his dying, but in his living.'

On the way back to the ashram, Sundarajan and the heart surgeon couldn't stop talking about the visit and commenting on it. With his large, round, blood-red mark and three sandalwood stripes on his forehead, Sundarajan's eyes, which were enormous at the best of times, were open even wider than usual now as though to underline his astonishment. He was quite convinced of the pyramid's power. He was already well acquainted with the powers of the mandram, and as an example quoted the magic formula to be recited in order to prolong the life of someone who is dying, or to chant during a marriage ceremony to ensure the couple's first child is a boy. The heart surgeon's only objection was that much of the effectiveness of the mantras depended on who it was that was using them. 'Like antibiotics,' he said, 'they can't be prescribed indiscriminately, and are only of use in certain cases.'

I listened to them as I watched the usual, despair-inducing scenes of Indian life pass by outside my window. I thought about how, with all the power of the mantras and pyramids, this is still one of the countries with the highest infant mortality rate and tuberculosis rate in the whole world. It was a country where, despite the power of prayer to bring rain or stop it, thousands of people die every year because of droughts or floods. Maybe this is precisely why we need mantras, pujas and all the poetry of their 'powers'. Or is the opposite true? Is it that everything is so desperate because of the mantras and pujas?

Each of us had bought our own little pyramid in the director's museum-cum-shop. Mine was a light blue plastic one, which I tried to put on my head a couple of times to help me meditate, but which ended up under the bed along with the cardboard box of medicine bottles from Kottakkal.

I increasingly began to skip the group meditation sessions, preferring instead to look at nature around me, and occasionally paint some very modest watercolours with the paints I had bought in the stationer's shop in Coimbatore. I have painted ever since I was a child. I have never been very good at it, but I do like trying to reproduce on paper not so much what I see, but the atmosphere I feel.

One evening at sunset I was up on my hill, painting the haystacks scattered across the plains below. I thought I was alone, but a woman came up to me. She was from the course. I had noticed her before: she was very thin, always on her own, with an elegant air and a pained expression.

'Do you mind if I watch?' she asked. Soon, we had unravelled a skein of coincidences and interests we had in common. She had heard that I had been to Kottakkal and guessed I had health problems. She did too. Ten years ago, she had been diagnosed with an incurable degenerative illness. Western medicine had brought her to the point of death faster than the illness itself. Someone had mentioned a tiny naturopathy centre to her, run by a couple in a village in the middle of Andhra Pradesh, and she had summoned her last remaining strength to go there. It was the poorest, most primitive region she had ever seen, but the couple had nursed her back to health and she stayed. She had turned her back on her former life and her evidently wealthy family in Delhi, and had gone to live in the centre trying to help others using naturopathy, which she was convinced was the best form of medicine in the whole world.

The most important stage in the treatment process is the analysis of the patient, she explained. It was necessary to talk to the patient for a very long time, sometimes hours on end, in order to understand how the one truly natural therapy available – fasting – should be applied in each case.

'Fasting heals,' she said, 'but it has to be established clearly how long the fast is to last, how much water should be drunk and with what, that is, with honey or lemon. Never with fruit juice. Fasting forces the body to use up what it does not need: growths, extras, malignant things and old reserves, never what is useful. Fasting doesn't take energy away from the body; it forces it to save what it would otherwise have to use for food. There must be complete concentration during the period of the fast: no reading, no writing, just meditation.'

She explained that it was vital to heal not just the patient's body, but also their psychic state and their spiritual development. 'Ultimately it is a question of faith in God,' she said. 'All illnesses can be cured, but not all patients can.'

I told her about Kottakkal, and asked her what she would do with the medicines I was storing under my bed.

'Only take them if you believe they will heal you.'

So I was back where I had started! If they had no effect on me or even proved to be harmful, it wouldn't be the fault of the cow's piss, it would be mine because I hadn't had enough faith! I knew how this line of reasoning went.

She invited me to go and see her in her village in Andhra Pradesh. If that was too far for me, I could get an idea of naturopathy from a centre near Bangalore, which she said was quite well known.

I took down the address.

Gradually the world of the ashram, which to begin with had struck me as being so unique and so special, started to seem not so different from the outside world after all. People who initially had been interested in solitude and taken with the subject they were there for, over time began to socialize and form cliques to keep each other company. One of the 'pensioners' brigade' who had come to hear of our trip to the pyramid was upset that he had been left out, and having noticed I hadn't spoken for a week, wanted to take me once the course was over to see his Mauni Baba, an old sadhu who had not spoken for twenty years.

The ashram was a form of society too, and after a while the same old tendencies seen in society started to emerge there as well. For example, a group of women very politely competed for the right to serve the visiting swamis, whereas others strived to ask the most intelligent questions during the satsang.

Anyone who thinks they can escape the snares of life by entering an ashram is mistaken. There might not be any tax or telephone bills to pay, or invitations to dinner with people, but there too, tensions and moral obligations can creep in unnoticed. Such as feeling obliged to attend the puja, or jostling to sit as close as possible to the Swami's feet. The ashram can become its own kind of trap. It was a haven that guaranteed protection and security, but at the same time involved curtailing certain liberties.

I had learnt a great deal there; my mind had been filled with lots of new ideas. I did feel like I was a member of the gurukulam; but the life of the ashram, learning holy texts in order to pass them on to others, was really not for me. I was very much indebted to the Swami, but I wasn't ready to become one of his followers.

Taking a shower one morning, using the simple but highly effective method of squatting down in front of a low tap and pouring buckets of cold water over my head, I realized I had begun to smell like a monk: the chastity, insipid food and blameless lifestyle. This worried me. Soon afterwards, in a fit of heretical rage and without sparing them so much as a thought, I killed a whole army of ants that had ventured into my room and attacked my precious stock of dates. Then at breakfast, rather than eating the three large semolina dumplings which the brahmachari serving had just dolloped into my bowl, I put them on my neighbour's plate while he was getting himself a glass of milk. He was one of the quietest, most respectable of the pensioners, and on his return was most confused to find his food had miraculously multiplied. He looked around, looked at me while I, proud of my naughtiness, pretended to know nothing about it.

One day, in the concrete area at the foot of the stairs leading up to the auditorium, I saw a beautiful rangoli, a decoration made with rice flour that the ants would come and eat up and remove all trace of. A rangoli is a geometrical design where everything is based on the number eight: eight sides, eight angles, eight internal lines forming eight triangles, eight points with a white circle in the centre, as though it were the sun around which the universe rotates, or the nucleus of an atom with its neutrons.

It was the day devoted to celebrations in honour of Shankaracharya, the great eighth-century commentator on the Vedas. There weren't to be any lessons, just a variety of pujas. For me it was a chance to escape from the ashram and get a breath of fresh air. I went up to Coonoor, the old hill station where the English used to go to seek refuge from the heat of the plains.

The journey was awful. The road was like a gas chamber. Tankers full of petrol and buses loaded with people were throwing out asphyxiating clouds of cancerogenous fumes as they snaked up the road to the top of the hill. I had heard Coonoor was one of the most beautiful, peaceful towns in the whole of India, but when I got there I thought I must have got the wrong place. It had just rained and the town was a mudbath, full of people who were soaking wet and looking somewhat the worse for wear. I had read that the Young Woman's Christian Association (YWCA) was like an old-fashioned hotel, and indeed it was a nineteenth-century building, but dilapidated and rotting, its walls painted the kind of blue meant to conceal and disinfect every type of imperfection. Bare light bulbs hung from the ceiling. The floor was covered with old, damp rugs only in some places. There was a piano in one corner and an unlit fire in another. Three young foreign travellers were sitting at the table, who declined to respond to my 'Namaste'.

With the old energy of someone who thinks there is still something left in life for him to discover, I headed off to the bazaar and saw Coonoor in the usual squalor. In the traditional Indian open-air sewers, I saw a child defecating, a dog drinking water, a crow poking its beak and a goat grazing on a few isolated blades of grass, all in the space of just a few minutes. At the bottom of this hellish pit was a stream that flowed under the bridge in the town centre, where the various streets converged in front of the bus stop. A rivulet of stinking, fetid water passed through the piles of rubbish, swarming with rats, dogs, crows, cows and buffaloes which fed peacefully on it. A band of emaciated, hairless monkeys with their young clinging to them around their bellies were on top of the bridge, waiting to cross the road as the lorries drove past. On the pavement a leper sat on a jute mat mending sandals, his hands covered in pink sores.

The speciality of this bazaar was its oils. Little bottles of eucalyptus, citronella, almond, sandal and carnation oils covered in dust were lined up in dozens of shop windows, each proclaiming its own qualities to help in treating various illness.

The ashram with its Brahminic order, its clean members dressed in white and intent on contemplating the self, seemed miles away from all this. I wondered what the point of all those fine ideas was, when the society they generated was ultimately so wretched. The best way of evaluating a cause is to look at the effects it produces. So, is it the fault of the Vedas, or the colonial regime which destroyed the Vedas and killed and polluted the Indian mind? I felt more and more confused, with none of those wonderfully clear ideas I used to have when I was young, and sure that I not only understood the problems, but I had the answers to them too.

I had dinner in a kind of greasy spoon run by a Muslim. At my table were also some young Indians drinking chai, and learning to use the great innovation of the moment – a mobile phone. Despite a bad tummy ache, I managed to sleep in a wide, rickety bed, with the light from the bathroom next door shining through the pane of glass above the door joining the two rooms. The only way to turn it off was via a switch in the hallway, which unfortunately turned off all the other lights on the floor as well.

I had breakfast in front of the piano with the husband of the woman who ran the hotel. He sat with me to give me company and told me he had a degree in Tamil literature, but now had reinvented himself as a 'holistic doctor', which was how he introduced himself to me. Health care has become one of the fastest-growing markets in the world, and he too was trying to carve out his own slice of this particular pie, which seems to attract so many good-for-nothings and swindlers. He dealt in yoga, siddha,[20] numerology, magnetism and a host of other odd things. To give me a demonstration of his abilities, from his armoury of plastic objects he pulled out his acupressure equipment and a battery-operated mask for massaging the eyes and restoring sight. There had been an alternative medicine fair in Madras to which he had gone to stock up on new products. He had already collected a series of statements from people claiming they had been healed of this or that illness. The list of diseases he claimed he could cure was impressive. He was about to buy some land, on which he wanted to build a holistic health centre. The bungalows for the inpatients were to be built as pyramids, a shape which he said 'had great healing powers in itself'. He had heard a lot about a pyramid with such properties at the Perks school near Coimbatore and intended to go there soon to find out more about it.

I didn't know whether to laugh or strangle him, especially when he asked me to help by sending him foreign patients. In the end, I did neither. Instead, I noticed a young man outside the door in a dreadful state, who looked Japanese, and chose to talk to him. I asked him to come and eat with me. I wasn't wrong: he was from Tokyo and was thirty years old. He had been horrified by the way his compatriots lived, 'working all their lives just to die',

[20] An ancient system of medicine originating from Tamil Nadu, which is similar to Ayurveda, but which some maintain is influenced by Chinese medical practices.

and had decided he would 'rather die than work', which was why he had come to India. He had no money and said he was sleeping in stations, churches and temples. He was dirty and sickly, and didn't look like he was that far away from reaching his goal.

I got back to the ashram soaked to the skin. The sudden torrential monsoon rains had begun, and I had been caught in them. I took this as an advantage to do my washing, change my sheets and mop out the room before starting up with the life of the ashram again, suitably refreshed.

The noxious fumes of the lorries and the polluted atmosphere of Coonoor had set my old allergies off again: one of my sinuses was blocked, my eyes were watering and I was sneezing constantly. This was one reason not to take part in the group meditation, which I would otherwise have disrupted, and to go and sit instead on my own in the temple up on my hill, which was open to all the horizon and to every breeze. From up there, the world looked so beautiful, when contemplated with the detachment of one who wants nothing from it and has no desire to change it.

But the world did have a way of creeping into the ashram. One day, a famous businessman from Madras arrived with his family. They were devoted followers of the Swami, and among his most generous benefactors. I had to go to dinner with them. Another day, around a dozen of the Swami's ex-pupils arrived. They too had become swamis, and were themselves now teaching the Vedanta in various cities around India. They were there to discuss a subject which I too got involved in: conversions. This was a topic I realized the Swami cared deeply about, for all his feigned detachment from the things of this world. He had written articles and spoken on the subject throughout India. He had submitted a formal petition to the United Nations several months ago in a speech when he asked the international body to step in to block the number of conversions to Christianity in India.

His argument was that conversions constituted an act of violence; they changed the shape of the local culture, bringing about tensions and conflicts which during these days in particular it was preferable to avoid. He said that religions generally fell into one of two categories: those which are aggressive and missionary in nature, such as Christianity and Islam and those which do not seek to proselytize, such as Judaism, Zoroastrianism and Hinduism. The former category comprised 'strong' religions while the latter comprised 'weak' religions. In instances of conflict between the two categories, the latter was always bound to lose. This was particularly true of Hinduism, which has no centralized structure, and one of whose principles is to recognize the freedom of all to worship whichever god they want under whatever name they like.

This wasn't the position that previous swamis had adopted. In the nineteenth century, for example, the great mystic Ramakrishna, who during his spiritual preparation had spent time in a mosque as a Muslim, and for a while embraced Christianity too, maintained that all religions were equal. It was like water from the same pond being used to fill different buckets, and being called by different names according to which words meant 'water' in the respective local languages. But times had changed, the Swami said.

He felt that the Catholic Church and several Protestant denominations, especially those from the United States, were taking advantage of Hinduism's natural tolerance to invest huge amounts of capital in winning over Indian souls. This he found unacceptable. Hinduism had become a victim to genuine acts of aggression. He wasn't asking for Christians to leave India. He recognized they had been there for 2,000 years, and that they were welcome to stay another 2,000. He was only asking for them to stop destroying Indian culture, as in the past they had destroyed the ancient cultures of Africa and Latin America.

I told him that ours was the age of the free market: products, ideas and religions too. What made him think he could stand against this tide? 'The market is not free,' he replied, 'because the weak is not free in relation to the strong. Non-aggressive, non-combative religions such as ours cannot compete against rich, aggressive religions. This is why they require protection. Someone has to take action, perhaps the United Nations, but above all it is the church that must put an end to its proselytizing. If it does not, grounds will be laid for a violent reaction in India.'

I felt he was right. Conversions are just a new form of colonialism. The Swami opposing them was one attempt to re-establish the Indian tradition, as was bringing the Vedanta back into people's lives, or P.S. Varrier's attempts to re-establish Ayurveda and Kathakali theatre.

Another visitor was the doctor treating the Swami's diabetes. The Swami had a very high opinion of him: he knew the shastra, the sacred scriptures, by heart. He certainly was special. He came from a small village just a few miles from the southernmost tip of India, where he ran a small Ayurvedic clinic that he had inherited from his grandfather. We fixed an appointment – I was to go and see him at the end of the course.

Yet another visitor who stayed in the ashram for four days was a well-known Indian psychiatrist, who was working on an international, Harvard-funded project on marginals. Some of his colleagues in America and Europe were researching into drug addicts, dropouts and tramps; his task was to research sadhus and sanyasin in India.[21] When he heard I was there, he insisted on talking to me.

I think he felt I was an interesting case, a marginal who somehow straddled both East and West. I don't know how I was supposed to contribute to his research, but he certainly contributed to mine. He told me he had spent a long time in the Himalayas looking for people with powers, and as a scientist, had been forced to admit that he hadn't met any. He also said he had been to see Sai Baba, again for research. Sai Baba is the most famous holy man around at the moment, with millions of followers in India and elsewhere. This man appeared to have taken a real dislike to him: Sai Baba was vain and wore make-up. He said many of the followers he surrounded himself with were psychologically childish, in need of a father figure and something to play with. And magic is a wonderful toy!

What worried him most as a psychiatrist was the fact that some of his patients had gone off to become disciples of Sai Baba. The holy man had persuaded them to abandon their therapy and stop taking medicine, and by the time they came back to him for treatment, they were often in a more terrible state.

Regarding Sai Baba's miracles, the psychiatrist told me that a famous magician from Calcutta, P.C. Sorcar, had once gone to visit him at his ashram and concealed himself among the faithful who were there for the darshan. When Sai Baba stood before him, like

---

[21] Sadhus renounce the world, often at a very young age, and go around India living as 'holy beggars'. They are often people of low social rank. Unlike sanyasis, who usually become such in an initiation ceremony at the end of a more or less normal life, sadhus do not always take formal vows. They too wear orange or red. There are several million of them in India. All sanyasis are sadhus but all sadhus are not sanyasis. Both may become swamis once they have been recognized as teachers.

he did with everyone else, to give him some of the vibhuti that rained down 'miraculously' from his fingers, out of nothing the magician produced a rasmalai – the sugary sweet which Sai Baba is notoriously fond of – in the palm of his hand. Magician versus magician. Sai Baba's bodyguards immediately grabbed hold of him and frogmarched him out of the ashram. The psychiatrist said the other magicians had challenged Sai Baba to 'miracle' contests, but he always declined the invitations.

'I'd better go and see him for myself!' I thought. At this point I realized my old desire to travel wasn't dead after all. Getting rid of my desires had proved harder than I had thought.

One morning as I left my room, I noticed someone else had left their washing out to dry on the line where I hung mine. They were female items of clothing and my mind immediately turned to the attractive belly dancer instructress who was visiting the ashram for a few days and who I knew was staying near me.

I went to the puja, the meditation and the lesson, but despite my best intentions, and almost unnoticed, that fascinating, indomitable part of us which is the mind, was off and running. It completely eluded my attempts to control it, and though I wanted it to be where I was, it was back at the washing line with the belly dancer; although I wanted to talk to no one, it was already immersed in an imaginary conversation, asking questions, giving answers and expressing desires.

Of course I had a choice, as the Swami used to say. I could be the 'me' that desires or I could be the 'me' that laughs at the 'me' that desires. But this was easier said than done. I could have gone to the Swami with my problem, and I would have done so ... even without going to the lengths that a pupil of the founder of Zen Buddhism went to in the temple of Shaolin in China centuries ago, or so the legend goes.

The master, an Indian named Bodhidharma, who in China was known as Da Muò and then in Japan as Daruma, was always deep in meditation and no one ever managed to get to talk to him. One time, his pupil, exasperated by this, chopped his left arm off to attract his master's attention, allowing the blood to leave a great red stain in the snow.

'What do you want?' the master finally asked him.

'To quieten my mind.'

'Fine. Bring me your mind, and I'll quieten it.'

The pupil set off. 'I can't find it,' he said when he returned.

'See?' the master said. 'Your mind has been quietened.' And he went back to meditating.

What the pupil was looking to escape from was the network of his thoughts. What the master helped him see with this discovered is that it is the thought itself which is the problem.

Could I really go to the Swami and tell him what I was thinking? I knew only too well what the thought in question was. Exactly the same which the moralizing monk in another well-known Zen story was thinking.

Two monks were walking along a road that had flooded following a downpour. After a while, they came face-to-face with a beautiful girl, who was dressed smartly and hence had some difficulty in crossing a large puddle. One of the two monks took her in his arms and put her down where it was dry. The other monk said nothing, but that evening, in the temple where they were to spend the night, he couldn't help but say by way of a rebuke:

'We monks are supposed to steer clear of women, especially young, attractive women. Touching them is even more dangerous. Why did you do it?'

'I left the girl on the other side of the puddle,' the accused replied. 'You appear to have brought her with you.'

This was the state I was in. A couple of items of clothing hung up on a washing line had reactivated a mechanism which I thought I was free of forever. More than the thought itself, however, what humbled me was the fact that I had been unable to control my mind and that the more I attempted to control it, the more it played new tricks on me. Then I remembered Sundarajan.

One time, when we were up on the hill together, he told me of his love for his statue and said he 'had never known a woman'. He alluded to some kind of power which he had used all his life to keep his instincts at bay. I went to see him and shared my problem with him very openly.

'Don't you know the exercises?'

I had to confess, I didn't. He did these exercises along with his yoga every morning, just after getting up. They were extremely effective, he said, in making the sperm reascend and be transformed into spiritual energy, thus removing from the mind the stimulus which unleashed it.

'Kneel down. I'll teach you.'

He got me to kneel down and lean forward, with my head and hands on the ground. He explained how I was to curl my tongue as far back as possible towards the throat, showed me how to breathe, what to do with the muscles in my lower abdomen and with my sphincter. He also confided another couple of secrets and had me watch him perform each of the movements so that I wouldn't make mistakes. I was to begin with just a few moments every day, then gradually build up.

The very idea of this power fascinated me. Isn't the world great? On one hand, you've got someone inventing Viagra, and on the other there are people looking for ways to muzzle this impertinent part of our biological equipment. Man really is amazing!

I don't know whether Sundarajan's exercises did cause my

semen to reascend like he claimed, but once I had added these exercises to my potpourri routine in the mornings – some yoga, qigong, a few exercises for the eyes, the prostate and the backbone, smiling and saying hello to my stomach, and Master Hu's 'ball' – I was able to report, truthfully, as it happened that the system he had taught me had the desired effect.

Day after day, week after week, almost three months had now passed. The weather had changed. The monsoon season was here and the winds brought short, sharp, wonderful downpours of rain. The mountains I looked at everyday for company had also changed colour. They had turned grey and were shrouded in mist. And I too was once more calm and at peace. I felt as though I had got to know India a bit better, it had been the most unusual experience; and if I had ever been tempted to consider the possibility of living a life of pure contemplation, now I knew that it wasn't for me. The Vedanta? In the end, it felt like something to which I was already naturally sympathetic: I didn't feel like I was separated from the world, nor that I was a little wave that had been overcome by the ocean. Deep down, I was no longer scared by the idea of dying.

As far as my desires were concerned, I had decided to try and control some of them and just live with some of the others – the ones which I had consciously decided I wanted to keep. As for jagat, the world, I agreed with the Swami that it had been put together very, very cleverly. In which case, I might as well try and enjoy it. In denying themselves, I felt the brahmacharis were missing out on something wonderful.

I was spending more and more time with nature. From my hilltop, I would stand and watch the white froth and foam of some of the waterfalls; and further down in the lush, verdant valley, I would look at the distant outline of an old, majestic, solitary tree. The Swami said that the trees are like sadhus, in the sense that while everything around them is moving, they remain magnificently still, aware of themselves, without the need to run here and there in search of something else. I could never become like that. It just wasn't my nature. I wasn't born to be a monk, but I could try. I might even enjoy it. But it wasn't for me, and the most ludicrous thing that could happen to me was that someone would take me for one.

But that was exactly what happened. A group of peasants in a neighbouring village had come to the ashram to ask for an offering to go towards helping them rebuild their temple. As I walked past, an old man called me 'Swamiji', touched my feet and then the tip of my beard. Then, with his hands suitably blessed, he touched his own face, head and chest, as if to infuse my wisdom and 'holiness' into himself.

The course was coming to an end, and as it did so, the closing ceremonies started. The most interesting of these, at least as far as I was concerned, was that of the mantra japa, where we had to repeat, hundreds of thousands of times, a prayer of thanksgiving to Dakshinamurthy, the goddess of the ashram, and protector of the Vedas. We had been given the words of the mantra in Sanskrit the previous evening, printed on a little sheet of paper for us to study and memorize. There was nothing very special in the meaning of the words: 'Om ... I prostrate myself before you, oh Dakshinamurthy, who lives in the roots of the banyan tree with all concentration ... Before the destructive power of Shiva I bow ... Om.' But as usual, the sound of the words was beautiful, with a power of their own, due particularly to the circular effect of the 'Om', the first and last syllable of the mantra as it was repeated. Repeating the same phrase hour after hour had the effect of emptying and calming the mind.

The ceremony took place in the temple. Thirteen special pujaris had come down from Coimbatore for the occasion – Brahmin priests, along with at least a hundred of the Swami's followers. Some of them were there for the darshan, to look at him, to be in his presence, the presence of one who knows himself. They had come from as far as Madras. The focus of the ceremony was the square hole for the sacred fire in the floor of the arcade to the left of the temple. The Swami was sitting there in front of it in his armchair. As a sanyasi, free of all ties with the world, including religion and its rites, he was not formally involved in the ceremony which was presided over on behalf of the shishyas by the secretary to the ashram, an elderly, very distinguished-looking gentleman, next to whom sat his wife as prescribed by the Vedas. The thirteen pujaris were all in a circle around the hole. We were behind them, and behind us was the public, many of whom were standing in order to get a better view.

The start of the ceremony was a complete disaster. According to the rules of the Vedas, the fire had to be kindled in the time-honoured fashion, by rubbing together two sticks of wood. But for some reason the spark just would not take. A brahmachari began to pray: 'Come, come soon ... don't make us wait.' All together, we repeated the mantra 'Om Namah Shivaya' in various keys, under the direction of the two widows/Vergers. But there was nothing doing. Sweaty and breathless, the pujaris took it in turns, forcibly pulling a rope tied around a stick of wood spinning on top of another covered in little strands of coconut hair that should easily have caught fire. All eyes were on it. There was a bit of smoke, the smell of heated wood from the stick which one of the pujaris was so lovingly blowing on, but there was still no spark.

'Do you have anything like this in your country?' one of the shishyas from the pensioners' brigade asked me.

'No, we have matches,' I couldn't help replying, rather rudely.

They went on like this for the better part of an hour. The poor Swami waited ashen-faced. Just a few evenings ago during the satsang, he had answered in the affirmative when I had asked him whether or not he believed a puja truly could bring rain. He said he himself had been sceptical, but had once taken part to see it duly come. So why no fire now?

I wished I myself had the power to kindle it, if only to put everyone out of their misery. And if that power consisted merely in putting some camphor oil or alcohol on the coconut hairs, as at one point it seemed to me that somebody did, discreetly passing a white ball of cotton wool to one of the pujaris responsible for rubbing the sticks together. Suddenly there was a little red glow, the smoke became denser, and soon the most gorgeous tongues of fire began to devour first the bits of wood, then the butter, the sprinkled water, the rice, and all the other things which the pujari offered up to the gods, accompanying each offering with an invocation.

Eventually they blessed us too, with a mango branch dipped in a bucket of water, and we were able to begin our great litany amid the increasingly dense clouds of smoke which the wind was blowing into our faces: 'Om hrim Dakshinamurtaye tubhyam ... Om hrim Dakshinamurtaye ...'

The mantra lasted around twelve seconds. In an hour, everyone would be able to recite it 300 times, and with 100 or so shishyas present, someone had calculated that, if account were taken of the fact that every now and again someone would have to absent themselves, in total we would have recited the mantra more than 100,000 times. And so it was. We spent four hours repeating the same words over and over again ... like a worker on a production line repeating the same actions time after time in order to assemble some useless gadget to be bought by others with the money they have earned from making equally useless things.

So life passes without meaning – I reflected to myself – both inside and outside the ashram. A succession of delays and rituals, whose only significance lies in the fact that they appear to give some meaning to the useless passing of life. In the outside world, people go to work, exchange pleasantries and play about with things which we label 'necessary'; inside the ashram, a phrase in honour of a goddess who represents knowledge is repeated thousands and thousands of times. Outside, people tremble with fear if their son or daughter fails to return home in time; here in the ashram people shudder if a fire won't light.

If we had spent our time digging a well, rather than reciting the mantra so many times, maybe two-thirds of India's population would less likely be without drinking water. But this too was a part of the madness of India that I loved so much! And anyway, Brahmins don't dig wells. I looked at the hands of those fine men, my companions dressed in white, and the pujari: clean fingernails, slender fingers. None of them looked like they had ever so much as seen a hoe, pickaxe or hatchet.

So much of India could be understood in that ceremony: the revolution of the Buddhists who had rejected all forms of ritual, the practical common sense of the Tibetans who for the purpose of reciting a mantra ad infinitum had invented the prayer wheel into which they put hundreds of little notes with the sacred formula, so that with every turn its effect is multiplied.

At least the whole ritual reminded us of how difficult it was once upon a time to kindle fire and how sacred the duty of keeping it alight was.

At the end of the last lesson of the course, one of the

brahmacharis reminded the Swami that he had promised to perform the 'miracle' of the vibhuti for us.

'Do you really want to see me do it?' he asked, smiling.

A huge chorus of 'Yessssss!!' arose from the auditorium.

'One of you come here, then.'

There was a moment's hesitation. No one had the courage. So up I leapt from my place against the wall and ran to the podium. I held my hand out to him: he smiled at me and, from the open fingers of his right hand, began to pour the sacred ash into mine. At first a sprinkling, then gradually more and more. He was rubbing his fingers together gently and the ash continued to fall. I was dumbstruck. I turned around with my hands outstretched to show my companions, and dozens of them threw themselves at me to grab a pinch of it and put it on their foreheads. It was utter chaos, practically the entire class crowded around me, while the Swami tried to calm the proceedings, saying, 'It's a joke, it's a joke! Please don't take it seriously!' He was upset, but no one was listening to him. In fact, we all liked the idea, myself included, that the Swami was able to do miracles, just like Sai Baba. Undoubtedly the biggest sceptic there, I was the one who had always refused to touch the Swami's feet, the prodigal son who had had the honour of being on the receiving end of such a 'miracle'.

By the time I returned to my desk, my hand had been wiped completely clean by the dozens of others who had taken all there was to be had of the magical vibhuti. All that was left for me was the distinction of being the most sought-after of the shishyas for the rest of the day.

After lunch, many of them came to recount their version of the events to me.

'How lovely. I don't want to know if it was a real miracle or not ... but it certainly was a prasad, an aspect of Ishwara,' the old head of the nurse's home said to me. A young female doctor had no doubt on the subject. 'Those who are further along the spiritual path acquire such powers. There's nothing odd about it.' Meanwhile, the brahmachari who had reminded the Swami of his promise, explained how it had all been a set-up and how the Swami had hidden the powder under the table he used to pull his various objects out from. All to no avail: the 'believers' didn't want to renounce their faith. I understood them: it is nicer to believe than not to believe. But it all seemed stranger and stranger to me.

When the heart surgeon came to ask me not about the vibhuti, but about whether or not I had been using the pyramid, I really did feel as though I had ended up in a madhouse. Everyone was mad in their own way and anyone who had seen me that evening in my room sitting on the floor, using an immersion heater to boil a pound of onions in a pan to help get rid of my allergy which simply wouldn't go away, would doubtless have thought the same about me.

Dawn on the last morning was crystal clear. There was a group photo, with the usual little struggle between a handful of the most 'enlightened' disciples to get as close as possible to the Swami. Then the diplomas were handed out. The Swami, suitably bedecked for the occasion like one of the statues in the temple, with a huge garland of flowers around his neck, was sitting on a chair. One by one, we paraded in front of him. A swamini, one of his pupils who had gone on to become a teacher, gave everyone petals to throw at his feet. He pronounced the name of each shishya one by one and handed over the certificate, along with a banana. Many were overcome with emotion.

'This is the most important event in my life,' Sundarajan said. Some were unable to hold back their tears. Their devotion was moving. Most of them really did see Bhagawan in the Swami. And me? At the end of these three months, I felt like a spy who had infiltrated the ranks of the enemy in order to try and learn its secrets. When they asked me to make a speech, I refused. The old paediatrician made a very nice one, on behalf of him and his wife, mixing his praise for the Swami with irony and gratitude, and quoting great Indian poets such as Kabir. Others read out poems they had dedicated to him.

Someone asked the Swami for one last piece of advice. He didn't disappoint them. 'Live a life in which you can recognize yourselves!'

This was the Swami as I knew him and would remember him.

As for us, after three months, we each departed on our various ways, each asking ourselves a bit more consciously than before, the fundamental question which in my view not all of us had received an answer to: 'Who am I?'

A DOCTOR FOR THE HEALTHY

When I arrived, the hill on the right-hand side of the road was just an ordinary hill, albeit long, with boulders strewn about it, whose odd form stood out against the horizon. By the time I left one week later, it had become a giant woman lying on her back in the rice fields, looking up to the void above her. I could make out her knees, her hips, her breasts and the outline of her chin, lips and nose against the sky.

The village was an enchanted place: the most unusual and certainly the most peaceful and tranquil I have ever been to in India. But please, do not go there hoping to find what I found. We all make of things – places, people, events – what we will, and what at any given moment we might happen to need. And nothing on earth can help us to see reality in the same way our imagination does.

The village, all white, was set against the vast, dazzlingly green expanse of rice fields, dotted here and there with the odd row of palm trees. These two colours alone were sufficient to generate a sense of peace. An asphalt road which the odd car, bus or herd of buffaloes would occasionally pass by on, came up to within a few hundred feet of an inhabited part of the village, and another, flagged with stones also used to beat rice and dry grass on, wove its way through the identical low-roofed, one-storey buildings. It finally came to a large old temple with dark, echoing caverns which seemed to be charged with some mysterious force. The temple looked to be outsized, compared with the rest of the village as though it belonged to some previous age, when all men were giants.

In front of the temple there was a patch of bare earth, in the middle of which stood an old peepal tree, a *Ficus religiosa,* majestically wide, strong and with luxuriant foliage, surrounded by a walled ledge on which old men were sitting and children were playing. Apparently, it does good to those with breathing difficulties to sit under the tree and chant mantras, for the tree itself is alive and breathes, and a great power reputedly emanates from it. A few feet away there was also a lovely trough of fresh water, closed in by an amphitheatre of steps leading downwards. That was where the village itself ended. Beyond this there were more rice fields, more rows of palm trees, and behind them, as if protecting them, the rocky hill.

According to legend, the temple was one of the two which Rama, the hero of the Ramayana, founded on his way through India. He was heading towards the island of Sri Lanka to rescue his wife, Sita, whom the evil Ravana had abducted. Rama stopped under a tree to rest, but a female demon, notorious for bothering the rishis during their meditation in the Himalayas, came and disturbed him. Rama recognized her, took hold of his bow, and 'ping!' let fly one of his unerring arrows. The she-devil was struck right in the heart, fell down dead in the rice fields and has stayed there ever since, in petrified form.

In commemoration of that event, Rama had built his temple and given the village its strange name, Derisanamcope, meaning 'the place where the arrow was fired from'.

It was also the place where L. Mahadevan lived, the young Ayurvedic doctor I had met in the ashram whom the Swami held in such high regard, not merely because he was treating him for diabetes, but also because he knew the shastra, the holy scriptures, by heart.

'Come and spend at least a week in my hospital, and we will see what we can do,' he had said when we spoke of my illness. And here I was.

I had a camp bed with a very thin, plastic-covered mattress to sleep on, in a bare room with blue walls, a black stone floor and an open window which looked out on to a little patio, a wall, a pond covered with lotus flowers, and beyond them the rice fields. I also had a Turkish-style toilet and tap in a concrete courtyard.

At lunch and dinner time, a man would come on a bicycle to bring me a three-layer dish with some chapattis, dal (the classic Indian dish made from pulses), and a portion of highly spiced vegetables.

The hospital itself had just six rooms and was some fifty yards from the tarmac road where the clinic proper was located, which it overlooked. This was where Mahadevan received his patients and where from morning till night, the servants prepared the medicines in what was generally referred to as a large 'kitchen'.

Steaming bronze cauldrons were heated over log fires, as tradition demands, with each cauldron containing its own potion. Around a dozen men and women were squatting on the floor, grinding the herbs, mixing them in the vats, filtering the oils or making balls with the compounds that had dried out in the sun as they chanted their mantras. The kitchen walls were shiny with soot, but the air was thick with aromatic fragrances which themselves seemed therapeutic.

'That is exactly how it is,' Mahadevan said to me as he took me on a tour of his little kingdom. 'The people who work here never fall ill. They do not even catch cold,' he said.

Perhaps I should have spent more time in that kitchen. It might have helped me get rid of my chronic sinus allergy that had been playing up for weeks now, giving me a streaming nose, watering eyes, sneezing fits and headaches.

On the road in front of the clinic, there was a stall serving tea to patients waiting to see the doctor, and those who had already seen him and were waiting for the bus home, pleased with their paper bags full of powders, their pills and their medicine bottles.

If it had not been for a couple of street lights which hardly ever worked, the bus itself and the small generator powering the fan in the tiny room where Mahadevan received his patients beneath a picture of the god of Ayurveda and a black-and-white photo of his grandfather who had founded the clinic. You might have thought you had stepped into one of those sepia-coloured postcards from the early nineteenth century. I had never seen India so authentic, simple and unaffected. Then, there was the doctor himself, Mahadevan, who was also rather special. Tall, thin, clear-skinned with black bushy hair and the kind of rapt expression typical of the believer, he was only thirty-five, but had the confidence of one who knows he has found the answer to everything.

'I know the scriptures, and the scriptures tell me what to do in every situation. For every patient, I have a cure, even if sometimes I do not know how it works,' he replied when I asked him if he ever had any doubts. 'But let me make this much clear: I do not cure people, it is I who cure myself. The real healer is the one we all have inside us, and above all it is him,' he said pointing to the benevolent god in the golden picture-frame hanging above him.

The first two days I spent the whole time in Mahadevan's office, morning to evening. I sat in a corner, observing him at work as he saw his patients, one after the other: some for just a few minutes, others for much longer. In each case, he managed to give the person concerned the impression that he was more interested in them than he was in anyone else in the whole world at that time. With all his patients, he asked questions first and felt their pulse afterwards. 'The left hand for women and the right hand for men,' he explained to me. Then he would gather his thoughts, lean his head to one side, close his eyes and enter what looked like a state of meditation. 'If I concentrate, by feeling a patient's pulse it is as though I can sound their entire body. I can tell so much about them this way,' he said.

Many of his patients were amazed that it was he who could tell them what it was they were experiencing, and the symptoms they had which they themselves had not been able to articulate. For everyone he had a smile, a word of advice and some medicine to collect from the chemist's adjoining kitchen.

The clinic was well known throughout the region and people came to it from far and wide. Two women said they had travelled nine hours by bus to see Mahadevan. The cases he found himself confronted with were most varied. In the course of a day, some of the many patients I witnessed included a woman with an outsized thyroid gland, one with menstrual problems, an older woman with suspected bowel cancer. There was also a man who said he had become impotent following a vasectomy in a government hospital, a young man who had returned to show the doctor how his leg had healed up after it had almost got gangrene, when shards of glass had become stuck in it following a car crash, then a diabetic, an old man suffering from the after-effects of a heart attack, one with high blood pressure and two instances of psoriasis.

Between the patients coming and going, I would ask Mahadevan questions and he would give me answers. But in his view, this was not the right way to understand his 'science'. He was very concerned that I should not get the wrong idea. So at the end of the first afternoon, he took some time to give me a proper introductory lesson on Ayurveda as I took notes.

'Ayurveda is not an alternative form of medicine; it is not in competition with Western medicine. It is merely a different type of medicine with a different philosophical basis, a different vision of the world and life,' he began.

Mahadevan knew I had spent three months with the Swami, so I was no longer unfamiliar with the Indian vision of 'the world and life'. But still, he wanted to go over some of the main points again.

'First of all, we are convinced that the sensory world is not the only form of reality and that our senses are not the only way of obtaining knowledge. For us, the shastra, the sacred scriptures which were handed down to us by the rishis, are also an instrument of knowledge. And the shastra proves to us that there is unity over and above all that which to our senses appear separate. We look at the world and it appears to be made up of separate parts. We ourselves think we are a part of it, but the truth is that the universe is a single, independent whole, and certainly not just the sum of its parts.

'In medical terms, this means that you and I and all the

other living beings, human or non-human, are mini-universes encompassed within the fullness of the larger universe. We are the microcosms which are not at all separate from the macrocosm. This means we are subject to the same influences and cosmic laws. As a science of life, Ayurveda sees man as a whole, not as a collection of parts, and argues that his health cannot be maintained independently from his social and spiritual context, nor from his connection to the rest of the cosmos.

'This approach, which you in the West refer to as "holistic", is the exact opposite of that adopted by "modern" medicine, which sees illness and disease as a dysfunction of one of the mechanisms that go to make up man.

'One can, of course, make comparisons between Ayurveda and Western medicine, they can compare a patient's clinical condition, but after a while you come to a halt because we believe it's impossible to find the answers to human problems in science alone, at least science as you define it.

'I know modern science does admit there are certain phenomena which it has not yet worked out, for which it claims the cause is unknown. We say the unknown cause is karma. But karma cannot be seen under an ordinary microscope, which is why you westerners say it does not exist. All you have to do is look at it through the microscope of wisdom and you can see it very clearly.

'Take the problem of illness. Why should an illness affect me rather than someone else? At present, Western science explains it all by genetics and there is definitely some truth in this. However, my question is: what is it that causes genes to be different? We don't know. And even if one day we do discover it, we will, afterwards, still have to find out what it was that was the cause of that cause. We can go on looking for the cause of the cause of the cause ad infinitum. But what is the ultimate cause? The rishis knew: they said it was karma.

'So where modern medicine ends is where Ayurveda begins. Modern medicine begins and ends with the physical body; Ayurveda goes beyond the body. If we look closely, we will see that you and I are more than just bodies: we are minds, selves, souls and, above all, karma.'

I liked listening to Mahadevan. It was almost as though he had been with me during the months I had spent in New York, sharing my doubts and second thoughts on the MSKCC's methods of treatment. He seemed to have answers to all the questions I had entertained and challenged my fixers with. But was it really like this? A part of me rejoiced at feeling understood, but the rest of me, as usual, remained sceptical. Certainly, the rishis understood a good deal about human nature, but was it possible to translate these fine words into a medicine for me that would be more effective than the phosphorescent liquids used in chemotherapy? After all, what the fixers had used on me was the fruit of many years of study, research and clinical testing.

'I too admire certain aspects of Western medicine,' Mahadevan said, when I put this thought across to him, 'and I too, like any Western doctor, learn from practice. But what I learn more than anything else is how right the rishis were and how clearly they saw. Sometimes I am genuinely surprised by the insights contained in the shastra, and I am happy to have them and be able to respect them. Just think, they managed to predict the hereditary consequences of certain diseases, they classified the various forms of diabetes, they knew what stress was – such a fashionable concept nowadays – they were able to describe what we now refer to as psychosomatic illnesses, and they also had a clear grasp of the idea of immunity which they set great store by.

The rishis knew about the transmission of diseases through sexual intercourse, through physical proximity, through use of the same clothing; they knew about illnesses deriving from the pollution of water and soils; they knew about epidemics. It is incredible if you think about how they got there without the help of medical instruments.

'In the shastra, there are many wonderful verses describing mental illnesses. There are much better descriptions than those found in modern medical textbooks,' he said, and to prove his point, quoted some of them to me in Sanskrit.

Then, while still on the subject of mental illnesses, but clearly referring back to my remark about of 'a medicine for me', he explained that when the shastra speaks of therapies, they do not only refer to those treatments which take effect at the physical level, as modern science does, but also psychological and spiritual levels. The three of them go together, hand in hand.

'Being treated does not mean taking a pill every six hours,' he said. 'It means purifying one's mind and then using it to sustain the healing process. It can mean bathing in a holy river, going on a pilgrimage, taking part in certain rituals or reciting mantras. Being treated means putting oneself on the path to the right lifestyle. This much was obvious to the rishis. They realized that the most important thing was not to treat illnesses as and when they arose, as Western medicine was increasingly doing, but to prevent illnesses by living a life where the body is in harmony and the mind is at peace.'

He looked at me and then added, as if to challenge my 'Occidentalism' in a friendly fashion, 'The pills you see me giving the patients are not just chemicals like yours are. They contain pranashakti, the force which gives life. They are pills for the soul as well as for the body.'

Once again, he quoted me some Sanskrit verses from the shastra, then explained that while ayurvedic medicines were indeed made from herbs, plants, sometimes minerals, powders made from precious stones and certain very special animal products, they were also impregnated with mantras, and in certain cases were prescribed on the basis of the patient's horoscope.

'It's true,' he said. 'Our medicines do not have instant effects. By their very nature they work slowly, giving the patient time to come to terms with his or her karma. Once this has been worked out through suffering, the illness passes. I admit, Western medicine is more effective in the most serious of cases, in situations requiring urgent action, such as surgery. But what Western medicine fails to understand is all the rest, especially the spiritual side of life.'

Mahadevan was a man of great faith. In his view, his science, i.e., Ayurveda, came from Brahman, the divine, omniscient creator; three or four thousand years ago the rishis had received it in meditation and some of their followers had handed it down in the shastra several years before Christ.

Maybe because I have never had faith myself, I instinctively feel sympathy for those who do. However, I ask, 'Doctor Mahadevan, you are a man of my time. How can you possibly believe that a few thousand years ago, men such as you and I managed to understand everything that we would ever need to know, even if we did have some connection with the divine? How can you believe that the shastra contains such a wealth of knowledge, including scientific knowledge, that is unchanging and hence has no need of being updated?'

'That is how it is. Ayurveda is an eternal science, for the simple reason that it does not depend on research. Science is changing all the time, but Ayurveda is not. Ayurveda is the fruit of a vision, and that vision is eternal. It cannot be altered or updated. We doctors are like birds that come and go, but Ayurveda is the tree which remains forever. The logic of this vision that the rishis had has been used now for thousands of years. My grandfather used it, and so too shall my grandchildren.'

'What about new illnesses?' I asked. 'The world we live in is changing all the time, and medicine has to adapt and respond to new requirements. Don't you think?'

'No. Circumstances may change, but the basic theory does not, for it has to do with nature. And no one has the power to change nature. Illnesses come after that. My duty as a doctor is to eliminate the suffering caused by illnesses, not the illnesses themselves. People ask me if we Ayurvedic doctors can treat AIDS, leukaemia or diabetes. My answer is that we do not treat illnesses at all; we treat people. Sometimes our patients are healed of illnesses that I do not even know the names of. You must understand this: the end of Ayurveda is to have a healthy world to live in, where all living creatures, including animals and humans, can be healthy. And healthy in this sense does not just mean in terms of the body, but especially in the case of man, in terms of our whole being.'

I asked him how he would define a healthy man. This was music to his ears. 'Swasta!' he said, then rattled off some more beautiful Sanskrit verses penned by a famous doctor who had lived at Benares in the sixth century BC. He translated them as follows:

'A person is healthy when he or she is in a state of swasta, when all the vital elements, fire and function, are in a state of equilibrium; when his or her bowel movements are regular; when his or her mind, senses and soul are calm.'

'Wonderful, don't you think?' Mahadevan enthused. 'Being healthy does not always mean all the various tests which Western medicine carries out show normal results: CAT scans, blood tests and cholesterol levels. A person can be absolutely normal in all these respects, yet still not be well. This is particularly true when the mind is not stable. Swasta means harmony and stability in the realization of the Self. This for us is true health.

'You see, in Ayurveda, the concept of health goes far beyond the normal level of consciousness. It goes beyond, shall we say, health as Western medicine understands it. The rishis truly were "seers" in the sense that they saw beyond appearances and saw inside man. They understood that human suffering is not merely physical, and that the greatest source of unhappiness is spiritual ignorance, the feeling of being separated from fullness. You know, only knowledge of the Self can solve all our problems.

'It is only in this sense that Ayurveda is interested in physical health, for physical health is important even to a yogi who turns his mind to the Ultimate Reality of Knowledge.

'It is this vision which is the basis of ayurveda. A doctor has to get into the mind of his patient using the light of his knowledge, to eliminate the ignorance which is the ultimate reason for all illnesses. Knowledge is what matters, for only knowledge is able to satisfy the mind. So you see,' Mahadevan concluded, 'Ayurveda is not a system of medicine with merely a practical, material end, namely physical health. It is a spiritual system, the purpose of which is moksha, the freedom from rebirth. Shall we continue tomorrow?'

The following morning, Mahadevan made his queue of patients wait, as he wanted to give me my next lesson first thing to help me understand more clearly how he would treat the various cases that would present themselves in the course of the day.

'When a patient is new and I have the notes I may have taken during previous examinations, the first thing I do is observe the person carefully, subject them to a series of questions and then decide what their constitutional model is,' he began. 'Everything else follows from this.'

The question of models interested me, for I too am convinced that God does not make all men completely different from one another, that he uses various models and types which result in some people being extremely similar. Each of us, in the course of our lives, discovers that we tend to make friends with the same kinds of people, i.e., with people who tend to bear the same imprint as ourselves, regardless of size, shape or colour.

'According to Ayurveda,' Mahadevan said, 'the whole universe, with all its objects and living beings including man, is made up of five different elements: earth, air, water, fire and ether. These five elements are the basis for the physical reality of the cosmos. Hence, they are inside as well as outside us; they are in the food that we eat, in the plants and herbs; they are in everything that we see and touch.

In the human body, these five elements are manifested in the tridosha, the three functional principles – vata, pitta and kapha – which govern all our physical and mental functions.

'Ether and air are elements without form, so in terms of the body they represent everything that is unstable or restless. This is vata. Meanwhile, pitta is produced by fire, and kapha comes from water and earth. These three principles are manifested in different forms in every organ and cell of the body. In the body, one element generally ends up prevailing over the other two, or two together over the third. This dominant element is extremely important to an ayurvedic doctor. It determines a person's constitutional model. Hence, we say a person is vata if the ether or air element predominates in him or her. A person is pitta when the element he or she primarily manifests is fire. And so on. We are given these constitutional models when we are born and they remain more or less constant for the rest of our lives. Some factors which determine this model are hereditary, astrological factors linked to a person's physiology or their karma.'

'Astrological factors?'

'Certainly,' he replied. 'The planets' influence also determines a person's character with regard to their health.'

I didn't understand how, but with just three models it was possible to establish who was made with which model, so I asked Mahadevan to describe a vata person to me.

'A person who is vata,' he said, 'is thin, has no fat and little hair, and what hair he or she does have tends to be dry and prone to dandruff. Their eyes are small and gloomy. Vata is a person who can eat as much as he or she likes, but never gets fat, is usually tall and has long hands and feet. He or she has a weak immune system. Sometimes they have a healthy appetite, sometimes not. Sometimes their bowel movements are regular, sometimes not, precisely because of the unstable nature of vata. Instability is the consistent feature of the vata person; he or she is restless, never sits still and is indecisive. Such a person has difficulty in sleeping and tends to speak a great deal. Some of their limbs may not be straight. They dream, but have lots of nightmares. Their first reaction to anything new is fear. They have poor memories, they earn lots of money, but never manage to save. They spend all they have right away. They hate the cold and want to be protected. They believe in an imaginary world. They can spend long periods of time in meditation.'

This didn't sound like me. 'And pitta?'

Pitta is a manifestation of agni, meaning fire. So a person who is pitta is full of energy, warm, greasy and intellectual. He or she has a healthy appetite and find it difficult to sleep. They tend to sweat a lot, they get grey hair while still young, cannot bear the heat, don't like being in the sun, adore ice cream, are irascible and quick to lose their temper, but it all blows over equally quickly.'

This didn't fit me completely, either.

'Kapha is the opposite of vata,' Mahadevan went on. 'A person who is kapha is fat, often obese, very stable. He or she moves slowly, has a red face and greasy hair and the whites of his or her eyes tend to be very pronounced. Kaphas are perfectionists, calm and tolerant.' Clearly I didn't think I was a kapha either.

When one of these elements increases in relation to the others, it gives rise to illnesses,' Mahadevan continued. 'Illnesses cause a breakdown in the original equilibrium between the three constituent elements. There are many possible causes for this, but some of the most important include the wrong diet or lifestyle, trauma, some external factor or a factor linked to supernatural forces. We believe emotions are often responsible for the breakdown of this equilibrium. Emotions have their own tastes, just like food does, which influence these three constituent elements and forces one of them to increase at the expense of the others. Pain is bitter, desire is sweet, anger is spicy; greed is salty, which aggravates kapha.'

He reminded me of Dan Reid, who used to quote the Chinese medical tradition in saying that it was necessary to pay attention to those emotions which are the cause of illnesses: anger, fear, hatred and jealousy all contribute to ill health, whereas others such as charity, compassion, joy or mad laughter – as Norman Cousins had discovered – help a person to remain healthy. All this made sense to me.

Did my grandmother not encourage me, when I was small, to go to the toilet immediately after I had had a fright? This was an old-fashioned way of clearing out the residual negativity from the system, while its staying there might have had harmful consequences. I mentioned this to Mahadevan, who said, 'It is the same in India with adults as well. If a person who has lost someone dear to them and is unable to cry, their relatives use onions, put smoke in their eyes, or if that does not work, start hitting them in order to release their pent-up emotions.

'Illnesses also have their own nature linked to the three different categories,' Mahadevan went on, 'so there are vata, pitta and kapha illnesses. On its own, an illness is neither serious, curable nor incurable. Everything depends on the context it occurs in. A kapha illness is serious when it occurs in a person who is of kapha constitution. From this, you may infer that in Ayurveda there is no generalized treatment for one and the same illness. Not even for a cold. The same illness in people of different constitutions must be treated differently, even if a surplus of one constituent element in different persons is manifested in different illnesses, which are nonetheless to be treated in the same way. This is because the treatment involves re-establishing the balance between vata, pitta and kapha, whatever the illness may be. Such treatment is allopathic, if you see what I mean, in the sense that it involves using the opposite constituent to the person's constitution rather than the same one, as in homeopathy. For example, a kapha person who is predominantly damp and cold, is treated using a remedy that involves heat, dryness and spicy flavours. A person who is pitta, who is fiery and hot, is treated using refreshing herbs. Food with different flavours is an important medicine in its own right.

'Once the patient's constitutional model has been established, and once an idea has been formed of what might have caused the imbalance, where the illness began, in what season, what the patient's immune system is like, their willpower, their diet, their lifestyle, and so on, the rest becomes easy. For every case there are only two forms of treatment: what has increased must be reduced, and what has reduced must be increased.'

'Using what?'

'Anything can be useful because nothing in the universe is useless. We might think we can do without scorpions or poisonous snakes, but this is not so. Everything has value and exists in order to nourish all other things, and in return is nourished itself. Nothing is entirely good or bad. Everything in the universe may be used as a medicine. In some situations, we prescribe nothing, for nothing too can be something.'

How could I fail to be fascinated by such a vision of the universe? The day before, I had seen a man bringing leeches to the clinic and I wanted to know what they were for, given that modern medicine has now written them off as an example of the barbaric treatments of the past.

There were two kinds of leeches, Mahadevan said. One was poisonous, which he used in certain instances of arthritis, and the other, more common ones were good for eye cysts. Both types came from the pond with the lotus flowers near the hospital where I was staying.

We could hear the number of patients waiting outside beginning to grow, so to bring our conversation to a close, Mahadevan turned to his beloved scriptures once again.

'Sukarta sarva bhutanam ... The purpose of my science is to create the conditions in which all living creatures can be healthy. The best way is not to cure illnesses, but to prevent them. The duty of an Ayurvedic doctor is to teach people to live with balance, judgement and awareness.

'Until 200 years ago,' Mahadevan continued, 'the wisdom of the shastra had been a part of people's everyday lives, especially in southern India. Every family's kitchen had been equipped with herbs and spices to be used in the preparation of food. Everyone knew what to avoid and what would be good for them, given their own constitution. For example, someone who is vata naturally had to steer clear of dry, cold foods. But first colonialism, then modernity had caused people to depart from their own millennial, Ayurvedic tradition, especially in the cities.'

Today, Ayurveda was under threat from a new danger, Mahadevan said; commercialism, he called it. The term 'Ayurveda' was now liberally used to advertise all kinds of products, in particular cosmetics which had nothing to do with Ayurveda at all. Indeed, Ayurveda had become a kind of tourist attraction in Kerala, with various centres offering massages of every kind. An ashram purporting to call itself 'Ayurvedic' had become very popular with foreigners, especially as it practised free sex as a way of helping people 'detach themselves from their desires'.

I had been at Derisanamcope for three days when Mahadevan finally said he would deal with my case. It would be impossible to do so in the clinic itself, where there was always something else demanding his attention. Only at his home were we assured the peace and quiet we would need. He let his cousin, himself a doctor, handle all the other patients for him that afternoon, and invited me to his house.

The Mahadevan family – the name means 'Great God' and also another term for Shiva – was one of the most important in the village. But their house, one of the low buildings which lined the flagstoned road, was in no way distinct from the others. Like all the rest, it had a little porch in front of it with a raised concrete patio, where visiting sadhus could stop and rest or even spend the night, sheltered from the elements. This was a traditional way of extending hospitality to holy beggars; as Mahadevan explained to me, the women of the house could bring them drinks and food to eat without their actually having to come in.

Mahadevan's house was also built around a central courtyard, overhung by the roofs of the various surrounding rooms. The whole family lived in those apartments, with none of the absurd distinctions we take for granted in the West between sitting room, bedroom and kitchen. The courtyard served to collect the rainwater for washing clothes and bathing. Only when returning from a funeral, Mahadevan told me, was it necessary to perform one's ablutions on the porch, i.e., outside the house. The toilet had to be at least 200 yards away from the house, and I did not even see it.

I detected a certain amount of pride in the way Mahadevan explained to me the various customs of his family and village. It was the pride of the Brahmins who had remained faithful to their traditions and had managed to keep their way of life stable and healthy over the centuries. The holy scriptures had been their guide in this. Indeed, the Vedas laid down the rules for every kind of activity, and the solution for every circumstance with the utmost precision. The Vedas contained instructions on what was to be said and done, and how and when it was to be said and done. By adhering to this code of conduct, they were able to ensure order, harmony, and even good health.

The old ways still dictated the rhythm of Mahadevan's days. The whole family would wake up at 4.30 a.m. for the morning religious ceremony. The first act this involved was to look at the palms of their hands before joining them together in a sign of greeting, to remind themselves that the 'I' which is symbolized by the hands is not the one which dies or decides things.

'Anyone who thinks they themselves are the author of an action has understood nothing,' said Mahadevan, paraphrasing a verse from the Gita. 'The "I" should not be repressed, but made subordinate to the fact that everything is Ishwara, God, and that the only thing we should aspire to is moksha, or release from having to be reborn.'

Mahadevan's father, a retired lawyer responsible for running the clinic, wanted to show me the corner of the house where the puja was performed, and the old drum that had been in the family for generations and which they used to strike the note which the mantras were chanted at. It appeared to be the only valuable item the family possessed. All I could see of the rest of the house was tidy and clean.

It was Mahadevan's father who explained to me that in Kerala, some Brahmin families had kept the Ayurvedic tradition alive even during the times of decline, by handing down the sacred scriptures which they had learnt by heart from generation to generation. As Ayurveda was divided into eight sections, each family was responsible for one of them. This was how things had gone until the time of his own father, who had founded the clinic in 1924. His son, my doctor, Mahadevan, had been blessed from birth with an outstanding memory. From his early days he had learnt the scriptures from his grandfather, had gone on to study at one of the leading schools of Ayurveda and now knew virtually all the sacred texts by heart.

When the old lawyer went off to the clinic, Mahadevan and I sat down before the portrait of the family's protector god, an incarnation of Shiva. Both of us had our notebooks at the ready.

Mahadevan said that he had been watching me over the past couple of days, but had not been able to classify me yet. He was unsure of what constitutional model I belonged to, but the way in which he was to help me would depend on this classification. So he began to subject me to a barrage of questions which touched on every aspect of my life: my tastes, preferences for different kinds of foods, my habits – especially those of my bowels – my way of sleeping and dreaming, my sex drive, my memory, my ability to sit still for long periods of time deep in meditation, or not as the case may be; my way of sweating and responding to external stimuli. Did I prefer to remain silent or to talk? Was I curious? If I got angry, did it blow over immediately?

This interrogation extended even to the medical history of my family, hereditary diseases and what had left the deepest impression on me when I was a child: the funerals of my aunts, both of whom died of tuberculosis, then my maternal grandfather who had died the same way. On returning from the cemetery, I recalled how they had madc a huge bonfire to burn everything of his so that the infection would not be passed on to anyone else, and how straight afterwards my grandmother, my wonderful farmer's wife grandmother, came to live with us, bearing only the clothes she was wearing at the time. And then, the constant fear that I too would fall ill, and the blood tests that had made my arm burn. These were the most memorable experiences of my childhood, but Mahadevan didn't seem in the slightest bit interested. But as for my haemorrhoids, now those really did interest him!

'What? You've been operated on twice? One time twenty-five years after the other?' He wanted as much information as possible.

In his view, haemorrhoids are a maharoga, a major illness. He recited scriptural verses in Sanskrit on this subject, as if to confirm the sanctity of what he was saying. Then he looked at the notes he had made, focused himself, and said that 80 per cent of my answers were those of a person who was vata and the rest were those of who was pitta, plus the odd kapha element which he reckoned had come in with my illness and did not really belong to my constitutional model. So I was a halfway house – a vata/pitta.

The rest would all follow from this diagnosis.

'On the basis of what you have told me,' he said, 'I don't think your vital elements have been in equilibrium since the time of your childhood. Your immune system has always been weak. There has always been interference from kapha, which has meant you have lung problems. Then there are your haemorrhoids, which for us is an important sign that something serious is wrong in the lower part of your abdomen where vata is concentrated. In your case, vata is not flowing in the right direction, so has started going another way and begun to rise upwards, producing an amalgamation of kapha and pitta in the stomach. This is what caused the serious illness from which you are now suffering. This is the pathology.'

The seriousness of my situation derived from the fact that there was an imbalance between the three vital elements, vata, pitta and kapha. To make matters worse, he felt there was a serious constitutional lack of agni, the internal fire on which our entire metabolism depends.

'Aham vaishvanaro bhutva praninam deham asritaha ... I am fire, and I manifest myself in digestion,' he declaimed.

'Gita, Chapter 15, sloka 14,' I replied. I had just been studying it and was happy to show off. He liked this – it meant I understood!

'Agni is Krishna,' Mahadevan continued. 'It is a god, to which we devotedly offer our food, as water, butter, fire and the rest are offered to him during a puja. We make offerings to the god and the god protects us. But when a person's agni is abnormal for long periods of time, a large build-up of toxins accumulates.'

'Where?' I asked. 'In which organ?'

'No, no, this type of toxin cannot be demonstrated,' he replied. Then he explained that all the pathologies of the gastro-internal system have to do with agni, and seeing as I had a kapha pathology and a weak agni, I was destined to have a serious illness; it could have been leukaemia or any other form of cancer.

Could anything be done about it?

'Yes,' said Mahadevan. The answer was to increase my digestive fire in order to build up my resistance and hence, reverse the trend towards imbalance. The treatment was simple: it was a question of taking agni, fire, from herbs and plants, and getting it into my body by means of a potion which he himself would prepare for me.

'I will mix all the herbs together which have fire in them, plus a plant which in Sanskrit is called agni. When you take this medicine, you must avoid all foods containing sugar or ghee (clarified butter), and eat as many citrus fruits as possible, such as pomegranates, lemons and oranges.'

He felt that in this way I would be able to solve the basic problem because illness is not the natural condition of man, as he said to me. I had a strong will to live and the healer within me would soon spring into action to help me.

I asked him what he thought of the tangible increase in cancer rates among the populations of industrialized countries. He felt it was due to what he described as the 'perverse' use of people's time and intelligence – he gave the example of the mindless jobs so many of us are forced to do – and becoming increasingly enslaved by the objects we relate to via our senses.

'The more people move away from nature, the more they get ill. Man today is becoming increasingly selfish. He thinks only of having fun, of enjoying himself and indulging in eating and drinking. Many illnesses are caused by eating too much. It uses up too much agni. Eating in moderation causes no illness whatsoever. The old rules of social and personal behaviour are being followed less and less ...'

According to Mahadevan, the proper method of eating involves only half of the stomach actually being filled with solids; one-quarter should be filled with liquids and the other quarter with air. It is necessary to drink while you eat, but talking should be avoided at all costs so as not to increase the amount of air consumed. No more working lunches, then!

He concluded, in the now familiar way, by quoting from the same great Ayurvedic doctor from Benares, who compared the human body to the axle of a cart. In the sixth century BC he wrote:

'As the axle is worn down and eventually snaps if the cart is loaded too heavily, if the road is too bumpy, the unskilled driver or the wheels are not strong enough, so the length of human life is reduced or even halved if the body is subjected to excessive strain, if its diet is not congenial, if meals are taken irregularly, if the correct positions are not maintained, if sex is indulged in with excessive frequency, if the body is exposed to noxious gases or fumes, if those desires which are able to be suppressed are not suppressed, or if those which may not be repressed are repressed, and if the company of unworthy people is kept.'

'You see,' Mahadevan went on, 'it is from behaviour such as this, which is contrary to the morality of life, that illnesses arise. But Western medicine takes no notice of this; it fails to look for the true cause of the illness and ends up sweeping things under the carpet.'

This all seemed a bit superficial to me. I remembered my fixers in New York, who all things considered, had done lots of tests and thought long and hard before subjecting me to their various potions. I felt moved to defend them.

'Doctor Mahadevan, with your methods you would never have discovered my cancer of the kidney. An extremely sophisticated test was required to do that.'

'So what? I often see patients with congenital cysts in their kidneys which they themselves are not aware of. They live perfectly happy lives.'

'But what I had wasn't a cyst. They analysed it in a laboratory and discovered it was cancer,' I said to him. I lifted up my kurta to show him exactly how much work had gone into getting that thing out of me.

'So if a person is living their life quite happily, why bother removing a part of their body and sending it to a laboratory? I think those doctors disturbed you unnecessarily. Look here,' he said, pointing to my hernia.

I liked his choice of the word 'disturb'. They had indeed removed me from a state of peace. Perhaps he wasn't so mad after all. Even the fine fixers hadn't been able to tell me how long that particular foreign body had been residing in my kidney, or how quickly it had grown. Maybe it could have stayed there for the rest of my days, without me having to be cut up so much or go through so much trauma, perhaps also without the hernia that had ripped such a nasty hole in my belly.

Maybe young Mahadevan was not wholly wrong. While I was still in New York, I had read of a study commissioned by the American Senate, according to which virtually half of the operations carried out in the United States were pointless. On an average they cost more than 10,000 people their lives in the course of each year. Had mine been one of them?

'What actually is illness?' I asked.

'Illness is a form of disharmony with the cosmic order,' Mahadevan replied convincingly.

To suggest my illness was as grand as this seemed a bit too much, but the idea appealed, not because, if true, it would mean I would no longer need to put myself under the surgeon's knife, have phosphorescent liquids pumped into me, or fall back into the Spider's clutches.

The whole afternoon had now passed and Mahadevan's father,

who had returned from his clinic, suggested I stay and eat with them rather than sending me food via a man on a bicycle.

As we sat waiting for Mahadevan's mother and young wife to prepare the dinner, the father wanted to talk to me about the temple. This was one of his great concerns. It was falling apart, there was no longer a pujari, and if restoration work was not carried out on it soon, the roof would cave in when the rains started to come down.

He told me that for many generations, the local king's family had taken responsibility for it, but now that this had lapsed, the temple had passed into the custody of the village Brahmins. However, since these were mostly people of very few means, he had now taken it upon himself to raise funds to restore it, and pay for one pujari to perform at least one of the necessary rites each day.

From a distance I was introduced to Mahadevan's young wife. They had been married for just a few months. She had been chosen for him by his parents and he seemed happy enough with this arrangement.

The dinner was very simple. The men ate first, attended to by the women. When Mahadevan finished eating, I noticed he passed his dirty plate to his wife, who without washing it, dished out her own portion of food on to it. She then went and sat next to her mother-in-law who was eating out of her husband's dirty plate. I had never seen this done before.

'They see it as an honour,' Mahadevan explained to me. 'Another old, traditional custom.'

I imagined the response this scene would provoke among European or US feminists, and the responsibility they might have felt to 'liberate' the two women concerned from the sexist oppression of their respective husbands. Then it occurred to me that the same feminists might at the same time have been very interested in Mahadevan's medicine, because it tends to be Western women who are most open to things that are new, who are more flexible and willing to see the world in an alternative light. But can we embrace one aspect of a civilization which has remained unchanged for centuries while rejecting another? Surely the whole is linked together by ties that cannot be severed at whim according to our own preferences. Take it or leave it was how I saw it.

Mahadevan insisted on accompanying me back to the hospital. It was dark, and there were no lights. He was afraid I might fall. I took advantage of our walk together to ask him what he thought about courses such as Ramananda's one on yoga and sound. Could music help even cells like mine that had gone mad?

'Certainly. Cells too have a conscience,' he replied. 'Only two parts of our bodies do not have a conscience: our nails and our hair. This is why it does not hurt when we cut them.'

It took a while for me to fall asleep that evening. My nose was blocked because of my sinusitis, my mouth was dry and my head was spinning with all that we had talked of that afternoon. My mind kept returning to the same old question: what was illness? I had asked Lucio Luzzatto that question while in New York, and recalled how he had sought to cover himself by responding that he preferred to talk about cancer than illness, for he felt that he knew at least something about that. I wondered how, as a scientist, he would have reacted to Mahadevan's definition of illness as being 'a state of disharmony with the cosmic order'. And yet ...

While I was a patient/client at the MSKCC, I had become interested in a story about a community of Cambodian refugees who had ended up in America after surviving the massacres perpetrated by the Pol Pot regime and the Khmer Rouge. They were living in a town near Los Angeles, when it emerged that many of them had gone blind, especially the women. There was no apparent explanation for this. One hundred and fifty women had been subjected to a series of detailed tests, which proved that they were clinically healthy, in the sense that their eyes were sending regular light and motion signals to their brains. However, they were unable to see. Perhaps they had already seen too much? They had watched as so many of their relatives had been tortured and executed in Cambodia, and now, in America, they found themselves in an entirely alien environment. Although their eyes were fine, they did not want to see any more.

Then, while in India, I had been struck by a story told by Jim Corbett, a British hunter, who had gained something of a reputation for himself through his books on jungle animals and escapades to hunt man-eating tigers. One night, while Corbett was camping at the feet of Trishul, one of the highest peaks in the Himalayas, the men in his expedition party began to dance and celebrate by the light of their bonfire. One of them was his longest-serving attendant and trusted hunting assistant. All of a sudden, this man took ill, fell to the ground and lost consciousness.

'The spirit of Trishul entered him when he opened his mouth to sing,' said the other servants and bearers. Corbett sent the man back to his own village, had him examined in a couple of hospitals, and then took him to an English doctor, who said nothing could be done.

'For the spirit to leave his body, he has to die,' the people said. And he did. The man allowed himself to die. As far as the doctors were concerned, he was healthy. So what illness did he have?

Everything was fine in terms of his body, but in terms of the man as a whole, which is what Mahadevan had been talking about, an equilibrium had been broken, the cosmic relationship had been disturbed in some way. The man, most likely a result of something other than the spirit of Trishul, had lost contact with that universal consciousness which, according to the Swami, holds the entire universe together so intelligently, and manifests itself in man as the power to live, the instinct to survive.

For science, this ayurvedic way of thinking, of seeing health and illness in terms of balance and imbalance, of broken and restored harmonies, is absurd. But I felt there was some truth in it. Illness is never an objective fact; it is above all a personal experience and is different for all of us. Each illness is the fruit of our own lives: it is *our* illness. What is absurd is not to realize this, and to think as science does, that all it takes is some medicine to put an end to our sufferings.

I liked the rishis' idea that above all, it was necessary to live properly in order to stay healthy. But are we really prepared to change our lives, which in the majority of cases are not lived properly? Change is one of the hardest things of all. It frightens us; no one ever really wants to change their way of living. This is why we're increasingly in favour of objective forms of treatment; this is why we prefer to treat asthma with nebulizers, allergies with anti-histamines and headaches with aspirin. It's so much easier and quicker than trying to understand what actually causes these illnesses in us. If we were to discover that they are caused by us living in a house that is not suitable, keeping company with the wrong kind of people, eating the wrong kind of things or doing a job that is meaningless, would we really be willing to make the change? Anyway, how does one actually go about changing? This feeling of impotence merely increases our propensity towards disease.

The following morning when I went to the clinic, Mahadevan took me into the kitchen to show me his servants working hard around a cauldron, where they were busy preparing the potion that would put the 'fire' back into me. I didn't want to go through the same experience as in Kottakkal, so I didn't ask what the herbs were being mixed with. I had decided I would take it anyway, and just seeing the devotion that went into preparing it made me feel better. Anyway, there was nothing suspicious about its smell: it was peppery, strong, but not at all unpleasant.

When I told Mahadevan I had slept badly that night because of my sinuses, he had them bring me some aromatic herbs rolled up like cigars, which he told me to burn and inhale the fumes. So I spent the rest of the day attending to my nose. I lay on my camp bed, read, burnt my herbs and enjoyed the smells and sounds which the breeze brought in through my window: children's voices, birds singing, a dog barking in the distance, noises of pans and prayer chants that arrived from the houses in the village.

By now I felt as though I had got to know this village: it was simple and tidy, without any exceptionally rich or exceptionally poor people. It was marked out by tried and tested rhythms, in harmony with the gods to whom everyone in one way or another turned their thoughts each day. Among the various acquaintances I had made, there was a retired teacher who had undertaken to look after a small shrine dedicated to Ganesh where the flagged road began. Every morning at half past six, regular as clockwork, he would open the gate, wash out the bowls and change the flowers. In the evening, he would close the gate and light a small oil lamp. This was his way of putting something back into the community, he said.

This, I imagined, was the world in which the Vedas were born. This was the environment in which Mahadevan still moved, with his medicine for the poor. Here, in conditions such as this, Ayurveda made sense. Here, one could speak of prevention, of a proper way of living and a cosmic connection. But in a modern city, everyone lives for themselves as strangers among strangers. There, health care consists solely of responding to individual illnesses, in an attempt to re-establish some semblance of normalcy in such a way as to enable the sufferer, a cog in the productive machinery, to set off once again the following morning, to be hemmed in on the underground, do his or her job and come back to his or her box flat in the evening just to flop in front of the television set. In conditions such as these, you have to have fixers; you need to use chemicals, tranquillizers, phosphorescent liquids and all the rest.

Were they of no use to me, Mahadevan and his science then? Of course they were. Mahadevan is the ideal doctor to meet while you are healthy. A doctor you should get to know while still young, so that he can teach you how to eat and fast, how to walk and stand still, how to stand and how to sit, posture being of utmost important, how to breathe using all and not just a part of your lungs, how to make love not as a kind of gymnastics but as a yogic act – seeing as so many of us know so much about yoga – and an act of union. We needed a doctor to teach us how to live our lives properly.

I took a good look at myself. Deep down, for all my openness to this culture and willingness to those who talked to me, I too was little more than a pirate from the West, who had set off for an adventure on the last ship bound for the Orient, ready to carry off some medicine as his booty. I could have found it and used it, but could I honestly hope that, as a patient from another world, it would have the same effect on me as it would have on someone else from this world, someone who had also bathed in a holy river, taken the trouble of going on a pilgrimage, or even simply chanting mantras.

In other words: can we entrust ourselves to holistic medicine, at the same time without living a holistic lifestyle? To do that would take much more than meditating, drinking infusions, doing yoga and using herbal remedies just so that we can call ourselves 'holistic' from the thirty-seventh floor of a skyscraper in New York, or even from some fashionable apartment in Milan! Was Ayurveda not just another example of the de-territorialization – or de-temporalization – of which Leopold had spoken?

There was a surprise for me on one of my last evenings at Derisanamcope, when I returned from the temple which had become the preferred destination for my daily walks at sunset. There were two new guests in the room next to mine: the old paediatrician and his wife, my fellow shishyas from the ashram. I had always liked them and it was a real joy to see them there. He was short, strong and dignified; his farewell speech to the Swami had been a masterpiece of intelligence and devotion. She was taller, upright, always an affectionate helpmate to her husband.

We sat on the patio in front of our rooms, waiting for the man on his bicycle to bring us our dinner. We recalled some of our experiences at the ashram, then his wife began to speak about her family, something the Indians do with as much ease as the Italians. But this is where the comparison ends, for the conversation which ensued could never have taken place in Italy nor, for that matter, anywhere else on this planet.

The wife was still busily telling me how many children and grandchildren they had and what each of them did, when her husband interrupted her to inform me that just before they had left home to come for the Vedanta course, they had summoned everyone – children, sons and daughters-in-law, grandchildren – to tell them that from that day onwards, after a life in which neither of them had eaten meat and only he had drunk alcohol, they had now come to a joint decision to abstain from sexual intercourse as well. He, aged sixty-two and she aged sixty, they had taken a vow of chastity so as to be able to devote all their energies and attentions to spiritual objectives. The children, sons and daughters-in-law and grandchildren all congratulated them on their decision and threw a huge party in their honour.

'The feeling of power you get from taking a decision like this is almost as great as the pleasure itself,' he said, as he concluded his account. Then he recalled how, when he was a child, his father always used to tell him that a man could capture and milk a tiger if he was determined enough.

'Our minds are incredibly powerful. We can do anything with them,' his wife added. She had been a nurse, and for years had run a school for nurses. Now she and her husband had only one goal: to attain moksha in this life.

They had come to Mahadevan's clinic to undergo the panchakarma, the five purifying treatments with oils which, according to the classical yogic tradition, serve to strengthen the body so that the person can devote himself or herself more completely to liberation.

'When the one who meditates retreats from his senses, like a tortoise withdrawing its limbs, his vision becomes fresh and stable,' the old paediatrician said, quoting verses from the Gita.

I was fascinated; inwardly I admired them for their determination. There was nothing holier-than-thou in what they were doing, merely the conviction – pretty obvious, really – that if one wants to pursue an objective, they must channel all their energies in that, rather than in the opposite direction. Their objective was to be released from their bodies, so there was no reason why they should continue to pay heed to the senses of those bodies.

Indian tradition has always held abstinence to be an indispensable prerequisite to knowledge. The young person who went to live in a gurukulam took vows as a brahmachari because at that time his goal was to get to know the inner world, the self, not the external world which is perceived through the senses. Once his time with the guru had come to end, so too did the commitment to being a brahmachari, so from that moment on it was right for the young man to pursue all kinds of pleasures.

Sex itself has never been seen as wrong or an instrument of the devil in India – at least, not until the Muslim conquest. For centuries, the Kamasutra has been carved into the stones of the temples in India at Khajurao. Even today, they sell erotic engravings etched in bamboo leaves at the markets in the countryside, so that mothers can teach their daughters how to be good lovers when they get married.

Together, the paediatrician, his wife and I recalled how the Swami would playfully compare the Indian attitude towards genitalia with that of the West. He himself spoke freely on the subject, saying how wise the ancients had been to place the lingam and the yoni at the centre of their religion. They had realized there was nothing more perfect and sacred than those two organs to which we all owe our lives. Westerners cover their genitals with fig-leaves, he said; Indians adorn them with flowers!

I was surprised at how easy I too found it to discuss such matters with them. There was wisdom in their decision to distance themselves from something that usually takes up so much time and attention in life. They saw their vow of chastity as a part of a new kind of balance they were seeking. The basic idea was that everything in the universe is in harmony and that it is sufficient to follow nature and to do what is right. Fruits and vegetables ought to be eaten in season, for the earth produces hot things when the weather is cold, and cold things when the weather is hot. The season for them was no longer the season of the senses. I could see their point clearly.

What does this mean for those of us who live in the West and who eat what we want when we want? Cabbage in the spring, cherries in the winter? Who, with the help of Viagra, carry on making love until we are eighty? We may have this freedom, but what are the consequences? In the long term, they are hard to predict. In the short term, however, and in the case of Viagra, one very real possibility is that of a heart attack. The old paediatrician would at least be spared this. The following day he would begin the series of purifying massages in the company of his dear wife. After sharing their lives, now they were also sharing this last adventure of the spirit.

After a week of such peace and order, it really was a wrench to leave 'the place where the arrow was fired from'.

When I boarded the bus heading north with a group of other patients, I saw Mahadevan, his father and cousin, some of the servants, the paediatrician and his wife lined up on the steps outside the clinic to bid me farewell. Above all, however, I saw her, the she-devil, motionless and looking up at the sky. While alive, she had disturbed the rishis and Rama; dead, as if to atone for her misdeeds, I was convinced she was protecting this cocoon of tradition and those few faithful followers of the great ancient masters of life.

It took just a few miles of tarmac road for me to realize how unique and blessed Derisanamcope was. Soon, we began to drive through villages where the neon crosses of the new churches built by Protestant denominations, of which the Swami had been so critical, towered above the palm trees. These churches, with their ostentatious opulence, were large and out of place there. They were also closed, as it was not Sunday.

Would Mahadevan's father manage to find enough money to repair the old temple of Rama at the end of the village and keep it alive for a while?

SEVEN

THE HIMALAYAS

MERCURY POWDER

A tiger had two followers, a leopard and a jackal. Each time the tiger caught its prey, it ate as much as it could and left the rest for the other two. However, one day, the tiger killed three animals: one large, one medium-sized and one small.

'Now, how shall we divide them up?' the tiger asked.

'Simple,' replied the leopard. 'You take the large one, I'll take the medium-sized one and we can give the small one to the jackal.'

The tiger said nothing, but ripped the leopard into pieces with its paws. 'Now, how shall we divide them up?' the tiger asked again.

'Oh Majesty,' the jackal replied, 'take the small one for breakfast, keep the large one for lunch and eat the medium-size one for dinner.'

The tiger was astonished. 'Tell me, jackal, from whom did you learn such wisdom?'

The jackal paused for a moment, then with the humblest

expression he could muster, answered: 'From the leopard, Your Majesty.'

I had brought a copy of the *Panchatantra*[22] to keep me company, and in the evening before falling asleep in my room at the small hotel that I was staying at in Rishikesh on the Ganga, I had started to read some of this entertaining collection of animal stories written, legend has it, more than 1,500 years ago by an old hermit, to give a king's three ignorant, unwilling children some rudimentary lessons in life in order to prepare them for their succession.

I had come from Delhi, and in the morning would continue my journey to Dehra Dun where I had an appointment with a well-known Ayurvedic doctor who had recently been at the centre of a great deal of attention, as he claimed to have an original cure for cancer.

What struck me the most in these ancient stories of animals was their absolute lack of any moral, unlike the fables we in the West are familiar with. Indeed, their very purpose was to impart practical lessons on the art of survival, starting from an objective and dispassionate observation of life. The conclusions which the old hermit helped the three unwilling young princes to reach might not have been ethically inspiring, but they did contain their own form of pragmatic wisdom.

And me? Had I not managed to draw at least some wise conclusions from my life over these last years? Travelling around the world, meeting doctors, magicians and teachers, I had certainly learnt that there was no point in continuing to travel, that there

---

[22] Some argue that the author of these tales, Vishnu Sharma, was in fact Chanakya, the 'Indian Machiavelli' and author of the *Arthashastra* on the art of government.

was no such thing as cure for cancer. The only thing to do was carry on living as consciously and as naturally as possible, to live a life that was simple, to eat healthily and not in excess, control my desires and in so doing expand the horizons of my freedom. In which case, what was I doing on the trail of yet another doctor?

What had inspired me to set off for Dehradun was not so much as a patient, but the old passion of a journalist: the pleasure of setting off to find out whether or not there was any truth in a story one had heard or read. And the story in this case was most interesting.

Unlike the 'doctor' from Kakinada or young Mahadevan, Vaidya Balendu Prakash was already famous. The press had covered him, he had a national honour bestowed on him and he enjoyed the protection of the then president of India. One of the many patients who had used his remedies was the multi-billionaire Sir James Goldsmith, who had brought him to Britain and sent his private plane to get him. Vaidya Balendu Prakash's fame had licked off in 1987, when he had managed to cure a Pakistani boy aged two-and-a-half from leukaemia, after a big London hospital had given up all hope. The story had been all over the newspapers.

What made Vaidya Balendu Prakash's treatments so unusual was the fact that he did not use any herbs or plants, but metals. The idea that metals could play an important part in the upkeep of the body has been common to all civilizations, and the copper jugs which our grandmothers used for water and the iron pans they used to fry eggs in were doubtless the remnants of some ancient form of wisdom now swept away by modern industry, replacing them with utensils that are infinitely more practical, but less healthy.

But it is one thing to make saucepans out of metals, quite another to ingest them. And this, which Western medicine considers to be a sure form of poisoning, is exactly what Vaidya Balendu Prakash has his patients do. Using a highly complex system described in some Ayurvedic texts, he reduces the metals to powder and then administers them to his patients to drink. I had read that of all the metals, the one he used the most was mercury. This was another reason why I was curious to meet him. According to Indian mythology, mercury is the sperm of Shiva, 'the seed of pure consciousness'. Was there, in Vaidya Balendu Prakash's medicines, something that went beyond mere appearances? Like in alchemy, for example?

Thousands of years ago, priests and magicians from civilizations as remote and distinct from each other as the Maya and the Chinese, the Egyptian and the Indian, had sought to transform ignoble metals such as lead and copper into precious metals such as silver and gold. This mysterious art, later dubbed alchemy, formed a part of man's never-ending attempts to discover something more about himself. The putative material transformation of one metal into another was a way of concealing a more spiritual transformation – one of the soul – the procedure for which was linked to a form of esoteric knowledge accessible only through a lengthy and demanding initiation process. It was no coincidence that the terms in which the accounts of this art were couched were highly allusive. For example, they spoke of 'killing' the vile metal in order for it to be 'reborn' as noble gold, which was another way to killing the ego, so that the self of pure consciousness could be born.

In China, alchemy became a part of the Taoist tradition, where the claim that they were producing 'the gold of immortality' clearly masked an objective that was anything other than metallurgic. In Europe, alchemy became an art for preparing medicines by mysterious means, which was later identified as the philosopher's stone. Medicine for both body and soul? Maintaining this ambiguity was essential as far as the medieval mystics were concerned. They managed to avoid being persecuted in their search for a direct relationship with God by barricading themselves behind a mass of stills and mortars, and hiding their true labour as spiritual seekers behind their apparently material endeavours as scientists.

Could there be something similar lurking behind the practice of the doctor of Dehradun, who claimed to transform the 'sperm of Shiva' into a type of medicine?

The following morning I arrived at my destination in the customary old Hindustan Motors' Ambassador. But this was no doctor's surgery: it was a farm outside the town, at the end of a dirt track right out in the sticks. A white retaining wall, a gate, a couple of buildings, a large lean-to over rows of black holes in the red earth, and lots of animals – chickens, ducks, peacocks and cows – peacefully wandering around a small pond.

'Welcome to the smallest, least-funded cancer research centre in the whole world!' said the doctor as he approached me. He was smiling, short and in a Western dress. He greeted me with a handshake, rather than a 'Namaskar'. There was nothing holy or mystical about him. The marked affability with which he greeted me was more of the public relations variety. He was certainly not an alchemist. He was not even a vegetarian. When I pointed to the chickens and asked if he ate them, he replied: 'Certainly!' with the kind of conviction that suggested it would be foolish not to.

When I had spoken to him on the phone, I had not introduced myself as a potential patient. I had merely told him I was intending to write about alternative medicine, and he had left his whole day free to explain his work to me. So there were no patients queuing up to see him, but the phone in the little office we were sitting in rang constantly, with people calling from all over the world to arrange consultations and request appointments. In the majority of cases he said 'no'.

He was no longer interested in treating individual cases, he told me. His priority now was research. He wanted his treatments to be accepted by the scientific community, which for the moment was studiously avoiding him. Doctors with Western training considered it anathema, whereas those steeped in the Ayurvedic tradition, he felt, avoided allowing their practices to be subject to proper scientific controls and experiments.

Balendu Prakash himself had studied in the classical, Ayurvedic way and had earned the degree which allowed him to add the prestigious title 'vaidya', meaning doctor, to his name. However, he had been at loggerheads with his colleagues for some time now.

'Ayurvedic doctors are fundamentally conservative and opposed to all things modern. They continue to treat their medicine as though it were a religion, and to speak of the ancient texts as "sacred scriptures". By doing so, they prevent these texts from being criticized and questioned,' he said. 'For my part, I consider myself most fortunate to be living in India, but most unfortunate to be Indian. India is a country full of wisdom, but today there is more help for religion than there is for science. New ideas are not welcomed, or financed. Ayurvedic research is virtually non-existent and not a single new form of medicine has been produced for years now.'

Before going to see him, I had read of his public attacks on the Ayurvedic schools, which in his view merely churned out 'doctors' who ended up illegally practising Western allopathic medicine for which they were unqualified. I had seen that he had also railed against products that exploited the 'Ayurvedic' tag, and deceived those who bought them while making charlatans rich.

Vaidya told me that certain tonics which were famous in India and increasingly popular as well in other countries, where they managed to avoid the stringent controls on medicines by being marketed as 'dietary supplements', are in fact nothing more than saccharine mush, and that 'Ayurvedic' cosmetics are fraudulent, pure and simple.

'Oils that are described as vegetable-based are in fact synthetic, while shampoos supposedly made of herbs actually contain the most ordinary chemicals. Ayurveda is merely a fashion which people follow slavishly. Given that such products constitute no real threat to the pharmaceutical industry, they are not removed from circulation. But with medicines for treating cancer, it's different. With them, the pharmaceutical industry rakes in huge profits and since a treatment like mine costs at most a couple of dollars per day, it is seen as a threat. Do you have any idea how much a course of treatment at the Memorial Sloan Kettering Cancer Center in New York costs?'

His was a rhetorical question, so I didn't tell him I knew. But I did know – boy, did I know!

Vaidya gave me an example of a former officer in the Indian Army, who had been pronounced incurable in Delhi, had come to him and been restored at a cost of twelve rupees, around fifteen pence, per day. What was the medicine which brought about this miracle? Simply a combination of different metals!

His treatment was based on a very simple theory. An illness such as cancer is caused by some form of imbalance – a deficiency or an excess – of essential metals: copper, silver, lead, gold, iron, tin, zinc and mercury. Accordingly, the treatment consists of re-establishing the very balance in the body.

'I'm well aware that the metals themselves are toxic, and that those in car exhaust pipes can be lethal, but metals can also restore life if they come from the hands of a vaidya,' he said. 'As is written in the ancient texts: "Mercury a thousand times refined is able to treat any illness, if the patient abstains from sexual relations, from eating salt and from any form of bitter food." I myself have experienced it and seen the results with my own eyes.'

He pulled a sheaf of papers from his desk. These were the records of more than fifty patients whom he had treated successfully in recent months. As he handed them to me, he said something striking: 'I know the treatment works, but I don't know exactly how or why. I'm not sure of the doses and I'm not sure of the length of time the treatment ought to last.' He appeared to be sincere when he said, 'This is why I need help – funding – to be able to continue with my research.'

The moment had come to see his famous 'medicines'. The lean-to I had noticed on arriving sheltered the furnace where the metals were 'refined a thousand times'. The holes in the ground were of differing sizes: some were a span deep, others two spans, others went down as far as your elbow. These were the units of measurement described in the ancient texts. A fireclay container sealed with mud was placed in each hole every evening. Inside it was the correct quantity of metal that was to be melted into liquid form by the fire and have all its impurities removed. In the morning, the metal was poured into stone mortars, and pounded by hand for the rest of the day. In the evening the mixture was again placed in the holes over the fire, and in the morning it was back in the mortars once more. After months of this process, the metal was reduced to an extremely fine powder, a kind of ash, referred to as bhasma.

Vaidya Prakash, took me to see his 'pharmacy'. Rows of men

sitting on the ground were slowly pushing steel wheels back and forth in the black pulp at the bottom of the mortars. There were lots of jars stacked up on the shelves, each with a label stating what it contained and the date on which it had been produced. Vaidya said that at the end of the procedure, the powder was not to be touched for at least two years prior to being taken. Every medicine required at least three years' preparation.

In a bowl, he showed me what mercury in its pure state looked like. I picked up the bowl and found it was extremely heavy. Then Prakash, using the tip of a teaspoon, took the bhasma from the same mercury out of a jar: it was a black, very fine, almost ethereal powder. 'In water it floats, because the mercury has lost its nature as an earth-bound metal which sinks, and has taken on the nature of fire which rises,' said Prakash, quoting a verse from one of the ancient texts.[23]

He had studied these texts and now knew them well. But this had not been the starting point for him in discovering this form of medicine. It had all begun with his father, and the story, as Prakash recounted it to me, sounded like an Indian fable for all the word.

His family came from Meerut, a small town to the north of Delhi. They were simple folk, but very devout, and many of his forefathers at the end of their lives had become sanyasi. When Prakash's father was twelve years old, someone forced him to drink alcohol. His parents were horrified and made him leave home. A sadhu popularly called Maharaj, one of those who lived off nothing but bananas and milk, took him in as his disciple, introduced him to the study of the sacred scriptures and Ayurveda,

---

[23] The Ayurvedic texts which deal with the use of metals go by the name of *Rasa shastra*, literally 'knowledge of mercury'. They date back to roughly the eighth century AD and are much more recent than the classical Ayurvedic texts. Some believe this use of metals came to India from China.

and taught him the secrets of the strange black powder which he, the Maharaj, kept with him in a bag at all times and used it to heal people's bone diseases.

When he grew up, the Vaidya's father became a healer. With the help of a complicated purification process for several metals which he had learnt from the Maharaj, he built his own store of black powder which he used to treat various types of patients. In 1960, he had a government officer referred to him; the local hospital had said it could not do anything for him because of a disease that had already got into his bone marrow. His father gave the man the Maharaj's powder and he was cured. Many other such instances followed, and his father became famous as the one who could heal those for whom other treatments did not work. His father died in 1984, and in the meantime the Vaidya had taken Maharaj's advice and studied Ayurveda with the view of taking his place. In order to have more space to perform his experiments, he had moved to the farm at Dehradun where he had set up his own research centre.

The Pakistani boy had been his first great success. He had cured him using a blend of mercury, arsenic and silver. Since then, the Vaidya claimed he was able to cure at least thirty-five different types of cancer. He knew perfectly well that his system did not work in all cases; he admitted he had made mistakes, and had no difficulty in speaking to me about his critics.

It was the Vaidya himself who told me that the health authorities in Australia had made announcements on television to warn the several dozen Australians taking his medicines of the risk of poisoning. He pointed to a photo of a blonde girl on his office wall. Her name was Catherine, he said; she was English and had come to him looking for a cure for leukaemia. She had stayed with his family for several weeks, but in the end he had not been able to save her.

'At that time, there was something wrong with my medicine stocks,' Vaidya admitted. Once it had happened with his father too. After years of good results using the Maharaj's powder, suddenly people stopped being cured. It took time to discover that the problem was the quality of the copper being used. The copper in new coins was not as pure as that in the old ones, and it was only once that his father had begun to use copper from electricity wires that the medicine started working again.

'What about Goldsmith?' I asked him.

He said that when he called him, it was already too late. There had been disagreements with the team of French and English doctors treating him too.

The Vaidya knew very well that he had had many failures, as well as successes. What he did not understand, though, was why the scientific community was not interested in the cases where his system had worked, and why it did not want to help him discover the reasons why in others it had not. After the case of the Pakistani boy, some doctors from England had gone to visit him and study his methods of treatment, but after that there had been no one. Now the only doctors who turned to him were the ones who no longer knew what to do with their patients.

In the meantime, he went on conducting his experiments and recording the details of every case that he dealt with. 'Keep on feeding the jackals, and one day the lion will come looking,' his father would always say to him. The Vaidya was convinced that sooner or later someone would step forward to help him.

As we walked around the farm, we approached the pond where some fine-looking chickens and ducks were scratching around, while pairs of doves were cooing in the trees up above.

'Imagine if we lived in a forest in ancient times,' said the Vaidya. 'One can learn a lot just by observing nature and animals. We see that a cockerel eats one thing in one season and another thing in another season. We see that an elephant only eats the exterior of certain plants. We copy the animals, we do what they do, but we don't always obtain the same results. We discover that the grass which grows in one place doesn't necessarily have the same properties as the same grass growing elsewhere

'You take a rock, heat it, and it produces a metal. You eat that metal and you die. Then you discover there are earthworms in the ground that absorb that metal, say, copper, and you realize that the colours of the cockerel's wings, so strikingly mauve and black, are due to the copper it ingests when it eats the worms. This is the cycle: the worm eats the copper and recycles it, the cockerel eats the worms and absorbs the copper. The rishis understood all this. Certainly, copper is poisonous in its natural state, but it also has anti-inflammatory properties, and when it is reduced to powder form, it is able to impede the growth of certain forms of cancer.

'The same thing happens with mercury. When people died of mercury poisoning, they discovered that the mercury had got into their staminal cells too. From this they deduced that it could be used as a vehicle for getting substances into the deepest recesses of the human body. Ayurveda has known this for centuries, just as it has known about the properties of zinc and iron which Western medicine has only recently discovered. But Ayurveda came into being without any knowledge of chemistry, physics or electronics. My purpose is to bring these sciences into Ayurveda in order to refine it, explain it, improve it, and move on.'

Vaidya was a modern thinker, but he also had his doubts about modernity. For instance, he was very suspicious regarding everything produced by industries, the food industry in particular. He was convinced that the earth was losing many of its ancient properties, largely due to the use of fertilizers, and that the food produced today no longer contained those substances, especially minerals, which the human body needs. For this reason he was especially proud of his ecosystem, as he described his little farm, where he was able to produce everything he and his family needed as naturally as possible. Everything there was recycled, down to the cow and bull dung which was used as fuel for the furnaces.

We spent the whole day talking. He was very happy to have someone to share his thoughts with, and I was happy to take notes.

Just before sunset, the daily ritual of kindling the fires took place and every member of the family was involved. I too was invited. A burning coal was placed in each hole, and this, without the need for bellows, caused the cowpats placed under the containers to burn at a slow, constant heat.

A man would stand guard over them all night. In the morning, the metals would be left to cool, poured into the mortars, ground slowly for hours on end and in the evening they would be heated again. This would be the pattern for weeks and months.

'Only in India is the labour cheap enough for us to afford to produce medicines of this kind. But maybe it is because the medicines are Indian that they won't be taken seriously by the people at the Memorial Sloan Kettering Cancer Center,' he added.

He had mentioned my beloved institution on several occasions in the course of the day. Without divulging anything personal, I asked him why he kept referring to it. He said he did not know the New York hospital himself, but had many patients who had been there, and then come to him once the MSKCC had said there was no cure for them. He understood they were pinning all their hopes on genetic research, but he felt they would not find the solution to cancer there. He had seen many patients who had had bone marrow transplants at the MSKCC which, in his view, had served no useful purpose whatsoever.

'I don't mind patients whose bone marrow has already been infected,' he added smiling, as a kind of a challenge. 'In that case, I'm not quite ready to be one of your patients yet,' I ended up telling him. Briefly I recapped my clinical history.

The Vaidya said nothing, but this 'confession' of mine had established a greater degree of intimacy between us and he invited me to stay for dinner.

The Vaidya sat at the head of the table, his wife to the right of him, then his three children, two girls and a boy, all of whom were certain that they wanted to follow in their father's and grandfather's footsteps and become Ayurvedic doctors. I noticed that the Vaidya took several pills before eating, which he washed down with water from a silver goblet: zinc, gold, pearl, coral and mercury, he explained. He even took a good dose of black pepper because, as he put it, 'you need fuel to make a good fire'.

The rotis, or the flat, round, flour breads, we ate were not in fact made from wheat, but from a very ordinary plant that grew in the fields. 'It's the cheapest flour of all, the one poor people eat,' the Vaidya said. 'And poor people fall ill less often if they stick to their traditional diet. Unfortunately we've become richer, more stupid and less healthy.'

It was only when we sat down together in his little living room to drink herb tea that he went back to what I had said.

'One day, you will have to come back here as my patient because the people at the MSKCC will fail with you, as they have failed with so many before you. They have no answer to the one real question worth asking: what is it that causes your cancer?'

I was familiar with this line of argument. I myself had used it during my months in New York. But he added another point which focused the question more clearly.

'A cancer sufferer is bound to die if he or she is treated according to the Western style of medicine, i.e., by fighting the cancer, rather than its causes. Some manage to survive because they change their way of life.'

'Well, that's what I've been trying to do.'

'Yes, then the people at the MSKCC will say it's all due to them! You know how they do things: they take five years' survival as an indication of success. Then you die in the sixth year. Is that still a success?'

In his view, one of the main causes of my kind of illness was an imbalance in the metallic content of my body. This was partly due to pollution, to the fact that the earth is increasingly bereft of its natural constituents and increasingly imbued with artificial chemicals.

I agreed.

He asked me to return the next day on an empty stomach. He wanted to check the state of my blood. To do so, he used a special type of microscope which performed its best 'in the dark'. 'The stars are only visible at night-time, when it is dark,' he explained to me. 'But the stars are there during the daytime too. The same is the case with the signs of cancer. When I look at your blood, I can see the signs of your cancer and how it will develop more clearly and quicker than Western doctors can.'

This I was less keen on. Was he some kind of a charlatan?

That evening, once again in a hotel but this time in the centre of Dehradun, I read other entertaining if not desperately edifying stories of animals from the *Panchatantra* before falling asleep. One of them went as follows.

An old lion went for a nap every day in its lair after lunch. However, it was regularly disturbed by a mouse which got into its ears and nibbled on its fur. The lion was big and strong, but was still unable to catch the tiny rodent. So it asked a cat to stand guard. Everything went according to plan. The mouse, when it saw the cat, did not come out of its hole and the lion carried on sleeping. The lion was so grateful that it praised and thanked the cat constantly for all its help. One day, the mouse, who by this stage was hungry, came out of its hole regardless. Without thinking twice, the cat pounced on it and killed it. When the lion awoke from its slumber, the cat, all proud of itself, told the lion what had happened. There and then the lion said nothing, but its attitude towards the cat changed completely. It stopped speaking to it and did not even give it so much as a crumb to eat. The cat was confused.

'I did what I was told to. Why are you treating me like this?' the cat asked eventually, after several days' famine.

'Vile little beast, you are but a servant and no longer needed. Go away and let me sleep,' the lion replied.

The next morning I arrived at the Vaidya's house, having eaten nothing since the previous evening. The family was still having breakfast with him at the head of the table, and the door of the room open, out on to his ecosystem: pigeons, chickens and ducks all claiming their share.

The Vaidya entrusted me to the young microbiologist in charge of the microscope. She took a drop of my blood, put it on the glass and minutes later I was witness to the magnificent spectacle of hundreds of different shapes, all different colours, all moving, touching, embracing and devouring each other, changing shape and colour. Such incredible life was moving in that projection of a mere drop of my blood!

The girl said that everything was in order. Then the Vaidya came along and found that there were traces of the food I had eaten twelve hours ago still in my bloodstream, a sign of bad absorption. He said my blood cells were not perfectly round, which was a sign of iron deficiency; my resistance was low, and that rather than surviving for five hours, my cells were already dead after just one.

It occurred to me that the whole spectacle, with that modern touch brought by the television screen, might just have been a set-up to lend greater credibility to the metals he would prescribe me. Was this a trap? Just like the phone call that arrived while I was in his office (one of the many) from the mother of the Pakistani boy, who was calling from Dubai to say hello to the Vaidya. He got me to talk to her. The boy was now sixteen and perfectly healthy. They were eternally grateful to the Vaidya for what he had done for them.

Coincidence? Or had he arranged that phone call just to impress me? I inclined towards the former alternative. Instinctively, I liked Vaidya. And his system had certainly been successful in the sense that it had given hope to people who had lost it and maybe even helped cure the odd one or two people. But deep down, his approach as a doctor towards illness was no different from that of the fixers in New York he was so critical of. He too saw me merely as a body, deficient in some metal or another, and nothing else. At most, he wanted to put some more matter into me in order to help with the rest of my matter. I was no longer interested in all that.

When he told me I should start taking one of his combinations of metals to strengthen my immune system, I replied that I didn't want to take any more medicines and that I had come to him thinking I would find an alchemist. The idea made him laugh, as though he was amused by it. But I think he understood what

I meant, and in the end we said our goodbyes very cordially. I promised him I would write about him as honestly as possible.

I had a seven- or eight-hour drive ahead of me to return to Delhi, so I lay down on the back seat of the old Ambassador. The road was full of potholes, so I was unable to read. To help myself get to sleep, I told myself an animal story. Not one from the *Panchatantra*, the aim of which was to teach material, practical lessons, but one of the much older, simpler tales from the Vedas intended to impart a much loftier moral.

A falcon was flying high above the countryside one day when it saw a fish come to the surface of a pond. It swooped down, caught it in its beak and flew away. A group of crows watching the scene flew off in pursuit of him, and tried to steal his lunch from him. The falcon attempted to fly, but they jumped on him and attacked him, pecking at him and giving him no rest. When the falcon realized that all this was happening because he was still attached to his prey, he let go. The crows all descended on the fish, while the falcon soared away. Nothing and no one could disturb him or distract him any more. Finally, he could rise higher and higher towards infinity. He was free; at peace.

A FLUTE IN THE MIST

The forest kept its ancient promises. All that was needed was to walk into it. With every step I took, it became more and more animated, mysterious and sacred. Its trees looked like the nave of some huge cathedral; the sun filtered obliquely through the branches, as though it were shining through magic glass windows. Soon, there was nothing of our own time around me. The only trace of human life was the path I was walking on, which went upwards then plunged downwards into a deep gorge, before rising again, higher and higher.

The trees were old ilexes bearded with musk, and lichens hanging from their contorted branches; giant rhododendrons whose bark bore an infinite variety of greys, pinks and violets. Each of them had its own personality and history, with scars from lightning and fire imprinted in their antediluvian trunks.

This forest on the slopes of the Himalayas was the forest of all legends. Every herb could have been a remedy, every cave the refuge of some holy man, every hole in the ground the lair of some bear or leopard. We are no longer accustomed to such natural majesty, and the wonder, along with a slight feeling of anxiety, left us speechless. We walked in reverent silence, attentive to the sounds of the rustling of the leaves, the distant pitter-pattering of an animal or the cry of a bird. The forest spoke whisperings of a thousand different lives and altogether of one single life.

In ascending a mountain, one often thinks of the reward they will receive, if nothing else, at least that of being able to gaze down at the world from high above. Our surprise came somewhat sooner than this. In the middle of the wood, we saw a large stone wall covered in stonecrop, then an iron gate which was rusty and closed.

I opened it and we made our way through two imposing trees, which stood like guardians on either side of the path, then went on perhaps another fifty feet. The forest ended, the path curved and all of a sudden, in broad daylight, there was an amphitheatre of bright green meadows in terrace formation. Above them, as if on the last battlement or the saddle of the mountainside, there loomed the outline of a chimney, a roof, a house squatting in the shadows of the tall cedar trees.

Everything suddenly went still and silent, as though it were no longer real but painted on a large canvas which we, as if enchanted, were about to enter. It was a vision outside time, like the depiction of a peace which we no longer know.

A dog barked, and an old man who had been sleeping in the sun stood up.

We had to climb a little further in order to reach those two black silhouettes which stood out against the skyline. When we got to the ridge, what we saw before us took the little breath we still had away: along the entire horizon, above an ocean of hills and valleys, above banks of clouds, higher still where the world appeared to have already ended, mountain peaks soared as far as the eye could see; remote, dazzling white against the azure backcloth.

'Tell me the truth, it's a painting, isn't it?' I said to the Old Man who was waiting for us, motionless, outside the porch of the house.

He chuckled heartily. 'Of course. The Divine Artist painted them. And every day he paints them again for me, different each time.' Then he stared at me and added: 'The truth? Why? Have you come here looking for the truth?'

How could we say no?

'The truth is like beauty. It has no limits,' he continued. 'It cannot be imprisoned in words or in forms. The truth is without end.'

Angela and I looked at each other. There was no longer any need for introductions.

The Old Man invited us to sit down on two wicker chairs and offered us water.

'It comes from a spring down here in the forest,' he reassured us.

Dry-skinned and wrinkled, the Old Man himself looked like a tree in the forest we had just left behind. He wore dark brown trousers, a dirty green sweater and a woollen beret the colour of foliage. A pair of glasses were perched on his large nose and a white beard framed his swarthy, Indian face, which had been tanned still more deeply by years of sunshine. Ropes, baskets and bunches of dried herbs hung down from the porch roof.

It was December and the sun was warm, the air crystal clear and the mountains behind us as much of a presence as if they themselves had been another invited guest, or as if they were the real hosts. The dog calmed down after seeing us and went to sleep at the feet of the Old Man who began to slowly roll himself a cigarette. Long branches of little purple-and-white flowers were sprouting from the wild sage bushes in front of the porch; the rose bushes, which had not been pruned for some time now, were full of tiny overblown flowers. It seemed as though every blade of grass and stone was enjoying their peace in the sunshine.

We barely had time to take out the bread and cheese which we had brought with us, when two jet black crows descended upon us from the top of a cedar tree, cawing, coming to claim their share. The Old Man said they had been eating from his table for years now.

'Male and female?' I asked.

'That's their problem, not mine!' he replied, with an amused laugh.

Angela and I continued to look at each other. What had brought us here? At first it appeared to be the usual random chain of little steps, coincidences and decisions that only with hindsight are revealed to have been arranged by someone other than ourselves.

In so many years of visiting India, Angela had only seen the Himalayas from afar, from Dharamshala. So we decided to spend Christmas in Almora, an old hill station on the great mountain barrier where India borders with China to the east. We were staying in a nineteenth-century bungalow that had been converted into a hotel. It bore the name of the majestic cedar trees that had once covered the whole area: The Deodars, the trees of the gods.

Almora has a long history. Mention of it is made as early as in the Puranas, the ancient legends, and for centuries it has been the gateway to some of the most sacred peaks in the Himalayas and their secrets. The sanyasis who decided to 'go to the forest' used to stop there, as did the holy men who retreated even higher up on the glaciers. Poets such as Tagore stayed in Almora, as did mystics like Vivekananda, who founded one of his ashrams here. Gandhi too spent several weeks here, pronouncing it the ideal place for the health of both mind and body.

In terms of sacred geography, Almora is located at the centre of a tantric triangle – others say a swastika – which contributed to its reputation as a place especially well suited to concentration and the spiritual life.

With the Himalayas everywhere on its horizon and its forests still virtually intact, in the nineteenth century Almora also attracted a small number of non-Indians in whose footsteps I had decided to follow. They had all gone to live along a narrow ridge between two deep valleys which extended for several miles from The Deodars to the old temple of Kasar Devi. It was because of the eccentric foreigners who sought refuge here that in the course of time it came to be known as 'Cranks Ridge'.

One of them was the theosophist W.Y. Evans-Wentz, an American of German descent who was responsible for the first edition of the classic *Tibetan Book of the Dead* and *Tibet's Great Yogi Milarepa*. There was also Lama Anagarika Govinda, born in eastern Germany, who had arrived on the Ridge after studying Pali, the language in which the earliest Buddhist texts were written, in

Naples. After an extended residence on the island of Capri, some had taken him for the reincarnation of Novalis, the first German romantic poet. Novalis had died of tuberculosis in 1801 at the age of twenty-nine, leaving a minor novel half-written. Bizarrely, Lama Govinda wrote the ending to it while still very young, without knowing anything about Novalis or his unfinished work.

Another character who arrived here via Capri was the American painter Earl Brewster, friend of D.H. Lawrence and Aldous Huxley. Yet another was a Dane named Alfred Sorensen, who had been lured to India by Tagore. For several years, he worked as a gardener in his academy at Santiniketan, then moved to the Ridge and became a sadhu by the name of Baba Sunyata, or Father Zero.

I too was looking for some kind of refuge, and the idea of spending some time on the Ridge appealed to me, maybe even in one of the cranks' own habitations. But here too everything had changed. The house that had belonged to Evans-Wentz and then for some forty years to Lama Govinda had been divided up and ugly concrete houses had been erected on the site where these two scholars had lovingly sought to recreate a mini-Tibet. Where the bungalow, in which Brewster had lived for almost half a century and died aged eighty-one, had stood, there was now a modern house. And right behind Kasar Devi, one of the most sacred temples in the whole region, in the centre of the tantric triangle a signal repeater for telephones had been installed, thus desecrating the entire panorama with its enormous metal pylon.

In the world's biggest democracy, everyone is free to do as they please, especially when it involves pursuing their own interests. This is how the Ridge, which once upon a time was covered with dense woodland, came to be deforested and is now dotted with white concrete cubicles to be rented out to the new generation of cranks – no longer the cultured, eccentric personalities of some decades ago, but crowds of hippies attracted primarily by the good quality hashish that grows wild along the walls here, including those of the police station.

I had gone to see if I too could rent one of those cubicles, but had fled in despair. Until one morning, while having breakfast on the sun-kissed terrace which, like the deck of a ship, looked out over the sea of mist that was filling the valley, the owner of The Deodars, Richard Wheeler, pointed out to me behind the other mountains fading away to blue, a peak in the distance that was darker than the rest.

'See, up there nothing has changed. The forest is the same as ever, and I believe an old Indian man still lives right at the top,' he said.

That peak began to speak to me. I watched it, and as I did so I heard these lines from Kipling's *The Explorer* whisper:

Something hidden. Go and find it.
Go and look behind the Ranges –
Something lost behind the Ranges.
Lost and waiting for you. Go!

So one morning we went. The car climbed up the hills and down the valleys, then took a little road which continued on upwards through a forest, first of pine trees, then of ilexes. In under two hours we reached an opening, in whose moist belly a mandir, or Hindu temple, squatted, white and orange. It was dedicated to Shiva and was tended to by an elderly lady sanyasi. There we left our car and walked along the path leading into the forest. Up and up we went for more than an hour, until we reached the rusty gate, the Old Man and his house.

'This is the ideal place for anyone who wants to separate from the world,' I said to him.

He had been fasting here for the best part of half a century. He too had lived on the Ridge once, but when the old generation of cranks had begun to disappear to be replaced by the new arrivals, when the old dirt track that runs along the Ridge had first been widened and then asphalted, he decided to move higher up. The cranks of yesteryear, he said, had come to the Himalayas in search of something outside of themselves; the new cranks were only looking for illusions. Timothy Leary, the American LSD guru and former Harvard psychologist, had arrived on the Ridge in the early 1960s. He and his tablets had symbolized the start of the revolution.

The Old Man had met all the characters I was interested in. He had come to the Ridge as a young painter, and his first contact had been with Brewster who was already well on in years by that stage. Brewster, from a wealthy American family, had written a book on Buddha and made some sculptures while in Capri, in the so-called House of the Four Winds. From Capri he moved to Colombo on the island then known as Ceylon. From there he had moved to the ashram of Sri Aurobindo in Pondicherry, and towards the end of the 1920s had come to Almora where he had started to paint. The Old Man felt that Brewster had managed to capture the spirit of the mountains better than anyone else, faithful to the end.

The Old Man told us about Rudolf Ray, a Jew of Russian/Polish descent known on the Ridge simply as 'Ru'. He had made a name for himself as a portraitist in Vienna, but under the influence of Freud, had stopped painting 'what was visible'; he devoted himself instead to depicting the subconscious. Thus, he ended up among the cranks. He painted in the dark, sometimes for hours on end, without even being sure that the colours had actually ended up on the canvas. 'Ru,' the Old Man said, 'was drunk with beauty.' For him, everything was beautiful. He never saw anything as existing in its own right; he saw the link between things, which for him was true beauty.

Li Gotami, the wife of Lama Govinda and a rich Parsi from Bombay, was also a painter. She wanted to see the world from 'a different point of view', and to obtain this view she used to paint with her head down between her legs. But according to the Old Man, the strangest of them all was the Dane, Father Zero. Like the others, he too was seeking to 'transcend the self', and never spoke of himself in the first person. He had written a book on this subject entitled *Why We are Called Us*. Father Zero had a dog he was very attached to who was named Wu, which is a privative in Chinese meaning 'that which is not'. He used to say, 'In the summer he's my guru; in the winter he's my hot water bottle.'

Despite being over eighty years old, the Old Man had a wonderful memory. He could remember names, dates, conversations and details. It was as though his mind were continually focused. And it was then that he mentioned the 'candle trick' for the first time. 'I have done nothing else in my life,' he said laughing, and recited two lines from the Gita:

Like a flame which does not move in the wind
Is the mind that is focused on Brahman.

He told us how, shortly after arriving on the Ridge, he had taken the most important decision of his life: rather than 'becoming' a painter, he wanted to just 'be' himself. He had burnt all his paintings and devoted himself to focusing his mind, to 'going beyond'. He never used the word meditation. He did say, however, that every night he got up to spend two or three hours in silence, to sit still in front of a lit candle. This exercise was what he referred to as the candle trick.

I asked him which other Indians lived on the Ridge. One he had been friends with was Boshi Sen from Bengal, who had married an American, the grand-daughter of Ralph Waldo Emerson. The Old Man's passion had been botany. Right from his youth in Calcutta, he had sought to show that plants had feelings too. He was convinced that there was another world beyond the material one, and that the whole of creation was pervaded by a form of consciousness similar to that which human beings had.

When he spoke of the people he had known, the Old Man often ended up describing their laugh. A person's laugh was a significant indicator of their character, he felt. An 'intellectual' laugh was a bad thing; a 'genuine' or 'simple' laugh was good. Those who were also able to laugh at themselves, like Brewster, he described as having a 'pure' laugh.

He himself had a lovely laugh, I noted, despite his emphysema caused by the cigarettes he had rolled himself and smoked for several decades now.

In his view, the person with the most unusual laugh – unusual in the sense of being so profoundly genuine – was Krishna Prem, an Englishman christened Roland Nixon, who had been an air pilot during World War I before teaching at the University of Lucknow in India. He came to Almora in 1929 to found the ashram of Mirtola, some miles from the Ridge, along with his female guru. The Old Man had gone to the ashram, but had never become a member. For his own spiritual quest, he preferred the silence of his home.

As we talked, the Old Man spotted my Soviet watch bearing an image of Buddha, his right hand touching the ground to call it as witness that he had attained enlightenment.

'Ah, eternity trapped in time ... and what time!' he said. 'Had it at least been the time of experience. But no, it's the time of a watch, with its hands coming out from the heart of the Enlightened One!' He thought it was dreadful.

I decided not to tell him where I had bought it. That was one of the repertoire of anecdotes I had now given up recounting. I told him that all I had done in my life was travel and that now I wanted to stop.

'It's the only way there is to know oneself,' he observed. And to explain what he meant, he told us a story, all the while pointing to the Buddha wrapped in an orange tunic on the dial of my watch.

One day, Buddha was travelling and wanted to cross a forest. Everyone advised him against it. The forest was extremely dangerous. A wicked bandit was hiding there who enjoyed attacking travellers, robbing them and cutting off their fingers to add them to the garland he wore around his neck. Indeed, his name was Angulimal: anguli, meaning fingers, mala, meaning garland. However, Buddha would not be distracted from his purpose and set out alone. As soon as the bandit saw him, he threw himself into chasing him, but was unable to catch him. Angulimal went one way, but Buddha went another; Angulimal ran in one direction, but Buddha was not there. Exhausted, Angulimal cries out:

'Who are you? Man or superman? God or the devil? I chase you, but never catch you. How can you be so much quicker than me?'

'You're the one who is running. I never moved,' Buddha replied. 'Here I am.'

So Angulimal stopped and in this way finally 'caught' Buddha. He understoond, threw himself at Buddha's feet, and became his disciple.

'The point of the story,' the Old Man concluded, 'is that you need to stop in order to know yourself, to be yourself.'

I certainly understood that! I had felt this need for years now and had been trying to stop somewhere. When I had first come to India, I had asked around if there was a place I could retreat to in order to write. Some acquaintances in Delhi had mentioned an isolated old house up in the mountains to the north, where Nehru had been held prisoner by the English.

'But if you use a computer to write, it's not the place for you,' they said. 'There's no electricity.' The whole thing finished there.

I told the Old Man I had studied the Vedanta with Swami Dayananda for three months, but that the ashram was not the place where I felt like I could stop.

'Swamis place too much faith in words,' he said. It was as though he had read my mind, and before I had time to say how much the Vedanta had helped me, he added: 'The Vedanta is an excellent place to start, but it's too intellectual. True knowledge does not come from books, not even holy ones, but from experience. The best way to understand reality is through feelings and intuitions, not via the intellect. The intellect is limited.'

I couldn't work out exactly where he was coming from. He was not dressed in orange like the renouncers, nor did he bear the red mark of the Hindus on his forehead. There was nothing in his appearance or in what he had said to indicate that he belonged to one faith or another. So what was his position?

'Vedanta, Buddhism, Hinduism, Jainism: one does not automatically preclude the others,' he answered. 'This is India, a civilization made up of many religions, all of which are founded on several basic ideas that no one since Buddha has ever sought to dispute.'

He paused, and looking at me as if to be sure that I had understood and agreed with him, he began to list those ideas:

'This is not the only world,' he said, indicating the entire universe with a broad sweep of his arm.

'This is not the only time,' he said, pointing at my watch.

'This is not the only life,' he said, pointing at himself, Angela, me, the dog and everything around us.

He stopped, as if to cause us to reflect. 'And this is not the only consciousness.' Tapping his chest, he added, 'What is outside is also inside; what is not inside is not anywhere.'

Then, as if to lighten the atmosphere, he roared the most delightful laugh, turned to me and said, 'This is why there is no point in travelling. If you haven't got anything inside, you won't find anything outside, either. It's pointless going to look in the world for what you're unable to find within yourself.'

What he said spoke to me; he was right.

The hours had passed as we talked. In winter, the days here are short. As the sun lowered towards the horizon, the air got colder and the Old Man invited us into his home. We went from a dark, primitive kitchen into a basic dining room with an oval table, four chairs and a wineskin in one corner. We then came into a room that was like a treasure vault, with the treasure on full display on the back wall, where a large window framed the most exceptional picture: in the foreground, the trunks and dark limbs of the two cedars; behind them, the chain of mountains with the Nanda Devi mass in their midst which the setting sun was already tinging with pink. This was no still life, but it was life in full, glorious motion, changing constantly before our astonished eyes.

The room had a high wooden ceiling, darkened by years of smoke. The walls were ochre and the floors made of old beams. An iron stove had been installed in the fireplace. It was round like a demijohn and gave off a fragrant warmth. A small bronze Buddha meditated on the mantelpiece. An old, dark brown sofa stood at the back of the room as though it were the stage of honour in some theatre, before the window itself where the mountain spectacle continued unabated. To the sides, there were two armchairs made of inlaid wood; a black-and-white photo of an old Indian man stood on a small piece of furniture along with a brass vase from which a yellow flower peered out.

I turned around. On the wall facing the window, there was a picture framed in grey of the same mountain scene, viewed from the same window at the same time with the same colours. I went closer. There was a signature in blue in the bottom right-hand corner: E.H. Brewster.

The picture itself had its own silent force; it gave off a light which appeared to be a reflection of something outside the window. There was something bewitching, inconceivable, even vaguely disquieting in all of this: the picture of the picture in the picture which I had felt like I was entering right from the start. For a moment, I felt as though I had almost lost myself in this strange game of mirrors off which my consciousness appeared to be bouncing.

'This is the most beautiful house I have seen in my whole life,' I ended up saying to break the silence, but also to reassure myself that everything that was happening was not a hallucination.

'I love this house, and my love is not unrequited,' the Old Man replied, 'for it too loves me.' He told me it had been built at the beginning of the nineteenth century by an English colonial officer. Then he added, 'The English held Nehru prisoner here during World War II.'

Angela remembered the story as I did. We looked at one another incredulously. How could this be? In a country as huge as India, with hundreds of millions of houses, this was the very same house I had heard of years ago, before I had fallen ill, before all the medicines.

I got the feeling that something, or someone was playing with me, some kind of power which I could not, and should not, resist. It was as though everything had already been decided.

In the atmosphere that had been created, to not mention something that regarded me personally would have been tantamount to lying. So I briefly told the Old Man about the journey I had begun in Bologna, which had taken me via New York to Almora in search of a refuge.

'Oh, cancer!' he said, his words once more accompanied by his raucous smokers' cough. Then he asked me a question, one which since then I have thought every medical student should be forced to answer on the first day of their university course: 'Is it illness which causes death, or is it death which causes illness?'

He went on: did I really want to stop travelling? Was I honestly looking for a retreat? If so, there was one not far away from there. Initially, it had been a kind of storeroom, but it had since been rendered habitable.

We went to see it immediately. It was a modest, low stone hut, its roof covered with slabs of slate. It had a low doorway and a steep, narrow staircase that led up to a wooden mezzanine floor with a small fireplace. The walls were made of mud and cow dung plaster, and there was a large window with a view over the Nanda Devi, the second highest mountain in India.

'You can come here whenever you want,' the Old Man said to me. I nodded in thanks.

Life is a mystery and it is better that it remain that way. Something, someone was holding the strings of my life in its hands, like it might hold a sleepwalker on the edge of a roof and lead him away to prevent him from falling.

'When the pupil is ready, the master appears,' the Indians say about their gurus. But the same is also true of a loved one, a place or an event, which only becomes significant under certain circumstances. It is pointless to look for reasons or go hunting for facts and explanations. We ourselves are living proof that there is a level of reality beyond that of our senses, that there is truth which lies beyond the facts. If we stubbornly refuse to believe in it, we lose that other part of life and with it, the joy of mystery.

It had got late. Angela and I had to go back through the forest to the mandir, and we ended up leaving in so much of a hurry that we were spared the usual round of thank yous.

'See you soon!' I called out as we headed off. Before going down into the basin of meadows, we looked at the mountains one last time. The sun had disappeared, but the Divine Artist was putting the finishing touches of warm pink to the tips of the glaciers after having covered the gorges and crevasses below with a dark, frozen veil. We almost ran back, light-headed, as though slightly tipsy or having just got off a roller coaster. We couldn't stop talking.

We had so much to talk about and decide, Angela and I! She was so generous. For forty years, I had shared the most varied, and virtually all the most wonderful, experiences in life with her. However, the adventure I was about to embark on was different. This was a journey we could not go on together. She knew it and she too, like me, had been struck by the verses from Attar[24] which the Old Man had quoted to us as a kind of blessing when we said goodbye:

The Pilgrim,
The pilgrimage and the journey:
None other than me
Travelling towards myself.

We returned to Delhi and from there she left for Florence. In many ways, it was like a separation. Angela was returning to the life that we knew, whereas I was going in the direction of a life which not even I was sure really existed. But I had to try and without any time limits or deadlines. Doctors, medicines, healers and miracles interested me no longer. I had had enough of these effective treatments for my body. Now I was looking for something different. Like Father Sogol, in René Daumas's allegorical story 'Mount Analogue', I didn't want to die without having understood why I had lived. Or in other words, I had to find within myself that seed of peace which could germinate and grow wherever I was.

Normal daily life had become a many-tentacled monster for me. I couldn't escape it. My head was constantly full of thoughts of defence, organization, plans and hopes; it was never empty, and hence never ready for anything bigger. In Florence, Anam was an even more ridiculous character than the one he had replaced, even as far as I was concerned. I felt I was neither one thing nor another. So who was I?

---

[24] Farid Uddin Attar, the 'Perfumer', was a twelfth-century Persian Sufi and author of the religious/philosophical poem '*Mantiq-ut-Tair*', the 'Conference of the Birds'.

The sanyasis cut all ties with the world when they leave it, and 'die' to their past. For this reason, they go and live as far away as possible from everything that was theirs: family, work and friends. I hadn't reached that stage yet, and nor did I want to, honestly. But I had to move away, put some distance behind me. I had to attempt this solitary journey I so felt the need for. That rusty gate in the forest might just be the visible door to an invisible world.

I stayed in Delhi for another ten days. I bought a solar panel, a battery and a converter to power the laptop I was intending to write on. I stocked up on food and incense and had supplies of the best oolong tea delivered from Chiangmai. Then I went around the house a couple of times, choosing the few things I wanted to surround myself with, out of all the books and objects I had accumulated in the course of a lifetime.

I took the tanka with the Buddha of medicine that had been painted for me at Dharamshala, a small, modern bronze bust of Milarepa, and the 'travelling' (as I liked to call it) Buddha I had put on my window sill in New York. I didn't forget my old teapot, made in Yixing at least 100 years ago, and two tiny bowls of very fine white China. From the books, I chose a copy of the Gita and a few collections of poems, mostly Indian.

I stayed one last night in the old, ex-colonial luxury of The Deodars in Almora. I bought a copper container for filtering water, and to sleep on the wooden floors I bought some rugs and some thick woollen blankets woven by the Bhothia, the shepherds of Tibetan descent who live on the Indian side of the Himalayas.

When my baggage was unloaded at the mandir and the porters piled it on to their shoulders, setting off into the forest ahead of me, the image of Lao-tzu came to my mind, sitting side-saddle on his buffalo as he passed through the Jade Door and disappeared into the Himalayas.

For as long as man has existed and has lived in the lands we now know as India, Nepal, China and Pakistan, those remote, immaculate mountains with their Sanskrit name meaning 'snowy region' ('hima' meaning snow, 'laya' meaning dwelling) have been the symbol of human aspiration to the divine.

Up there, on those remote peaks covered in ice, shrouded in snow and unattainable by mere mortals, men have sensed the presence of all that was missing from their own lives. The very remoteness of those mountains and their purity have led people to imagine that the things not found in the valleys might be found up there: the answer to all the natural desires of existence. There, the treasures of creation, the secrets of power, wisdom and serenity were hidden, which only a few were allowed to understand after great effort and much searching, and to pass on to others equally committed to the cause.

The Himalayas are the focus of all myths, the source of life and knowledge. They are the source of all of India's great rivers. It was there that the rishis lived, who conceived the Vedas. It was at the foot of the Himalayas that Vyasa wrote the Gita and the Mahabharata, that compendium of all ancient, but still relevant, philosophical, political and psychological knowledge, not just of India but of all mankind.

In their ascent of those barren, icy peaks, not with the Western idea of conquering them but of being conquered by them, for centuries the sanyasis undertook the journey in the knowledge that there would be no coming back. They broke with the past, burnt all their bridges with the world, not having anything to go back to, only the self.

Their ascent, and perhaps also mine, was an allegorical rite of renunciation of the material world, a rite of initiation into the desired world, if nothing else, of the spirit.

I had only one fear as I walked behind the porters in the forest: everything would not be as I had left it. I went through the gate and walked between the two great guardian trees. Everything was still there, motionless and silent. I saw the Old Man's silhouette, but I couldn't hear the dog barking.

'He's been eaten by a leopard,' he said, as I approached him. 'I've lost a lot of them that way. This one at least survived four years. It's a shame, but the leopard has to live too.' He didn't seem unduly sad.

I moved into my retreat, went to enjoy the sunset from the highest point on the Ridge, then at the Old Man's invitation shared a bowl of vegetable soup with him, in his lovely apartment, by the light of an oil lamp.

The mountains in the window frame had just vanished into the dark and been extinguished, but those in Brewster's painting continued to emit their own dim glow in the grey frame on the wall. The Old Man resumed the conversation of our first encounter. He was a great raconteur, and began with a story.

A disciple went to his guru and said that what he wanted more than anything was the truth. His master did not answer. Instead, he took him by the scruff of the neck, dragged him to a nearby waterfall, and held his head under the water until the poor thing was on the verge of drowning. Then, at the last minute, he pulled him out.

'Tell me, what was it that you wanted most all while your head was under the water?'

'Air,' the disciple struggled to reply.

'Good. When you want the truth as much as you wanted air a minute ago, that's when you will be ready to learn.' But was I ready?

I would have liked to have answered with a laugh, but I preferred to be honest. I didn't know if I was ready. And anyway, the truth has always seemed to me too big a thing to look for on my own.

It was then that the Old Man came out with one of his characteristic, wheezing laughs.

'Of course,' he said, 'it's not we who find the truth, it is the truth which finds us. All we have to do is prepare ourselves for it.'

Then he explained: 'Can you invite a guest you don't know? No, you can't, but you can at least get your house tidy, so that when the guest finally does arrive, you'll be ready to welcome him or her in and become acquainted.'

What relationship did he have with the truth?

He said he had glimpsed it from afar on a couple of occasions. But that had been sufficient for him to ascribe to it a certainty that came not from faith, but from experience; not other people's experience, but his own. It was that certainty which kept him committed to the search. As for tidying up his own house, he still had a lot of work to do.

He pointed to the old black-and-white photo above a piece of furniture. The man in the picture had been his first guru, Swami Satyananda, the man who had opened up his mind. He took another photo, also black-and-white, out of a drawer. This was the man who had opened up his heart: Krishna Prem, the Englishman-turned-sanyasi he had mentioned previously. He said Krishna Prem had died of cancer in the ashram he had founded.

He too died of cancer? How could this be? People in the West thought that cancer was linked to stress, I said, but in India many holy men from the last century died of cancer, all of them after living in blessed peace, far removed from the tensions of modern life. The mystic Ramakrishna, and Nisargadatta Maharaj, the man who made cigarettes on the streets of Bombay, both died of throat cancer; Ramana Maharshi died of a painful form of cancer of the arm and J. Krishnamurti, although already an old man by this stage, died of cancer of the gall bladder.

'Stress can be internal as well as external,' the Old Man said. 'Those who are searching for the truth often suffer a great deal. Krishna Prem managed to integrate his illness into his life, to see it as part of the whole and to reach a higher level of consciousness thanks to his illness.'

'Do you mean he accepted it?'

'It's not a question of accepting or not accepting, it's about making the illness a part of yourself. He managed to do this, and it became proof for us of everything that cannot be proved.

'In every generation and every continent there are characters such as Krishna Prem and Ramana Maharshi, whose lives demonstrate that it is possible to go beyond. All it takes is to be determined, to persevere and be fearless.'

Clearly he was giving me discreet advice. Did I have a lot of books in the bag I had brought with me? Then I should be careful. 'The knowledge you find in books is all second-hand, borrowed. It's not worth much at all.' And he went on to tell me another story.

A man went into a large library, and after much studying and searching, decided to take three books with him. He went to the counter to check the books out, and asked the librarian, 'How many books are there in this library?'

'Tens of thousands,' he said.

'And how long would it take to read all of them?'

'Oh, several lives.'

'In that case, I don't want these either,' the man said. 'There has to be another way.' And then he departed.

This other way, according to the Old Man, was the way of experience, experienced personally. True understanding never takes place in the mind but in the heart. One only really understands what they have experienced personally, what they have felt inside themselves. There are various ways in which one can attain such experience. His was the candle trick, practised regularly, without tiring or losing heart. 'For at least ten minutes a day,' he said.

His first guru had forced him to do those for ten minutes, and thinking about it, that was the best advice he had ever received. As the years had gone by. Those ten minutes had turned into hours, but he had never forgotten the importance of taking that first step. I should try it too.

'At least ten minutes to begin with. Force yourself.'

It was the kind of encouragement that comes from someone who believes they have discovered something, and do not want to keep it to themselves. I was very interested in this discovery and as the Old Man could sense it, he continued, 'Above all, you have to quieten your mind. Only then will you be able to hear the voice inside. You must not be impatient, for the intuition which opens up your consciousness only arrives infrequently. Perhaps it's just a drop, but when that drop comes, it comes like the ocean. What speaks to you then is the voice of the inner man, the cosmic man, the self. You can call it the Beloved, like the Sufis do; the philosopher's stone, like the alchemists do; call it Buddha; call it Him, Her. But know that it is there, and that it is the real you.' His throaty laugh was full of warmth and friendliness.

I returned to my retreat without lighting the torch I had used on my arrival. The moon had not yet risen, but the sparkling of the firmament was sufficient for me to be able to see where I was putting my feet. Before going into the house, I stopped. It was cold, but the ground was dry. I lay down on the grass and looked at the stars. I felt I was looking at them for the first time. In one sense I was, for I was looking at them without thinking of their names, without looking for the North Star or the Ursa Minor. I imagined I was released from all 'knowledge', I lost myself in the marvellous, comforting immensity of the universe. I was no longer looking at it. I was now a part of it.

One of the many resolutions I had made when I departed was to keep a record of all of my dreams. I knew that the only way to do so was to make notes as soon as I woke up. I had read somewhere that in order to dream more, and hence become 'witness to the nocturnal journey of the soul', it was necessary to have just a light meal in the evening, to sleep on a hard surface and to fall asleep consciously, rather than allowing oneself just to drift off. The Swami too used to say that the only experience comparable to death was the passage from the normal state of consciousness to sleep, and that anyone can get an idea of what it is like to die by paying special attention to that moment, remaining conscious of it right to the very last moment. I tried too, but was so tired and the room was so cold that I drifted right off under my heavy Tibetan blankets and slept like a log. A very happy sleep.

I had two dreams, which I forced myself to write down. In the first I was with friends on the Peak tram, the funicular railway that goes up Victoria Peak in Hong Kong. I was looking for a hospital, the address of which I had in my pocket. But at one stop I jumped off the tram, pretending I had arrived and left the others to continue on their journey. From the platform I gestured to them as to how we could meet up, but inside I knew that I had given them the slip and would never see them again.

In the second dream, I was in a city in Central Asia. There too, I was looking for a hospital, which Doctor Bringluck had given me the address for. I was crossing a square where two large bulls were fighting, one of them black and the other white. A man intervened, a kind of magician with a red bandana around his forehead. He separated the two animals using a machete, cut the head off the white bull, pulled its tongue out of its mouth and offered a bite to a child, who I realized was the real leader and magician of the ceremony. This child had 'solved the problem' and was able to teach me the secret of his powers. I knew I didn't have time because I had to go to the hospital, but thinking I might be able to go and see him afterwards, I asked the child for his name and address. He smiled at me and wrote them down in my notebook. I felt I was holding something important in my hands, as though I had come close to some inexplicable but mysteriously effective power.

Usually it is Angela who helps me to interpret my dreams. Who knows what implications she might have shown me in these? But she wasn't there, she was miles away, and deep down I felt it was this too that I had dreamt of. I got up feeling very positive. I felt the dreams boded well. I saw them as confirmation that I wanted to be alone, that I had the 'address' for where I was going, and that approaching the 'power of magic', something outside the realm of reason, was the right thing for me to be doing at this time.

Dawn was breaking. I wrapped myself in a blanket and went up to the highest point of the ridge to greet the mountains. They were not there yet. A veil of opaque haze shrouded the entire horizon. Slowly, imperceptible shadows began to emerge from the semi-darkness, followed by white, cold silhouettes. Suddenly, the peaks were illuminated with pink and orange. In the valleys the haze turned to violet, then gold, and the glaciers were set on fire against the lapis lazuli sky. The world had become an apotheosis of light and joy. Balancing on the tops of the cedar trees, the birds began to twitter and my heart was with them.

The simple, remote beauty of the mountains awoke a sentiment in my heart which was akin to the emotion one feels when in love: a feeling of completeness, invincible strength and almost immortality. I had never before felt so in the presence of the divine. Heaven was within reach and the mountains appeared to be the way to attain it.

I didn't need to think of myths, wise men in ice caves or hidden treasures in Shangri-La. I didn't need to hope for any miracle. It was all there, in the life around me. I lacked nothing, feared nothing, worried about nothing. Even my death seemed to me to be a part of that infinite perfection.

The days passed one after another, in absolute peace, without plans, expectations or deadlines, apart from the comforting rising and setting of the sun. I could sense the discreet presence of the Old Man in his house, but he too wanted to be alone, and neither of us were tempted to keep each other company. However, I would subsequently discover that he nonetheless spent a part of his time entertaining some rather odd visitors.

More than anything, I wanted to fast. I wanted to rid myself of everything that the world down in the valley stuffs and distracts itself with: news, desires, hopes, gossip. Up there, with no electricity, telephone, newspapers, anything or anyone to take account of, it was easy to get some clearing out done. As soon as you depart from your routine, you notice how little freedom, including inner freedom, there was in your everyday life, and how what you do and think is often merely the result of automatic mechanisms. We take the reasoning of reason for granted, the notions of science, the needs of our bodies and of logic. In so doing, we prevent ourselves from seeing the world and ourselves in any way other than how we normally see it.

How many ideas and convictions, how much 'knowledge' had I acquired in the course of my life! How nice it would be to go back to being a blank sheet of paper on which to write something completely new! This is a problem which Zen Buddhism in China tackled right from the outset, and one of the simple yet apt anecdotes used for centuries to indicate the path to be taken by novices makes precisely this point.

A learned professor went to see a monk.

'Tell me, what is Zen?' the professor asked.

The monk did not answer. Instead, he invited him to sit down, put a pot of tea in front of him and started to pour him some from it. The cup was soon full, but the monk carried on pouring regardless. The professor was speechless, for a while said nothing, then seeing that the monk was not stopping, warned him, 'It's full, it's full!'

'You're right,' the monk replied. 'Like you: you're full of opinions and prejudices. How am I supposed to tell you what Zen is if you don't empty your mind first?'

The monk in this story did not explain how one was supposed to go about emptying their mind. But I found the night was a great help in this respect. Everything that stimulates our senses by the light of day recedes in the night and disappears into darkness, leaving the individual alone. The night is his time, the individual is the only spectator and the only one being observed.

Perhaps because I was sleeping in the ideal conditions for dreaming, or perhaps because, having decided I wanted to record my dreams, a part of me remained alert through the night, but I have never dreamt as much as I did while I was there. Every night was a spectacle, usually an unpleasant one. While during the daytime I felt calm and relaxed, as soon as I fell asleep I was assailed by anguish, conflicts and obsessions. The 'awake-I', which had the impression it had distanced itself from the anxieties of the world, was goaded and contradicted by the 'asleep-I', from whose concealed sewers the most unbridled passions scuttled forth.

If I still had any doubts that the world of our senses is not the only form of reality, at night I found myself confronted with another which I was forced to reckon with. In the same way that snails are made to eat only lettuce leaves and are immersed in vinegar prior to being eaten, I too was being cleansed and flushed out. The irrigation was not colonic, it was the bowels of my long-term memory, where the emotional debris of a lifetime had ended up, that were being washed out. I found much more real, powerful toxins and poisons in the sieve of my consciousness than I had ever imagined. And I had unlimited time and leisure to reflect on them.

The Old Man got up to do the candle trick in the middle of the night, and I tried to do likewise. It was bitterly cold, but I forced myself to get up. All wrapped up in a thick blanket, with a woollen beret on my head which I pulled right down to my ears, I lit the wick of my candle and sat on the ground, straight-backed, in front of that little orange flame with the blue-coloured soul. I closed my eyes and observed with detachment the thoughts, memories, images and remains of my dreams. At no time did I step in to change, direct or refuse them. I observed them without identifying with them, as if I had nothing to do with them.

I sat like this for much more than ten minutes, and felt like things were beginning to become a bit tidier.

There was also another thing that I found up in the mountains and which became increasingly important to me: silence. We are no longer used to it, but up there it became the background music to all the experiences that I had.

There were various types of silence and each of them had its own qualities. In the daytime, it was the sum of the birds' twittering, the animal cries and the wind blowing. No other unnatural sound was added to these – no man-made sounds. At night, the silence was a single, dull echo which came up through the walls from the bowels of the earth and reverberated everywhere. There, silence itself was a sound. A symbol of the harmony between opposites I so craved. My ears heard absolutely nothing, I realized, but the echo was outside and inside my head. The voice of God? The music of the heavenly spheres? As I listened, too tired to define it, all I could bring to mind was an enormous fish singing on the ocean floor.

Glorious silence! Yet, we modern individuals instinctively avoid silence and are afraid of it, perhaps because we associate it with death. We have lost the habit of being silently on our own. If we have a problem or are scared by something, we prefer to distract ourselves with noise, to blend into some crowd rather than stand out from it in silent reflection. I am sure this is wrong because silence represents man's original experience. Without silence, there are no words and no music. Without silence, nothing can be heard. Only in silence is it possible to go back in time with ourselves, to rediscover the link between our bodies and us as bodies plus all the other stuff that goes along with them.

For some time I had been preaching the sanctity of silence to anyone who would listen to me, until eventually I found an old Indian tale that explained everything succinctly.

A king went to a famous rishi in the forest. 'Tell me, what is the nature of the self?' he inquired.

The old man looked at him, and did not reply.

The king repeated his question. Still the old man did not reply. Again he asked the same question, and again the rishi remained silent.

At this point, the king became angry. 'I ask you a question and you do not even answer me!'

'Three times I answered you, but you were not listening,' the rishi said calmly. 'The nature of the self is silence.'

Ramana Maharshi, the Indian mystic who died in 1950 in his ashram at the foot of the mountain which he had chosen as his guru, used to say, 'There are various different ways of communicating with someone: touching them, speaking to them, but above all, silence.'

Ramana's silence was powerful and many visitors were overcome simply by his presence. The writer Somerset Maugham came into a room where Ramana was sitting and fainted.[25] The psychologist Carl Jung refused to go and meet the great mystic during his journey to India, despite having arranged to do so beforehand, possibly out of fear that Ramana's silence would destroy his theory of the psyche.

---

[25] Maugham wrote about the experience in his book *Points of View*. It also inspired one of his most famous novels, *The Razor's Edge*.

As the days went by, I got the impression that the silence outside my mountain refuge was being matched by the silence within me. This, along with the solitude, gave me moments of sheer exaltation. Without external distractions or stimuli, my mind was free to follow each of its thoughts, escape from its limitations and then ultimately be quietened. To have a silent mind does not mean to have a mind with no thoughts. It means the thoughts occur in peace and quiet and may be observed better – thought better – because of it.

Never have we needed such masters of silence more than we do today. Never before have we been so bereft of these masters. We could do with them in our schools: 9 a.m., maths; 10 a.m., silence. It is a hard lesson to learn because, attuned as we are to the constant din of city life, we no longer manage to 'hear' the silence. Yet it is worth trying. When I was a child, if I had been taught that philosophy begins with making myself silent and asking myself who I am, perhaps I might have learnt something from the lessons in the end; if nothing else, at least the fact that all those theories really did have something to do with my life were maybe less boring than they were made to seem.

The other main feature of my life up in the mountains was nature. I came to realize why certain people have no need of sacred scriptures, of messages brought by someone else from another world. The book wide open before their very eyes is the only one that is worth reading. Every message you could ever want is written there. There is something profoundly sacred in nature; man has not yet put his grubby hands all over, to exploit it and bend it to serve his own purposes.

In its primordial purity, nature has the balance and fullness that we human beings aspire to. Simply by observing it, I got the impression that I had found some long-lost homeland, a sense of harmony that I had long forgotten. Getting my life back in step with the rhythms of nature was like a form of medicine. In the cities, we do not notice such things. When the day ends, without thinking we switch on the lights, carry on reading, walking, working just the same. We could even turn the whole thing around, as many are forced to do by their jobs, and stay awake by night and sleep by day. But in doing so, it is ourselves that we are turning upside down and around. The more civilized we become, the further away we get from nature.

Sitting on a rock high up on the Ridge, at times for hours on end with none of the anguish induced by the sense of time passing, all wrapped up against the cold as I looked out over the horizon criss-crossed by chain after chain of blue and white mountains, I had moments of sheer ecstasy. The same wind caressing me was the one swaying the blades of grass at my feet and driving the clouds in the sky. The life that I sensed all around me in the plants, flowers and animals was the same life that coursed through my veins. Nature helps us to expand our consciousness. All of a sudden mine seemed able to perceive fullness. In nature, there is nothing small or petty, nothing that afflicts us or impoverishes us. In nature, we are led to entertain notions of grandeur, and we instinctively allow our lungs to expand and breathe in deeply, as though wanting to allow what is outside to enter us.

I was alone, but wherever I looked there were dozens, hundreds, an infinite number of other existences. Everywhere there was life, in various forms and at various stages coming into being. The Cosmic Spider at that moment was spinning the web of the universe, each part of which was held together by the same thread, like the pearls on Indra's necklace, each capable of reflecting the others.

And this spider had no need of a seventh day to rest. It just carried on spinning.

What wonderful visions of creation these are! A creation which is taking place right here and now, taking place continuously. Not one that is lost in time and which took place over six days only. Not man being created before woman, and not even man created in the image and likeness of his creator. Precisely the opposite is true: it is man who has conceived his creator in his own image and likeness!

For who else is the god of religions, but the projection of man's own ego and passions? Jealous of other gods, selective in whom he loves, vindictive to the point of condemning anyone who might have offended him in the short span of their lives to an eternity of suffering in hell. Those passions which religions attribute to the creator are entirely human. They do not exist anywhere else in nature.

What a pleasure it was to be able to observe my own thoughts! Even more so surrounded by such beauty, which I was free to enjoy without having to try and make it my own. This is another calming aspect of nature: its immense beauty is there for all. No one could think of picking up a dawn or sunset and taking it home with them.

The Divine Artist was a never-ending source of surprises: a dark cloud which obscured the sun and created a golden waterfall on the glaciers; a sudden wall of rain, behind which the sun shone as though made of metal, or the emergence of the world from the cosmic dark of night which was different every time.

There were things that filled me with wonder, just in looking at the span of earth I bent down towards in order to find something to put at the foot of the Milarepa I kept on my table. The colours, shapes and veins on the leaves seemed to be infinite, as were the varieties of grass and flowers, sometimes minuscule. Large and small: a simple shrub and the vast chain of the Himalayas; both an expression of the same beauty and a part of the same never-ending spectacle.

One morning, as I was doing my exercises with the sunlight on my back, I saw myself reflected in a bank of fog rising up from the valley below the Ridge. The fog was moving in great clouds, and all of a sudden a halo formed around the silhouette of my head with all the colours of the rainbow. But I didn't have much time for indulging in notions of possible canonization. The crows, clearly laughing at me, started cawing from on top of a nearby tree.

The Old Man's two dining companions had forced their way into my solitary life. I soon came to realize how inquisitive they were. When I was in my room, they peered over the roof and looked in through the windowpanes. I couldn't go outside to paint without one or the other of them descending on me and commenting on the picture, or so it seemed. One afternoon, I heard them calling like mad. I looked out of the window and saw they were up a tree, but a large monkey sitting on the fence was picking all my flowers off one by one. They had been warning me!

If I managed to reach the top of a nearby mountain after a long walk, still I found them flying over me and calling out from above. They had got there with just a few flaps of their wings, carried by the wind. I looked at myself with their eyes: how heavy I was, how earth-bound! When they rose up on their wings or allowed themselves to plunge to the depths of the valley below the Ridge, it was hard not to envy them, so light in comparison.

That valley contained a wealth of life that eluded me. Down there, I could hear the raucous cries of the Himalayan deer; I could hear the wild she-goats leaping around at the sound of my footsteps. Them too! I could barely make out their shadow. The ancient Chinese got it right when they painted the horse of Fergana with wings. How else would it be possible to depict the sudden and light way they rise up from the ground?

One afternoon, when a thick fog had risen up from the valley and I was walking along the Ridge as though on a tightrope suspended over a void, I heard the sound of a flute rising up from the abyss below. I stopped. That sound was speaking to me. And despite the fact that music has never particularly affected me emotionally, I felt as though I were on the point of tears. The flute, perhaps of a distant shepherd, struck a chord with me. I stood there, listening. Then, like everything, perhaps simply because the wind had changed direction, the sound stopped too and I instantly missed it.

Then I used my mind to hear it again.

Sometimes I can still hear the sound of the flute playing in me. Basho, the samurai-turned-hermit who wrote haikus, knew all about this type of experience, which is why he wrote:

The gong of the temple
Has fallen silent
But the sound continues
To come from the flowers.

Without us organizing it, the Old Man and I allowed our meetings to be determined by chance. Our paths crossed during our walks in the forest or we would visit each other when we had something to ask for or share. No regularity, no sense of obligation, no routine.

So when we did see each other or sit on my landing drinking the China tea I would pour for him from my beautiful Yixing teapot, it was always an event for which he gave the credit to 'all the forces of the universe – visible and invisible, tangible and intangible, male and female, positive and negative' that had combined to make the miracle of that moment possible. He was joking, of course, but not entirely.

For him, everything was related. He was convinced that everything that happens to us has a meaning, even if much of the time we are unable to see it. He felt that my illness too had a meaning. The important thing was to become aware of it and this would mean embarking on one final journey, the return journey, as he called it. It was the journey of every man who awakes from the sleep of the senses.

'Do you see? It is time to go home, to go back to your roots. And your roots are divine, you know, because while on the scale of time we have descended from the apes, on the scale of being we have descended from God. Going home means claiming your divine inheritance.'

'How?' I asked.

'By digging deep inside yourself, gradually getting rid of the layers of make-up that are your personality and knowledge to reach the essence of your being. It takes courage,' he said, 'because it involves throwing away one thing after another, until you have nothing left to hold on to and you realize that in fact something is holding on to you. Only then do you realize that thing is what you were looking for.'

Another time, he pointed to one of the large cedars outside his house and said, 'You see? In all cultures, the tree of life is depicted as being like that cedar: its roots in the earth and its branches in the sky. That's what life is like. It begins in darkness and looks for the light. But the rishis also describe another tree in the Upanishads. This tree has its roots in heaven and its branches turned towards earth. This is the tree of spiritual life, which begins with matter and reascends to heaven via its divine roots.'

The Old Man always spoke very slowly, making long pauses as if to give time for what he said to go right through me, not just my ears.

'It is this life, the spiritual life, which matters. And the first step is the most difficult. It involves removing oneself from the earth and all its certainties. It involves avoiding the snare of the intellect. We owe the intellect a great deal. It helps us analyse, select, judge, and extend the realm of our knowledge. But for what purpose? Man can make great discoveries and advance enormously in terms of what he knows, but whatever progress he makes, he will almost always find the unknown lurking on the frontier of knowledge. We have to admit it: there is a mystery, and our minds are unable to solve it.'

One evening, it was already pitch-black when I heard him arrive. He had come to ask me something, but was distracted when he saw a bowl with half an apple in it on the floor.

'Ah yes, it's for the mouse,' I said, finally getting a chance to tell him of the problem I had been looking for a solution to for the past few days.

Every night, a mouse appeared in my house and went around nibbling at whatever it could find and hence ruining all my precious supplies of fruit, potatoes and tomatoes. I didn't want to kill it and was trying to persuade it to eat what I put out in the bowl for it, rather than it going for my other things.

The Old Man laughed heartily at my good intentions, and told me what had happened to Lama Govinda one time when he was his neighbour on Cranks' Ridge. He too had a mouse which kept coming into his home, and the people there used to say to him, 'Lamaji, there's nothing else to do, you'll have to kill it.'

But Lama Govinda was a Buddhist and the idea of killing another living being was anathema to him. So he bought one of those cages with spring doors which trap the mice but do not kill it. It worked perfectly. In just a few days Lama managed to catch several of them. Each one was duly taken outside into the wood and set free once again.

'Don't you see? It's the same mouse each time,' people said to him. 'You have to kill it. Wherever you take it, it'll keep coming back.'

Lama Govinda refused to believe it. But when another mouse ended up in his cage, he borrowed one of his wife's brushes and painted its tail green. Then he went for a walk, going even further than usual before releasing the mouse. By the time he got home, empty cage in his hand, a little mouse was there waiting for him at his doorstep. 'He had a green tail and was grinning at me,' Lama Govinda would say when he told the story.

The Old Man thought my non-violent solution might work. 'Basically it's all a question of the psyche,' he said.

'The psyche?'

'Yes. The psyche is not in us, it is us who are in the psyche. It is everywhere, in everything that surrounds us. It's neither Western nor Eastern; it's universal. The psyche is one: for animals, plants, rocks and humans, and always the same psyche. Take a creeper: it finds a place in which to take root, then reaches for the light. Take the bees, all kept together by their queen, or the storks which pass by every year on their flight from Lake Mansarovar in Tibet towards Rajasthan. What makes all this possible? The psyche! The consciousness which underlies them all, the cosmic consciousness which holds the entire universe together and without which nothing would exist. The whole point of yoga is to get into contact with the cosmic consciousness.

Once you succeed in doing so, there is no more time, no more death.'

'But the mouse?'

'The mouse too is in the same consciousness of which my consciousness, yours and his are all but reflections.' Then he laughed. And as though to challenge me, he added, 'These aren't even Indian ideas! In the West, your rishis have said the same things as ours, the same as in the Vedanta. It is just that you have forgotten your rishis and have put them in libraries and museums and the books of professors. For us, the rishis are always there, companions and masters of life. That is the difference.'

'Western rishis?'

He had a long list of our 'seers'; from Heraclitus to Pythagoras to Boethius; from Giordano Bruno to Bergson. But Plato was easily his favourite.

'Take him as your guru and you will see that he accepts you as his disciple and speaks to you.' This was what the Old Man himself had done. He confessed that for a while now he had been receiving Plato in his delightful apartment and spent many hours in silent discussions with him. According to him, Plato had gone much 'further' than many others. His *Republic* was one of the finest, most inspiring visions of that 'inner republic', the republic of the self. The fact that Plato had described it all so well should be a great encouragement to others to seek it too, the Old Man believed.

He felt that there was a common thread linking people across millennia and continents, thinkers as diverse as Plato and Gurdjieff, Plotinus and Sri Aurobindo, the Sufi masters, Meister Eckhart, Ramana Maharshi and Krishna Prem. 'They are all on the same path; some of them are further ahead than others, some of them get lost along the way, others eventually reach their destination, but what all of them are looking for are our roots.

This is the meaning of the question: "Who am I?" Those who do not ask themselves this question cannot understand, and maybe they think we are all mad, but we must persevere. We are going home ... Come on, you come too!' he said.

Perhaps he felt he had been rather too personal with this final exhortation, so he returned to the question of the mouse. He wanted to tell me 'another of those stories which the mind cannot understand', but which he himself had been witness to. I put some more water on to boil for our tea, he rolled himself another cigarette, and ...

In the ashram at Mirtola, Krishna Prem had around ten disciples with him. There was also a large Tibetan dog which was never left outside at night because a leopard had become accustomed to roaming around the grounds of the ashram and stopping to look in through the large window. The leopard would roar, the dog would bark, and everyone would have to get out of bed and shout and make noise to send the leopard away. Each night it was the same story and no one could get any sleep.

'I'll try and do something about it,' said Krishna Prem eventually. He went to the temple and stayed there for around ten minutes. That evening the leopard did not appear, nor the evening after that, nor the one after that. It had vanished.

'What did you do?' one of his disciples asked the former English lecturer-turned-*sanyasi.*

'I didn't do anything,' Krishna Prem replied. 'I merely spoke to Lord Krishna and said, "Your leopard is disturbing your dog."'

'That is all there is to it,' the Old Man said to me. 'The psyche is everywhere, and the leopard, the dog, your mouse, we are all in the psyche. To deny this means wishing to remain blind, to stay in the darkness.'

Blindness, darkness. These words reminded him of why he had come around to visit me in the first place. He needed matches. He didn't even have one left for his candle trick, as he called his regular night-time appointment with the self. I gave him a box and he set off home into the night.

Every two or three weeks, I went down to Almora to stock up on provisions. The bazaar there extends along a narrow, stone-clad alley which leads uphill and remains one of the more old-fashioned ones. Some of the houses there are still made of wood with inlaid windows. The workshops, some of them minuscule, are all in a row, each a mini-stage with its own solo actor-merchant-philosopher. Buying and selling are marginal activities. Everywhere a great sense of peace reigns. Even the dogs there are not like other dogs: they don't bark or attack, but peacefully share the pavement with the cows and small crowds of men squatting to warm themselves around small fires.

Bazaars are a reflection of the communities; the one in Almora appeared to possess some special air of wisdom and serenity, accumulated over the centuries of its existence at the foot of the Himalayas. Many of the men sitting in their workshops seemed to be just waiting for an opportunity to hold forth on the destinies of the world and the soul.

One of the shops I stopped at, I talked with the owner, Said Ali, a thin, unkempt Muslim with a very warm smile. He repaired watches in a small hole in the wall to which he had given the name: 'A Million Tick-Tocks'.

Life had been hard for Said Ali, but he was not angry. His two children had suddenly developed schizophrenia, and neither magicians nor doctors had been able to do anything, apart from make Said Ali a bit poorer. His wife was inconsolable as a result of their misfortune, and spent hours of her day praying to Allah to heal them. Said Ali too was a devout Muslim and did not miss any of the five prayer times each day, but on the matter of their children, he and his wife did not see eye to eye.

'You cannot ask Allah to intervene in human affairs. When I have a watch to repair, I can pray all I want. He will not do it for me. He has already done so much. He has given me eyes, ears, hands and a brain. The least I can do is repair the watch myself,' he said.

One day I asked him how he managed to never let himself be overcome by the unhappiness. 'Every morning after my prayers, I sit down on the ground and hold my back straight. I follow my breathing, listen to my blood as it circulates in my veins, empty my head of all thoughts, and concentrate on Him. He who is without time and space; he who leaves no trace, who is unknown but who is always present. I spend some time with Him. Then I come to work,' he said to me.

Apart from his devotion to Him, Said Ali also had another secret that kept him alive: music. He composed ghazals, musical poems, and forgot his troubles as he sang them. Once a year he even performed on stage. Every February, an Italian came to Almora; with a touch of genius, mystical and practical, musician and poet who called himself Krishna Das, the servant of Krishna. He would stay for some time at the old Savoy Hotel and provide guidance to his initiates who were looking for peace. Every morning during those days, Said Ali would add his own fine voice to the one with which Krishna Das would make his sitar sing, and the poetry of the old Sufi hymns would fill him with joy and a zest for life until the following February. When I passed by his shop, he was always smiling.

The bazaar was full of surprises. One day, as I approached the chemist's shop, I noticed Balbir was making all his usual expansive 'Namaskar' gestures to me, but without the many words he customarily greeted me with. He smiled and held up a notice that said, 'Six weeks' silence'. However, he continued to work and ordered his two assistants about by means of loud grunts and great gestures.

'He's probably doing it to atone for some huge lie or swindle,' the Old Man commented when I went to see him and give him news from the world.

He invited me to share his dinner with him again that night, so I told him of the 'orphans' who had appeared on the Ridge. Most of them were middle-aged foreigners who had spent years as disciples of Osho at Poona and then Babaji at Lucknow, and who had been utterly lost since these gurus had 'left their bodies'. Two of them had taken me into their white cubicle on the Ridge, to have me listen to a cassette in which Osho spoke of death as being like 'an enormous orgasm with God'. Hearing that voice for the hundredth time, the two of them fell into an ecstatic trance, while I was struck by the degree of psychological dependence these people had on their guru. Was it worth all the trouble of living in an ashram for years and following a master, if all it meant was to become enslaved again rather than liberated?

The Old Man was amused, and answered me the way he liked best. With a story.

A man woke up in chains one morning, and did not know how to free himself. For years he was looking for someone to release him. Then one day he passed by a blacksmith's workshop, saw him forging a piece of iron, and asked him to help. With two blows, the blacksmith broke his chains. The man was so grateful that he began to work for the blacksmith, became his servant and spent the rest of his days ... chained to the blacksmith.

'The guru is important,' the Old Man continued. 'He expresses in words what you feel is true inside. But once you have had that direct experience of the Truth, you do not need him any longer. The guru points to the moon, but woe betide you if you mistake his finger for the moon. The guru shows you the way, but you yourself have to walk on it. Alone.'

Then, as though the moment had come to tell me something that could prove to be genuinely useful to me, he added, 'The real guru is the one you have inside, here,' and he prodded my chest with one of his bony fingers. 'It's all here. Don't look for anything outside yourself. Everything you can find outside is by its very nature transient, impermanent. You can deceive yourself into thinking you may find stability in wealth, but then it ends. You may think you find it in love for a person, but then they go away. You can give your life to a guru, but then they die. Nothing outside your body will ever satisfy you. The only stability that can ever truly satisfy you is internal. Gurus who make themselves completely indispensable serve their own egos more than their disciples' searching.'

The Old Man wanted to lend weight to what he had said, so he reminded me of Buddha's last words. When he was about to die, surrounded by a select group of followers, all of whom were in tears, his cousin and disciple Ananda said to Buddha, 'Now who will lead us?'

'Be a light unto yourselves. Take refuge in the self,' Buddha had replied.

The self he spoke of was the same as that in the Vedanta, according to the Old Man. 'And without knowledge of that self,' he concluded, 'there is no knowledge at all. Only information.'

'WHAT ABOUT THE GLASS OF WATER?'

The mouse and I had come to an understanding. He ate what I put in his bowl every evening and did not touch the rest. But I do believe he told some of his friends and relatives about my land of plenty, for one of them took up residence in the ceiling above my bedroom and made a right racket every morning before sunrise, as if to remind me it was time for the candle trick. Or at least that was how I liked to see it.

Even the stone table I had laid for the two crows in front of my house had, over time, turned into a kind of general mess at which all types of different 'people' came to eat. All I had to do was stand quite still at my window and watch the various comings and goings: so many different types of animal, each with its own personality, colours, behavioural patterns and habits.

One morning, I was sitting on the grass warming up in the sunlight, when a tiny grey bird with white and red stripes and a little crest of black feathers arrived. I sat quite still. It looked around, flew down on to my feet and unashamedly began pecking at my woollen socks. When its mouth was full of thread for its nest, it departed, only to return immediately in search of another mouthful.

This reminded me of the Zen master, whose disciples were lined up in front of him ready for him to begin his evening sermon, when a little bird came to rest on the ledge of his open window. The bird looked around, chirruped for a while and then flew away.

'Here ends today's sermon,' the old monk said, and departed too.

How many lessons have the Asians learnt by observing the lives of the animals? Many more than any of us in the West have. The monks at Shaolin invented kung-fu by combining the various methods of self-defence adopted by animals, so as not to succumb to the bandits who plagued the forests surrounding their temple. The Indians developed hatha yoga to control their bodies by copying the animals' most important activities: stretching, washing, breathing and so forth. Animal behaviour is determined by instinct rather than thought, so their life is in absolute harmony with nature. Ours is less so. We no longer 'feel nature'; we do not take it seriously or try to learn from it. Yet it is there, a great museum with no opening hours or curators, a university with free access to all and lectures at every hour of the day and night.

'When you touch a stone, you feel something. Try and imagine what the stone feels. It too has a conscience,' the Old Man once said to me. Then, perhaps so that I did not think him quite mad, he explained that according to the shastra, the mineral world is no different from the rest of the universe. No Indian sculptor of antiquity would ever have dreamt of making a statue of a god out of stone that was deemed to be female, or one of a goddess out of a stone held to be male because of its consistency, colouring and veins.

I had gone to see the Old Man to tell him about a dream I had. I wanted him to help me interpret it, but he was not interested. The content of dreams was stuff for psychoanalysts, he said, who considered it their duty to re-educate their patients to society rather than change and educate society towards the needs of mankind. What he was interested in was whether or not I had discovered who it was actually dreaming.

'If it is you in the dream, who is it that is dreaming about you while you are in the dream? Keep digging. Dig in one place only and go deep down, down, down. You'll see, you'll find water eventually,' he said.

For days now I had been having problems with the candle trick. Everything went fine as long as it was dark outside, but as soon as it became light, I could feel the sunshine and my mind could see the mountains. I preferred to look at the world outside with my eyes wide open, rather than keep them shut in contemplation of an inner world which at times truly did feel like I was making it up. I made no attempt to conceal my frustration from the Old Man. He smiled, and rather than replying directly, told me an anecdote from the life of Rabia, a well-known saint from the Sufi tradition.[26]

Rabia spent a good deal of her time shut indoors, lost in contemplation. One day, a friend of hers was out walking beneath her window and called out to her, 'Rabia, come outside and see the beauty of creation!'

From behind the closed shutters came the answer, 'You come inside and see the beauty of the Creator!'

It was a nice story. But my contrarion spirit had sprung back to life with a vengeance, and my reaction was, 'You're always going on about inside and outside. But where on earth is this inside?'

'It is certainly not inside your body. There it stinks just as much as it does outside,' the Old Man retorted. Then he continued, 'There is an inside which is nowhere, like silence, like the afterworld.

[26] *Rabia* means 'fourth', because her father had already had three daughters by the time she was born in 717 AD at Basra, now in Iraq.

Where is that? If you were a fish that was given to reflection and metaphysical speculation, you would have said, "There must be something beyond this water." There you have it: the inside is somewhere near there.'

Soon it snowed. It started during the night and when I got up for the candle trick while it was still dark, the silence outside had stopped echoing. Now it was a muffled sound. At sunrise I looked out of the window: everything was white, the cedars had become even grander with their frozen branches, the surrounding meadows formed an even more pronounced amphitheatre and the horizon was covered in a flickering curtain of snowflakes that continued to fall. The sun appeared around mid-morning for just a few moments and the mountains suddenly seemed to be very, very close. The snow gave them a lightness I had never seen before. But the spectacle was short-lived. A large cloud dampened the proceedings; it turned dark again and it started snowing once more. It continued all day, all night, the day after that and the one after that too. My window was half-covered and my door was blocked. The animals had all disappeared and all that was left was the immense silence.

Someone came up from a village in the valley below the precipice to see if the Old Man was alright and to give him news that the lady sanyasi from the mandir had died. They had found her in the forest with one of her legs ripped off. The police were trying to establish whether she had died of exposure and the animals had sunk their teeth into her once she was already dead, or whether it had been the leopard that had attacked her and eaten her. If it was the leopard, they would have to organize a hunt, for once a leopard has begun eating people nothing will stop it. It would start prowling around houses too, looking for prey. It would have to be killed.

Two days of sunshine thawed the snow slightly, so the Old Man and I decided to go down to Almora to stock up on our provisions. It was hard work walking through the forest to the mandir. No one had yet walked on the path, and at some points the snow reached up to our knees. However, there were lots of animal footprints and the Old Man pointed out the leopard's footprints to me.

'It'd be nice to see it – though perhaps from a distance,' I volunteered.

'Before you see a leopard, three leopards have seen you at least three times,' he replied.

Neither of us said so, but we were both obviously thinking of the lady sanyasi from the mandir. The Old Man, partly in jest and partly to frighten off any leopards that might have been watching from their hiding places, began to declaim loudly the opening lines of William Blake's famous poem:

Tiger! Tiger! Burning bright
In the forests of the night,
What immortal hand or eye
Could frame thy fearful symmetry?

I too joined in, and the two of us walked on with renewed vigour reciting loudly: 'Tiger! Tiger! Burning bright ...'

The light in the forest was dazzling, reflecting off the whiteness of the snow. The trees were motionless and frozen. Curiously, some of the rhododendrons had begun to flower and the clusters of bright red buds were like handfuls of rubies scattered over the ice.

We amused ourselves by shouting 'Tiger! Tiger! Burning bright ...' until we reached the mandir where a jeep was waiting for us. We did our shopping in the bazaar and returned home safe and sound that evening, with our supplies of vegetables, rice and flour. We celebrated our successful expedition by dining together in his lovely warm room perfumed by the iron stove in the fireplace.

The Old Man pulled an old edition of Blake's poems out of a little cupboard, one with gold lettering etched into the blue cover. Together we re-read the poem that had 'saved' us. It really was beautiful, especially the part at the end where Blake realizes that the same hand created both the fierce beast and the meek lamb.

'You see? An Englishman living in the eighteenth century saw to the heart of things, just like the rishis did,' the Old Man enthused. 'He realized that the divine is that in which opposites coexist: beauty and horror; hatred and love. It's all there. There is no duality. The rishis had the courage to see evil as a part of God. But they were not the only ones. It is simply that in India, this vision is more explicit: Kali, the goddess of destruction, the one whose tongue drips blood and who has a chain of skulls around her neck, is also the mother of the universe, for the very reason that there is no creation without destruction. Duality is merely an illusion. It is we who wish to distinguish between happiness and unhappiness, joy and pain, life and death. But such distinctions are false. The truth is that they are all one.'

He quoted a verse from the Vedas: 'The day is the shadow of the night, life is the shadow of death.' Then he added, 'Achieving this means entering into contact with the Spirit, Him, or whatever else you want to call it.'

'And if He too were just an illusion?' I asked. 'If the life of the spirit were also just hearsay? Where actually is this spirit?'

He looked at me in amusement. 'Tell me, Tiger: where is it *not*?'

And from that moment onwards, 'Tiger' became his affectionate name for me.

Days, weeks, months passed; peacefully, in a harmonious

succession of thoughts, walks, silences, the odd conversation, and above all a whole lot of time devoted just to time itself. I had to go to New York for my regular check-ups with the fixers – one time Folco came with me, another time it was Leopold – but it was as though, by virtue of living on my own and sitting in front of a candle, I had actually succeeded in dividing myself. My body was travelling, being anaesthetized, inspected, woken up and put back on an aeroplane, but my mind was still there, in the peace and quiet of my stone house 9,000 feet up. So I returned there without ever really feeling as though I had left.

I wished to have less and less to do with New York and even the world down in the valley. I felt as though I had understood how it worked now and did not like it. Even my beloved hospital, which by this stage I had grown quite fond of, I realized was first and foremost a big business, run according to the same logic as a supermarket or a diamond mine. When a deposit I had put down on an operation was delayed as a result of the banks' usual machinations, I was informed my name would be removed from the list of patients due to be operated on that day.

On the other hand, even the respectable, traditionalist MSKCC had adapted to the times during my absence, to the extent that it had opened a Complementary Medicine section, adopted reiki, was researching into a possible cancer treatment based on arsenic and sent young people with guitars through the wards to cheer the patients up and speak to them about holistic medicine. The fixers themselves had no faith in any of that 'stuff', as they put it, but the hospital had evidently given in to the requests of a good number of patients. Or, more to the point, it did not want to lose their market share to the healers and their like.

At the end of the second visit, my residence permit for the state of limbo between illness and wellness had been extended from three to six months, but I was careful not to pay undue attention to this news. I felt as though I had reached my own form of wellness; silence, the sight of the mountains and my own company was all that I desired now.

If travelling had once been a kind of drug I was addicted to, now I was able to say that I had kicked the habit completely. There was not a single story of some possible medicine or healer that could persuade me to set off again. The only journey that interested me now was the 'return' journey the Old Man had spoken of. I had found a perfect description of it in Lao-tzu, which under different circumstances I might barely have noticed.

Legend has it that when the old Chinese philosopher who lived in the sixth century BC arrived in the northernmost part of China on a buffalo, before heading into the Himalayas from where he was never to return, the guardian of the Han Pass told him he would let him through on one condition only: before disappearing, he would write down his most important thoughts. This was how the Tao-te-Ching came to be written, the classic work of Taoism which begins with the words: 'The Tao which can be told is not the eternal Tao'.[27]

At one point in this book, Lao-tzu said that the end of man is to bring his own life into line with the Tao, with no striving, without wanting to achieve anything, but in simple recognition of that which is. Whoever practises Tao has only to be at peace with themselves for:

Without going out of the door,
He knows all that is to be known;

---

[27] Tao in Chinese means 'the way' and is broadly similar to the concept of dharma in the Vedas and Buddhism.

Without looking out of the window,
He sees the ways of heaven;
For the further you go,
The less you understand.
The wise man arrives without leaving,
Sees without looking,
Does without doing.

At Benares, I had allowed myself to be encouraged by the exhortation which Indra, the god of travellers, made to the young Rohita to set out on his journey. This, on the other hand, was the perfect exhortation to an old man who had already stopped to stop.

Spring came, so too did the monsoons. With each change in the climate new birds, animals and colours arrived in the forest and heavens. The road to Almora also changed with the passing months. First, it was set ablaze by the flowering of the rhododendrons, then it became yellow and hazy as the mimosas exploded into bloom, then it was dotted with blue by the clusters of jacaranda blossom.

One morning, as I bent down to pick a flower I had never seen before, I noticed that the grass all around me was full of ladybirds. In Hindi these are called 'Ram ki gai', the cows of Ram. Goodness knows why, someone's imagination must have done a few somersaults to come up with that. Mine did some too as I stopped to look at one and became distracted. The ladybirds climbed up a blade of grass, moved on to another, climbed down it, went back and forth on to another. At one point, wrapped in the slender tip of a blade of grass that appeared to yield to its weight, it pulled its tiny transparent wings out from under its shiny red shell with black spots and flew off, not to a bush nearby but far, far away, high up in the sky towards the mountain, without knowing anything at all of the laws of gravity, without wondering whether or not its mind could conceive of infinity, simply doing what it was born for, following its own nature.

Upon hearing that I have spent a large part of my life in Asia, on more than one occasion I have been asked if I have ever seen any 'miracles', unusual things such as a yogis levitating, walking on water or making themselves invisible. In fact, I have never seen anything of the kind. But the Ram ki gai flying off towards infinity? Is that not a miracle? One does not need to go off in search of the extraordinary, when the ordinary, if properly observed, can be so surprising, so divine.

My occasional visits to the world, especially to New York, where not only my dear hospital but everything else too, representing the most advanced tip of what Western society was supposed to be capable of producing, merely confirmed to me that the solution to man's problems cannot come from reason; it is reason itself which is the cause of so many of these problems.

Reason is the cause of the efficiency which is increasingly dehumanizing our lives and destroying the earth that we depend on. It is the cause of the violence we deploy in the hope of putting an end to all violence. It is behind all the weapons we build and sell in ever-increasing quantities, only for us then to wonder why there are still so many wars and children being killed. Reason is behind the cynical cruelty of economics, which makes the poor believe that one day they will be rich, while in fact the world is being divided more and more clearly into those who have more and those who have less.

Reason, which has been of great help to us and contributed to our well-being, particularly our material well-being, has now made us slaves. Having denied any role whatsoever to our emotions and intuition, having rendered the language of dreams thoroughly extinct, reason now forces us to think and talk only as it does.

It has removed all the mystery from our lives and has caused us to forget fables, made redundant the fairies and witches that used to do so much to people the otherwise barren panorama of our existence.

But what of all the alternatives? I too, could tell that they had limits. Words such as 'heart', 'intuition' and 'energies' had always left me cold, but given the disastrous results produced by the objective truth of reason, it seemed right to me to explore the terrain, however uncertain, of subjective truths instead. Not so much in order to find an alternative, but rather, as in the case of medicine, to find something complementary.

If reason and its products operating in the outside world, such as ideologies and religions, have failed to such an extent in their task of improving the human condition, which increasingly seems to be controlled by feelings of separation and violence, it makes sense to look inside man himself in order to seek another solution. Maybe we ourselves are the answer, provided we are able to escape from the slavery of preconditioned thought and experience, what we think we know, in order to recapture the freedom of our imagination and regain a space in which it can work.

Sometimes it may seem, and it certainly seem so to me, that to leave behind the terra firma of reason in favour of the shifting sands of non-reason is risky. But if you think about it, is it not a risk we are all already familiar with, despite the fact that we tend to forget it? For what is love, if not the negation of reason?

So why not seek to be 'unreasonable' in the way one is unreasonable when in love? Why not reject the automatic mechanisms of the rational mind which are the basis for our whole way of seeing the world?

'Tell me, what is the truth?' a monk asked his master.

'First you must drink all the water in the river with just one sip,' he replied.

'I've already done that.'

'Fine, and I have already answered your question.'

This was one example of the 'non-reason' practised by Zen Buddhists, who devoted themselves to this activity with passion. They too felt they would not be able to reach up to grasp the Ultimate Reality in one sole leap, as they dreamt of doing, without first leaving behind their normal way of thinking.

It was the Zen Buddhists, first in China at the Shaolin monastery, then in Japan where the tradition flourishes to this day, who developed the idea of the koan, a paradox which the rational mind is unable to deal with. It is an apparently absurd question that it is impossible to answer in a logical fashion. But this is precisely the meaning of it.

The best-known koan story is the one where a young novice saw his fellow monks every morning and evening going in and out of the rooms of the head abbot named Mokurai – his very name is a paradox, meaning 'silent thunder'. The young monk was envious, for he realized that Mokurai was giving the others special instruction on the art of meditation. One morning, he plucked up the courage, and he too went to see Silent Thunder.

'Not you. You are too young. Go away,' the abbot said when he saw him.

The boy was insistent and the old man gave in. 'Come back this evening.'

That evening he returned to Mokurai's door, struck the gong three times and went in. The monk said only this to him, 'Do you know what the sound of two hands clapping is like? If you do, what does one hand clapping sound like? Come back when you have found the answer.'

The boy was perplexed and returned to the master each day with a different answer: the sound of a drop of water falling on a stone; the music of a geisha; the song of a cricket; the breath of the wind. Lots of different sounds, but all of them wrong. None were the sound of one hand clapping. The young man was distraught, thought a lot, despaired. His torture continued for more than a year. Every day he went through all the various types of sounds, until one day, he managed to transcend them all. He ran to Mokurai, saying, 'Master, I have it. It is the sound which has no sound: it is silence.'

'Well done, young monk. That is indeed the sound of one hand clapping.'

The answer was obvious, but finding it was difficult. This was the real meaning of koan. The secret is not so much in the answer, as in the process that keeps the mind occupied. In looking for the solution, the young monk had had to come to terms with a variety of emotions, ranging from arrogance to anger, desperation and hatred for his master, until he reached a state of enlightenment which pushed his mind beyond its customary, linear way of reasoning and enabled him to think differently, rather than think and see things as they are. One hand clapping on its own makes no noise.

The mind is the fruit of time. It is a storehouse of experience; it works with what it knows, and by its very nature does not go beyond that with which it is familiar. When it has reached its rational limit, having failed in its attempt to find the solution within itself and what it has accumulated, the novice's mind finally retreats and allows him to go further and make the step up in terms of consciousness which enables him to see things differently. Today, this may involve the issue of non-sound; tomorrow, it might be a vision of the Ultimate Reality, the mystery of the great 'beyond', the unknown, which is always far vaster than that which is known, as the Old Man said.

We often have this kind of experience in the course of our lives: a problem appears to have no solution and the solution suddenly materializes outside the logic of the obvious ones.

I was thinking of koans one evening, when finally I realized that the question which had bothered me for three months in the ashram and which I had brought up into the mountains with me, namely 'Who am I?', was in fact the koan of koans. Despite the words of the Upanishads and the Gita, what the question triggered in me was not so much an intellectual process to be sealed with an answer – not even the answer of the Vedanta, 'You are that'. No, what it triggered in me was the process of questioning my own identity.

The answer lies in asking a question, in realizing that I am not my body, I am not what I do nor what I possess, the relationships I have, nor my thoughts, experiences or the self we all so dearly cling to. The answer has no words: it is the silent immersion of the 'I' in the self.

I realized that a part of my instinctive attempt to change my identity, renounce my past, go to the ashram and become Anam sprang from this need to escape from what I knew, to see things differently without the burden of the 'knowledge' I had accumulated in my life.

I had spent hours in front of a candle, trying to get the muddy waters surrounding the problem of the self to settle. One day I asked the Old Man what he thought of those practices that were intended to annihilate the self and sometimes had disastrous consequences.

As usual his reply came in the form of a story. This was one Ramakrishna himself used to reply to precisely this question concerning the self.

Outside a village, there lived a terrible snake which attacked and bit anyone who went near it, and with its hissing even managed to terrorize those who kept their distance. The villagers were at their wits end. Fortunately, one day a sadhu passed by, and he was asked to intervene. He went up to the snake, and spoke to it very civilly saying, 'You must leave these country folk in peace. They are not your food. They are not threatening you. Why should you threaten them? I realize you must eat mice and the other little beasts in the forest, but why should you terrorize these poor people? Do it for me; stop now.'

The snake agreed. A year later the sadhu returned to the village on his wanderings and saw the snake again looking decidedly the worse for wear. One of its eyes was hanging out of its socket, its mouth was bleeding and its whole body was covered in wounds.

'What happened to you?' asked the sadhu.

'Your words truly changed me, Master. I did exactly as you said and now everyone comes here and beats me. Even the children find it amusing to throw stones at me. But I, Master, shall continue to do just as you told me.'

'Idiot!' the sadhu blurted out. 'I never told you to stop hissing!'

What Ramakrishna meant, the Old Man concluded, was that the 'I' can come in useful. Indeed, a bit of ego can be indispensable for self-protection if we are to live in this world. What matters is that it should not take itself too seriously and that we realize eventually it is only a mask.

Every coin has two sides, and even the solitary life spent in peace and quiet and focused on itself has a dark side, even in a place so illuminated by the joys of nature. In my case, this took the form of hallucinations.

They began one night. I was sitting in front of the candle, as usual doing my exercises to calm my mind and dispassionately observe the dance of my thoughts against the backdrop of silence, when I suddenly heard the voice of a woman. It was not the voice of anyone I knew, nor Angela's, but a clear, distinct voice coming from nowhere in particular, which spoke the following words to me in Italian: 'Carry on this way. I will help you.'

This voice was the result of the situation I had put myself in. Prolonged solitude and silence create a void that can lead to psychological giddiness. With no distractions, the mind concentrates on itself and becomes a kind of magnifying glass in which small things can appear to be enormous. The mind then gets the impression that it can understand everything, see more clearly and have experiences that it could not otherwise have. It is a sensation akin to that produced by various kinds of drug, as I understand it, when even time loses its usual rhythm and becomes like a concertina where past, present and future are all bunched up.

I heard that same female voice on another couple of occasions, but never as clearly or dramatically as the first time. It was obviously me playing tricks on myself.

Then something else happened which was clearly connected to the exercises I was doing to detach myself from my body and identify myself not with it but with my consciousness. I began to get the feeling that there was something inside me, like a seed which was trying to germinate, but with was being strangled by several different layers: of knowledge, certainties, notions and rules linked to my previous life. This seed was like a prisoner now seeking to escape from the burden of matter.

One evening at sunset, I went down to a part of the forest I had never been to before and saw a strange old rock there on top of which a dwarf ilex was growing like a natural bonsai, its silhouette standing out against the pink handwriting of the mountains. I climbed the rock, sat down next to the ilex and the void of the precipice opened up right beneath my feet, at once frightening and appealing. High up in the sky, my two crows appeared and began to call me. I answered, and they came and flew nearby. Wonderful, the way they flew through the wind that had blown up with the sunset! They let themselves swoop down into the chasm, then just a moment later were back high up in the sky. It was delightful to watch them! Time does not repeat itself, it is only ever in the present, for that is when we experience it. They were calling me and the answer seemed obvious: to take the plunge, to go and join them. Behind me I could sense a presence encouraging me to do so, a hand pushing me to jump, a mind repeating to me that time exists only in the present, that the body is just a burden which is easy to get rid of in order to become lighter and to fly like the crows. I turned around, frightened. I saw no one, but I was sure I was not alone. I made an effort to remain calm, to concentrate, back away from the precipice and then slowly retrace my steps.

It was easier to climb up there than it was to descend and I had to be very careful of where I put my feet. I felt as though I had been wrestling with someone, while the crows up above laughed at me, earth-bound as I still was.

I had not seen the Old Man for several days, when one afternoon I met him at the gate as we were both heading into the forest for our walks.

'How's your friend, Tiger?' he asked me.

I assumed he must have been referring to the mouse, so I began to tell him of our agreement. But he added: 'Are you still thinking about cures?' at which point I realized he meant my cancer.

'You have to reach the point where being cured is no longer what matters, for you have realized that there is a deeper cure than those which medicine is able to offer. If you were able to come into contact with the unity of life, you would realize that to be cured physically no longer has any meaning,' he said. 'See, there are two types of health. Low health which means being fit, like an athlete is fit, and high health which is the integration of the illness.'

We walked on for a while without saying anything, but he was clearly pursuing this line of thought inwardly, for at one point he stopped and asked me, 'Have you discovered yet who it is who dies when you die?'

I could give him all the right answers, I said, because I had read so much on the subject recently and had given a great deal of thought to it. I had been intrigued by the exercises recommended by a variety of traditions to acquaint oneself with death, to 'die before you die' like the Sufis, but I honestly was not sure if all this had actually changed anything within me. In my mind it was clear to me that when we are born, we begin to die just as much as we begin to live. It was clear to me that life and death were but two aspects of the same existence. Intellectually, I understood that when we die, all which we identify with dies too: our bodies, thoughts, human relationships, experiences, the self we set so much store by. So it is right to say every morning: 'I am not this. I am consciousness', and in this way teach ourselves not to be too attached to what we are not. But was all this sufficient to take away my fear of death?

What about him? Had he never experienced that fear?

Yes, when he was young, he said. But not any longer. In fact, he was now curious about death. And I was right, it was not about understanding it intellectually. The only way to truly know it is to die.

We carried on walking slowly, the same theme in our minds. I said one of the loveliest things I had read recently was the *Katha Upanishad*, where the young Nachiketas went to Yama, Death, sat in front of his house and for three days begged him to tell him what the Truth was. Death wanted nothing to do with him and hid instead. Then he offered him gold and riches in an attempt to get rid of the boy. Death even offered him his own kingdom and exceedingly long life. But Nachiketas refused them all. All he wanted was what lay beyond the reach of Death itself.

Death was moved by this. He agreed to take Nachiketas on as his disciple, and once he became his guru, taught him what, once it is known, 'can release every knot in the heart and render useless every other form of knowledge'. The lesson is the same as that in all the other Upanishads and the Gita. It is the lesson of the Vedanta: everything that is born also dies and everything that dies is reborn. Only the self, pure consciousness that is never born, is outside time and therefore remains.

I recalled those verses from the Upanishads and quoted them:

Like the wheat,
Man ripens,
Like the wheat,
He too is reborn.

The old man was amused. The *Katha Upanishad* was also his old guru, Krishna Prem's favourite Upanishad.

'You see? Death is not negative. It can be the great teacher. In fact, it is Death which causes us to ask all the great questions about life,' he said. 'If you think about it, it was Death that brought you here.' He was right.

As we returned home, we passed near where I had left the path the other evening to go towards the odd-shaped rock with the dwarf ilex. I told him what had happened.

'Oh yes, I forgot to mention that. That's a place where you should never go,' the Old Man said. 'It has bad vibes from all the murders that have been committed there. When the English lived here, they used to stand on that rock and shoot animals in the forest. They perpetrated slaughters in that spot too. One shepherd once took his wife up there and threw her down into the chasm. It's a place to steer clear of, believe me.'

After months of isolation, it was time to go home. There was to be a family reunion at Orsigna, our home in the Apennines between Tuscany and Emilia, and I could not miss it. In fact, I was delighted at the prospect. I missed Angela so much that at times it was like physical pain. I ached to be with my children whom I had not seen for so long. But it was not easy. I had become so used to silence now, to being on my own and to having my head focused in only one direction that I was frightened at the idea of returning to the daily routine.

After all my various ups and downs, alone in my stone house, I felt I was finally on the trail of something I cared deeply about, something that seemed to me more important than all the rest and I absolutely did not want to let it go. Basically, I was frightened, frightened of losing myself, as Narada did in another old Indian tale.

Narada was a very devoted follower and disciple of Vishnu. One day he went to his master, and asked him what the difference was between maya, the world of illusion, and the truth. Vishnu had no desire to set about explaining it to him. It was a very hot day, and he was thirsty.

'Listen,' he said to Narada, 'first go and get me a glass of water.'

Narada ran off. He came to a village, knocked on a door and a beautiful girl opened it. Narada asked her for water and the girl invited him in. The two of them started talking and Narada fell in love, married her, and had several children by her. Twelve years went by, and one day a terrible hurricane followed by a deluge struck the village. The river broke its banks, the houses were carried away and Narada saw his wife and his children being dragged off one by one in the floods. Only the youngest of them remained, whom Narada tried to save by holding high above his head. But the water continued to rise, it reached his throat, and not knowing what to do, Narada turned his eyes to heaven and cried out: 'Please, Lord, help me!'

Suddenly, amid the thunder and lightning a voice is heard: 'What about the glass of water?'

The meaning of the story was that in sending Narada to get water for him, Vishnu gave the pupil the answer he was seeking. The village, the pretty girl, the family, the children ... all these are maya, the world of becoming and change. It is not the truth, that which does not change. Experience taught Narada the difference between the two, far better than any explanation could do.

Orsigna too was a village, but I did not even get as far as acting the part of the good Narada. I did indeed spend the summer with my family, but my presence was not a source of much pleasure for anyone. I was grumpy the whole time and I wanted to be on my own. Everything and everyone got on my nerves. Over the Bank holiday weekend in the middle of August, there was dancing in the square outside in the evenings. At one time, the music coming up through the valley and the voice of some local singer in the star-lit night sky would have brought me joy. But not any more. Now they were 'disturbing my peace'. I even had it in for the church bells which, as there was no longer a proper bell-ringer, now chimed automatically by means of some electronic device. I found it all pointless and cumbersome. I had no time for anyone: the complete opposite of what I wanted to achieve.

If all these months of solitude and concentration had served only to make me so unbearable, it had truly not been worth the effort. I realized that requiring solitude to be at peace like this was a sign of immaturity, but to be aware of this was not enough. I realized that solitude itself was not the answer, merely a starting point that I had not yet got beyond. In the Himalayas, I had always found peace in externals, but I had not succeeded in making peace inside myself. My only thought was to go back there and 'get back to work', as the Old Man put it.

The straw that broke the camel's back was the shopping trolley in the supermarket. I had gone there to get the shopping and was wandering about through the aisles. Slowly, my eyes scanned the shelves to find the things that we needed, and threw them in the trolley. I looked at everyone else doing the same thing and the queues at the check-out. I heard the noise of the tills opening and shutting. I felt the call to buy all those tins and boxes, of all different colours and shapes. And I just could not take it any more. Was it me that was mad or the world? I left my trolley right where it was and went back to my car. Within twenty-four hours I was on a plane bound for Delhi and two days later was back in my stone house in the mountains.

I spent another winter alone, with lots of snow, then another lovely spring. This time there were no hallucinations, just the feeling that I might actually be getting somewhere. I was soon put to the test again. With years of hard work, Angela had organized a great exhibition to commemorate her father's paintings at the Zitadelle in Berlin, following on from another exhibition held at Palazzo Pitti in Florence. Hans-Joachim Staude had been born in Haiti to a German family from Hamburg, but had come to Florence at a very early age. His friends in the city called him 'Anzio', and he remained there as a painter for the rest of his life.

This exhibition was to mark his posthumous return to Germany as a famous artist. It was a major event. All the German relatives were there as were the family, press, television, my former colleagues from *Der Spiegel*, and lots of friends and acquaintances. I felt like I had been catapulted into some play in which I had forgotten my part. I sat there on the stage like an idiot, unable to remember my lines. The few I did manage to blurt out were all wrong, imbued with that arrogance which only the austerity and asceticism of the solitary life can produce. Those who make sacrifices and renounce the pleasures of this world occasionally develop a sense of their own superiority as if to compensate, and if they themselves are not basically humble people, they can delude themselves into believing that they are saints.

I realized the same thing. Angela, without having hidden herself away on any Himalayan mountain or severed her ties with anything or anyone, was far more serene, balanced and at peace than I was. This merely increased my frustration. I should have looked to her as my guru. Instead, I got to the point where I saw her, whose presence was drawing me back into the world, as a hindrance to my 'work', the final temptation that prevented me from really taking flight. And with the nastiness whereby one is able to destroy what one loves, I thought even of severing that last bond. I had managed to master so many desires already; there was no reason why I could not sever the remaining ones too.

In forty years of companionship, this was the most difficult moment in the whole of our relationship.

'The river does not need to be directed; it flows on its own,' the Indians say. Angela had understood this and allowed me to leave without making me feel guilty. Did I need more time on my own? Then I should take it, with no deadlines and no strings attached. I returned to my stone house, knowing I had to find a solution to the problem of my restlessness, one that was not linked to some place or another, for all places belong to the external world and hence, are impermanent, changing.

I sought to focus on the themes that at the time bothered me most: love, detachment, freedom. What is love? Is it simply desire, and hence also dependence? Or is it one of the utmost expressions of freedom in the sense that it is a bond that does not tie the lover down, which accounts for its strength; like an elephant agreeing to be tied by a thread of silk?

Does to detach oneself from the things of this world mean to become indifferent to them? Or does it simply mean to no longer be enslaved by them? If the former were true, detachment was not what I wanted; if the latter were true, I could identify with it.

Once I asked the Old Man if one's family could be an obstacle in pursuing the inner life.

'It was for Buddha,' he answered. Then he realized that I was talking about myself, so the comparison with the Enlightened One was not appropriate. So instead, he told me of one of Tagore's stories about an aspiring ascetic. 'This is more appropriate to your situation,' he said.

A man decided to leave his family to become a sanyasi. One night, when he was on the point of leaving in secret, he cast one last glance at his wife and children who were asleep and said, 'Who are you, to keep me chained here?'

A voice in the dark whispered, 'They are me; I am God.'

The man paid no attention. He did not listen and left. So God was forced to conclude, 'Here is a man who abandons me in order to seek me.'

No. In the long run I was not cut out for asceticism and renunciation. Life was still wonderful as far as I was concerned; it held too strong a fascination for me. The fact that I was enjoying nature so much confirmed this. One day, I was struck by how some little flowers grew – so touching! – in the cracks between the stones of my house. They were tenacious and inventive and I shared in their determination to live life while enjoying the sunshine.

I realized that it was much more in my nature to include than to exclude, which was what I had been doing recently. Indeed, I came to the conclusion that it was more sensible too.

Slowly, and without anything in particular happening, I noticed that I was beginning to smile more. Even sitting in front of the candle became more of a relaxing experience. From a distance, and without the added complication of words which always end up saying too much or too little, my relationship with Angela began to smoothen out. The next time we saw each other, when she came with me to New York, being together was the most natural thing in the world. There were no recriminations whatsoever, just lots of laughter.

The fixers said I was fine and that they wanted to see me again after a year. By that time, a total of five would have passed.

As the doctor of Dehradun said, I could have died immediately afterwards and still the fixers would have been able to class me as one of their success stories. That is how statistics work.

I spent the summer with my family at Orsigna. I began to see people and friends again, and got involved in a project to save an old watermill down by the river. Occasionally, I even answered the phone, a sure sign that my neurosis was by now at least in part under control.

My plan was to return to the Himalayas in the autumn and wait for Angela to join me there for Christmas. But as the Swami used to say, 'Do you want to make Bhagawan laugh? Very well; tell him your plans.'

Bhagawan clearly had other ideas for me.

The fateful day of 11 September 2001 was a turning point in the lives of so many people; it certainly was in mine. I simply could not go back to the mountains and look on, while mankind was facing decisions of such historic importance. In view of what was happening, and even more so in view of what I was sure was about to happen – it is never easy being a prophet of doom – it seemed frankly unacceptable to go back to being a hermit. I felt there was something terribly arid in solitude, in seeking myself, at such a time, like the love that was being preached by the clergy. I still felt I was a part of the world, even if I did not want to be a slave to it. What I wanted was to live a better life in it. If I had learnt anything from those years of solitude, if I had learnt not to judge too much, to not react according to the usual mechanisms of reason, to be free from what I 'knew', to feel mankind as a whole, not to accept the divisions of religion, race or nation that are bringing us to ruin – this was the moment to start giving back a little of what I had taken. If indeed a little light had been kindled in my heart which did not flicker with the first passing wind, now was the time to use it to kindle lights in others so they may kindle others still, then the would may be a little less in darkness.

It was my grandson Novalis who provided the inspiration. Aged just two, inquisitive and unknowing, full of enthusiasm, he was still untroubled by the emotion that stifled others: fear. I wanted to leave him something more than just the memory of his old grandfather with a beard. This was how I got the idea of going to see with my own eyes the cause of all fear: violence. The book that derived from the journey I made, *Letters Against the War*, is dedicated to him.

In the three months that I spent travelling around Pakistan and Afghanistan, I would think of my stone house and the Old Man every so often. I could see him, smiling at my ardour for the cause of non-violence. I could hear him saying that everything I was doing was of no use, that this civilization is not worth saving, and that it is certainly not by running around plugging holes in a sinking ship that is to be saved. I knew he was convinced that humanity, whose only concern now was to pursue the pleasures of the senses, was on the verge of a major breakdown. He saw all that was happening in the light of eternity, where the world has already been born seven times, and has been destroyed seven times.

In truth he was possibly right. The forces at work are indeed much bigger than we are. But I could not just accept it. I am sure that if he had me there in front of him, he would have quoted some saint to me, even that intelligent crook and mystic Gurdjieff who had said that 200 enlightened people were enough to change the history of mankind. Better then, to seek to become one of them. But under such circumstances, inaction was action which I felt was immoral.

Deep down there was something profoundly Indian in his

eulogy of inaction which was not in my nature. If my roof was letting in water, I felt the need to go and repair it, whereas he, I know, would manage to remain indifferent.

On my way back from Kabul I passed through Delhi and went up to my stone house to write the last of the letters. When I saw the Old Man, it was as though we had actually had all those conversations I imagined.

'If you have to write, at least be sincere,' he said. I sought to heed him in this. Then he asked me a question which I found very hard to answer sincerely.

'With this book, are you writing for Him or for you?' he asked, staring at me. In other words: was I devoting myself to That, to Consciousness, Bhagawan, the Voice; or was I doing it all for my own ego? Was I writing because I thought it would bring me closer to the truth or because I liked seeing my name in the newspapers and having people come and listen to me?

It was an extremely pertinent question and in asking it, the Old Man effectively set a guardian angel on my back whom I still feel protecting me everywhere I go, most useful so as not to lose control of what is happening to me and to keep my Self at bay. The Old Man thought it would have been much better for me to 'dig in just one place rather than go around collecting pebbles thinking they are precious stones'. But his was not a binding judgement.

'You'll find the Way eventually ... if you are courageous enough to lose yourself,' he concluded, quoting an Urdu poet.

I owed a lot to the Old Man. He had pointed me in the right direction for the return journey. Above all, he helped me understand that I should not depend on anyone else's idea, not that of any guru, not even his. I had to experience everything myself, directly. It was I who had to listen for the Voice, not have someone else tell me what it says.

He and India had proved to be a great opportunity for me, but in the end what I think I learnt was not specifically Indian. It was a part of that perennial philosophy which is without nation and is not linked to any religion. It is concerned with the deepest aspirations of the human mind, that eternal need to know why we are in the world, to come into contact with what it was that put us here.

In India, where nothing is ever completely wasted, the various answers to these questions are still on people's lips and in their way of living, as once upon a time they were in ours too. But it is not necessary to travel physically to India to find them, nor indeed to travel at all. Anyone dying of thirst for knowledge has only to rediscover the source. Their own source. The water is always the same.

EIGHT

ARRIVAL

IN THE CLOUDS

Ultimately everything has to be tested: ideas, intentions, the things you believe you have worked out, the progress you think you have made. And the only place to test them is your own life. What use is it sitting cross-legged for hours and meditating, if it doesn't improve you, if it doesn't remove you, even just a little bit, from the things of this world, from the desires of your senses and the needs of your bodies? What use is it preaching non-violence if you continue to make use of the inherently violent market economy? What use is it reflecting on life and death if, when faced with a life-and-death situation, you fail to do what you always said you should, and instead fall back to the old, preconditioned way of reacting?

For as long as I was hidden away in my mountain retreat 9,000 feet up, there was never any contradiction between what I thought and what I did, between the person I was and the person I wanted to be. I was alone, living practically exclusively in the dimension of consciousness, with never any major decisions to make. But the moment of truth came for me too, and it came in the way I had always imagined: on a trip to New York.

It should have been a routine visit. It had been more than five years since I had started my journey. I felt fine, and the fixers could class me as one of their success stories, although, as the mercury doctor at Dehradun said, I could have died a year later without this affecting the MSKCC's statistics. I was expecting to stay in New York no longer than the week these things usually took, and be back in Florence in time to take part in the Social Forum and the massive demonstration for world peace. But Bhagawan, who like me is clearly not a fan of routines, must have had a good laugh at the plans I had made and, maybe to teach me another lesson, made quite sure that everything went wrong. Starting with my arrival at New York.

Angela was in front of me in the immigration queue. Her passport had already been stamped with a three-month visa, when the official took mine, looked through it page by page, stared at me, entered my name in his computer and somehow came to a conclusion that led him to take back Angela's passport too, step out of his cubicle and say to us: 'Follow me.' Was it my beard? My various Pakistani visas? My Afghan visa? Or maybe a note from the American embassy in Rome, which had publicly recorded its protest against some passages of my *Letters Against the War*?

We were handed over to another official, and shown into a room with row after row of plastic chairs, where the other suspects – terrorist suspects – were waiting nervously in silence. Many of the men had long beards like me, but their wives had their heads covered with black headscarves. They were Pakistani, Saudi or Yemeni Muslims.

We waited for half an hour, then another official called me to a counter from which he sat above me, while I had to speak to him with my nose sticking up. He said I was not authorized to enter the United States, and it was up to him whether or not to grant me an entry visa. I explained that this was the hundredth time I had been there; I showed him the email confirming my appointments at the MSKCC, and my air ticket with the return flight confirmed. There were questions, answers and lengthy negotiations, before eventually he said: 'Next time, you have to apply for a visa before leaving,' and handed the passport back to me, duly stamped. We breathed a sigh of relief. I had been lucky. Or had I?

If that official had put me on the first plane back home rather than let me in, at the time it would have felt like a disaster. But now? It is so hard to grasp the meaning of what happens to us when it happens. We must learn, once and for all, to set less store by distinctions such as good and bad, pleasure and displeasure, given that these things change over time and our judgements often end up being worthless.

When I look back now, I see that if I had been prevented from entering the States and going to the hospital, I would have been spared everything that came afterwards. Would that have been a good thing or a bad thing? Good luck or bad luck?

Anyway, I now had the visa, and the morning after I arrived at the hospital on the dot for my appointment. I saw my fixers, told them I felt fine, full of energy, had a healthy appetite, had no aches or pains, could go for long walks without feeling tired and, above all, was at peace. They examined me and appeared to agree with me. Unfortunately, however, their machines did not; especially not the rubber snake with the light bulb on its head, which was manoeuvred into the darkest recesses of my anaesthetized body. The machines said I was far from well, that my inner friend had come back to take up residence in one of my organs, and that it would have to be cut out and quickly – this was the bad news.

But I was in luck: the best surgeon in the hospital was free and available to take care of me – this was the good news.

Was this an operation that Mahadevan, the doctor from the 'place where the arrow was launched from', would say would 'disturb' me unnecessarily? Maybe. Was it one of the thousands of operations which everyone knows take place for no good reason in the States every year? The pressure to have it was immense. They said I would recover in a month and a half, and that I would slowly get used to life without this vital organ. I gave in.

Fortunately, a friend of ours from Florence offered us her studio flat high up among the city rooftops in an apartment block overlooking Gramercy Park, which meant we were able to leave our hotel. But this too, was the kind of adventure you don't know whether to laugh or cry about. When our taxi pulled up outside the old, elegant building where, in accordance with the complex rules of New York cooperatives, we had to be accepted as 'temporary and trustworthy guests' of our friend, the car door suddenly slammed shut on me, bashing me on the head in the process. This meant I ended up introducing myself to the pompous concierge half-dazed and dripping with blood. We left our bags and rushed off to the nearest hospital which, we later discovered, mostly treated urgent cases involving drug addicts, and where the hole in my scalp was sewn up with six stitches by a very young trainee doctor who admitted he was performing the task for the first time in his life.

Back with the concierge of the old apartment block for ex-artists, writers and actors, we were amazed to see a white coffin in the entrance hall from which death itself emerged in the form of a skeleton, wrapped in a black cloak, scythe in its hand and two flashing red light bulbs shining out of its skull like eyes of fire. America was celebrating Halloween! What kind of omen was this?

I met the surgeon and liked him. I told him to take out all the bits of me he thought needed removing, and while he was at it, to do something about the nasty hernia I'd been carrying around with me. He laughed. He couldn't do anything about that.

All that followed – the preparations for surgery, the prayers, the tubes, the anaesthetic – went along the lines I was already familiar with. I wasn't even curious any more. But when I came round, still half asleep from the effects of the drugs, the first thing I asked was how many bits of me they had taken out. 'None,' I heard a voice reply.

None? Had it all been for nothing?

Indeed it had. When he opened my belly up, the surgeon had been so shocked by what he had seen, that he had preferred to leave everything as it was and close up the wound he had just inflicted with fifty-eight stitches.

Was he right or wrong to do so? Was it a good thing or a bad thing?

The old fixers who had kept me alive for an extra five years and who, with their treatments, might also have been responsible for my new predicament – I had always known that might be a risk – were very upset and somehow, when they came to see me, it was I who ended up consoling them. I was no longer one of their cases. From now on, I would be looked after by one of their colleagues, an expert in this new combination of diseases.

When I met him, I took an instant dislike to him and knew I wanted nothing to do with him. He was sprawled over an office chair, wearing sneakers and chewing gum. So when, after reading my notes and files, he proposed a powerful new dose of chemotherapy, the conversation was abrupt and to the point.

'What do I get out of it?' I asked.

'Six more months, maybe,' he replied.

'And if not?'

'If not, you won't make it.' Then he added one of those statements which any doctor worth his salt really ought to avoid, but which are increasingly heard in the United States, for legal reasons especially: 'If you're still around in a year's time, you'll enter the medical history books.'

This, I confess, had never been one of my ambitions, but it became one there and then. When I replied, 'No, thank you, I won't be having any more chemotherapy,' the Gum-Chewer looked upset, like someone who had lost a client to the competition.

But the competition in this case was not a doctor with a better bedside manner, or some form of alternative medicine. It was peace, rather than more war. I was not giving up on treatment – it was just that now I wanted treatment of a different kind. The kind I wanted this time was to get back in harmony with … the cosmic order.

My belly might have been a battlefield, but my head certainly was not. I made up my mind quickly and never once changed it. I was not turning my back on my doctors or medical science, but I did not feel as dependent on them as I had five years ago. Doctors may give advice, but ultimately the decision as to what or what not to do rests with the patient, for the issue is not scientific or practical, it is existential. Everyone has the right to decide themselves how they want to live the rest of their own lives.

I had basically stopped looking for medicines since meeting the doctor at Dehradun, and was not about to start all over again. Five years ago, I had done everything I was told. At that stage I wanted to live longer, and America, with its state-of-the-art science, had seemed like the best solution. I had bought into it then. But not this time.

Anyway, did I really want to have more chemotherapy in

the States? No, I did not. Everywhere I went the talk was only of war. I could not relate to a post-9/11 America preparing to invade Iraq in the same way as I had before. The hospital itself had changed. So too had the atmosphere in New York. The violence I had previously felt bubbling under the surface was exploding everywhere. I wanted nothing more to do with American wars. I had had enough of their smart bombs that killed innocent citizens, their depleted uranium weapons which killed their own soldiers with cancer – and that's just for starters. I had had enough of their powerful chemotherapy cocktails and their cancerous radiotherapy. I wanted peace.

All the experiences I had collected in these years, on the road and in my Himalayan retreat, everything I had thought or understood, was now coming to a head. This was the great challenge I had been preparing for. The rest was mere literature.

The old Sufi masters saw sudden death as a misfortune, a curse from God, as it prevented them from preparing for it and savouring it in full. This was one problem I did not have. I had thought about it, prepared for it, and the sentence pronounced by the Gum-Chewer would now serve to test how much truth there was in the detachment I claimed.

Patients tend to remember this kind of 'sentence' and give up, as if it were final. Often such words become a kind of self-fulfilling prophecy because they take away a patient's last remaining strength, on which their salvation ultimately depends much more than on medication – their will to live. Of course, I too remembered the Gum-Chewer's prediction, but I lumped together with the others I already had regarding my future, and did not let it bother me. I filed it along with the Swami's prediction that I would live until at least 2006, and that of the Chinese lady doctor in Hong Kong, who said she felt there was a lot of life in me yet. What if they were wrong? I realized that did not matter. After all, one of the many exercises I had been devoting myself to recently involved reducing my needs and not giving into my desires. This meant not giving into any of them – including the desire to live longer.

Angela and my children understood. So too did Leopold. I wrote and told him I wanted to live now with more joy than ever before. He emailed me back from Odessa, where he now lived, to say, 'I can't offer you any advice – advisors rarely pay, after all – but I do feel strongly that you're right to choose watchful peace ahead of chemical or surgical war. There's nothing to be gained from war, and everything to be gained from peace.'

Even the surgeon who opened me up and closed me back down again understood this. I wanted to thank him before I left New York. He'd been great. He had kept his ego under control and gone against his professional pride as a surgeon. He had stood up to the organization. Everything had been set up for an operation lasting several hours: medicines, assistants and nurses had all been lined up. Everything, including his own fee, had been paid in advance, but at the last minute, and with one of my dear old fixers pleading with him on his mobile to go ahead and 'try anything and everything', eventually he decided to do nothing at all.

I went to tell him that I was grateful, that I was going back to live in the Himalayas and my treatment from now on would be to live in peace and solitude. He looked at me curiously, as though he had caught a glimpse of something that intrigued him, shook my hand and said, 'Ah, mind over matter? Do let me know how you get on.'

We went back to Florence. I had managed to miss all the wonderful new things that had taken place in my city during the Social

Forum, but at least I was in time for the massive peace march. On that occasion, I took part in the first and last rally of my life on the steps of the church of Santo Spirito, with two drunks intent on wresting the microphone off me so that they could give their views on the world to all and sundry. It was night-time, and the square was a shimmering sea of lights and multicoloured banners, all bearing the word PEACE. A moving experience.

If my old hometown, once so sober and dignified, now so slovenly and commercialized, was able to put so many people, especially the young, out on the streets, all moved by the same rejection of war, clearly there was still hope that man could make some kind of progress. I saw similar things happening in other parts of Italy too, when I went to speak about non-violence to young people in schools before their minds became irrevocably globalized. It could happen anywhere – not just to us, not just in Europe.

The signs of that inner revolution, as opposed to political, which now seemed to me to be the only viable option and certainly the only kind of revolution I was interested in being involved in, were increasingly visible everywhere I looked. Visible even among institutionalized religions – including Islam – in the anti-globalization movements, human rights groups, volunteer and environmental associations, among the young, who were not prepared to give up on their dreams, and women who had resolved to bring the feminine touch back into human affairs. I am convinced that around the world today, among the most diverse people, a new awareness is growing of what is wrong but also of what is needed in order to put it right. In my view, this is the best thing to happen in our times and needs to be encouraged.

It is from this new awareness, rather than from any new religion, prophet, dictator or deliverer, that the spiritual direction for our future will come. The answer is within us; to attain it, we must get some order in our lives, throw out everything that is useless, and arrive at the very core of our being. Rather than storming the bastions of power, we ought to be putting up a lengthy resistance. We must resist the sirens of prosperity and packaged happiness; resist the temptation to want only what we like. We should not abandon reason and give into folly, but must understand that reason too has its limits, that science can save many lives but it can also kill. We will not make any real progress until we give up on violence. Not by shouting it from the rooftops or setting it down in stone, not in constitutions or laws that no one takes a blind bit of notice of, but in our own hearts.

The path we must take is clear: live more naturally, desire less, and love more. If we do this, diseases such as mine will not occur so often. Rather than seek medicines for illnesses, we ought to try and live in a way that the illnesses do not occur. Above all, it is time to stop playing around with weapons and war. Time to stop fighting 'enemies'. Whatever it was that caused my cells to go mad was no enemy. At the moment, we are enemies of ourselves.

We have to bring a spiritual dimension back into our lives, trapped as we are in the snare of mere matter. We have to be less selfish, less taken up with our personal interests and more mindful of the common good. We must rediscover the meaning of that marvellous, concise message inscribed on the façade of the cathedral at Barga, Garfagnana, in my home region of Tuscany, which so struck me when I read it as a child on a school trip and which I have never forgotten:

'Small is mine; great is ours.'

I left for India and my Himalayan retreat just before Christmas. The idea was to go and live healthily, write some more of this book and silently breathe in the clean air and grandeur of the mountains. I added more and more bits of myself that I had to smile and say hello to every morning as part of my exercises, and spent several hours a day sitting in front of my little solar-powered laptop. I supplemented my diet, still vegetarian, with a potion of herbs which Angela, who was rather less sceptical about miracles than I was, had procured for me first in Hong Kong and then northern China where it was produced. As far as I was concerned, it was not that different from the cloud mushroom potion, but charged as it was with her love and determination to help me, I resolved to take it regularly without protesting. I still do.

Snows, the first rains, the monsoon, the autumn and then again snow. Time flew by without my noticing or feeling any different, and before I knew it I had 'entered the medical history books'. I have no way of knowing how long I will stay there, nor do I care much. At the moment I have more pressing problems to deal with.

One of which is that I still have not managed to develop the right attitude towards time, to see my time as time which is for others, as the Swami did. I'd love to be able to do that!

Another problem is my continuing to identify inner peace with solitude, to equate harmony with living in a mountain retreat. I have to separate myself from the world to feel at peace. This shows how much work I still have to do. This is why I have recently started to do an exercise which the Tibetans, Sufis and others have performed for many centuries.

I lie flat on the ground and look up at the sky. The clouds float by against the blue background. I fix my gaze on one of them, follow it with my eyes and identify with it. Soon I become that cloud and like it, weightless and without thoughts, emotions, desires, resistance or direction, I let myself go in the vast expanse of the sky. There are no paths to follow, no destinations to be reached. I just wander and float, as empty as the cloud. And like the cloud I change shape, take on different ones, become evanescent, melt away and disappear. The cloud is no more. I am no more. All that remains is consciousness: free, unbound and expanding.

I first started doing this exercise high up on a mountain ridge above a sheer precipice. Now I must learn to do it anywhere: in a meadow up in the Apennines, on the terrace of my home in Florence, on the side of a motorway. If I manage to get hold of this sense of the emptiness of matter, as I believe I have managed to finally grasp that silence as an inner rather than a physical state, I really will have begun to make some progress. I will be able to stop seeing every day as a many-tentacled octopus, stop seeing time as 'mine' and stop having to run away to the Himalayas every time I want to feel at peace. I'm working on it.

So is this a happy ending?

What exactly is a happy ending? Do all stories have to have one? What would be a happy ending in the case of a journey such as the one I've just recounted? 'So they all lived happily ever after?' This is how fairy tales end which are outside of time, not real-life stories, which are in time and consumed by it. Who is to judge what is happy and what is not? And at what stage?

When all is said and done, has the disease I've been writing about been a good thing or a bad thing? It's *been*, that's the most important thing. It has helped me, for without it I would never have embarked on this journey, nor would I have asked myself the questions which, for me at least, were the ones that really mattered.

This is not an apology for evil and suffering – even now I cannot say I've had much of that. It's merely an invitation to look at the world from a different point of view, not just in terms of what we like or don't like.

Again, would it be a blessing or a curse if life were just a bed of roses? Maybe the latter, because if you live without ever asking yourself what you're living for, you're not making the most of a great opportunity. Only pain leads you to ask the questions.

Maybe it's a privilege to be born human, with all that it entails. According to the Puranas, the ancient popular Indian tales, even the heavenly creatures to whom all things were given and who know beauty, prosperity and joy, at some point had to be born as human beings so that they could also know what their opposites were like, and understand the meaning of life. You can only test these things in your own life. You have to experience them personally to understand. Otherwise it's all words, which in themselves are meaningless and do neither harm nor good.

Gandhi knew this, and practised what he preached.

One day, a mother brought to him her son. He was fifteen years old and the doctor had ordered him to eat no more sugar, otherwise his life would be in danger. The boy refused to listen to reason and continued to gorge on sweets. His mother hoped Gandhi might be able to help her. He listened, then said, 'At the moment I can do nothing; come back in a week's time.'

When they returned, Gandhi took the boy to one side and spoke to him. From that moment on, the boy never touched another sweet. 'Gandhiji, how did you do it?' his followers asked him. 'Simple,' the great soul replied. 'For one week I myself didn't touch sugar either, so when I came to speak to the boy I understood what it meant not to eat sweets and was more persuasive because of it.'

Just before Gandhi was killed, someone asked him what his life's message was. He replied, 'My life is my message.'

Very few people can say such a thing, but each of us in our own way can aspire to something that sums up our lives. I sometimes think of it in terms of a circle. I see a Chinese painter holding a large brush soaked in ink, concentrating hard before a large sheet of ricepaper. Suddenly inspired, but his mind perfectly at peace, with one broad sweep of his hand he paints a complete circle. At other times I think of the Zen Buddhist monk who laughed and laughed until he breathed his last breath, so that not even his closest disciples were able to weep when he departed this earth.

Why should we weep? Death isn't always bad news.

On the way from Delhi to Almora, once the road has left the plains and begins to climb the gorges of the Himalayan torrents, an ashram with bright red roofs can be seen, nestling in a valley. This ashram is famous for having been home to a great sadhu, Neem Karoli Baba. A large, warm-hearted man, Baba with his simplicity and 'powers' attracted a following of several dozen Western hippies, including Richard Alpert, an American psychology professor who was kicked out of Harvard in 1963 for having experimented with the effects of hallucinogenic drugs together with his friend and colleague Timothy Leary. It is said that once Leary, to challenge Baba's powers in controlling his state of consciousness, gave him a handful of LSD tablets – as many as ten, perhaps – and Baba swallowed them and felt no effect whatsoever. Alpert became a faithful follower of Baba and under the name Ram Das, servant of Ram, he wrote of his experiences in several extremely popular books which changed the way many

Americans viewed India and spirituality. One of the stories Ram Das told concerning his guru was this.

One day a man rushed to the ashram and begged Neem Karoli Baba to go with him to a relative's house. The relative was very ill and only Baba could help. 'No, I won't come,' Baba replied abruptly. 'But when you go back, give him this banana, then everything will be fine, you'll see.' The man rushed home and gave his sick relative the banana to eat. As soon as he had finished the last mouthful, he passed away peacefully.

Everything had indeed been fine, just as Baba had predicted. The man had died peacefully. Yet we still think that, for things to be fine, he ought to have been healed and lived for many more years. But why? This is precisely the root of all our unhappiness: continuing to distinguish between what we like and what we don't like. It's only by accepting that everything is one, and not refusing anything, that we might be able to quieten our minds and calm our anxiety.

Hundreds of pilgrims still visit Neem Karoli Baba's ashram, even though he 'left his body' in 1973. 'Left his body' – what a lovely expression with which to take the sting out of death! We try to do something similar with expressions such as 'he's gone to a better place', or 'he's at peace now', but deep down we're still sad.

I'm certainly not indifferent to what happens to me, but I try not to be a slave to it and I would like to reach the same state of detachment which a great poet once expressed in the following haiku:

The shadow of the bamboo sweeps the stone stairs
But the dust remains.
The moon is reflected on the bottom of the pond
But it does not touch the water.

I have not told the story of this journey in order to try and prove that there is no cure for certain diseases or to show that everything I did was of no use. On the contrary, it was all extremely useful, including the disease. It was this that made me review my priorities, reflect on things, change my point of view and, above all, my way of life. And this is all the advice I can offer: change your life to heal yourself. I cannot offer any shortcuts. Holy books, gurus, and religions are all useful, but only in the same way that elevators are useful because they take us up a floor so that we don't have to walk. The last part of the journey, that small ladder which leads to the roof from which we can see the world or lie down and become a cloud, has to be accomplished by each of us on foot alone.

I'm trying. I feel okay, I am still strong, though I don't boast about it nor rejoice in it. I continue to do what feels right at the moment, without necessarily expecting any results or hoping to get anything back in return, without formulating desires apart from that of no longer needing time for myself and devoting whatever time remains to others. I was very envious of the Swami's attitude, and I really would like to make moksha the goal of my next journey, although I'm still a long way off. Sometimes, even just a word or a gesture are sufficient to change the direction a life and many people, especially the young, are on the lookout for just this opportunity.

When Angela came to see me in my hermitage, she was entertained to see how I caught the flies that came into my room with a handkerchief before releasing them out of the window. I enjoyed it too, not because I thought they were the reincarnation of someone, but because it was one way of feeling in harmony with other living beings, an opportunity not to remove life from life for once. Merely an intuition, as I have no need to believe or have faith or be sure of anything. I live here and now, with the feeling that the universe is extraordinary, that nothing ever happens by chance and that life is one long discovery.

And I'm especially lucky because, really, every day now, more than ever before, is one more ride on the merry-go-round.